G. WILSON KNIGHT
COLLECTED WORKS

G. WILSON KNIGHT
COLLECTED WORKS

VOLUME X

LORD BYRON

Christian Virtues

London and New York

First published 1952 by Routledge & Kegan Paul Ltd

This edition published 2002 by Routledge
2 Park Square, Milton Park, Abingdon, Oxon OX14 4RN

Simultaneously published in the USA and Canada
by Routledge
270 Madison Avenue, New York, NY 10016

Routledge is an imprint of the Taylor & Francis Group

Transferred to digital printing 2010

© 1952 by G. Wilson Knight

Typeset in Times New Roman by
Keystroke, Jacaranda Lodge, Wolverhampton

British Library Cataloguing in Publication Data
A catalogue record for this book is available from the British Library

Library of Congress Cataloging in Publication Data
A catalog record for this book has been requested

ISBN 978-0–415–27896–6 (Set)
ISBN 978-0–415–29079–1 (Volume X) (hbk)
ISBN 978-0–415–60668-4 (Volume X) (pbk)

Publisher's Note
The publisher has gone to great lengths to ensure the quality of this
reprint but points out that some imperfections in the original book
may be apparent.

LORD BYRON

Christian Virtues

by

G. WILSON KNIGHT

ROUTLEDGE & KEGAN PAUL
London

LORD BYRON
by E. H. Baily, R.A.

For

my Mother

CAROLINE KNIGHT

in whose thoughts the name of

BYRON

throughout a long life shone to the last as

a star

PREFACE

THOUGH Byron has been for long one of my major interests, this is my first full-length study. Of the poetry alone I have in *The Burning Oracle* already published a general survey which I hope eventually to reprint as part of a more extended investigation. I would point also to my article 'The Plays of Lord Byron' in *The Times Literary Supplement* of 3 February, 1950, with its plea for a Byron festival; and to the scattered comments throughout *Christ and Nietzsche*.

My present volume is conceived as the first of a trilogy on Byron as man and poet, to which there will probably be added a fourth on the *Don Leon* poems. The sub-title 'Christian Virtues' strictly limits the field of this first study. Of Byron's vices I hope to say more hereafter: given the necessary support, I shall not be backward in discussion of them. Meanwhile, we may suggest that the recognition of virtues should surely take precedence over any enquiry into our subject's vices. The negative must, here and elsewhere, be studied in terms of the positive and not *vice versa,* or we risk getting everything out of focus.

I cannot, it is true, make any pretensions to biographical skill of the more conventional kind; and I confess to being not always at ease with the details of time-sequence and locality. If I have made any mistakes of consequence, I hope that they will be quickly brought to light. Authorities are, however, given for almost every statement; the evidence is there. Indeed, we have in the past had perhaps too much biographical skill with too little reliance on evidence; and I would here emphasize that the wholesale acceptance of Lady Byron's unpublished account of her husband's domestic behaviour suggests a certain confusion regarding both the nature of evidence and the nature of marriage. In the following pages both narrative and comment are reduced to a minimum; the aim is, to let the evidence speak, as far as possible, for itself. The result is less the story of a life than a mosaic of evidence regarding *qualities,* both the art and the argument lying rather in selection and structure than in any explicit deductions. The massed quotations are not really expected to prove anything beyond themselves: the evidence is itself the argument. Such a book cannot, I know, make easy reading, but the serious study of genius has as much right to demand an effort from the enquirer as the study of physics or astronomy: it is certainly no less important. My references are placed directly beside the statements they support, so that each statement can be simultaneously read and, if need be, modified by knowledge of its date and source: this cannot be done if we use footnotes, and the irritation of notes at the end is surely something to be avoided. The eye soon gets used to the brackets, and those who wish to can ignore them altogether. The same is true of some of the evidence: there is no necessary compulsion on everyone to read every word of it, but it is there if required. Part of my purpose is, indeed, to map out and make available for future students the main trends of evidence in the original source-books, and some pains have accordingly been taken with the index, which is intended to act as an elucidation in retrospect of the complexities already handled. Anyone who has studied our subject must be aware of the distressing accumulation of facts, quotations and judgments with no references at all; and I would warn future students never to accord an uncritical acceptance to any statements whatsoever that are not fully documented.

Not only has a whole mass of generally accepted opinion and belief been constructed on the shakiest of foundations, but many rock-like substances appear to have escaped attention. A number of the most significant judgments and recollections of Moore, Lady Blessington and Medwin have been passed over; but probably the most important divergence from recent tradition in the following pages will be found in the high value set on the authority of Teresa Guiccioli. My own book was substantially in its present form before I turned to her study, when it was at once clear that this was, with the possible exception of Moore's *Life*, the most important storehouse of all, apart from the writings of Byron himself. I found, moreover, that not only the Countess's opinions, but even her exact choice of supporting evidence and quotation (as with Byron's help of Moore and Coleridge, and the FitzGerald Sonnet) corresponded, time and again, with my own; and it was no small encouragement to discover that my understanding of the evidence matched so exactly the considered judgment of one whose intimacy with Lord Byron over a number of years was unrivalled.

It has not been possible to give any adequate account of the various people and events referred to. As it is, my text had to be severely curtailed for publication. I must assume that my readers know their Nicolson, and also their Drinkwater, Maurois, Quennell or Vulliamy; and there is always the *Cambridge History of English Literature,* the Oxford *Companion,* and the *Dictionary of National Biography.* I have, accordingly, assumed that the outlines are known without pausing to explain that Hobhouse and Moore were Byron's friends; that Gamba, Parry and Stanhope served with him in Greece; that he married Miss Milbanke, and was for some years the lover of Teresa Guiccioli. Many details will be clear enough in the context; and many others of a more strictly narrative kind are not really germane to our enquiry.

I would express my grateful acknowledgments to Mr. Reginald Groves for giving me a useful reference to John Clare; to Mr. Wilfred Childe for reading and remarking on part of my text; to my brother for reading the book in proof; to Sir John Murray for permission to use copyright material; to the Editor of *The Times Literary Supplement* for permission to quote from the review of Makriyiannis' *Apomnimonévmata*; and to Mr. Richard Rieu for allowing us to use a photograph of the fine but little known bust in his possession by E. H. Baily, first exhibited at the Royal Academy in 1826.

G. W. K.

PS. On p. 248 I have substituted *feeling's* for *feeling* to correct what appears a syntactical impossibility in the *Monody on the Death of Sheridan.*

I would direct attention to certain interesting contacts with my present thesis in Dr. R. J. Z. Werblowsky's important new study of Milton, *Lucifer and Prometheus.*

May 1952

For the present reprint I have corrected a few minor errors.

The book was composed under pressure from the seeing of so many new significances in a superabundance of material. I apologise for its failings. Every reference was originally checked, but after triumphantly tracing down an inaccuracy one too often checks the discovered quotation without altering the numeral; and I fear that errors may survive. Index A confused me: I can only hope that it is in the main reliable.

October 1966 G.W.K.

LIST OF AUTHORITIES

Works will normally be cited under the author's name. Where there are exceptions, or a possibility of doubt, the designation chosen is given below in brackets.

This is not a formal bibliography: the dates given are simply those of the editions used.

The Poetical Works of Lord Byron; Oxford, 1926.

The Letters and Journals of Lord Byron; ed. R. E. Prothero (Lord Ernle), 6 vols., 1898–1904 (LJ).

Lord Byron's Correspondence; ed. John Murray, 2 vols., 1922 (C).

Byron: A Self-Portrait; ed. Peter Quennell, 2 vols., 1950 (SP).

The Last Attachment; Iris Origo, 1949 (including new letters).

The Life, Letters and Journals of Lord Byron; Thomas Moore, 1 vol., 1866.

The Life of Lord Byron; John Galt, 1830.

A Narrative of Lord Byron's Last Journey to Greece; Pietro Gamba, 1825.

The Last Days of Lord Byron; William Parry, 1825.

My Recollections of Lord Byron (for the title, see p. 40); Teresa Guiccioli, 2 vols., 1869 (Teresa).

La Vie de Lord Byron en Italie; Teresa Guiccioli (unpublished; quoted via Origo).

Conversations of Lord Byron; Lady Blessington, 1834.

Conversations on Religion with Lord Byron and Others; James Kennedy, 1830.

Journal of the Conversations of Lord Byron (with, as an appendix, an account of Byron's Greek Campaign, reprinted from *The Westminster Review);* T. Medwin, 1824 (octavo edn.).

Records of Shelley, Byron and the Author; E. J. Trelawny, 1905.

Lord Byron and Some of his Contemporaries; Leigh Hunt, 1828.

Recollections of a Long Life; J. C. Hobhouse, Lord Broughton, 4 vols., 1909 (Hobhouse).

Travels in Albania and other Provinces of Turkey; J. C. Hobhouse, Lord Broughton, 2nd edn., 2 vols., 1858 (*Albania*).

Astarte; Lord Lovelace, 2nd edn., 1921.

To Lord Byron (letters addressed to Byron); Paston and Quennell, 1939.

Also the following more recent works: *The Real Lord Byron,* J. C. Jeaffreson, 1883; *Byron: the Last Phase,* Richard Edgcumbe, 1909; *Byron: the Last Journey,* Harold Nicolson, 1924; *Byron and Greece,* Harold Spender, 1924; *The Pilgrim of Eternity,* John Drinkwater, 1925; *Byron,* André Maurois, 1930; *Byron and the Need of Fatality,* Charles du Bos, 1932; *Byron in Italy,* Peter Quennell, 1941; *Byron,* C. E. Vulliamy, 1948; *The Life of Lady Byron,* Ethel Colburn Mayne, 1929; *Shelley and the Unromantics,* Olwen Ward Campbell, 1924; *Shelley: a Biography,* Newman Ivey White, 2 vols., 1947.

Works by Edward Blaquière, R. C. Dallas, George Finlay, Caroline Lamb, Charles Mackay, Julius Millingen, and Leicester Stanhope are quoted through other authorities. Teresa Guiccioli's *Recollections* are quoted directly; her *La Vie de Lord Byron en Italie* and other statements indirectly.

N.B.—All page references prefixed by 'p.' or 'pp.' refer to pages in my own study.

CONTENTS

I
CURRENT MISUNDERSTANDINGS

I

THIS is a work on Byron as a man in whom poetry has become incarnate. Of the poetry I have already published a preliminary study,[1] and intend a more thorough investigation later on. With our current assessment I disagree totally. Byron appears to me our greatest poet in the widest sense of the term since Shakespeare; and I do not know where we shall look for his master in prose. But, great though the literature be, it is outdistanced by Byron's importance as a man; an importance, I believe, so great that it has been difficult to focus, like the large letters on a map. Biography in our time has proved sadly inadequate; and I hope I shall be forgiven for prefacing my own attempt at a reassessment of Byron's significance by drawing attention to what appear to me certain typical examples of a current misunderstanding. In selecting my main examples from the work of Mr. Peter Quennell's *Byron in Italy,* I would offer an apology. I have the greatest admiration for his fine editorial selection and commentary in the two volumes of the *Self-Portrait.* Nevertheless, the biographical method of his *Byron in Italy* appears to me, on occasion, dangerous. In criticizing, therefore, certain chosen passages, whether from his own work or—later—that of Mr. Harold Nicolson, I am attacking less an individual writer, or writers, than the mind-structure of our time. With this reservation, I shall attempt to indicate what appear to be certain vital misjudgments. It is simply my purpose to show, with exact reference to one of its accredited representatives, that our generation has not faced the truth of Byron.

Writing of Byron's menageries, Mr. Quennell observes:

'It pleased him to live surrounded by dependant creatures: and to this trait, rather than to any genuine love of animals (though he had appreciated the companionship of several enormous and devoted dogs) may perhaps be attributed that weakness for forming

1. See below, p. 24, note.

3

menageries which added so much to the discomfort and confusion of his domestic background' (*Byron in Italy*, III, 127–8).

The passage subtly conveys an impression of self-indulgence, and disintegration. One feels that Byron is ill-treating these amiable and forgiving beasts for his own selfish satisfaction.

It is, of course, true that all menageries may be called an unkindness. Also we can admit that the keeping of pets often involves a pleasure in the creatures' dependence; so does a mother's care of her children. But what white perfection is it we are demanding? Let us turn to the facts. In a letter to his sister dated 22 May 1809, C. S. Matthews tells of the dangers of a visit to Newstead. On entering the hall you may run into a bear—or wolf. The animals are fierce, and roam freely (LJ, I, 154, note). Nor was this a mere youthful whim: whatever the pressure of his later fortunes or misfortunes, Byron loved having animals round him. Newton Hanson describes his visit to Byron at Venice in the year 1818, observing that 'the basement contained his lordship's carriages, two or three kinds of dogs, birds, monkeys, a fox, a wolf, in different cages', and that, 'as his lordship passed to his gondola, he used to stop and amuse himself with watching their antics, or would feed them himself occasionally' (LJ, IV, 266, note). When he moved to Ravenna Byron took his menagerie with him, and on such occasions the cavalcade of carriages, servants, horses and animals made an amazing spectacle (Medwin, 1–2; Galt, XL). On 15 August 1821 Shelley gave Peacock his first impressions of Byron's Ravenna establishment, noting that it 'consists, besides servants, of ten horses, eight enormous dogs, three monkeys, five cats, an eagle, a crow and a falcon; and all those, except the horses, walk about the house, which every now and then resounds with their unarbitrated quarrels, as if they were the masters of it'. In a postscript he adds: 'I find that my enumeration of the animals in this Circeaean Palace was defective, and that in a material point. I have just met, on the grand staircase, five peacocks, two guinea-hens and an Egyptian crane. I wonder who all these animals were before they were changed into these shapes' (LJ, V, 339, note). The phrase 'as if they were the masters of it' is important: the human inmates of such a household were certainly in part dependent on the *beasts'* behaviour. Such establishments, with all the appalling trouble of transporting the creatures concerned from place to place as Byron changed his residences, might be considered a reasonable test of 'love of animals'.

Byron's prose writings bear out his extraordinary regard for his often ferocious and undisciplined pets. His innate sympathy is shown in a note from his Swiss Journal for Augusta, 20 September 1816: 'Strolled to river: saw boy and kid; kid followed him like a dog; kid could not get over a fence, and bleated piteously; tried myself to help kid, but nearly overset both self and kid into the river' (LJ, III, 356). The same sympathetic care is given to his own charges: 'The crow is lame of a leg—wonder how it happened—some fool trod upon his toe, I suppose. The falcon pretty brisk—the cats large and noisy—the monkeys I have not looked to since the cold weather, as they suffer by being brought up. Horses must be gay—get a ride as soon as weather serves.' That is purely a piece of self-communing, written for his own private satisfaction (Journal, 6 Jan. 1821; LJ, V, 155). But his affection is not limited to an oppressive care; he does not humanize the relation: 'Fed the two cats, the hawk, and the tame (though *not tamed*) crow' (Journal, 5 Jan. 1821; LJ, V, 152). Byron's italics here are important.

He seems to have liked his animals fierce. Pigot tells us that at Harrogate in the year 1806, Byron, then a young man of nineteen, possessed a very ferocious bull-mastiff, Nelson, as well as his Newfoundland, Boatswain. Nelson always wore a muzzle, though sometimes Byron sent for him into his room and to Pigot's embarrassment had the muzzle removed. The dog and his master amused themselves by 'throwing the room into disorder'. Nelson and Boatswain sometimes fought and then everyone, hotel waiters included, had to assist in parting them. Finally, Nelson attacked the horses and was shot by a stable-boy (Moore, IV, 37–8). Byron was never afraid of animals. On sailing from Genoa in 1823 he spent the night controlling the horses who had broken loose and were kicking each other in terror during a storm (Gamba, I, 11–12). Indeed, his pets were in part loved for their ferocity and forgiven for any hurts received. He had a bulldog called 'Savage', 'the finest puppy I ever saw', and dangerous: 'In his great and manifold kindness he has already bitten my fingers, and disturbed the *gravity* of old Boatswain, who is *grievously discomposed*' (Elizabeth Pigot, 11 June 1807; LJ, I, 129). Much later, included in a letter to Murray from Ravenna, is a request for some bulldogs to be sent from England (1 March 1820; LJ, IV, 415). That Byron's fondness for animals was not, as Mr. Quennell suggests (VIII, 252), 'capricious and self-centred', may be further supposed from another attacking creature, a parrot. James Nathan tells of the 'beautiful parrots' with which Byron amused himself during composition, and especially notes his patience when once, on leaving the room, he was so fiercely attacked that the blood flowed 'copiously': 'Instead of being excited by the pain produced, his Lordship was only lost in admiration at the strong attachment of the bird, which he instantly caressed, and, in the words of Macheath, exclaimed, "Was this well done, Jenny?"' (LJ, III, 75-6, note).

To Byron animals were half-human; they are not humanized, they are their own wild selves; but even so he feels their kinship with the wild selves of mankind. Such touches, though often light, are significant enough. Here is one, from a letter to Moore, 24 May 1820: 'I have just been scolding my monkey for tearing the seal of her letter, and spoiling a mock book, in which I put rose leaves. I had a civet-cat the other day, too; but it ran away, after scratching my monkey's cheek, and I am in search of it still. It was the fiercest beast I ever saw, and like —— in the face and manner' (LJ, V, 31). He could visualize Count Guiccioli as a pig (Teresa, 15 July 1820; Origo, V, 193) and Italian peasants as 'a fine, savage, race of two-legged leopards' (Journal, 24 Jan. 1821; LJ, V, 185). After visiting a zoo he compares the beasts to his various acquaintances:

'Two nights ago I saw the tigers sup at Exeter 'Change. Except Veli Pasha's lion in the Morea—who followed the Arab keeper like a dog—the fondness of the hyaena for her keeper amused me most. Such a conversazione!—There was a "hippopotamus", like Lord Liverpool in the face; and the "Ursine Sloth" had the very voice and manner of my valet—but the tiger talked too much. The elephant took and gave me my money again—took off my hat—opened a door—*trunked* a whip—and behaved so well, that I wish he was my butler. The handsomest animal on earth is one of the panthers; but the poor antelopes were dead. I should hate to see one *here:*—the sight of the *camel* made me pine again for Asia Minor. "O quando te aspiciam?"' (Journal, 14 Nov. 1813; LJ, II, 319.)

Later, writing from Venice to Murray on 14 April 1817 on his response to painting, Byron notes that most things in his life have proved disappointing with the exception of mountains and seas, 'two or three women', 'some horses', 'a lion (at Veli Pasha's) in the Morea'; and 'a tiger at supper in Exeter 'Change' (LJ, IV, 107).

To Byron animals radiated vivid significances. He admired especially their energies and strength. From Venice he described the breaking loose of an elephant who 'ate up a fruit shop, killed his keeper, broke into a church', and eventually had to be killed by cannon. Approaching him in a gondola, Byron was greeted by a shower of hurled beams—his strength was 'extraordinary'—and later saw him dead, 'a stupendous fellow' (Kinnaird, 6 March 1819; C, II, 105). This admiration of animal power was one with Byron's interest in the vital stuff of men and nations. He enjoys using terms of warfare to describe a fight between his great dog Matz and a mountain pig: 'The Pig was first thrown into confusion, and compelled to retire with great disorder', but later faced about and 'drove Matz from all his positions, with such slaughter that nothing but night prevented a total defeat' (Hobhouse, 22 April 1817; C, II, 50). We hear of Matz again: 'I have got two monkeys, a fox, and two new mastiffs. Matz is still in high old age. The monkeys are charming' (Kinnaird, 6 March 1819; C, II, 106). One of Byron's most lovable characteristics is his habit of referring to his dependants' well-being, whether servants (e.g. Fletcher) or animals.

Animals were felt as close, intimate beings, like lovers: he compared his first Italian mistress to an antelope (Moore, 17 Nov. 1816; LJ, IV, 7) and his second to a pythoness and tigress: 'I like this kind of animal', he says, and calls her 'a fine animal but quite untameable' (Moore, 19 Sept. 1818; Murray, 1 Aug. 1819; LJ, IV, 262, 332). Animals resembled himself: 'I am like the tyger (in poesy), if I miss my first Spring, I go growling back to my Jungle. There is no second. I can't correct. I can't and I won't' (Murray, 18 Nov. 1820; LJ, V, 120). He saw himself when attacked by his enemies as a bear or a bull being baited, and possessing the 'united energies of those amiable animals' (Murray, 1 Aug. 1819; LJ, IV, 326). Driven from London, he compared himself to a hunted stag that 'betakes him to the waters' (*Blackwood's* Defence, LJ, IV, 479). He was, from the start, a lonely animal ('The lion is alone and so am I', *Manfred,* III, i), and the friend of animals: 'I have got a new friend, the finest in the world, a *tame bear*' (Elizabeth Pigot, 26 Oct. 1807; LJ, I, 147). He had a painter down to Newstead to do its and his wolf's portrait (LJ, II, 57, note; Finlay, quoted Edgcumbe, I, VIII, 99); and some people thought the *Thyrza* poems recorded a perverted love for it (Medwin, 277, note). From his early travels he brought back four live tortoises and a greyhound which died on the passage (Drury, 17 July 1811; LJ, I, 318). Strangers made him 'sick': 'For my part (since I lost my Newfoundland dog) I like nobody except his successor, a Dutch Mastiff, and three land Tortoises brought with me from Greece' (Augusta, 9 Sept. 1811; LJ,

II, 31). To make a friend of a dog is natural; but to find romance in tortoises is rarer. He was deeply concerned about them: 'My tortoises (all Athenians), my hedge-hog, my mastiff and the other live Greek, are all purely (poorly?). The tortoises lay eggs, and I have hired a hen to hatch them' (Hodgson, 25 Sept. 1811; LJ, II, 46). He was often in the mood of a hermit, of a Robinson Crusoe, a Timon, alone among the beasts: 'I am now', he writes to Lady Melbourne, 'quite alone with my books and my Maccaw' (17 Oct. 1814; C, I, 281). Again, he tells Murray that he couldn't write, his vein being gone: 'my principal conversation is with my Maccaw and Bayle' (26 April 1814; LJ, III, 75).

We have already observed Byron's reference to his Newfoundland, Boatswain. 'Byron', writes Maurois, 'nursed him like a friend, and with his own bare hands sponged the froth that ran from his gaping jaws' (I, XII, 99). The dog's death was a severe blow to him. To Hodgson he wrote on 18 November 1808: 'Boatswain is dead! He expired in a state of madness on the 10th after suffering much, yet retaining all the gentleness of his nature to the last, never attempting to do the least injury to any one near him. I have now lost everything except Old Murray' (LJ, III, 171, note); and added, on 27 November (LJ, I, 200), that he 'is to be buried in a vault waiting for myself', and that he has composed an epitaph. The epitaph is in both verse and prose. The verse, published originally with *The Corsair* in 1815, is entitled *Inscription on the Monument of a Newfoundland Dog*. A titled man, whatever his worth, receives honour in burial—

> But the poor dog, in life the firmest friend,
> The first to welcome, foremost to defend,
> Whose honest heart is still his master's own,
> Who labours, fights, lives, breathes for him alone,
> Unhonour'd falls, unnotic'd all his worth,
> Denied in heaven the soul he held on earth:
> While man, vain insect! hopes to be forgiven,
> And claims himself a sole exclusive heaven.

Next the poet, in the manner of Timon, denounces man's insincerity and vice in direct comparison with the integrity of the brute creation. The conclusion runs:

> Ye! who perchance behold this simple urn,
> Pass on—it honours none you wish to mourn.

To mark a friend's remains these stones arise;
I never knew but one—and here he lies.

The prose inscription is in similar vein:

Near this spot
Are deposited the Remains of one
Who possessed Beauty without Vanity,
Strength without Insolence,
Courage without Ferocity,
And all the Virtues of Man without his Vices.
This Praise, which would be unmeaning Flattery
If inscribed over human ashes,
Is but a just tribute to the Memory of
Boatswain, a Dog
Who was born at Newfoundland, May 1803,
And died at Newstead Abbey, November 18, 1808.

(Moore, VII, 73.)

The thoughts of this inscription recur in Byron's remark, when visiting the house of Petrarch and seeing the embalmed body of his cat, 'that the hearts of animals were often better than ours, and that this animal's affection may well have put Laura's coldness to shame' (Teresa, quoted Origo, III, 116). In setting out directions for his will (12 Aug. 1811) Byron stated that he was to be buried without ceremony or service and that no inscription except his name and age was to be written on his tomb, adding: 'it is my will that my faithful dog may not be removed from the said vault'. This was his 'particular desire'. Though his solicitor urged that the request be left as a letter and not in the will, Byron insisted: 'It must stand' (LJ, I, 329–30).

He probably had Boatswain in mind when, on 5 May 1823, just before his last expedition, he wrote from the Villa Saluzzo to Edward Le Mesurier expressing great gratitude for the gift of a Newfoundland dog, a breed for which he asserted his especial fondness (LJ, VI, 203). This was, presumably, Lyon, the dog Byron took with him to Missolonghi and of which Parry writes:

'With Lyon Lord Byron was accustomed, not only to associate, but to commune very much, and very often. His most usual phrase was, "Lyon, you are no rogue, Lyon"; or "Lyon", his Lordship would say, "thou art an honest fellow, Lyon." The dog's eyes sparkled, and his tail swept the floor, as he sat with his haunches

9

on the ground. "Thou art more faithful than men, Lyon; I trust thee more." Lyon sprang up, and barked and bounded round his master, as much as to say, "You may trust me, I will watch actively on every side." "Lyon, I love thee, thou art my faithful dog," and Lyon jumped and kissed his master's hand, as an acknowledgment of his homage. In this sort of mingled talk and gambol Lord Byron passed a good deal of time, and seemed more contented, more calmly self-satisfied, on such occasions, than almost on any other. In conversation and in company he was animated and brilliant; but with Lyon and in stillness he was pleased and perfectly happy' (Parry, IV, 75).

At Missolonghi Byron told George Finlay that Newfoundland dogs had twice saved his life, and that 'he could not live without one' (Finlay, quoted Edgcumbe, I, VIII, 99).

Byron's sympathy with animals was one with his sympathy with men and peoples. 'Lord Byron', wrote Gamba, 'never could be an idle spectator of any calamity. . . . The slightest appearance of injustice or cruelty, not only to his own species, but to animals, roused his indignation and compelled his interference, and personal consequences never for one moment entered into his calculations' (quoted Edgcumbe, I, VIII, 80 and Teresa, I; IX, 387; no refs.). Once, thinking of an execution, he soliloquized on his own reluctance to attend: 'Now, could I *save* him, or a fly even, from the same catastrophe, I would out-match years . . .' (*Detached Thoughts,* Oct. 1821; LJ, V, 439). 'Tears of mental or physical suffering', wrote Teresa, 'make him almost ill—the dread of treading on an ant makes him go out of his way—a scene at the play, a sad story or a melodious tune bring tears to his eyes' (quoted Origo, II, 87). When, after the failure of the rising in Ravenna, Teresa was imploring Byron to join her at Pisa, his continued delay was prompted by his concern for certain delicate 'Dutch horses' for whom the condition of the roads was regarded as unsatisfactory. To the last he showed, says Iris Origo, a 'greater concern for the Dutch horses than for his mistress' impatience' (Teresa, 12, 23, 26 Oct. 1821; Origo, VI, 288–90). Byron loved horses and liked comparing himself with Alfieri, whose tastes likewise included a love of liberty and a fondness for animals, 'and above all, for horses' (Blessington, 96–7).

His menagerie caused him continual anxiety: 'It is troublesome' he told Medwin, 'to travel so far with so much live and dead stock as I do; and I don't like to leave behind me any of my pets that have been accumulating since I came on the Continent. One cannot trust to strangers to take care of them. You will see at the farmer's some of my pea-fowls *en pension*' (Medwin, 8). Medwin tells us that he bought a monkey in Pisa in the street, because he saw it ill-used (9, note); and quotes *Don Juan*, where Juan's love of pets ('let deeper sages the true cause determine') is emphasized:

> He had a kind of inclination, or
> Weakness, for what most people deem mere vermin,
> Live animals . . .
>
> (x, 50.)

There is, too, the interesting affair with the geese. Byron believed that one should eat a goose at Michaelmas (Gamba, quoted Origo, IX, 365). Nevertheless the phraseology of a letter to Teresa on 11 October 1820, 'Pray do not have such a massacre of geese as I cannot come for several days' (Origo, V, 228), subtly suggests a reluctance. On his journey from Pisa to Genoa, he had some geese with him for Michaelmas. I follow Teresa's account, drawing variously on her two studies. The geese 'swung in a cage behind his carriage, punctuating the journey with their cackling'. But Byron, says Teresa, 'felt sorry for them', and 'when the time came to wring their necks, he would not give the order, and decided instead to keep them, "to test the theory of their longevity"'. On arriving in Genoa, 'they at once became the guardians and mistresses of the yard, as sacred as those of the Capitol, and waddled about in the garden and the lower floor of the house, accompanying Byron wherever he went'. Notice Byron's rationalization of his instincts in 'in order to test their longevity': it happens elsewhere. Byron was always 'caressing' the birds and when he left for Greece boarded them with his banker, Mr. Barry, who was told to take good care of them, it being Byron's intention 'to keep them as long as they lived' (Origo, VIII, 325, 344; Notes, 513; Teresa, I; IX, 388–9).

Naturally enough, Byron repudiated field-sports. Teresa notes how he regularly refused the 'pleasures of the chase' (I; IX, 387). As early as 2 April 1804, he complained to Augusta that the sole pleasure of some of his neighbours, themselves 'only one degree removed from the brute creation', consisted in 'field sports' (LJ, I, 25). As he grew older, his antipathy hardened. On 14 December 1808 —again to Augusta—he wrote: 'I hate all field sports' (LJ, I, 205). He kept no guns at Newstead (Dallas, 27 Aug. 1811; LJ, II, 9). Once, in supporting the values of paganism, he asked: 'Is there a Talapoin or a Bonze who is not superior to a fox-hunting curate?'

(Hodgson, 3 Sept. 1811; II, 22). He sensed a hideous discrepancy in the conception, his revulsion from the cruelty involved being the clearer from his lines on angling in *Don Juan:*

> And angling, too, that solitary vice,
> Whatever Isaak Walton sings or says;
> The quaint, old, cruel coxcomb, in his gullet
> Should have a hook, and a small trout to pull it.
>
> (XIII, 106.)

On the last line his own note reads:

'It would have taught him humanity at least. This sentimental savage . . . teaches how to sew up frogs, and break their legs by way of experiment, in addition to the art of angling, the cruelest, the coldest, and the stupidest of pretended sports. . . . The whale, the shark and the tunny fishery have somewhat of noble and perilous in them; even net fishing, trawling, etc. are more humane and useful. But angling!—No angler can be a good man.'

His dislike of blood-sports started early and continued throughout his life. His clearest statement occurs in his Journal of 20 March 1814:

'I remember, in riding from Chrisso to Castri (Delphos), along the sides of Parnassus, I saw six eagles in the air. It is uncommon to see so many together; and it was the number—not the species, which is common enough—that excited my attention.

'The last bird I ever fired at was an *eaglet,* on the shore of the Gulf of Lepanto, near Vostitza. It was only wounded, and I tried to save it, the eye was so bright; but it pined, and died in a few days; and I never did since, and never will, attempt the death of another bird' (LJ, II, 404).

We have a letter to Moore on 15 September 1814 (LJ, III, 136), written at a time of mental 'confusion' when distraction was apparently sought in fishing and 'firing at the fowls of the air' as well as at 'soda-water bottles', probably without much expectation of catching or hitting anything; both the phraseology and 'bottles'—Byron's usual target—suggesting a random and haphazard activity with pistols. The action was certainly exceptional. Witness after witness records Byron's love of pistol practice, and each in turn notes his use of inanimate targets (bottles, coins, etc.; see pp. 106–7). The only exception is one recorded by Trelawny (XVIII) whose reminiscences are notoriously unreliable (see Nicolson's reference to 'his

usual inaccuracy' (VI, 130)). When associating with Teresa Guiccioli and the Gambas near Ravenna in the year 1820, at a time
when it was in his interests, both as lover and revolutionary, to
appear among his foreign friends as a man of iron, he stuck to his
principles: 'From the bowling-green the company passed to a trial
of marksmanship—a sport, Teresa added, in which Byron excelled,
but in which he refused to take part whenever the target was a living
bird.' The guests were later taken to the river and 'provided with
fishing nets', but 'before then Byron had had enough of it' and
returned to Ravenna. His behaviour must have surprised his friends,
Teresa noting it as 'a weakness, but the weakness of a great heart!'
(Origo, following Teresa, V, 217).

Among the various causes that raised British society against
Byron, Jeaffreson (XVII, 225-6) listed his aversion from blood-sports
(and see *Don Juan*, XIII, 75). Like his own Cain, Byron suffered
for his sympathies with the animal creation.

Among Byron's challenging eccentricities, Jeaffreson lists also
the poet's alienation of social feeling by his habit of 'sustaining life
on biscuits and soda-water' (XVII, 225). There were various causes
for Byron's almost suicidal diet maintained, with intermissions,
throughout; but his ingrained sympathy with animal life clearly
played its part. 'He ate little,' says Galt, describing the voyage from
Gibraltar; 'no animal food, but only bread and vegetables' (VIII). It
is not my purpose to prove Byron a theorizing or consistent vege-
tarian, but merely to observe a tendency noted by every one who
knew him; together with his instinct for living, as well as writing,
his convictions.

He could, however, and did, write them too. That Byron is our
greatest poet of animal life can scarcely be disputed. In revelation of
animal energy and animal pathos—for his animals are regularly felt
tragically—he has no equal in English poetry; and in deliberately putting much of his major work *at the service of* animals, he probably
stands alone in the literatures of the world.

Beside our prose description of the elephant at Venice we can
set the magnificent Bull of the bull-fight in *Childe Harold* (1, 74-9).
In each there is *both* a delight in the beast's strength *and* awe at its
agony and destruction. Each outlines the other, as again in the brilliant miniature of the dying war-horse in *The Destruction of Sennacherib;* or the fire-eye'd buffalo attacked by wolves, together with the
packed stanza of distraught animals at the poem's conclusion, in *The
Siege of Corinth* (XXIII, XXXIII). In close relation we have the fas-

cinating horror of biological energy in the quivering fragments of the severed viper in *Marino Faliero* (III, ii); and the agony of the scorpion ringed with fire and twisting round to inject itself with its own poison in *The Giaour*. No poet is so appallingly aware of animal suffering; the lioness robbed of her young in *The Giaour;* the over-worked post-horses in England in *Don Juan* (XIII, 42); the lamb 'bleating' before the butcher in *Marino Faliero* (V, I). The power of *Heaven and Earth* derives from its extraordinary realization of the Flood's impact on animals and birds (see pp. 111–12). Small creatures get equal notice with the greater: the wounded butterfly in *The Giaour,* the insect stinging in defence of its own in *The Corsair* (I, 13); most exquisite of all, that wonderful penetration of human psychology and animal companionship when the dungeoned Bon-nivard, after years of solitary durance, is anguished at leaving his long-loved friends, the spiders at their 'sullen trade'—the spiders' victims being also remembered—and the little mice at their moonlit play (*The Prisoner of Chillon,* XIV).

Three of Byron's late works—and two of them among his greatest —mature from this peculiar sympathy. We have, first, the nightmare ride and wild mustangs of *Mazeppa,* a narrative of suspended, sicken-ing excitement, based on a vivid apprehension of horses. Horses are, indeed, Byron's peculiar favourites, as with the magnificent, super-natural, coal-black horses of *The Deformed Transformed:*

> The mighty steam, which volumes high
> From their proud nostrils, burns the very air;
> And sparks of flame, like dancing fire-flies, wheel
> Around their manes as common insects swarm
> Round common steeds at sunset.
>
> (I, i.)

Our second is *Cain,* the impressions ranging from the tiniest to the most vast forms of animal life:

> The little shining fire-fly in its flight,
> And the immortal star in its great course,
> Must both be guided. . . .
>
> (II, i.)

From this we move to sight of great prehistoric monsters, mam-moths ten-fold greater than the forested roaring beasts of earth; to leviathans and the gigantic, dripping serpent rising from the abyss (p. 113). This serpent may be felt as the archetype of other Byronic serpents; and indeed the drama is at pains to assert that the serpent, not Lucifer, tempted Adam. The action, moreover, revolves precisely round the theme of animal slaughter. Cain instances a lamb stung by a serpent in accusation of Jehovah's cruel creation (II, ii); and his crime is, like Byron's, a refusal to participate in the accepted code. He will offer fruits, but not blood, to Jehovah:

> *His pleasure!* What was his high pleasure in
> The fumes of scorching flesh and smoking blood,
> To the pain of the bleating mothers, which
> Still yearn for their dead offspring? Or the pangs
> Of the sad ignorant victims underneath
> Thy pious knife? Give way! This bloody record
> Shall not stand in the sun to shame creation!
>
> (III, i.)

Abel's sacrifice is accepted, Cain's rejected. Biblical authority is closely followed. This drama, Byron's final statement of revolt against the religious and social traditions of Europe, specifically levels its indictment in terms of animal slaughter. Our third work is the lucid and compact *Sardanapalus*, probably Byron's most exquisite single creation, wherein all past themes of his life and poetry are beautifully and exactly harmonized.[1] The action shows us an enlightened emperor who refuses, like Byron himself, to conform to current standards regarding (i) blood-sports and (ii) imperial conquest; of which the respective symbols are his grim ancestors, Nimrod and Semiramis, whose ghosts in nightmare objectify the hero's sense of guilt:

> Hence—hence—
> Old hunter of the earliest brutes! and ye,
> Who hunted fellow-creatures as if brutes!
> Once bloody mortals—and now bloodier idols,
> If your priests lie not! And thou, ghastly beldame!
> Dripping with dusky gore, and trampling on
> The carcasses of Inde—away! away!
>
> (IV, i.)

As so often, no distinction is drawn between the sufferings of men and those of animals.

I have presented my case. Byron's interest in animals cannot be

---

1. My study appears in *The Burning Oracle*. *Sardanapalus* is unfortunately omitted from the *Everyman* Byron.

called 'capricious and self-centred' (p. 5). It is probable that no great man on record has left stronger evidence to the contrary.

Byron's insight into the energies of the animal creation is, as with Shakespeare, to be related to his understanding of man; as when he points a central human judgment by bitterly complaining that the 'lion' Napoleon is being replaced by enslavement to a number of 'wolves' (*Childe Harold,* III, 19). Being so closely in touch with natural vitality he is the better able to assess and place the energies displayed within any historic event. But here again we come up against Mr. Quennell, who has questioned Byron's historical knowledge. Basing his statements on Leigh Hunt's deliberately hostile account of Byron (which Hunt himself in part retracted), Mr. Quennell tells us that once, during an argument with Hunt on historical personages, Byron 'did not attempt to produce an answer'. Mr. Quennell adds: '*His own stock of historical parallels was not extensive*' (italics mine), and in conclusion informs us that Byron 'retired from the unequal contest baffled and irritated' (VIII, 249–50). Faced by this remarkable statement, one is tempted to do the same. For of whom is Mr. Quennell writing? Of some literary dilettante, some dandefied impostor, of contemporary fabrication? Or of Byron, the greatest historical poet in western literature? Let us enquire briefly into Byron's historical equipment.

Moore (V, 46–9) quotes from a rough notebook of Byron's, made in the year 1807, an account of his early reading. He observes that Byron's reading was 'far in advance of his schoolfellows', and that indeed, the poet's 'retentive memory' considered, it is doubtful if among the more regular 'contenders for scholastic honours and prizes, there could be found a single one who, at the same age, has possessed any thing like the same stock of useful knowledge'.

Here is Byron's account. First there is the 'List of Historical writers whose works I have perused in different languages'. It runs as follows:

'*History of England:* Hume, Rapin, Henry, Smollett, Tindal, Belsham, Bisset, Adolphus, Holinshed, Froissart's Chronicles (belonging properly to France)—*Scotland:* Buchanan, Hector Boethius, both in the Latin—*Ireland:* Gordon—*Rome:* Hooke, Decline and Fall by Gibbon, Ancient History by Rollin (including an account of the Carthaginians etc.), besides Livy, Tacitus, Eutropius, Cornelius Nepos, Julius Caesar, Arrian, Sallust—*Greece:* Mitford's Greece, Leland's Philip, Plutarch, Potter's Antiquities, Xenophon,

Thucydides, Herodotus—*France:* Mezeray, Voltaire—*Spain:* I chiefly derived my knowledge of old Spanish History from a book, called the Atlas, now obsolete. The modern history, from the intrigues of Alberoni down to the Prince of Peace, I learned from its connexion with European politics—*Portugal:* From Vertot, as also his account of the Siege of Rhodes,—though the last is his own invention, the real facts being totally different—So much for his Knights of Malta—*Turkey:* I have read Knolles, Sir Paul Rycaut, and Prince Cantemir, besides a more modern history, anonymous. Of the Ottoman History I know every event, from Tangralopi, and afterwards Othman I, to the peace of Passarowitz, in 1718,—the battle of Cutzka, in 1739, and the treaty between Russia and Turkey in 1790—*Russia:* Tooke's Life of Catherine II, Voltaire's Czar Peter —*Sweden:* Voltaire's Charles XII, also Norberg's Charles XII— in my opinion the best of the two—A translation of Schiller's Thirty Years War, which contains the exploits of Gustavus Adolphus, besides Harte's Life of the same Prince. I have somewhere, too, read an account of Gustavus Vasa, the deliverer of Sweden, but do not remember the author's name—*Prussia:* I have seen, at least, twenty Lives of Frederick II, the only prince worth recording in Prussian annals. Gillies, his own Works, and Thiebault—none very amusing. The last is paltry, but circumstantial—*Denmark:* I know little of. Of *Norway* I understand the natural history, but not the chronological —*Germany:* I have read long histories of the house of Suabia, Wenceslaus, and, at length, Rodolph of Hapsburgh and his *thick-lipped* Austrian descendants—*Switzerland:* Ah! William Tell, and the battle of Morgarten, where Burgundy was slain—*Italy:* Davila, Guicciardini, the Guelphs and Ghibbelines, the battle of Pavia, Massaniello, the revolutions of Naples, etc. etc. *Hindustan:* Orme and Cambridge—*America:* Robertson, Andrews' American War— *Africa:* merely from travels as Mungo Park, Bruce.'

Under Biography, we have noted:

'Robertson's Charles V, Caesar, Sallust (Catiline and Jugurtha), Lives of Marlborough and Eugene, Tekeli, Bonnard, Buonaparte, all the British Poets, both by Johnson and Anderson, Rousseau's Confessions, Life of Cromwell, British Plutarch, British Nepos, Campbell's Lives of the Admirals, Charles XII, Czar Peter, Catherine II, Henry Lord Kaimes, Marmontel, Teignmouth's Sir William Jones, Life of Newton, Belisaire, with thousands not to be detailed.'

The list continues with headings—not all so well-filled—of Law, Philosophy, Geography, and Divinity. Poetry is included as follows:

'All the British Classics, as before detailed, with most of the living poets, Scott, Southey, etc.—Some French, in the original, of which the Cid is my favourite—Little Italian—Greek and Latin without number;—these last I shall give up in future—I have translated a good deal from both languages, verse as well as prose.'

Under Eloquence he records: 'Demosthenes, Cicero, Quintilian, Sheridan, Austin's Chironomia and Parliamentary Debates from the Revolution to the year 1742.' He has also read to his 'regret', he says, 'above four thousand novels, including the works of Cervantes, Fielding, Smollett, Richardson, Mackenzie, Sterne, Rabelais, and Rousseau etc. etc.' Burton's *Anatomy of Melancholy* he regards as a storehouse *par excellence* of valuable quotations and anecdotes.

Concerning this reading he observes (just before mentioning the novels and Burton): 'All the books here enumerated I have taken down from memory. I recollect reading them, and can quote passages from any mentioned. I have, of course, omitted several in my catalogue; but the greater part of the above I perused before the age of fifteen. Since I left Harrow I have become idle and conceited, from scribbling rhyme and making love to women.' This is signed 'B—Nov. 30, 1807'.

In this same notebook Byron also wrote down 'a list of the different poets, dramatic or otherwise, who have distinguished their respective languages'. He enumerates first the poets, ancient and modern, of Europe, and continues with brief general comments on the poetry of Arabia, Persia, America, Iceland, Denmark, Norway, Hindustan, the Birman Empire, China and Africa. We are not claiming that he was properly read in these; but his awareness of them and interest are important. 'The works of the European,' he says, 'and some of the Asiatic, I have perused, either in the original or translations.'

The list is impressive enough. Byron was himself surprised at his precocity, and at pains to understand it; elsewhere his journals and poetry show him in this self-baffled mood. Moore was also impressed, noting that this early book-list helps to account for Byron's extraordinary command of language. Indeed, to any one well acquainted with Byron's work, this list should be less a surprise than a key. Surely we are all staggered by his wealth of historic reference, the easy command which enables him to raise the past in treatment of places and peoples, at—as it were—a moment's notice; fitting his references with all their weight of proper names, into, if need be, a complicated pattern of serious or humorous rhyme. The list is what one expects.

Nevertheless, since at every point the defence must be barricaded, let us answer a few objections. Is there any evidence, apart from general corroboration—and that lies everywhere—that his reading was so wide and so well remembered as he asserts? There is. We have seen, and may have questioned, Byron's striking claim to have read widely in Turkish history. Now in his account of Byron's last days in Greece Gamba describes a visit of Prince Mavrocordato to Byron on 31 January 1824:

'It must not be supposed that their conversations on all occasions turned on nothing but public affairs: on the contrary, they talked now and then upon general topics, and I remember very well, that one evening when they were together, they had a sort of trial of skill as to their recollection of Turkish history. Mavrocordato is esteemed very accomplished in this particular, and tried Byron on the genealogy of the Ottoman emperors. Wherever there was any difference of opinion, we always found, on reference, that Byron was right: his memory, indeed, was surprisingly accurate. He said "The Turkish history was one of the first books that gave me pleasure when a child; and I believe it had much influence on my subsequent wishes to visit the Levant, and gave, perhaps, the oriental colouring which is observed in my poetry"' (Gamba, III, 148).

That is factual evidence of the first order from an independent authority exactly corroborating, some sixteen or seventeen years later, what was perhaps the most striking feature in Byron's youthful claims. Those claims were definite: 'As to my reading,' he wrote to Dallas on 21 January 1808, 'I believe I may aver, without hyperbole, it has been tolerably extensive in the historical department; so that few nations exist, or have existed, with whose records I am not in some degree acquainted, from Herodotus down to Gibbon' (I, 172). He possessed, from the start, the *will* towards a comprehensive historical understanding.

Indeed, his historical memory was proverbial. His memory, says George Finlay, who knew him at Missolonghi, was 'very extraordinary'. Of all the 'innumerable' novels which he had read, 'he seemed to recollect perfectly the story, and every scene of merit'.

19

Once, engaged in a bet with a friend on the ancestry of Maurice of Orange, he applied to Byron, who had all the genealogical details ready. 'This', said Finlay to him, 'is the most extraordinary instance of your memory I ever heard' (Finlay, quoted Edgcumbe, I; VIII, 101–2). Another of Byron's Missolonghi associates was likewise impressed, Col. Stanhope noting that Byron's reading was extensive and also 'retentive' to an 'extraordinary' degree (Stanhope, quoted Edgcumbe, XVI, 213). And yet another, Millingen, refers to 'his wonderful mnemonic faculties, the rich and varied store with which he had furnished his mind, his lively, brilliant, and ever-busy imagination, his deep acquaintance with the world' (quoted Teresa, II; IX, 179). 'The memories of his heart', says Teresa, 'were even more astonishing than those of his mind' (I; VIII, 321). Byron's 'retentiousness of memory' from childhood may, wrote Jeaffreson—he is referring to emotional experiences—'be described as terrible' (v, 43).

Byron's Letters, Journals, and Notes tell the same story. When asking Murray on 9 October 1821 for a Bible to save constant wear—since he read the scriptures continually—on that given him by Augusta, he observes that he had read the Old Testament 'through and through' before he was eight, though the New was then a 'task' rather than a 'pleasure' (LJ, V, 391). He regularly corrected Kennedy's Biblical references at Cephalonia (Gamba, quoted Kennedy, App., 378). In *My Dictionary* (May 1821), he dwells on his early childhood at Aberdeen, remarking: 'The moment I could read, my grand passion was history'; and recalls that his imagination was peculiarly roused by the Battle of Lake Regillus, the site of which he has since visited (LJ, V, 406). At Harrow they wondered at his stock of general information, putting it down to a clever use of reviews, because he was 'never seen reading, but always idle, and in mischief, or at play'. But the real reason was that he 'read eating, read in bed, read when no one else reads'; and had read all sorts of books since he was 'five years old'. Thus he gained a reputation for the 'extent and readiness' of his 'general information'. Though Peel was his superior in some ways at Harrow, yet in 'general information, history, etc.', he was Peel's superior and ahead of most others (*Detached Thoughts*, Oct. 1821; LJ, V, 452–3). Galt (III) records his precocious studies in History and Scripture whilst at Harrow.

His wide learning and uncanny memory made him a frightening critic. Lady Blessington tells us that, 'having read perhaps more than any man of his age', he could immediately detect any plagiarism or want of originality in a writer and, whenever he did so, would throw away the book concerned in disgust (Blessington, 196). He could also spot mistakes, noting that Bacon was often inaccurate in his 'historical authorities' and drawing attention to certain errors in his *Apophthegms*, which he regarded as worthy of punishment in any 'fourth-form' school-boy. The corrections (which are given in full in a note to *Don Juan*, V, 147 and at LJ, V, App. VI, 597–600) are worth quoting here. Byron's corrections are given beside Bacon's statements, but to save space I quote the corrections only, the numbers referring to the apophthegms concerned:

'91— This was *not* the portrait of a cardinal, but of the Pope's master of ceremonies; 155— It was after the battle of Issus and during the siege of Tyre, and *not* immediately after the passage of the Granicus, that this is said to have occurred; 158— This was *not* said by Antigonus, but by a Spartan, previously to the battle of Thermopylae; 162— This happened under Augustus Caesar, and *not* during the reign of Adrian; 164— This happened to the father of Herodes Atticus, and the answer was made by the Emperor *Nerva*, who deserved that his name should have been stated by the "greatest— wisest—meanest of mankind"; 178— This was said by Anarcharsis the Scythian, and *not* by a Greek; 209— This was *not* said *by* Demosthenes, but *to* Demosthenes by *Phocion;* 221— This was not said of Caius (Caligula, I presume, is intended by Caius), but of *Tiberius* himself; 97— This reply was *not* made by a king of *Hungary,* but sent by Richard the First, Cœur de Lion, of England, to the Pope with the breast-plate of the bishop of Beauvais; 267— This did *not* happen to Demetrius, but to *Philip,* King of Macedon.'

Byron's reading, which served to select these errors out of a mass of statements, must have been wide and his memory exact. It is clearly a scholarly temperament that feels keenly about such errors, or he would hardly burden the notes of his poem with so laboured an account. He was, however, unwilling to parade his learning, writing to Murray, 'I had subscribed the authorities—Arrian, Plutarch, Hume etc.—for the *corrections* of Bacon, but, thinking it pedantic to do so, have since erased them' (8 Jan. 1821; LJ, V, 220).

Mr. Quennell has asserted that Byron's stock of historical parallels was 'not extensive'. But our recent quotations have shown that Byron had not only an astonishing historical equipment, but the ability to draw on that equipment for his immediate purpose with a careless ease. Here is another example, specifically concerned with 'parallels', from the Preface to *Marino Faliero:*

'I know not that the historical facts are alluded to in English, unless by Dr. Moore in his *View of Italy*. His account is false and flippant, full of stale jests about old men and young wives, and wondering at so great an effect from so slight a cause. How so acute and severe an observer of mankind as the author of Zeluco could wonder at this is inconceivable. He knew that a basin of water spilt on Mrs. Masham's gown deprived the Duke of Marlborough of his command, and led to the inglorious peace of Utrecht—that Louis XIV was plunged into the most desolating wars, because his minister was nettled at his finding fault with a window, and wished to give him another occupation—that Helen lost Troy—that Lucretia expelled the Tarquins from Rome—and that Cava brought the Moors to Spain—that an insulted husband led the Gauls to Clusium, and thence to Rome—that a single verse of Frederick II of Prussia on the Abbé de Bernis, and a jest on Madame de Pompadour, led to the battle of Rosbach—that the elopement of Dearbhorgil with MacMurchad conducted the English to the slavery of Ireland—that a personal pique between Maria Antoinette and the Duke of Orleans precipitated the first expulsion of the Bourbons—and, not to multiply instances, that Commodus, Domitian, and Caligula fell victims not to their public tyranny, but to private vengeance— and that an order to make Cromwell disembark from the ship in which he would have sailed to America destroyed both King and Commonwealth. After these instances, on the least reflection, it is indeed extraordinary in Dr. Moore to seem surprised that a man used to command, who had served and swayed in the most important offices, should fiercely resent, in a fierce age, an unpunished affront, the grossest that can be offered to a man, be he prince or peasant.'

Perhaps Byron could have loosed down on Hunt a similar avalanche, had he so wished.

Byron's historical interests were not merely academic. They are part of his immediate, personal, contemporary response to peoples and places. Here is an early example witnessing his passionate concern for suffering peoples, the style rising with a graceful ease and his habitual resource and felicity of reference to the passionate argument:

'Eton and Sonnini have led us astray by their panegyrics and projects: but, on the other hand, De Pauw and Thornton have debased the Greeks beyond their demerits.

'The Greeks will never be independent: they will never be

sovereigns as heretofore, and God forbid they ever should! but they may be subjects without being slaves. Our colonies are not independent, but they are free and industrious, and such may Greece be hereafter.

'At present, like the Catholics of Ireland and the Jews throughout the world, and such other cudgelled and heterodox people, they suffer all the moral and physical ills that can afflict humanity. Their life is a struggle against truth; they are vicious in their own defence. They are so unused to kindness, that when they occasionally meet with it they look upon it with suspicion, as a dog often beaten snaps at your fingers if you attempt to caress him. "They are ungrateful, notoriously, abominably ungrateful!"—this is the general cry. Now, in the name of Nemesis! for what are they to be grateful? Where is the human being that ever conferred a benefit on Greek or Greeks? They are to be grateful to the Turks for their fetters, and to the Franks for their broken promises and lying counsels. They are to be grateful to the artist who engraves their ruins, and to the antiquary who carries them away; to the traveller whose janissary flogs them, and to the scribbler whose journal abuses them. This is the amount of their obligations to foreigners' (Note to *Childe Harold,* ii, 73).

To such passionate pleas as this on behalf of suffering peoples was Byron's encyclopaedic reading regularly dedicated.

His life itself was so dedicated. Let us watch him at work, at a time of danger and tension when he was involved in both his liaison with Teresa Guiccioli and the Italian Carbonari movement. Action was hourly expected. Now, in his Journal for 5 January 1821, he amused himself with a random memoranda: 'Read Mitford's *History of Greece,* Xenophon's *Retreat of the Ten Thousand.*' This is at 6 minutes to 8. The clock strikes: 'Going out to make love. Somewhat perilous, but not disagreeable.' There are other jottings. On his return at 11, he notes, among other subjects discussed with Teresa Guiccioli, Sallust's *Conspiracy of Catiline* and the *War of Jugurtha.* On going to bed he returned to Xenophon (LJ, v, 152-3). On 14 January we have: 'Turned over Seneca's tragedies. Wrote the opening lines of the intended tragedy of *Sardanapalus.* Rode out some miles into the forest. Misty and rainy. Returned—dined—wrote some more of my tragedy. Read Diodorus Siculus—turned over Seneca, and some other books. Wrote some more of the tragedy' (LJ, v, 173).

Byron's early poetry and later dramas were all written with a keen historical conscience: he minded more about his local atmosphere and historical accuracy than about poetry, as such (see pp. 104-5, 113): 'There should always', he told Murray, 'be some foundation of fact for the most airy fabric, and pure invention is but the talent of a liar' (2 April 1817; LJ, IV, 93). His will to historicity in *Marino Faliero* and *Sardanapalus* is witnessed by his prefaces and notes. And yet both are more than historical dramas in the Shakespearian sense: history is felt prophetically, *Marino Faliero* dramatizing a revolutionary sovereignty and *Sardanapalus* an imperial pacifism.[1] Dramatic and tragic expression alone can, at present, define such profound and necessary conceptions and Byron was in such works investigating the conditions of man's advance beyond his past and present political and imperial limitations. He willed to transmute, without denying, the historic energies.

History was to Byron both a passion and a solace. In May 1821, after the Italian Revolution had failed, he started what he called *My Dictionary*. At this time of political disappointment and disillusion he turned naturally to his central passion: history. He starts by reviewing the character of Augustus, great but not 'one of *my* great men'. Sulla was the greatest character in history for laying down his power. As for the Roman republic, it was bound to go: 'its days ended with the Gracchi, the rest was a mere struggle of parties'. He meditates on despotism with reference to Caesar, Augustus and Napoleon, noting how values and views depend on a great man's *successors,* twining his thought into the mysterious mechanisms of history, with close reference to a number of emperors. He discusses the relative merits of hereditary right and popular choice in selecting sovereigns. The consuls made a 'goodly show', but their reign was short. It is hard to say what sort of government is the *worst* since 'all are so bad'; and 'as for democracy, it is the worst of the whole; for what is (*in fact*) democracy? an Aristocracy of Blackguards' (LJ, V, 405)—'democracy' meaning here rule by an oligarchy drawn from the lower strata of society (pp. 141-7 below); the 'democracy' that Milton likewise scorned. In such a passage Byron was studying man, especially the great man, as, so to speak, a political animal, assessing his powers and purposes. He never thought for long of movements as apart from men. To him heroes of the past were intimate, living persons:

'. . . If you mention Caesar, or Annibal, or Napoleon, you at

---

1. See my studies in *The Burning Oracle* and my article on Byron's plays in *The Times Literary Supplement,* 3 February 1950.

once rush upon Pharsalia, Munda, Alesia, Cannae, Thrasimene, Trebia, Lodi, Marengo, Jena, Austerlitz, Friedland, Wagram, Moskwa; but it is less easy to pitch upon the victories of Alcibiades, though they may be named too—though not so readily as the Leuctra and Mantinea of Epaminondas, the Marathon of Militiades, the Salamis of Themistocles, and the Thermopylae of Leonidas.

'Yet upon the whole it may be doubted, whether there be a name of Antiquity which comes down with such a general charm as that of *Alcibiades*. Why? I cannot answer. Who can?' (*Detached Thoughts*, Oct. 1821; LJ, v, 461).

From exactly such a vital human awareness flowered his historical dramas.

But, indeed, it is time to close. If we are still in doubt as to Byron as poetic—or other—historian, we have only to turn his pages. In his poetry alone a cursory reading introduces us, surely, to a store-house of geographical, ethnological and historical references of staggering range: *Nations and Peoples*—England, Scotland, Ireland, Germany, France, Russia, Spain, Portugal, Italy, Greece, Carthage, Turkey, Norway, Sweden, Denmark, Belgium, Albania, Morocco, America North and South (including Mexico and Peru), Palestine, India, China, Ceylon. *Stage settings*—Nineveh, Venice, the Alps, Silesia, Prague. *Great battles*—Thermopylae, Albuera, Lepanto, Marathon, Actium, Trafalgar, Thrasimene, Waterloo, the Spanish Armada, Talavera, Salamis and many more. *Soldiers and Sailors*—Miltiades, Mahomet, Alaric, Alcibiades, Epaminondas, Wellington, Alexander, the Black Prince, Pompey, Timur Leng, Scipio, Cortez, the Cid, Hawke, Leonidas, Napoleon, Nelson, Caesar, Wolfe, Marlborough, Pizarro, Juwarrow. *Sovereigns*—Xerxes, Queen Elizabeth I, Tiberius, Mithridates, Nadir Shah, Mary Queen of Scots, Barbarossa, George III and George IV of England, the Emperor Julian, Charles V (of Spain) and Charles XII (of Sweden), Trajan, Sardanapalus, Semiramis, Catherine of Russia, Nero, Cheops, Caligula, two Venetian Doges, Demetrius of Macedon, the Medicis, Numa Pompilius. *Great liberators*—Wilberforce, Cromwell, Wilkes, Brutus, Bonnivard, Rienzi, Washington, Franklin, Koskiusko, Bolivar, Thrasybulus, William Tell, Harmodius, Grattan. *Statesmen and Politicians*—Chatham, Burke, Marius, Themistocles, Draco, Pitt, Sulla, Cato, Demosthenes, Fox, Castlereagh, Canning. *Explorers*—Humboldt, Columbus. *Thinkers* —Bacon, Socrates, Diogenes, Dionysius, Archimedes, Rousseau,

Zoroaster, Hobbes, Locke, Newton, Epicurus, Rochefoucault, Aristotle, Tillotson, Berkeley, Machiavelli, Galileo, Plato, Aristippus, Kant. *Saints and Divines*—St. Augustine, St. Francis, St. Bartholomew, St. Anthony, St. Athanasius, Pelagius, Luther, Wesley. *Artists, Poets, Men of Letters*—Phidias, Rembrandt, Michael Angelo, Homer, Sappho, Pindar, Cicero, Vergil, Horace, Livy, Goethe, Aretina, Catullus, Cervantes, Longinus, Camoens, Sallust, Plutarch, Dryden, Pope, Swift, Martial, Crashaw, Tibullus, Dante, Petrarch, Boccaccio, Tasso, Ariosto, Fénélon, Sheridan, Voltaire, Schiller, 'Junius', Alfieri, Hafiz, Pushkin. *Biblical persons* —Saul, Potiphar, Nimrod, David, Solomon, Nebuchadnezzar, Belshazzar, Sennacherib, Moses, Christ himself. *Sacred books*—the Koran, Talmud, Kabbala. *Mythological persons*—Achilles, Orestes, Ulysses, Jason, Tiresias, Pygmalion, Prometheus.

Such, roughly, is Byron's poetic stock-in-trade, rich in the greatest figures, political, intellectual, and spiritual of the Western world; and the list could probably be trebled by reference to the Letters and Journals. Certain references are slight, but even so are used with skill and point to form part of some impassioned plea, pointed witticism or pictorial description. Some are major themes, as with the poems spoken through the persons of Dante and Tasso, the poem on Prometheus, the lines for Sheridan, the *Ode to Napoleon;* some are protagonists, the two Venetian Doges—Italian history was in Byron's blood as England's in Shakespeare's—and Sardanapalus. The whole history of Spain is amazingly compressed into a single page of *The Age of Bronze* (p. 164). As for the writers, Byron's poetic translations and imitations alone cover Aeschylus, Vergil, Anacreon, Catullus, Dante, Euripides, Horace, Martial, Pulci, Tibullus, Vitorelli, Ossian, together with pieces from French, Portuguese, Romaic and Arabic; besides his *Hebrew Melodies* and prose translations of the Pauline Epistles from the Armenian (LJ, IV, App. I).

All these literary references are *historically* relevant: first because many are used in connection with historic events; and second, because to Byron history is no mere record of kings and battles, but a spiritual challenge. History was the will to freedom, freedom is one with eternal power (*Childe Harold,* IV, 182–3), and the voices of eternity are men of letters. Once Byron remarked that, if the freedom of the press were discounted, 'there is an end of history' (John Hunt, 8 Jan. 1823; LJ, VI, 160). He willed to preserve, and lift, the soul of men, of nations. He was not content with reading; he would point historic energies to a supreme purpose. Nor was he content with poetry, even prophetic poetry; that was done with his left hand only, or less. His primary purpose and vocation was not merely to write, but to make, history; and he did so.

We have therefore to set against Mr. Quennell's remark that Byron's 'stock of historical parallels was not extensive' the neat *meiosis* of Byron's own claim, already (p. 19) noted, that his reading had been 'tolerably extensive in the historical department'; and even perhaps go a little further, and suggest that a proper appreciation of Byron is the last reward of historical scholarship.

My defence must be from now on compressed. Mr. Quennell, after observing that when in danger from assassination Byron 'did not discontinue his evening rides', adds: 'Like other neurasthenics, he possessed his full share of nervous courage; and it was with an elation not by any means unpleasant that he looked forward to the prospect of a dramatic "row"—whether with Guiccioli's hired bravos or the hirelings of the Austrian tyrant' (VI, 179). We are, it seems, to understand Byron's courage in terms of neurosis; while the 'elation' suggested is further robbed of any possible merit by the implied vulgarity of 'row'. Of Byron's courage we shall write later (pp. 114-20). Courage can be physical or moral; and each kind can be further divided into the 'impulsive' and the 'deliberate'. It is probable that these *four* varieties (two of which involve spiritual values) are together as variously and richly exemplified by Byron as by any man on record.

It is necessary to labour these points; and we have one other item outstanding. When in Italy Byron was told in a letter from Hoppner of a supposed intrigue between Shelley and Clare Clairmont. After rather carelessly agreeing to Hoppner's request that he should say nothing, he nevertheless told Shelley. On Shelley's denial, Byron accepted a letter to forward on to Hoppner explaining the truth, preferring to do this himself since an apology was due for his broken promise. The letter was found among his papers after his death, and it has been suggested that Byron avoided a difficulty by not forwarding it. Defence is, however, now scarcely needed, the explanation suggested by the editors of *Letters and Journals* (v, 74) and *Correspondence* (II, 191-4) and followed by Drinkwater in his excellent account of the incident (v, 312-14) being perfectly satisfactory; namely, that, since the letter, when found, had been both sealed *and opened,* it is reasonable to suppose that Byron had had it returned, since it cleared the mother of his natural daughter of a scandal.

Drinkwater considers that only 'wanton prejudice' can fail to see the truth. Suspicion would appear out of place, since no man ever lived less capable than Byron of such a dishonesty. Mr. Quennell, however, still suspects him, and even asserts that Byron, whom he calls 'bored and lazy', was—and this is *before* he could have done anything about the letter—'annoyed at being caught out' (VII, 200–1). As always in assessing Byron's personality, we must extract the simple facts from the fog of innuendo. From Mr. Quennell's phraseology you would think that it was Byron who was either the subject or the purveyor of a nasty scandal, and the careless reader certainly begins to feel that he had done something peculiarly nasty; whereas he had merely, at some personal inconvenience, given his friend a chance of disabusing the scandal-mongers. If he was 'caught out', he was only 'caught out' doing a good action.

In a completely different context Moore noted that all Byron's friends knew of his habitual 'frankness' in not preserving any confidences whatsoever regarding either others or himself (L, 573–4). 'There are no concealments in him,' Medwin tells us, 'no injunctions to secrecy. He tells everything that he has thought or done without the least reserve, and as if he wished the whole world to know it; and does not throw the slightest gloss over his errors' (Medwin, 334). Lady Blessington says that his own disclosures concerning others were given at random and never in confidence (Blessington, 259). Parry offers us an amusing example to illustrate the 'frankness' of a character who could not tolerate any sort of 'concealment'; and in whose presence scandal was accordingly a risky pursuit (Parry, VII, 158–62; V, 105).[1] This trait Shelley also observed as well known to all in connection with the scandal we are discussing (to Mary, 16 Aug. 1821; quoted C, II, 189). Is it likely, then, that Byron who, as Drinkwater insists, was certainly afraid of nobody, would on this occasion have felt any particular uneasiness about his habitual behaviour? But why then did Byron promise silence? Clearly because the confidence asked of him (Hoppner to Byron, 16 Sept. 1820; C, II, 180)—he was not told *on condition of* confidence—was only asked, and Byron only *gratuitously* gave it, *on the supposition that the scandal was true;* and he probably discovered Shelley's innocence before telling him of the rumour. We may therefore ask, could Hoppner admit to being angered by any

1. It was the same with Oscar Wilde, who, according to Lord Alfred Douglas, was always 'entirely natural', and said, utterly without fear or 'respect of persons', exactly what he thought on any given occasion (Hesketh Pearson, *Life*, XI, 169–70).

steps that ended by clearing a mutual friend of a misconception? That would be to admit that he wished the lie perpetuated. There is, indeed, something strangely lacking in our understanding of Byron. Mr. Harold Nicolson (II, 26) takes at its face value Byron's remark to Augusta: 'I don't know what Scrope Davies meant by telling you I liked Children. I abominate the sight of them so much that I have always had the greatest respect for the character of Herod' (30 Aug. 1811; LJ, II, 11). On internal evidence that was surely written by a man who did like children. That the love of children and youth in general was perhaps the central key to Byron's personality will be argued later, when the evidence will be set out (pp. 66–85). Meanwhile we may suggest that to base any general statement concerning a man's life and character on a semi-humorous remark in a letter to one's sister at the age of twenty-two shows a dangerous misconception regarding the nature of biographical evidence. Again, Mr. Vulliamy asserts (IX, 119) that Byron was 'unquestionably jealous of the reputation of other poets'. Byron was, as we shall see, strikingly, indeed almost inhumanly, non-envious of other poets, and at times almost pervertedly anxious to build up *their* work and reputation whilst neglecting his own. In his introduction to the Everyman collection of Byron's letters, M. André Maurois lets fall the extraordinary sentence that Byron 'was brave, frank, and, *though appearances belie it, capable of kindness*' (italics mine). As for Mr. Peter Ustinov's recent use of the phrase 'Byronic irresponsibility', in an article for *New Theatre,* that, as a generalized statement, scarcely applies to one who, with something of a Titan's endurance, lived out in his own person the guilt of European history, instinctively loaded his shoulders with the sufferings of persons and nations, and died in the cause of human advance.

As for Byron's true greatness, his generosity and kindliness, his chivalry, courtesy, humility and courage, though noted by those who knew him, by Moore, Rogers, Parry, Gamba, Lady Blessington, Medwin and others, what showing have they received? He was certainly a more kindly, probably a more innately Christian, man than Dante or Milton. The stories told of Dante suggest an appalling egotism; as in the remark 'If I go, who stays? If I stay, who goes?' (Boccaccio, XII) thereby equating himself with his city. On such a man the vice of lechery, noted by Boccaccio (XII) as his prevailing sin throughout his life, sits less creditably than on Byron's warm-hearted and generous temperament. But, indeed, much of what we hear of Dante may be untrue, or falsified in the telling. I merely argue that, if we must pronounce moral judgments, Byron need fear no competition from his peers.

On this matter he has himself, in a typically pregnant aphorism, said the last word: 'In fact (I suppose that), if the follies of fools were all set down like those of the wise, the wise (who seem at present only a better sort of fools) would appear almost intelligent' (*Detached Thoughts*, Oct. 1821; LJ, v, 460).

II

With Byron, misrepresentation, by himself and by others, started during his life. Walter Scott, for example, has recorded the impression that Byron's liberalism was superficial and mainly used as a vantage-point for attacks, while adding that his reading *seemed*—and it would not be hard to suggest the reason—not very 'extensive' (Mr. Quennell's exact word), and less than his own (LJ, III, App. IV, 412). Of Byron's reading we have spoken; and, as for his liberalism, what greater evidence has any man ever left, from his first political speech to his death, of sincerity? To live, write, ruin one's prospects, and finally die for a belief may not be absolute proof; but no greater proof on our plane of existence is in the nature of things conceivable. Nevertheless, Walter Scott was no fool. Moreover, these various misconceptions are merely symptoms of a profound discrepancy that assumed terrifying proportions at the crisis of Byron's life, when all, or nearly all, London rose against him.

The root of the trouble was not only social; it was also political. Jeaffreson neatly observes that 'had Byron voted with the Tories, treated the Prince Regent respectfully, and held his pen and tongue about matters touching the Thirty-nine Articles, England's higher society would never for a single instant have sided with Lady Byron in her domestic troubles' (XXVIII, 462).[1] Morally, socially, politically, Byron had struck fear into London: he was felt as, to quote Mr. Vulliamy's neat phrase, an 'insidious disintegrator' (x, 144). Politically, his fall was comparable with Dante's. Boccaccio in his *Life of Dante* laments the poet's 'unjust and mad condemnation' and the attempt at 'the tainting of his most glorious name by false accusations' (1). It is a pattern that, in various forms, repeats itself, being given dramatic expression in Shakespeare's *Timon of Athens* and *The Tempest*: 'Timon', I have written, 'is the inmost genius of man

1. This is not the place to discuss the separation, though I hope later to publish my analysis.

throughout the centuries unwanted and thence embittered by man's own degraded social consciousness' (*Christ and Nietzsche,* VI, 226). Especially does this pattern seem likely to present itself when poetry, or any higher wisdom, shows signs of getting out of books into life; as with Socrates; or Christ, in whose story a similar reversal from adulation to hatred accompanies the poëtic threat of an over-powering self-dramatization.

By 'self-dramatization' I mean some enlargement and adjustment of the personality to the richer dimensions normally associated with dramatic, and indeed all, art, in which oppositions are held in balance. This uncanny largeness strikes confusion into the beholders. The protagonist is at once accused of egotism or posing; or may be his most obvious qualities are turned inside out. He is a kind of devil. 'It is singular enough', Byron wrote to Lady Melbourne, 'that one whose whole life has been spent in open opposition to received opinions should be charged with hypocrisy' (undated C, II, App. A, 302). Shelley observed the 'ridiculous and unfounded tales' that regularly attach themselves to eminent men and in particular 'the absurd stories' which the 'multitude' believed of Byron himself (to Byron, 22 April 1818; C, II, 73-4). 'Without malice, or the instigation of any ill spirit', wrote Galt, 'he was continually provoking malignity and revenge' (XXIX). Hobhouse says that Byron seemed fated to continual misrepresentation (II; XV, 316). Such injustice tends, as Moore notes, to make its object in his turn unjust (Moore, XXXV, 416), with a blind fury against the intangibility and invulnerability of the opposing forces of innuendo and slander; of the normal, small, second-rate types closing their ranks with auto-matic impulse against the titanic, first-rate, genius. It happened with Pope, with Ibsen, with Nietzsche. Byron saw it happening with Shelley: 'There is thus another man gone about whom the world was ill-naturedly, and ignorantly, and brutally mistaken. It will, perhaps, do him justice *now,* when he can be no better for it' (Moore, 8 Aug. 1822; LJ, VI, 99). Sooner or later the genius hits back, his satire being the measure of the disparity existing between his super-status and the lower community. He is manoeuvred into greater and yet greater self-assertion by the patent iniquities into which his con-temporaries are driven through fear of a strangeness out-topping their comprehension. The relation is 'out of joint', and definition impos-sible by either side, genius being indefinable except in its own terms; the genius himself cannot understand it.

Our best way of assessing the extraordinary fear Byron struck into his contemporaries is to consider some of the revulsions caused by his mature work. A preacher commenting on *Don Juan* defined the author as a 'denaturalized being', no longer human and now deliberately showing himself as 'a cool, unconcerned, fiend'; on which Byron merely commented that other great names had endured the like (Kinnaird, 6 Feb. 1822; LJ, VI, 9–10 and note). Today bishops read *Don Juan* without anguish. Nor did Byron suffer merely from the misunderstandings of his enemies: his best friends were often at a loss. Moore saw *Cain* as a work full of 'blasphemies', striking a 'deadly chill' (16 March 1822; Moore, XLVIII, 554); he found *Don Juan* 'painful' and advised against its publication (Moore, XXXII, 386; XXXVI, 421). Hobhouse was always disapproving. During their early travels in Albania he succeeded in persuading Byron to destroy 'a very exact journal of every circumstance of his life, and many of his thoughts while young', thus robbing the world, as Byron told Finlay, 'of a treat' (Finlay, quoted Edgcumbe, I, VIII, 102); he called the early *Childe Harold* 'an extravagant conception' and persuaded Byron to put it aside, until Dallas' encouragement brought it to light (Teresa, II; III, 39); but he liked the 'air of mystery and metaphysics' of *Childe Harold III* even less (Hobhouse, II; VIII, 11). He thought *Cain* contained 'scarce one specimen of real poetry' and wrote to Byron 'remonstrating in the strongest terms'—the words are his own—against his publishing it, since it appeared to him 'a complete failure' (Hobhouse, II; XIV, 173). He was one of the circle of supporters who advised against publishing *Don Juan* (Hobhouse, II; XI, 110–11), and was a party to the destruction of the *Memoirs*. The friends of a man such as Byron are always likely to prove his greatest hindrance. Col. Stanhope, after recording that Byron 'never chose a nobler friend than Hobhouse', continues: 'Mr. Hobhouse has given many proofs of this, and among others I saw him, from motives of high honour, destroy a beautiful poem of Lord Byron's, and perhaps the last he ever composed. The same reason that induced Mr. H. to tear this fine manuscript will, of course, prevent him or me from ever divulging its contents' (Edgcumbe, XVI, 208). Teresa asserts that five more *Juans* and a Greek Journal were destroyed after Byron's death to avoid offence (I; Int., 40–1, and note). People's reactions were contradictory and confusing. Shelley thought part of *Childe Harold IV* the work of a peculiarly pernicious madness (p. 255), though he regularly spoke of *Don Juan* as a triumph (to Byron, 14 Sept. 1821; C, 200; and elsewhere). What was Byron to make of these diverse reactions? 'For my part,' he once wrote, 'I think you are all crazed' (Murray, 15 May 1819; LJ, IV, 295). 'I have no doubt', he would sometimes say of his wife in later years, 'that she really did believe me to be mad' (Moore, XXVII, 321). It was one thing or the other.

Subsequent criticism is not always enlightened; and with the impact on society of a Byron, the supreme genius of our era, justification and understanding have been slow. He himself feared that unreasoning hostility might 'continue to persecute his memory' (Moore, XXXV, 416). One of his own comments provides a valuable pointer: 'Do you think me a coxcomb or a madman, to be capable of such an exhibition? My sister knew me better and told you that *could not* be true' (Murray, 21 Sept. 1820; LJ, V, 77). Caution and humility are needed. Indeed, his friend Moore is not only Byron's first, but also his best, biographer, since he alone appears to possess the necessary philosophical equipment. Though often a conventional moralizer, he can, at the *limit,* take a Nietzschean, super-moral, view. He astutely discusses the unsuitability of genius in any age for marriage (XXIII, 267–71) in the manner of Boccaccio on Dante (Boccaccio, III).[1] He knows that genius regularly casts a 'shadow' in proportion to its own stature (XXV, 295); that in some degree 'an impetuous temperament and passions untamed were indispensable to the conformation' of such a poet, observing aptly 'the utter unreasonableness of trying such a character by ordinary standards' (XXV, 298). He sees Byron's faults as contributory to 'that whole combination of grand but disturbing powers' which so staggered his contemporaries (XXVIII, 328). His 'defects' were among the 'sources' of his 'greatness', his 'mighty genius' drawing its strength precisely from the combination and conflict of 'good' and 'evil' (XXV, 298; XIII, 149); an understanding which forecasts the philosophy of Nietzsche.

We must beware of premature impressions and premature conclusions. An objective understanding of Byron will only mature from direct contact with (i) his own authenticated actions—'Judge of me', he said to Stanhope, 'by my actions' (Gamba, II, 103); (ii) his Letters, Journals and Poetry; (iii) the impressions of those who knew him intimately.[2] Without such care, we shall never uncover the real Byron. One more caution: we must hold in reserve all nor-

---

1. Byron compared his fortunes with Dante's to Medwin (Medwin, 193). See also his note to *The Prophecy of Dante*, I.

2. We shall not, however, regard either Hunt or Trelawny as safe guides to Byron's personality. Here I cannot do better than point to Harold Nicolson's brilliant commentary (II; V, 95, 97–8).

mal moral judgments. That, if my argument be correct, if he be indeed a phenomenon larger than our reach, is our only sound course.

So prepared and forewarned, let us read Byron's grand defence, which I call throughout his 'Blackwood's Defence', since it was written in answer to an attack published by Blackwood's:

'My learned brother proceeds to observe, that "it is in vain for Lord B. to attempt in any way to justify his own behaviour in that affair; and now that he has so *openly* and *audaciously* invited enquiry and reproach, we do not see any good reason why he should not be plainly told so by the voice of his countrymen". How far the "openness" of an anonymous poem, and the "audacity" of an imaginary character, which the writer supposes to be meant for Lady B., may be deemed to merit this formidable denunciation from their "most sweet voices", I neither know nor care; but when he tells me that I cannot "in any way *justify* my own behaviour in that affair", I acquiesce, because no man can *"justify"* himself until he knows of what he is accused; and I have never had—and, God knows, my whole desire has ever been to obtain it—any specific charge, in a tangible shape, submitted to me by the adversary, nor by others, unless the atrocities of public rumour and the mysterious silence of the lady's legal advisers may be deemed such. But is not the writer content with what has been already said and done? Has not "the general voice of his countrymen" long ago pronounced upon the subject—sentence without trial, and condemnation without a charge? Have I not been exiled by ostracism, except that the shells which proscribed me were anonymous? Is the writer ignorant of the public opinion and the public conduct upon that occasion? If he is, I am not; the public will forget both, long before I shall cease to remember either.

'The man who is exiled by a faction has the consolation of thinking that he is a martyr; he is upheld by hope and the dignity of his cause, real or imaginary; he who withdraws from the pressure of debt may indulge in the thought that time and prudence will retrieve his circumstances; he who is condemned by the law has a term to his banishment, or a dream of its abbreviation; or, it may be, the knowledge or the belief of some injustice of the law, or of its administration in his own particular; but he who is outlawed by general opinion, without the intervention of hostile politics, illegal judgment, or embarrassed circumstances, whether he be innocent or guilty, must undergo all the bitterness of exile, without hope, without pride, without alleviation. This case was mine. Upon what grounds the public founded their opinion, I am not aware; but it was general, and it was decisive. Of me or of mine they knew little, except that I had written what is called poetry, was a nobleman, had married, became a father, and was involved in differences with my wife and her relatives, no one knew why, because the persons complaining refused to state their grievances. The fashionable world was divided into parties, mine consisting of a very small minority: the reasonable world was naturally on the stronger side, which happened to be the lady's, as was most proper and polite. The press was active and scurrilous; and such was the rage of the day, that the unfortunate publication of two copies of verses, rather complimentary than otherwise to the subjects of both, was tortured into a species of crime, or constructive petty treason. I was accused of every monstrous vice by public rumour and private rancour: my name, which had been a knightly or a noble one since my fathers helped to conquer the kingdom for William the Norman, was tainted. I felt that, if what was whispered, and muttered, and murmured, was true, I was unfit for England; if false England was unfit for me. I withdrew: but this was not enough. In other countries, in Switzerland, in the shadow of the Alps, and by the blue depth of the lakes, I was pursued and breathed upon by the same blight. I crossed the mountains, but it was the same; so I went a little farther, and settled myself by the waves of the Adriatic, like the stag at bay, who betakes him to the waters.

'If I may judge by the statements of the few friends who gathered round me, the outcry of the period to which I allude was beyond all precedent, all parallel, even in those cases where political motives have sharpened slander and doubled enmity. I was advised not to go to the theatres, lest I should be hissed, nor to my duty in parliament, lest I should be insulted by the way; even on the day of my departure, my most intimate friend told me afterwards that he was under apprehensions of violence from the people who might be assembled at the door of the carriage. However, I was not deterred by these counsels from seeing Kean in his best characters, nor from voting according to my principles; and with regard to the third and last apprehensions of my friends, I could not share in them, not being made acquainted with their extent, till some time after I had crossed the Channel. Even if I had been so, I am not of a nature to be much affected by men's anger, though I may feel hurt by their aversion. Against all individual outrage, I could protect or redress myself;

and against that of a crowd, I should probably have been enabled to defend myself, with the assistance of others, as has been done on similar occasions.

'I retired from the country, perceiving that I was the object of general obloquy; I did not indeed imagine, like Jean Jacques Rousseau, that all mankind was in a conspiracy against me, though I had perhaps as good grounds for such a chimera as ever he had: but I perceived that I had to a great extent become personally obnoxious in England, perhaps through my own fault, but the fact was indisputable; the public in general would hardly have been so much excited against a more popular character, without at least an accusation or a charge of some kind actually expressed or substantiated, for I can hardly conceive that the common and every-day occurrence of a separation between man and wife could in itself produce so great a ferment. I shall say nothing of the usual complaints of "being prejudiced", "condemned unheard", "unfairness", "partiality", and so forth, the usual changes rung by parties who have had, or are to have, a trial; but I was a little surprised to find myself condemned without being favoured with the act of accusation, and to perceive in the absence of this portentous charge or charges, whatever it or they were to be, that every possible or impossible crime was rumoured to supply its place, and taken for granted. This could only occur in the case of a person very much disliked, and I knew no remedy, having already used to their extent whatever little powers I might possess of pleasing in society. I had no party in fashion, though I was afterwards told that there was one—but it was not of my formation, nor did I then know of its existence—none in literature; and in politics I had voted with the Whigs, with precisely that importance which a Whig vote possesses in these Tory days, and with such personal acquaintance with the leaders in both houses as the society in which I lived sanctioned, but without claim or expectation of any thing like friendship from any one, except a few young men of my own age and standing, and a few others more advanced in life, which last it had been my fortune to serve in circumstances of difficulty. This was, in fact, to stand alone: and I recollect, some time after, Madame de Staël said to me in Switzerland, "You should not have warred with the world—it will not do—it is too strong always for any individual: I myself once tried it in early life, but it will not do." I perfectly acquiesce in the truth of this remark; but the world had done me the honour to begin the war; and assuredly, if peace is only to be obtained by courting and paying tribute to it, I am not qualified to obtain its countenance. I thought, in the words of Campbell,

> Then wed thee to an exiled lot,
> And if the world hath loved thee not,
>   Its absence may be borne.

'I recollect, however, that, having been much hurt by Romilly's conduct (he, having a general retainer for me, had acted as adviser to the adversary, alleging, on being reminded of his retainer, that he had forgotten it, as his clerk had so many), I observed that some of those who were now eagerly laying the axe to my roof-tree, might see their own shaken, and feel a portion of what they had inflicted. —His fell, and crushed him.

'I have heard of, and believe, that there are human beings so constituted as to be insensible to injuries; but I believe that the best mode to avoid taking vengeance is to get out of the way of temptation. I hope that I may never have the opportunity, for I am not quite sure that I could resist it, having derived from my mother something of the *"perfervidum ingenium Scotorum"*. I have not sought, and shall not seek it, and perhaps it may never come in my path. I do not in this allude to the party who might be right or wrong; but to many who made her cause the pretext of their own bitterness. She, indeed, must have long avenged me in her own feelings; for whatever her reasons may have been (and she never adduced them to me at least) she probably neither contemplated nor conceived to what she became the means of conducting the father of her child, and the husband of her choice.

'So much for "the general voice of his countrymen'" (LJ, IV, App. IX, 478).

How shall we receive these statements? Are they not borne out by his correspondence and what we know of his life? Where then are the charges, in his day and ours, of egotism? The truth is, men cannot stand too great a light; not even he who bears it. London and Byron alike were equally confused by the Byronic impact. We must beware of underrating both Byron's difficulties and also the difficulties of his contemporaries. They had reason to be afraid.

III

I conclude with a few notes on two central authorities: Lady Blessington and Teresa Guiccioli.

Lady Blessington's commentaries are extremely revealing. They show in Byron, as his letters rarely do, a man of genius fully conscious of his stature. The *Conversations* are repetitive, making and remaking the same points; but the points are valid.

She continually observes the contrast of (i) his bitter or witty attacks and (ii) his warm-hearted nature. Circumstances have soured his excessively 'tender and affectionate' heart (110). Over and over again she emphasizes the warmth and worth of his 'natural character', comparing it to a diamond breathed upon, which quickly recovers its original purity and lustre (283). 'Remember', she says, what 'heart-aches and corroding thoughts of a mind so sensitive' must have been experienced 'ere the last weapons of despair were resorted to' (383-4).

Her dislike of Byron's attacks on persons and society may appear strange to us, since it is precisely those attacks that are, to many readers, his most fascinating accomplishment. As an emissary from the society attacked she naturally stimulated Byron to do his best, and could scarcely be expected to submit, without protest, to his aspersions. But she makes an important distinction between his lighter thrusts and a far more deep-seated anger, as when, faced by an instance of uncharitable morality, his reaction was of withering impact (236-7). She saw his psychic discontinuities alternating from sentiment and generosity to satire and misanthropy and his general façade suggesting 'no fixed principle of conduct or of thought', and all the accompanying 'errors and inconsistencies' of his temperament, as redeemed by his *natural goodness of heart* (343-4); and here she has certainly detected at least *one* of Byron's basic, unifying, qualities. She records him as himself noting others: 'There are but two sentiments to which I am constant—a strong love of liberty and a detestation of cant, and neither is calculated to get me friends' (390).

The *Conversations* suggest that Byron's attacks were, his genius granted, justified. He is, moreover, recorded as himself fully conscious (in the manner of his *Monody on the Death of Sheridan*) that he had been slandered because of his genius, saying that the English instinctively 'depreciate' any sort of 'pre-eminence', preferring an amiable, good-natured, and colourless mediocrity, which they agree to admire since by that their pride is not hurt (173-4), 'vanity' being a central impulse in all men (215). Faced by any 'striking superiority', they accordingly search for some 'defect' or 'weakness' to counterbalance and console their envy (336). The 'herd' were, moreover, always ready to turn against their own idol with an irrational fury

(360). The man of genius may thus be rendered dangerous by the 'slander' and 'calumny' and distorted accusations of crime which, without any trial, have banished him from society, 'injustice rankling in his heart'; while his 'genius and power' merely add fuel to the flame of calumniation, acting as a continual reminder of his existence and his enemies' injustice (382–3). The trials of genius are under continual survey (124–6, 218, 222–4, 276, 280). Were he to revisit England, the press, 'that powerful engine of a licentious age', would merely return to its old misrepresentations and libels: 'This I could not stand, because I once endured it, and never have forgotten what I felt under the infliction' (401). Moreover, he felt that his works 'might have been one unbroken blaze of light' had not opposition and consequent resentment 'dimmed their lustre' (304); and it is true that Byron's basic poetic impulses were from the start those of a teacher; but it is hard to feel that Lady Blessington's counsel of a poem in which 'received opinions are not wounded' and 'morality is inculcated', with the assurance of 'universal applause' to follow (305), quite met the case.

She could, however, probe deeper, seeing, as did Moore, the good and evil—or what appeared as such—in Byron as mutually independent. Without his errors he might have been a 'more estimable man', but a 'less grand poet' (195); reverses served to temper his genius and that which marred the man perfected the poet (262); his every error was, indeed, *allied to some good quality*, and a final distinction seemed impossible (245). Clearly, she felt, without being able rightly to focus, the *kind* of good Byron radiated. She was never in doubt of his greatness; his astounding genius is *taken for granted*. He was beyond the understanding of 'commonplace people' (400). After describing what she considered the bad taste of his bed, carriages and liveries, she insists that she does it merely to show how even such a great man as he 'could be ordinary in trifles', observing that these were 'the only points of assimilation between him and the common herd of men'; and that he 'was only ordinary when he descended to their level'. Indeed, it was only his 'pre-eminence' that lent any interest at all to such details; and such defects were only to be noticed as an astronomer remarks the specks visible 'even in the brightest stars' (265–6). Byron's bed has had its full measure of attention; but how often has biography recorded these vital reservations?

Lady Blessington knew what she was about, and, apart from a certain blindness as to the positive value of Byron's satiric thrusts, understood the Byronic problem. She was on her guard against taking seriously what was merely Byronic mockery, describing his 'malicious smile' on occasions when he was enjoying a 'hoax' and thinking of the confusions of future biographers (66–7). But she was, once at least, herself taken in.

She describes his nervousness while riding; how he was discomposed if the horse stumbled and on 'any bad part of the road' walked his mount 'very slowly', though there was nothing to fear. Now we have the authorities of both Medwin and Kennedy that Byron was a good horseman (p. 107); we may also remember his extraordinary sympathy with animals in general and the Dutch horses (pp. 13–14, 10) in particular. Clearly, he was considering the safety and comfort not of himself but of his horse. Indeed, Lady Blessington gives the secret away:

'Finding that I could perfectly manage (or what he called *bully*) a very highly-dressed horse that I daily rode, he became extremely anxious to buy it' (56).

He pretended admiration of her horsemanship, asking her 'a thousand questions' as to *how* exactly she did it, and, when she at last promised to sell him the animal before he left for Greece, said that he would 'now feel confidence in action with so steady a charger'. She records her surprise, since she was 'by no means a bold rider' (56). Byron was enjoying a 'hoax' at the expense of his usually acute companion; and at the same time attempting to save her horse from ill-treatment.

We turn next to another lady, Teresa Guiccioli, whose *Lord Byron jugé par les Témoins de sa Vie* was published in French in 1868 and in English as *My Recollections of Lord Byron and those of Eye-witnesses of his Life* in 1869. The book is clearly of first importance, since her association with Byron was, in point of intimacy, unparalleled. It was an association, too, of love; and it should be recognized that any genuine insight into genius, whether in study of the man or of his art, demands something of a lover's intuition.

Teresa's work has scarcely received justice. It is a study composed of accumulated evidence presented by a mind of considerable penetration. The book, as a book, has faults. Drinkwater is correct in calling it an 'uncompromising eulogy' written 'on so tedious a plan as to be followed only by great perseverance' (v, 294). Nevertheless, the method in the main is, as we shall see, *implicit in the very nature of the attempt*. Probably more solid, factual, truth about Byron as a man has been recorded by Teresa than by any other of his biographers. The Marchesa Origo appears to deplore the fact that *this* study is not the personal study, *La Vie de Lord Byron en Italie,* which has hitherto been withheld from publication, and from which the Marchesa herself quotes freely. She blames our present study for being, among other things, 'a hotch-potch of other people's opinion' (x, 420), without seeing that in this lies the book's whole purpose and value. It is an accumulation of factual evidence concerning Byron's various *virtues* seldom depending on her own, Teresa's, authority. If, as Drinkwater says, Teresa's study has been held 'in general contempt' (II, 97), that contempt merely marks the folly of contemporary criticism. It is unwise to hold facts in contempt, since they tend to survive their despisers.

One can, indeed, see why this study has been ignored. In discussing the reason for the falsities of Byronic biography, Teresa observes that such falsities make better reading than a stern concentration on the evidence. Goodness, she admits, is dull; it lacks news-value, so to speak; and hence biographers prefer defects (I; V, 227). After suggesting that nobility is required to recognize nobility, and that noble minds are few, she continues:

'All that may well be, but I believe that what they especially feel is, that if their books were only written for noble minds, possessing such qualities as only belong to the minority of the human race, they might run the risk of being less sought after and less bought. Thus they search for faults with ardour, just as miners do for diamonds; and when they think they have discovered a vice in their hero, they look upon it as the "Mogul" of their book. They make it shine, polish it up, show it in a thousand lights, bring it out as the striking part of their work—the chief quality of their hero, who, unable to defend himself, is handed down, disfigured, to posterity. Such are the strange perils incurred, as regards truth and justice, and the wrong done towards the great departed; and this is why their surviving friends are called on to protest against the false assertions of biographers. Those who have written on Lord Byron, unable to find this great "Mogul" (for Lord Byron had no vices), have all, more or less, sought at least to draw the attention of their readers to a thousand little weaknesses, mostly devoid of reality. Upon what basis, indeed, do they rest?—almost always on Lord Byron's words'[1] (II; VI, 112–13).

1. Teresa's denial of 'vices' may appear strange; but she means it. She does not deny Byron's sexual irregularity—which she regards as perfectly normal for a 'young man'—at Venice (I; x, 443). For her full discussion, see I; x.

Teresa, as we shall see, lays, as do our other authorities, the heaviest emphasis on Byron's habit of self-denigration.

Moore and Lady Blessington were primarily interested in Byron's genius; Teresa in his goodness. All three are aware, of course, of both; but the emphases are different. To Teresa Byron's character was 'one of the finest that was ever allied to a great intellect' (I; Int., 10); and she insists on a steady facing of that character as witnessed by (i) his actions and (ii) his letters (I; Int., II). She is utterly at a loss to understand how Byron's critics have remained blind to the truth (II; VI, 112), and quotes Rogers' statement that he 'possessed an excellent heart' which had been *completely misunderstood*', by reason of his own 'lightness of manner' and persistent self-criticism (II; IX, 177–8). His goodness, says Teresa, 'shines as pre-eminently as does his genius'; it can bear any test at any epoch of his life (I; V, 227). These two volumes of some seven hundred pages are crammed with objective evidence from Byron's life and letters and the records of those who knew him indisputably supporting her case. I would point especially to the long chapter (I; IV) on Byron's Religion, to which I cannot myself give proper attention in my present study. It is for those who disagree to present a case with a similar abundance of documental proof.

Teresa saw Byron as a man of an anchorite's 'sobriety', showing a consistent will to make 'matter subservient to the spirit' (I; X, 448). This is certainly correct, at least with reference to exercise, bodily discomfort, endurance of physical hardships and fasting (see pp. 106–14, 265). Even in sexual indulgence, she witnesses, as do others, to the disparity between reputation and fact, at Cambridge, Newstead and elsewhere, the former housekeeper of Newstead, Nanny Smith, having told Washington Irving in 1830 that the young Byron and his friends were not licentious. She quotes Moore's statement that no anchorite who knew Lord Byron before and on his return from his early travels could have desired for himself greater indifference towards all the attractions of the senses (I; X, 411; Moore, IX, 95); and also Galt's statement that 'at no period' did he 'lead an irregular life', his excesses never being 'libertine' (I; X, 409). Teresa's emphasis is supported elsewhere. Hobhouse (II; XV, 196) tells us that on his marriage Byron, beyond being 'a man of the world', had 'no course of life to reform'. Byron's assertion that he 'never seduced any woman' (Medwin, 73) is passed by Maurois (I, XIX, 181) as correct. The trouble is, Byron seldom so defended himself; on the contrary, he *maligned* himself, as Moore observes on page after page. 'A single indiscretion in his hands', says Moore, 'was made to go farther than a thousand in those of others' (VII, 70). All our authorities, including Lady Blessington (see p. 264) and Stanhope (Edgcumbe, I, XVI, 209), were struck by this extraordinary propensity. He had, said Lady Blessington (293), 'an unaccountable passion' for misrepresenting himself, exaggerating his defects 'more than any enemy could do'. Teresa agrees: 'He invented faults rather than sought to extenuate them' (I; X, 404).[1]

As for Byron's supposed lack of feeling in certain letters regarding Teresa herself, she finds no difficulty, answering objections in terms of Byron's habitual 'mocking spirit' and 'horror of hypocrisy' (II; VI, 102). She recalls, quoting Finlay and Stanhope, how he checked himself in conversation at the approach of any 'sublime thought' and liked to hide 'the noble sentiments that filled his soul', being always ready 'to turn them into ridicule' (II; VI, 101–2).[2] Continually she reverses, with evidence, the current supposition. Though Kennedy had reported that Byron was irritable at a certain hour every night (and Byron had himself said as much; Murray, 29 Aug. 1819; LJ, IV, 353), Finlay and another called regularly at the dangerous hour to find him 'always pleasant and amiable' (II; VII, 129). As for his pride, one could scarcely better her account:

'And yet it is easy to understand how he might be accused of pride. His contempt for opinion, augmenting as he further appreciated its little worth; a certain natural timidity, of which Moore, Galt, and Pigot have all spoken, though without drawing thence the logical inferences; his eagerness to put down the unfounded *ridiculous pretensions of human nature;* his own dignity under misfortune; his magnanimity and passion for independence; all these qualities might easily betray those superficial minds into error, who do not study their subjects sufficiently to discover the truth' (II; X, 197).

For the rest, in so far as he was proud, that pride was the 'legitimate pride belonging to great souls' (II; XI, 216); or, as Moore puts it, 'It is, indeed, in the very nature and essence of genius to be for ever

---

1. For other supporting evidence countering Byron's reputation for licence, see *My Dictionary*, LJ, V, 445; Journal, 17 Nov. 1813; LJ, II, 328; Harness, quoted Paston and Quennell, 24–5; and also, among Byron's letters, Harness, 15 Dec. 1811; Murray, 9 Oct. 1820; LJ, II, 91; V, 115–16.

2. Compare Moore's similar statement noting Byron's habit 'of depreciating and making light of what intrinsically he valued' and in particular of 'throwing slight and mockery upon a tie' involving his 'best feelings' (XL, 470; see also XXXIV, 403).

occupied intensely with self, as the great centre and source of its strength' (XXIII, 268).

Teresa was at great pains to answer complaints regarding what she—or her translator—calls Byron's 'mobility'; that is, his chameleon changes that baffled Lady Blessington and which Moore likewise observes (LI, 582), seeing them in terms of his multi-facial genius. Now the contrast between Moore's view and Teresa's corresponds to the contrast between Shakespeare's work, with which Byron *as a man* holds so exact a correspondence, and the work of Pope, which Byron so greatly *admired*. In Byron we find various passions together with the will to unity, to ethic; and he admired Pope as the great moral poet of our literature (The Bowles Controversy, LJ, V, 554, 559). Teresa was throughout aware of Byron as a moral force; she denied his 'mobility'. Her diagnosis is, as usual, well supported. She quotes Stanhope's assertion that Byron remained always constant in religion and politics, and that his conversational scepticism was to be contrasted with his *actions* and serious sentiments (II; I, 3).[1] She admits his *intellectual* versatility, while regarding it rather as a virtue than as a vice, but insists that in all the central concerns of *life* and *action* he was constant:

'Were his principles in politics, in religion, in all that constitutes the man of honour in the highest acceptation of the term, at all affected by it?' (II; VIII, 152).

'Mobility' may have animated his writings, and still more often his conversations, but *never his actions* (II; VIII, 153); it was in him united with a constancy the more admirable for the difficulties involved:

'To overcome this difficulty, when one has a mind eager for emotion, variable, with width and depth capable of discovering simultaneously the for and against of everything, and thus being necessarily exposed to perplexity of choice, it is surely marvellous if a mind so constituted be also constant. Now Lord Byron personified this marvel' (II; VIII, 155).

'Such constancy', she writes, 'united to a temperament like his becomes positively wonderful' (155). These statements I would with

---

1. Stanhope remarked that to a *superficial* observer 'his conduct appeared to be quite unsettled', but that in reality 'no man was more constant, even obstinate', in the pursuit of certain 'great objects'. In religion and politics he was 'firm as a rock', always returning to certain fixed opinions involving 'liberty' and the existence 'of a God' (Edgcumbe, I, XVI, 207).

no reservations assess as the most profound, comprehensive, and important that have ever been made about Byron. They cover the whole of him—his inclusion of dramatic opposites, his Shakespearian variety, his will to unity and ethic, his admiration of Pope—while profoundly emphasizing *the unique importance and value of this peculiar balance or direction*. Here we have Byron as, not merely a genius, but as genius pointed towards ethic; one in whom the molten fluidities of great poetry were being steadily cooled, tempered and sharpened into a supreme instrument of good.

She blames Moore, not altogether justly, for emphasizing Byron's 'exuberance of faculties' without sufficient awareness of his integrity. Such various faculties 'united in one individual', she says, surely themselves constituted a 'character', a 'distinct personality, almost unique in kind'. But, she says, human nature is always compacted of mixed qualities; and could Moore 'not have found, towering above the rich profusion of qualities in his friend, one dominant passion?' What was that passion? This—

'The master-passion that occupied so great a place in Lord Byron's mind was his *love of truth, with all the qualities flowing from it*' (II; XV, 399–400).

To him, as to Swift's Houyhnhnms, untruth was intolerable: 'A lie was not only a lie to him, it was also an injustice, a cowardice, the mark of a corrupt soul, an inconceivable thing, and not to be forgiven' (II; XV, 400). It was a vice he 'never forgave' (II; I, 6). Clearly, such an uncompromising honesty was risky: 'Ever attracted towards truth, his first desire was to seek after that; and the better to do so, he searched into himself, analysed what was passing within and without, and finally proclaimed it without any consideration for himself or others.' She refers to 'that imperious *want* of scanning himself, of descending into the depths of his own heart, interrogating his conscience, and very often of writing down in his memorandum books the severe sentences pronounced by that inflexible judge'. Since he 'could not put away from his sight' his self-constituted, 'divine', model of goodness, he came out from these examinations '*humbled, dissatisfied, reproaching and punishing himself for having strayed from it*'. He found in himself too many egotistical elements, concerned with friendship, love, ambition, glory; and brought the maxims of the severe Rochefoucault to bear on his own soul (II; VI, 106–7). Hence (i) his distorted self-depreciation, and (ii), as a corollary, the opportunities given to scandal.

The passion for truth was, however, accompanied by a second principle, generosity. These two, she says, 'divided the empire of his soul' (II; IV, 51). Again, 'Had he known himself, he would have found that he realized one of the finest types of character that humanity can offer; for his two characterizing faculties were, his attraction towards truth and benevolence' (II; VI, 112). Certainly these dual qualities cover all the virtues; they are, basically, the love of God and of man demanded by Christ. More—they are, really, mutually independent, and so one can feel a unity, a central, inclusive, devotion at work; or, as Teresa puts it, throughout his works, letters, and life 'one perceives a golden ray, ever present', a kind of 'latent' religious 'faith' (II; I, 7). That golden centre, or heart, once recognized, all the various Byronic complexities fall into significant place.

It would be wrong to suppose that Moore had failed to observe these primary Byronic virtues, though his emphasis on Byron's variability—'a genius taking upon itself all shapes from Jove down to Scapin, and a disposition veering with equal facility to all points of the moral compass' (LI, 582)—may have been excessive. Moore also recognized a unity. Through all variations he observed 'a general consistency in the main, however shifting and contradictory the details, which had the effect of preserving, from first to last, all his views and principles, upon the great subjects that interested him through life, essentially unchanged' (LI, 585).

With so clear an intuition into the golden centre of Byron's personality, Teresa naturally shows little sympathy with the opposing forces; with the arts of popular biography; with what she calls 'that terrible English *law of opinion*', that 'phenomenon of a terrible character, a phenomenon almost peculiar to England, the tyrannical power of its public opinion' (II; IX, 165; XIV, 361); with the 'crime' of the destruction of Byron's *Memoirs* to screen certain 'insignificant beings' (II; XII, 254); and so on. In return, these forces, and their successors, have refused to face Teresa's book. It simply is not true that her study is the work of a second-rate, and sentimental, mind; and, even if it were, the greater part is plain, impersonal, evidence. When using the important witness 'Miss S' (pp. 228, 86 note) she gives strictly critical reasons for accepting the document concerned as reliable and free from exaggeration (II; IV, 57–8). She is throughout critically aware. At her best, she is incisive. Consider, for example, this pithy comment on Lady Byron, and see how well it applies to our own, steely-precise, brilliant, but deceptive and self-deceptive, twentieth-century intelligence:

'One of those minds that act as if life were a problem in juris-
prudence or geometry; who argue, distinguish, and, by dint of
syllogisms, *deceive themselves learnedly*' (II; XII, 230).

The words have the cutting edge of a Nietzsche. They are, moreover, written from a viewpoint constituting a threat to the established
mind-structure of our time; and that is perhaps why Teresa's work
has been so strangely ignored.

True, it is an untidy book. It is, like Lady Blessington's, repetitive, and to those who expect a normal biography strung out in
a time-sequence, will appear amorphous. But it is not a normal
biography: it is a piling up of evidence, irrespective of time-sequence,
regarding Byron's qualities. It will, of course, be obvious that
Teresa was here employing precisely the technique that I myself
have regularly applied to works of genius and am applying throughout this book; the technique of 'spatial' analysis. She knew what she
was doing: 'These pages, we again repeat, are not a biography, but
the picture of a soul' (II; V, 94). It could not have been better put.

IV

Teresa's difficulties resemble those of my present study; and it
may be as well to conclude with a word or two more regarding what
I have called the 'spatial' approach, defined best in my *Christian
Renaissance* and discussed and practised there and in other studies in
interpretation of poem, play, or poet's life-work.

Countering our temporal thinking by spatial emphases, it introduces us to the space-time, or eternity, dimension of artistic genius.
This approach we shall apply to both Byron's total literary, especially
his prose, output, and the events of his life. The method is simpler
than it sounds and indeed, like poetry itself, far easier to practise
than to explain. It involves the massed use of materials wrenched
boldly from their habitual associations and grouped about various
new centres of interest, often with little or no emphasis on the temporal succession from which they have been removed; thereby being
loosed from the trammels of false biographical or narrative accretion
to be seen afresh *as themselves;* or, to use a famous phrase, they stand
sub specie aeternitatis. But the temporal succession is not forgotten, and
its implications never contradicted; rather is it fused with this more
spatial awareness so that we view events as both temporal and co-

existent. Some such space-time fusion is necessary to any understanding of eternal life.

Byron, in whose poetic work the 'eternity' concept beats more powerfully than in other poets, may be felt, as a man, uniquely shadowed by the eternal. There is something non-temporal about his story, his end is implicit in his beginning; and he therefore lends himself uniquely to the spatial approach. 'At every single moment of one's life', wrote Oscar Wilde in *De Profundis, '*one is what one is going to be, no less than what one has been.' Before the deaths of his Mother and early friends, Byron was already associating, like Hamlet, with skulls; an instinctive *Macbeth*-guilt tortured him before he could be accused of any major sin; he was spiritually exiled, a Timon in soul, before the crash which, as Moore (XL, 469) notes, merely gave him a specific occasion for an ingrained antipathy. But this is not all; the reverse also is strangely true. Even on his last expedition to Greece, during the campaign itself, when so much that was superficial had been sloughed off and he felt the destinies of Europe on his shoulders, and his alone; even then his behaviour was characterized by Puckish pranks (p. 209) that would seem to suit better the Harrow schoolboy than the saviour of nations. In his comprehensive personality nothing is omitted. How much easier to assume saintly status if you avoid those too practical jokers on the soul of man, sex and politics: but Byron shirked nothing. At any instant of his life all ages, and both sexes, all human compulsions, good and evil, are co-present. In this sense he is the eternal, the universal, man.

II

PATRON AND PROTÉGÉS

I

CONTEMPORARY biography tends to assert that Byron was an egotist, that he suffered from literary envy, that he disliked children,[1] though he was, on occasion and in spite of appearances, 'capable of kindness' (p. 29). Let us inspect the evidence.

Teresa Guiccioli notes that Byron's manner and conversation were often misleading. Only 'mean minds and superficial observers' were, however, deceived, since you had only to consider his *actions* or any moments of spontaneous feeling to become 'aware of the stores of sensibility and goodness of which his noble heart was full' (quoted Moore, XLIX, 567). The warning is salutary. We shall first inspect Byron's instinct for patronage.

If we glance through his letters during the period of his success, when the first two cantos of *Childe Harold* had made him the most famous author in England, we meet the unusual phenomenon of a successful writer valuing his sudden eminence primarily as a vantage-point for the assistance of others.

In the vast extent of Byron's letters and journals there is no instance of what is usually meant by 'egotism'. He consciously avoided such faults. 'How I do delight in observing life as it really is!—and myself, after all, the worst of any. But no matter—I must avoid egotism, which, just now, would be no vanity' (Journal, 17–18 Dec. 1813; LJ, II, 378). His remarks 'You will, I trust, pardon this egotism' and 'excuse all this damned . . . egotism' after some very harmless references to his own poetry (Drury, 13 Jan. 1808; Murray, 20 Feb. 1816; LJ, I, 162; III, 264; see also Miss Milbanke, 26 Sept. 1813; LJ, III, 401) are characteristic. He disliked himself: 'You must excuse all this, for I have nothing to say in this lone mansion but of myself, and yet I would willingly talk or think of aught else' (Dallas, 25 Aug. 1811; LJ, II, 6). Composition

1. Mr. Quennell groups Byron's attitude to children with his attitude to animals as 'capricious and self-centred' (VIII, 252).

was to him only valuable as, in T. S. Eliot's well-known phrase, 'an escape from personality'; 'To withdraw *myself* from *myself* (oh that cursed selfishness!) has ever been my sole, my entire, my sincere motive in scribbling at all' (Journal, 27 Nov. 1813; LJ, II, 351). He referred instinctively to others as 'my elders and my betters' (Harness, 15 Dec. 1811; Moore, 28 Aug. 1813; Journal, 17 Dec. 1813; LJ, II, 91, 256, 378). 'It would but ill become me', he wrote to Goethe, 'to pretend to exchange verses with him who, for fifty years, has been the undisputed sovereign of European literature' (24 July 1823; LJ, VI, 237). Himself a writer of the first order, he could yet with extraordinary readiness submit to the judgment of others. Teresa recounts how promptly he reacted in youth to the Rev. Mr. Becher's criticism of his early work, how he withdrew *The Curse of Minerva* from the press on being told that it would pain Lord Elgin, and suppressed certain parts of *Childe Harold II* in deference to Dallas and Gifford; and so on (Teresa, I; IX, 377; II; X, 195). Though he could refuse compromise and stand alone against the judgment of the world, this natural tendency towards respect and submission was also genuine. His letters provide continual corroboration of that 'good-humour' and 'docility' attributed to him by Moore (Moore, XV, 167; see also Teresa, II; III, 46; Medwin, 338). It was the same with his life; he took a 'scolding' from Lady Blessington 'with his usual good-nature' (Blessington, 204) and showed an extraordinary humility in his willingness to listen to Kennedy's sermonizing at Cephalonia (Moore, LII, 599). His modesty, says Teresa with—his genius and the nature of his challenge and its reception granted—a far greater degree of truth than has hitherto been supposed, 'shines in every line of his poetry and his prose, at every age and in all the circumstances of his life' (II; III, 37).

He was averse to soliciting Gifford's interest on behalf of *Childe Harold* (Murray, 23 Aug.; Dallas, 17 Sept.; 1811; LJ, II, 1, 41). But that was not his attitude to the work of others. He was an eager patron, anxious and ready to see merit, thinking one of George Townsend's poetic plans 'borders on the sublime' (Dallas, 27 Aug. 1811; LJ, II, 9); writing kindly of H. G. Knight's *Persian Tales* and apologizing to the author for certain corrections (Murray, 4 Dec. 1813; LJ, II, 299); offering a careful and sympathetic criticism of the future Lady Byron's poems (Caroline Lamb, 1 May 1812; LJ, II, 118); and being instrumental in getting a reprint at Murray's for Bernard Barton (Barton, 1 June 1812; LJ, II, 123). His Journal for 1 December 1813 notes: 'Galt called—Mem—to ask some one to speak to Raymond in favour of his play' (LJ, II, 361). His literary interests were objective: he wanted Gifford's opinion on an old manuscript whilst characteristically remarking, 'It is not for me to hazard an opinion upon its merits' (Murray, 22 Nov. 1812; LJ, II, 183).

Whatever his success, he refused to compare himself with such literary giants as Rogers or Scott, remarking curtly of a review: 'The man's a fool. *Jacqueline* is as superior to *Lara* as Rogers is to me' (quoted LJ, II, 69, note). He was angered at being compared favourably with Scott: 'All such stuff can only vex him and do me no good' (Journal, 17 Nov. 1813; LJ, II, 322). Scott he regarded as 'Monarch of Parnassus' (Journal, 24 Nov. 1813; LJ, II, 343), and admired Gifford, Campbell, Coleridge and Crabbe. But here we meet a strange yet important characteristic. *English Bards and Scotch Reviewers* he quickly regretted, calling it, 'this miserable record of misplaced anger and indiscriminate acrimony' and writing against a passage on Wordsworth 'all this is bad, because personal' (Moore, VIII, 81; see p. 267 below). In it he had also admonished both Scott and Moore, urging these established authors to write more worthily of themselves, as a schoolmaster might advise, sternly, a couple of promising pupils. Now, that early poem repudiated, the young Byron still, as though 'by sovereignty of nature', showed a craving, as it were, to assist and encourage his seniors. After an unexpected introduction to the Prince Regent, who spoke praisingly of both his own poetry and Scott's, Byron quite unnecessarily hastened to Murray asking him to hand on the happy news to Scott, whom he had not met and who next wrote to Byron praising *Childe Harold*. In answer (6 July 1812) Byron apologized for his early satire, but showed little desire to discuss his own work: '. . . and now, waiving myself, let me talk to you of the Prince Regent'. He records, in spite of his political antipathy, his impression of the Prince's accomplishments and suggests that Scott should be happy at his sovereign's recognition (LJ, II, 131-5). Instead of himself luxuriating in the approval of either, Byron's one aim was the encouragement of an older writer.

This is no isolated incident. After some preliminary difficulties and the risk, owing to Byron's satire, of a duel, he and Moore became good friends. His letters to Moore, though characterized by an extreme literary modesty, were nevertheless written as by an established author to a junior of wavering confidence. He urged Moore to cash in on the popularity (created by himself) of Eastern subjects with a big work, a 'Shah-Nameh', decrying his own successes in this field as only worthy to break ground for better things, and apologizing for writing in such a style to one of his 'elders' and 'betters' (28 Aug. 1813; LJ, II, 253-6). When Moore showed a fear of competition, Byron could only suggest he must be joking: 'It really puts me out of humour to hear you talk thus.' He is as anxious for his new friend's success 'as one human being can be for another's. . . . The field of fame is wide enough for all; and if it were not, I would not willingly rob my neighbour of a rood of it.' There is no comparison between Moore's vast 'property' and his own 'wild common' (1 Sept. 1813; LJ, II, 256). Moore's reply was more confident and Byron answered: 'Your letter has cancelled all my anxieties. I did *not suspect* you in *earnest*. Modest again! Because I don't do a very shabby thing, it seems, I "don't fear your competition". If it were reduced to an alternative of preference, I *should* dread you, as much as Satan does Michael. But is there not room enough in our respective regions? Go on—it will soon be my turn to forgive' (2 Oct. 1813; LJ, II, 273). There was nevertheless a clash. Byron sent Moore *The Bride of Abydos* noting (30 Nov. 1813; LJ, II, 293) that it did not touch Moore's territory, and 'if it did, you would soon reduce me to my proper boundaries'. His own poem is a mere trifle; he adds hopefully that it may well lose him his new-found fame; it is 'the work of a week' only and 'the reading of an hour to you, or even less,—and so, let it go'. But Moore's true worry was not known to Byron. This very poem, *The Bride of Abydos,* resembled in narrative one which Moore was using for his major work *Lalla Rookh,* and which Byron's poem now caused him to reject. 'To aim at vigour and strong feeling after *you*', he wrote, 'is hopeless;—that region was made for Caesar' (LJ, II, 302, note). Here is Byron's reply:

'I certainly am of opinion that you have not yet done all *you* can do, though more than enough for any one else. I want, and the world expects, a longer work from you; and I see in you what I never saw in poet before, a strange diffidence of your own powers, which I cannot account for, and which must be unaccountable, when a *Cossac* like me can appal a *cuirassier*. Your story I did not, could not, know,—I thought only of a Peri. I wish you had confided in me, not for your sake, but mine, and to prevent the world from losing a much better poem than my own, but which, I yet hope, this *clashing* will not even now deprive them of. Mine is the work of a week, written, *why* I have partly told you, and partly I cannot tell you by letter—some day I will.

'Go on—I shall really be very unhappy if I at all interfere with you. The success of mine is yet problematical; though the public will probably purchase a certain quantity, on the presumption of their own propensity for *The Giaour* and such "horrid mysteries" . . .'

And a little further on:

'This last thing of mine *may* have the same fate, and I assure you I have great doubts about it. But, even if not, its little day will be over before you are ready and willing. Come out—"screw your courage to the sticking-place" . . .' (8 Dec. 1813; LJ, II, 302–3; *Macbeth*, I, vii).

He seems positively to want his own poem to fail.

These rather remarkable colours of sentiment are not just laid on for the recipient. In his own intimate journal we find him writing a schoolmaster's report on Moore: 'There is nothing Moore may not do, if he will but seriously set about it. . . . For his honour, principle and independence, his conduct to —— speaks "trumpet tongued"' (Journal, 22 Nov. 1813; LJ, II, 333; *Macbeth*, I, vii). The sentiment is as typical as the Shakespearian reference. He continued to keep Moore up to it: 'How proceeds the poem? Do not neglect it, and I have no fears.' Moore's fame was, he says, dearer to him than his own; he had lately begun to think his own things had been strangely over-rated; 'and, at any rate, whether or not, I have done with them for ever' (3 March 1814; LJ, III, 56). Again, 'Now is *your* time;—you will come upon them newly and freshly.' There is a scornful reference to his own tales and the general dearth of good things of late, and then (quoting *2 Henry IV*, V, iii), 'Now, Tom, is thy time—"Oh, joyful day!—I would not take a knighthood for thy fortune"' (10 Jan. 1815; LJ, III, 169). Byron continued to regard the success of *Lalla Rookh* as a personal responsibility (Murray, 25 March 1817; LJ, IV, 85). 'He almost', says Teresa, 'wished to be eclipsed, that Moore might shine the more prominently' (Teresa, I; VIII, 343).

Byron's literary unselfishness antedated his own success. Before the publication of *Childe Harold* he had insisted on Hobhouse making prior use for his *Travels* of certain material collected for the notes of the poem: 'I declare to you most sincerely', he wrote, 'that I would rather throw up my publication entirely, than be the means of curtailing a page of yours'; and again, 'The Devil's in it if there is not a field for both' (3 Dec. 1811; see also 20 Sept. 1811; C, I, 63-4, 47-8). There was nothing exclusive in him at all. He welcomed news of Maturin's dramatic success, as any one must, he said, who desired to see merit rise in—quoting Falstaff (*2 Henry IV*, I, ii)— 'these costermonger days' (Hobhouse, 27 May 1816; C, II, 10). His assertion to Moore (12 March 1814; LJ, III, 59) that he had 'no literary envy' is exactly corroborated by Gamba, who says that he prided himself on the successes of his friends, adding: 'This I know, that of envy he had not the least spark in his whole disposition' (Gamba, Notes, 289). 'I think', wrote Moore to Rogers of Byron's dedication of *The Corsair*, 'there are few more *generous* spirits than Lord Byron's'; it is what 'might be expected from a profuse, magnificent-minded fellow, who does not wait for the scales to weigh what he says, but gives praise, as sailors lend money, by "handfuls"' (13 Jan. 1814; LJ, III, 12, note). He loved, said Lady Blessington, to dwell on the merits of his dead friends (170) and, even after attacking people in conversation, could emphasize their 'good qualities' with just as much 'apparent pleasure', his 'candour and good nature' leading him to 'enumerate' and 'draw attention' to their virtue (246). Teresa's statement, though, as usual, uncompromising, says no more than the evidence supports: 'In his noble soul', she tells us, 'no feeling of jealousy could enter' (I; VI, 301); he was always depreciating his own 'genius' whilst praising 'his rivals' and assisting those in need of 'help or encouragement' (II; III, 40). After observing how much harm has been done on earth 'by the jealousies of artists and literary men', she adds: 'This right I claim for Lord Byron, that he was the least jealous of any man.' With him, 'to praise was almost a besetting sin'; and this generous appreciation extended to statesmen, soldiers, and women; 'he who was so sparing of answers to his own detractors could not allow a criticism against a friend to be left unanswered'; indeed, his freedom 'from all sentiments of an envious nature' showed itself 'so clearly in all his sayings and doings', that it appeared 'impossible to doubt it'; and yet some have done so (Teresa, I; VIII, 332-3, 352, 368, 371, 372). Hobhouse groups as one of Byron's finest qualities his praise of contemporary writers, though observing that 'exception must, of course, be made as regards Southey, who assailed him personally, with unsparing bitterness, and whose merit he would never acknowledge' (*Albania*, I, App., 542, note). Teresa, while likewise allotting the blame to Southey, makes an obvious but important distinction between personal rivalry and attacks in the cause of political principle and for the sake of mankind (II; VII, 131–4, 141–2).[1] Byron's private aspersions on Keats' early poetic manner must be understood in the light of his devotion to the school of Pope. But none of this is jealousy, or anything like it. One can only, properly, as Byron himself observed (The Bowles Controversy, LJ, V, 556), be called envious of those one admires. He particularly despised what he called 'the vindictive jealousy of *gens de plume*' (Hay, Sept. 1819; SP, II, 488). Speaking of Campbell he once wrote: 'Now this comes of "bearing no brother near the throne".' For himself, his throne, he said, was gone; he disclaimed all future poetic ambition and was at perfect peace 'with the poetical fraternity'. Besides, 'Surely the field of thought is infinite. What does it signify who is before or behind in a race where there is no *goal*?' (Journal, 6 Dec. 1813; LJ, II, 365). Even late in his life, when he had every excuse for both bitterness and poetic pride, he would not accept 'homage', since 'there is no sovereign in the republic of letters', and even if there were, he himself 'never had the pretension or the power to become a usurper' (Coulmann, 12 July 1823; LJ, VI, 230). Once only in the vast mass of his prose and poetry did he assert the opposite claim (*Don Juan*, XI, 55–6); once only, that is, did he admit the truth of his poetic eminence.

This literary benevolence extended to comparative strangers. His Journal for 20 February 1814 (LJ, II, 388), after recording his receipt and acknowledgment of 'young Reynold's poem *Safie*', notes that 'the lad is clever'. The poem's thoughts appear borrowed, but he hates 'discouraging a young one' and thinks the work shows 'talent' and 'fire'. He tells the young man of his approval, and continues:

'Whether you intend to pursue your poetical career, I do not know, and have no right to enquire—but, in whatever channel your abilities are directed, I think it will be your own fault if they do not eventually lead to distinction. Happiness must, of course, depend upon conduct,—and even fame itself would be but a poor compensation for self-reproach. You will excuse me for talking to a man, perhaps not many years my junior, with these grave airs of seniority; but though I cannot claim much advantage in that respect, it was my lot to be thrown very early upon the world, to mix a good deal in it in more climates than one, and to purchase experience which would probably have been of greater service to any one than myself.

---

1. See also 'The Quarrel between Byron and Southey', LJ, VI, App. 1; Teresa, I; VIII, 359–61; Drinkwater, V, 288–9; and Murray, 9 May 1817; LJ, IV, 117–18.

But my business with you is in your capacity of author and to that I will confine myself' (20 Feb. 1814; LJ, III, 46).

A strange letter from a man himself only in his twenties; but its humility, its rating of life and morality above poetic fame, its desire to help a young beginner, its touch of patronly, Timon-like benevolence, are all thoroughly Byronic. He warned Reynolds not to be discouraged, or angered, by adverse reviews, and next approached Francis Hodgson, asking him to write a kindly notice to avoid blighting the first-fruits of a '*young* mind' (28 Feb. 1814; LJ, III, 51). Byron's earlier phrase about discouraging a 'young one' was significant; but whatever the age, he tended to treat others as younger and deserving his care; he was pre-eminently tender. If he had a play to read, he remarked: 'I must read it, and endeavour not to displease the author. I hate annoying them with cavil' (Journal, 10 Dec. 1813; LJ, II, 372). Much later, at a time when his own literary affairs must have been an agonizing worry, he undertook the support of Taaffe, who was anxious for publication of his translation of Dante. Teresa has left us an interesting record:

'All the English at Pisa, including the kind Shelley, were turning him into ridicule. Lord Byron alone would not join in the laugh. Taaffe's sincerity won for him grace and compassion. Indeed, Lord Byron did still more; for he wrote and entreated Murray to publish the work, so as to give the poor poet this consolation. Not content with that step, he wrote to Moore to beg Jeffrey not to criticize him, undertaking himself to ask Gifford the same thing, through Murray. "Perhaps they might speak of the Commentaries without touching on the text," said he, and then he added, with his usual pleasantry, "However, we must not trust to it. *Those dogs! The text is too tempting*" ' (II; XIII, 287).

Byron wrote to Moore on 13 December 1821: 'You must really get Taaffe published—he never will rest till he is so' (LJ, V, 494); and again, with his usual *persistence* in the cause of others, 'It will make the man so exuberantly happy'; the work is full of the 'most orthodox religion and morality'; 'I make it a point that he shall be in print' (Moore, 8 March, 1822; LJ, VI, 39). On such occasions, Byron spared no effort. Lady Blessington tells us how, even after attacking some one, 'in half an hour he would put himself to personal inconvenience' to render a kindness to the person 'shown up' (59). Whatever the pressure of his affairs and the extent of his own personal sufferings he found time for such 'little, nameless, unremember'd acts of kindness and of love'; though he himself would no doubt have capped such a sentiment with an ironic comment.

Our Wordsworthian quotation may serve to introduce a greater name than those we have so far noticed. Coleridge, suffering from his long addiction to opium, solicited Byron's help in finding a publisher for his collected poems. Byron had already used his influence for the production of *Remorse* at Drury Lane in 1813; and now, on 31 March 1815, he answered with more than courtesy, saying: 'It will give me great pleasure to comply with your request, though I hope there is still taste enough left amongst us to render it almost unnecessary.' He was at pains to *comfort* Coleridge. He praises *Remorse,* urges him to work on another tragedy, and concludes by humbly apologizing for his lines in *English Bards and Scotch Reviewers:* 'The part applied to you is pert, and petulant, and shallow enough' (LJ, III, 190–3). On 18 October he was promising to use all his influence with 'the trade' and referred to an unpublished poem of Coleridge shown him by Scott—'the wildest and finest I ever heard in that kind of composition'. The poem was *Christabel,* and Byron urged its inclusion in the proposed volume: 'I do not know that even "Love" or the "Ancient Mariner" are so impressive—and to me there are few things in our tongue beyond these two productions.' As a member of the Drury Lane Committee, he next enquired after Coleridge's proposed 'tragedy' which he was 'very anxious' to have 'under consideration'. 'It is', he wrote, 'a field in which there are none living to contend against you and in which I should take pride and pleasure in seeing you compared with the dead' (SP, I, 316). A few days later (27 Oct. 1815) Byron had read the poem: 'I have the *Christabelle* safe, and am glad to see it in such good progress; surely a little effort would complete the poem . . .' (LJ, III, 228). He instinctively felt the older poet as one needing his help and encouragement. On 28 October he was soliciting Moore's aid as a reviewer: 'By the way, if poor Coleridge—who is a man of wonderful talent, and in distress, and about to publish two Volumes of Poesy and Biography, and who has been worse used by the critics than ever we were—will you, if he comes out, promise me to review him favourably in the *Edinburgh Review?* Praise him I think you must, but you will also praise him *well*—of all things the most difficult. It will be the making of him' (LJ, III, 232). The last phrase ('making') is peculiarly important.

Christabel appeared in 1816 with the other poems brought out by

Murray. *Kubla Khan* was only included at Byron's request, though Coleridge himself could make nothing of it (see Coleridge's preface to *Kubla Khan*). Byron told Medwin that *Christabel*, written in 1795, was the origin of all Scott's metrical tales; that it had a 'pretty general circulation in the literary world', but was not published till 1816, and 'then probably in consequence of my advice'. As for *Kubla Khan*, 'his psychological poem', he says, 'was always a great favourite of mine, and but for me would not have appeared. What perfect harmony of versification!' Asked what it possessed beyond verbal music, 'I can't tell you,' answered Byron, 'but it delights me.' Had Coleridge not ruined himself by German metaphysics, 'he would', said Byron, 'have made the greatest poet of the day'; he 'might have been anything; as it is, he is a thing "that dreams are made of"' (Medwin, 211–16; *The Tempest*, IV, i).

It is usual to decry Byron's merits as a critic of romantic poetry. His more general judgments against romanticism were, however, far from exclusive. He once coupled Crabbe and Coleridge as the first of contemporary poets (Moore, VIII, 81); while his selection from the mass of Coleridge's poetry of *The Ancient Mariner, Christabel* and *Kubla Khan* for primary attention showed, for a contemporary, a remarkable insight. Two of them appear to have found in Byron their main supporter, and probably owed to him their survival.

He was blamed for his support. On 24 December 1816, he wrote from Venice to Moore: 'When does your poem of poems come out? I hear that the *Edinburgh Review* has cut up Coleridge's *Christabel* and declared against me for praising it. I praised it, firstly, because I thought well of it; secondly because Coleridge was in great distress, and after doing what little I could for him in essentials, I thought that the public avowal of my good opinion might help him further, at least with the booksellers. I am very sorry that Jeffrey has attacked him, because, poor fellow, it will hurt him in mind and pocket. As for me, he's welcome—I shall never think less of Jeffrey for anything he may say against me or mine in future' (LJ, IV, 31). Byron's kindness to Coleridge has, except for the emphasis accorded it by Teresa (I; VIII, 348–50), who appears to miss nothing, received scant attention. Throughout we are aware of Byron's sympathy for one only on the edge of his acquaintance and whose lectures he found irritating (Harness, 6 Dec.; Hodgson, 8 Dec.; 1811; LJ, II, 75, 83).

Moore and Coleridge were important writers, but his benevolence functioned irrespective of literary merit, as when he urged

Thomas Ashe to leave disreputable and dishonest hack-work: 'Depend upon it they amuse *few*, disgrace both *reader* and *writer*, and benefit *none*. It will be my wish to assist you, as far as my limited means will admit, to break such a bondage' (14 Dec. 1813; LJ, II, 307). Ashe at once demanded a substantial sum and showed annoyance at the slightest delay, Byron answering his impetuosity and impudence with the extraordinary patience, tact and sympathy that characterized his behaviour on such occasions (Moore, XIX, 224–5; Teresa, I; IX, 391–2; Ashe, 5 Jan. 1814; LJ, III, 4). Behind his actions, here and elsewhere, was the will to make of persons, or nations—remember his phrase on Coleridge: 'It will be the making of him'—the best that it was in them to be. He was, in essence, and by instinct, an *educator*. On occasion he was forced into a false position by his own magnanimity. That was to happen later with Leigh Hunt. But their early relationship was happy enough. On 22 and 30 October 1815, Byron wrote enthusiastically to Hunt about his *Rimini*, and later, on 4 November, told Moore of it (LJ, III, 226, 242, 244). His readiness to engage in such enthusiasms even led him to write an unsolicited letter to an unknown author, praising his work and hoping to have the opportunity of smoothing his path (18 July 1815; LJ, III, 211). His general behaviour at this period is summed up in a characteristic letter to Murray on 4 November 1815:

'Dear Sir,—When you have been enabled to form an opinion on Mr. Coleridge's MS. you will oblige me by returning it, as, in fact, I have no authority to let it out of my hands. I think most highly of it, and feel anxious that you should be the publisher; but if you are not, I do not despair of finding those who will.

'I have written to Mr. Lh. Hunt, stating your willingness to treat with him, which, when I saw you, I understood you to be. Terms and time, I leave to his pleasure and your discernment; but this I will say, that I think it the *safest* thing you ever engaged in. I speak to you as a man of business; were I to talk to you as a reader or a critic, I should say it was a very wonderful and beautiful performance, with just enough of fault to make its beauties more remarked and remarkable.

'And now to the last—my own, which I feel ashamed of after the others;—publish or not as you like, I don't care *one damn*. If *you* don't, no one else shall, and I never thought or dreamed of it, except as one in the collection. If it is worth being in the fourth volume, put it there and nowhere else; and if not, put it in the fire' (4 Nov. 1815; LJ, III, 246).

For Coleridge and Leigh Hunt he was willing to act not only as patron but as an unpaid—indeed, paying, since he gave Coleridge £100 (LJ, III, 191, note) and planned to give more—literary agent. Byron's generosity was not confined to encouragement and recommendation; throughout his life he was lavish of financial assistance, both to writers, friends in general, strangers in want, and greater, communal, causes: 'Were it possible', said Hodgson, 'to state *all* he has done for numerous friends, he would appear amiable indeed' (Hodgson, quoted Moore, IX, 92, note). He at first regularly handed over his works' proceeds to Dallas, calling it assistance rendered to a worthy man by one 'not quite so worthy' (Dallas, 17 Feb. 1814; LJ, III, 43). Even when in financial difficulties, which, as he told Hobhouse, were 'such as to drive him half-mad' (Hobhouse, II; XV, 201), and which made him sell his library—and later Newstead itself, on which he had originally 'fixed his heart', determining never to sell (Mrs. Byron, 6 March; Hanson, 26 April; 1809; LJ, I, 216, 222)—he refused, on principles which need not here concern us, £1,050 from Murray for the separate publication of *The Siege of Corinth* and *Parisina* (3 Jan. 1816; LJ, III, 251). His help, however, being suddenly solicited for Godwin's distress, he reconsidered his attitude, deciding to make over £600 worth of the copyrights to him, the rest being purposed for the dramatist Maturin and Coleridge. On 20 January 1816 he asked Rogers to 'arrange it with him (Godwin) in such a manner as may be least offensive to his feelings, and so as not to have the appearance of officiousness nor obtrusion on my part', adding: 'Only don't let him be plagued, nor think himself obliged and all that, which makes people hate one another' (LJ, III, 255-6). Complications followed, since what Murray, knowing his embarrassments, had offered for Byron, and Byron had definitely asserted was far too much, he was less ready to hand over to Godwin. Byron's relations with his publisher were temporarily damaged. As Moore observes (XXV, 301), Byron's letter to Murray of 6 March 1816 referring to the seizure of his books during the 'tenth execution' in progress (LJ, III, 271), suggests the extent of his own pecuniary troubles while he was thus planning for others. Teresa notes that he was writing to Murray the letter already quoted on behalf of Hunt and Coleridge—both later on, she says, to prove ungrateful—during his matrimonial anxieties (II; III, 43-4). When he assisted Godwin, he was in a state of inward turmoil; his sanity was already being questioned by his own wife. But Byron elsewhere appears unnaturally considerate of others and inhumanly calm, just when he was himself—one would suppose—most tormented.[1] We noted an example with Taaffe's *Commentary;* we shall meet others.

The tact of his approach to Godwin—an excellent example of what Teresa calls his 'refined generosity' (II; V, 88)—is striking, and a similar fineness of feeling seems to have characterized his gift to Moore, who needed help, of the ill-fated *Memoirs* 'as a kind of legacy' (Hobhouse, 23 Nov. 1821; C, II, 205–6; Moore, 9 Dec. 1820 and 1 Oct. 1821; LJ, V, 131, 384; Moore, XXXVI, 422). Byron's financial generosity to his friends was continual. He lent Augusta Leigh, whose husband was in difficulties, £3,000, in reality a gift though nominally a loan (May 1814; LJ, III, 84, note). In similar fashion he lent, or rather gave, J. W. Webster £1,000 (Oct. 1813; LJ, II, 3, note; C, I, 207, note). Francis Hodgson blesses him for £1,500 given to clear his father's liabilities (LJ, II, 294–5, note). On one of these latter occasions Byron notes in his Journal for 17 November 1813:

'I wish there had been more (in)convenience and less gratification to my self-love in it, for then there had been more merit. We are all selfish—and I believe, ye gods of Epicurus! I believe in Rochefoucault about *men,* and in Lucretius (not Busby's translation) about yourselves' (LJ, II, 325).

This is quoted by Teresa as an example of what she called 'that extraordinary susceptibility of conscience which led to self-reproach for egotism, only because he felt pleasure in exercising beneficence, and that it did not contain enough sacrifice' (II; VI, 106, 111). Byron was expressing an instinct, as surely as Timon. It was scarcely 'charity'. He was annoyed with Hodgson for telling people of the gift: 'I obliged myself ten times more by being of use than I did him—and there's an end on't' (Journal, 1 Dec. 1813; LJ, II, 358).

Byron's remark, with reference to Godwin, that obligations led to hatred (see also Teresa, 17 July 1820; Origo, V, 194; and Blessington, 351) may assist our understanding of his later association with Leigh Hunt. We have already observed Byron's encouragement of *Rimini.* Afterwards, in 1822, he and Shelley collaborated with the Hunt brothers to launch *The Liberal.* Byron was embarrassed by the

---

1. Teresa gives striking examples of his extraordinary calm at times of danger (II; ii, 25–30). See also *Marino Faliero,* IV, ii, 'It was ever thus. . . .'

arrival in Italy of Leigh Hunt, his wife and six unruly children, whom he settled in his own house at Pisa; and by the subsequent death of Shelley, who was originally responsible for the scheme. Byron for two years continued his hospitality to Hunt, though *The Liberal* was a calamitous failure, John Hunt in London being prosecuted for Byron's *Vision of Judgment,* while the Hunt ménage, first at Pisa and afterwards at Genoa, grew more and more burdensome and distasteful. All his friends, Moore, Murray, Hobhouse and others, strongly disapproved of his association with the Hunts. Though the idea of such a paper was not new to him, collaboration with the Hunts was; he himself had little in common with the extreme radicals; he knew the danger to his reputation. Why then did he involve himself?

From the start Byron had admired Hunt as a man recalling the days of Pym and Hampden (Journal, 1 Dec. 1813; LJ, II, 357): and, being naturally loyal to such memories (Teresa, I; VIII, 321; see Blessington, 50 and Drinkwater, V, 334), felt himself bound to assist a man who 'stuck by me through thick and thin when all shook and some shuffled in 1816' (Kinnaird, 23 Feb. 1822; C, II, 217). Hunt travelled out at Byron's expense. On being asked for money or a manuscript, Byron, who already had doubts regarding *The Liberal* (Moore, 12 July 1822; LJ, VI, 97), 'reluctantly acceded', though he wished to drop the whole scheme and, in offering *The Vision of Judgment,* advised the omission of all actionable passages (Kinnaird, 23 Dec. 1822; C, II, 239–40; see also Kennedy, 251). In a number of subsequent letters (Murray, 23 Sept., 18 Nov., 25 Dec.; Kinnaird, 23 and 30 Dec.; J. Hunt, 8 Jan., 10 March; 1822, 1823; LJ, VI, 117, 138, 156; C, II, 239, 245; LJ, VI, 159, 171) Byron asseverated his determination to stick by the Hunts; and, since an action had been brought against John Hunt, who had neglected Byron's caution regarding *The Vision of Judgment,* arranged for his defence and repeatedly offered to return to England and stand trial himself should that be allowed. During the campaign of Missolonghi, shortly before his death, in ill-health and among all his other pressing engagements, he kept John Hunt in mind: 'We must pay the expenses of his fine' (Kinnaird, 13 March 1824; C, II, 290); though the value of the copyrights already given, which Harold Nicolson calls 'little short of prodigious' (II, 31), must have more than balanced them.

Byron's own expanded statements leave no doubt as to his self-less behaviour. He must 'do as he would be done by'; he could not turn out Hunt and his family to starve; whatever the odium he had incurred on their behalf, he regretted nothing (Murray, 9 Oct., 25 Dec.; 1822; Moore, 20 Feb., 2 April; 1823; LJ, VI, 122–5, 157, 167, 182; see also Kennedy, 251, and Shelley to Byron, 15 Feb. 1822; LJ, VI, 183, note). Lord Ernle justly comments on Byron's wholehearted generosity to the two brothers (LJ, VI, 123, note). *The Liberal* was set up 'for the advantage of a persecuted author and a very worthy man' (Lady ——; 17 May 1823; LJ, VI, 213). Byron was involved, through high motives, in disaster due partly to others' folly, his own caution having been disregarded. And that was not all. Mrs. Shelley (22 Dec. 1822; C, II, 242–4) told Byron that his acknowledged attitude of helper in a letter to Murray that had been shown around in London had hurt the susceptibilities of the helped. Could not Byron in some way openly explain the letter? Byron answered: 'I presume that you at least know enough of me to be sure that I could have no intention to insult Hunt's poverty. . . . On the contrary, I honour him for it.' But if asked if he would have joined *The Liberal* had Hunt been wealthy, he must answer, blankly, No (Mrs. Shelley, undated, LJ, VI, 174; see also Murray, 25 Dec. 1822; LJ, VI, 157). Byron's letters to Murray were all forced by his friends' objections to his altruism; but they merely involved him more deeply, till he ended by having to defend himself to the beneficiaries. We may compare the trouble he gets into with his biographers for clearing Shelley's name in the matter of the Hoppner scandal: had he kept silent, he would have been safer (see pp. 27–9). His own comment is typically apt: 'I have gotten myself into a scrape with the very best intentions (i.e. to do good to these Sunday paper patriots). . . . I have offended everybody, like the old man and his ass' (Hobhouse, 14 Dec. 1822; C, II, 238).

We need not, of course, deny that after Hunt had planted himself on him 'in such a disagreeable way as to become the plague of his life' (Teresa, II; XIV, 389), Byron's manner may well on occasion have shown, and roused, annoyance. Lady Blessington received the 'impression' that he had got into a false position before he could summon 'mental courage sufficient to abandon' the object of his original benevolence, 'though he has not said what might be called an unkind word of him' (77–8). As usual, the facts are in Byron's favour; but her 'impression' nevertheless bears the stamp of truth. The only courage Byron lacked was the courage to be unkind, as when, at Drury Lane, he sent unsuitable applicants up to Kinnaird, who, being 'a man of business', was 'sufficiently ready with a negative' (*Detached Thoughts,* Oct. 1821; LJ, v, 443). His best qualities manœuvred him into difficulties.[1]

He appears to have been regarded by everyone as fair game, a natural source of wealth and bounty, to be tapped when need arose. In thanking him for his offer to make possible her return to England, Mary Shelley wrote that she was aware of the 'many claims' always being made on him, while sympathizing with the position of 'one to whom all look up to as their prop' (*circa* June 1823; C, II, 266, 269). That is how those who best knew him saw him. But his assistance did not mature. Hunt wrote a peremptory and insulting demand on her behalf, threatening that Trelawny was quite ready to help her instead, with the result that Byron, who had already made 'frequent offers of money', was exasperated and refused. Hunt told Mrs. Shelley that Byron had called her visits 'tedious'; she was accordingly angered, though still generously promising to accept money provided that Byron would assert his friendship and show that he *enjoyed* helping her. Finally, she got the money from Trelawny, accusing Byron of 'inconquerable avarice' (Nicolson, II, 32–4; Origo, VIII, 328–32; both excellent accounts), though he had refused the £2,000 left him in Shelley's will (Hunt, 28 June 1823; LJ, VI, 227). As with the Hunts, Byron was put into a false position and his own irritation aroused by his original generosity and the universal assumption that he was there to be used. Contemporaries and commentators alike have been baffled by his quixotic behaviour: Byron knew that people 'will, of course, attribute motives, of all kinds' (Murray, 18 Nov. 1822; LJ, VI, 138). They have, indeed, done so. And yet these actions on behalf of 'radicals' with whom he was not really in sympathy were merely extensions of his attempt to save the indecent hack, Thomas Ashe, in 1813 (p. 61), when, in answer to Murray's expostulation on his generous intentions towards one 'whom nobody else would give a single farthing to', he answered: 'It is for that very reason *I* give it, because nobody else will' (Moore, XIX, 224; see also Teresa, I, IX, 391).

II

Byron's early heroes are, in part, self-portraits. Conrad in *The Corsair* was by 'nature' good, his soul having been deflected since

1. For a neat summing up of Byron's relationship with Hunt, see Teresa's letter to John Murray, Jr., of 2 June 1858 (Origo, X, 417); and also Harold Nicolson's excellent account (II).

his youth; he is 'doom'd by his very virtues for a dupe' (1, 11), and suffers from 'passions worthy of a fool or child' (1, 12). So, too, Lara possessed a heart 'not by nature hard' (*Lara*, 1, 17); he was one

> With more capacity for love than earth
> Bestows on most of mortal mould and birth;
> His early dreams of good outstripp'd the truth
> And troubled manhood follow'd baffled youth . . .
>
> (1, 18.)

So is it, too, with Manfred. This is Byron's central human metaphysic. His Juan and Haidée episode is composed to present a primal innocence, countering the Fall (*Don Juan*, II, 189, 193). Byron's clearest statement was written to Harness on 15 December 1811. Mankind, he says, is universally 'selfish and distrustful':

'The cause of this is the state of society. In the world everyone is to stir for himself—it is useless, perhaps selfish, to expect anything from his neighbour. But I do not think we are born of this disposition; for you find *friendship* as a schoolboy, and *love* enough before twenty' (LJ, II, 92).

Byron's youthful attachments are felt, rather in the manner of Dante, as his key to all ultimate human problems. The fault is somehow in 'society'; and much of Byron's life was certainly given to attacking society, though elsewhere his poetic diagnosis sinks deeper. At Cambridge he dreaded to feel himself no longer a boy; for age was not, to him, 'estimable' (*Detached Thoughts,* Oct. 1821; LJ, V, 445). He recalled how, in his youth, his 'heart overflowed with affection' to any one who liked him. He felt that '*the heart of man*' at *the age of* '*eighteen*' held a purity afterwards lost, and spoke of his youthful friendships with a feminine delicacy, indicating what must have been his tenderness before it was repelled by the world (Blessington, 169, 345, 112; italics mine). We shall next shortly notice Byron's youthful friendships.

We have observed Byron's gentleness, as of an elder brother, to the 'young one' Reynolds, the invalid Coleridge, and also—which is stranger—the established and able, yet self-doubting, Moore. At the heart of his romantic friendships lie the twin impulses of (i) protection and (ii) education.

Teresa devotes some valuable pages to Byron's friendships. The first concerns the son of a tenant at Newstead, addressed in the verses *To E——* (1802), published in *Hours of Idleness,* where the poet emphasizes the disparity in rank between lover and loved one, while asserting, as against his own 'gaudy state', the other's 'modest worth'. Another early friendship is more passionately ('bless my aching sight') celebrated in *Epitaph on a Friend* (1803). Later poems witness to the power of Byron's Harrow attachments, the most inclusive being *Childish Recollections,* whose various records and pseudonyms are interpreted for us by Teresa (I; V, 249). A chapter (I; VI) is given to his friendships. Other records are found in Byron's letters.

Charles O. Gordon, to whom he wrote of his score in the Eton and Harrow match (4 Aug. 1805; LJ, I, 69), was one of a list of 'juniors and favourites' whom Byron tells us that he 'spoilt by indulgence' (Moore, III, 21; LJ, I, 69, note; C, I, 57, note). William Harness was another, 'the earliest and dearest I ever had, from the third form at Harrow to this hour' (Moore, 11 Dec. 1811; LJ, II, 88; Teresa, I; VI, 279–81). Byron, who first saw him being ill-treated at Harrow (Moore, III, 23), immediately *'took pity upon his lameness and weakness and protected him from the bullies of the school'* (LJ, I, 177, note; italics mine). On his return from his travels he told Hobhouse, on 3 November 1811, that he now eschewed romantic friendships, preferring 'a man of calibre' and affairs (C, I, 57); but in a later letter (16 Jan. 1812; C, I, 68), remarked that Harness was 'a mighty friend of mine', and had meanwhile written to Hodgson, on 8 December 1811:

'Master William Harness and I have recommenced a most fiery correspondence. I like him as Euripides liked Agatho, or Darby admired Joan, as much for the past as the present' (LJ, II, 83).

The romantic colouring co-exists with a sense of almost schoolmaster-like responsibility. On 6 December 1811 (LJ, II, 74), he advised Harness, who was at Cambridge, to study mathematics and leave Southey's poems alone, the former being more intelligible. Again, two days later:

'And now, child, what art thou doing? *Reading I trust.* I want to see you take a degree. Remember, this is the most important period of your life; and don't disappoint your papa and your aunt, and all your kin—besides myself. Don't you know that all male children are begotten for the express purpose of being graduates? and that even I am an A.M., though how I became so the Public Orator only can resolve. Besides, you are to be a priest; and to confute Sir William Drummond's late book about the Bible (printed, but not published) and all other infidels whatever. Now leave Master H's gig, and Master S's Sapphics, and become as immortal as Cambridge can make you.

'You see, *Mio Carissimo*, what a pestilent correspondent I am likely to become; but then you shall be as quiet at Newstead as you please, and I won't disturb your studies as I do now' (Harness, 8 Dec. 1811; LJ, II, 79).

This peculiar sense of educational responsibility, observed already in his more literary relationships, may help us to understand that in Byron which, in both his life and his work, devotes itself to the protection and raising of suffering classes and suffering peoples.

The most ideal of such romances was probably his love for the young chorister of humble birth, Edleston, at Cambridge, whom Byron had saved from drowning (LJ, I, 130–1, note). As with Harness, the romance was started by an act of protection. Byron compared the romance to the love of Orestes and Pylades, or David and Jonathan, saying of his 'protégé', 'I certainly love him more than any human being'. They met every day at Cambridge and Byron parted with his 'Cornelian' amid 'a chaos of hope and sorrow' (Elizabeth Pigot, 5 July 1807; LJ, I, 133–5). As always, he was an eminently practical patron, offering his interest (LJ, I, 134) to help Edleston in the city:

'I quit Cambridge with little regret, because our set are *vanished*, and my *musical protégé* before mentioned has left the choir, and is stationed in a mercantile house of considerable eminence in the metropolis. You may have heard me observe he is exactly to an hour two years younger than myself. I found him grown considerably, and, as you will suppose, very glad to see his former *Patron*. He is nearly my height, very *thin*, very fair complexion, dark eyes, and light locks. My opinion of his mind you already know;—I hope I shall never have occasion to change it' (Elizabeth Pigot, 30 June 1807; LJ, I, 132).

This passage, with its terms 'patron' and 'protégé', stands at the heart of Byron's life; though with him the term 'patron' is more than social, and his protégés extend, and expand, indefinitely.

To this romance Byron later referred as 'a violent, though *pure*, love and passion'[1]—which was, together with the friendship of

1. These words have been taken by the Editor of *Correspondence* to refer to Mary Chaworth (I, I). Mr. Vulliamy (IV, 62) is surely correct in referring them to Edleston. I postpone discussion of *Thyrza* and the relevant stanzas in *Childe Harold II*.

Edward Noel Long, the 'romance of the most romantic period of my life' (Journal, 12 Jan. 1821; LJ, V, 169). That it is to be given precedence over all other such relationships is suggested by Byron's statement: 'I don't know what to say about "friendship". I never was in friendship but once, in my nineteenth year, and then it gave me as much trouble as love' (Moore, 22 June 1813; LJ, II, 225). Against this we must balance his clear statement elsewhere:

'My School friendships were with *me passions* (for I was always violent), but I do not know that there is one which has endured (to be sure, some have been cut short by death) till now. That with Lord Clare began one of the earliest and lasted longest, being only interrupted by distance, that I know of. I never heard the word "*Clare*" without a beating of the heart, even *now*, and I write it with the feelings of 1803-4-5 *ad infinitum*' (*Detached Thoughts*, Oct. 1821, LJ, V, 455).

Meeting Lord Clare in Italy, after a long separation, he notes, 'We were but five minutes together and in the public road; but I hardly recollect an hour of my existence that could be weighed against them' (*Detached Thoughts*, LJ, V, 463). Writing to Clare from Missolonghi on 31 March 1824, his phraseology was, to the last, that of a lover, quite different from his address to, for example, Moore (LJ, VI, 366).

He probably loved Clare, as he did Harness, as 'much for the past as for the present' (p. 68); that is, for reawakening school-memories; and it is important to realize the close connection between such romantic attachments and the inmost principle of education, in direct descent from the *pederastia* of those world-educators, the ancient Greeks;[1] and hence the recurring scholastic touch in Byron's approach. It is accordingly right that, in Byron's story, itself so closely involved with Greece, ancient and modern, he should have experienced some interesting boy-friendships on Greek soil.

First there was 'my dearly beloved Eustathius', an 'unbroken colt' of wayward propensities whose passionate kisses and embraces —for Byron's boy-lovers, even perhaps Edleston (Elizabeth Pigot, 5 July 1807; LJ, I, 135), seem, like the ladies, normally to have taken the initiative—alternated with less amiable traits. Though certain pills, which Byron, who regularly doctored his favourites, as he doctored Boatswain (p. 8), his servants (Augusta, 9 Sept. 1811; LJ, II, 31) and Allegra (Murray, 4 Dec. 1819; LJ, IV, 382), admin-

1. For an expansion of this thought, see my *Dynasty of Stowe*, III.

istered for the boy's headaches, appeared also to improve his disposition, he was eventually sent home: 'He plagued my soul out with his whims' (Hobhouse, 29–30 July, 16 Aug. 1810; SP, I, 74–9).

More important was Byron's association with Nicolo Giraud. Moore was for once baffled:

'During this period of his stay in Greece, we find him forming one of those extraordinary friendships—if attachment to persons so inferior to himself can be called by that name—of which I have already mentioned two or three instances in his younger days, and in which the pride of being a protector, and the pleasure of exerting gratitude, seem to have constituted to his mind the chief, pervading charm. The person, whom he now adopted in this manner, and from similar feelings to those which had inspired his early attachments to the cottage-boy near Newstead, and the young chorister at Cambridge, was a Greek youth, named Nicolo Giraud, the son, I believe, of a widow lady, in whose house the artist Lusieri lodged. In this young man he appears to have taken the most lively, and even brotherly, interest' (x, 114).

We recognize the recurring elements, though Moore's interpretation appears biased. Let us turn to Byron's account, given to Hobhouse on 23 August 1810, observing again the *educational* context: 'I am most auspiciously settled in the Convent, which is more commodious than any tenement I have yet occupied, with room for my *suite;* and it is by no means solitary, seeing there is not only "il Padre Abbate", but his "schuola", consisting of six "Ragazzi", all my most particular allies' (C, I, 14). He arranged a boxing match for the boys, three Catholics against three Greek Orthodox, the Father Superior being duly gratified by the Catholics' victory. These boys, almost his 'only associates', Byron describes in turn, calling them 'sylphs', how one kisses him and another calls him his *'philos',* with rivalry for his friendship:

'But my friend, as you may easily imagine, is Nicolo, who, by the bye, is my Italian master, and we are already very philosophical. I am his "Padrone" and his "amico", and the Lord knows what besides. It is about two hours since, that, after informing me he was most desirous to follow *him* (that is me) over the world, he concluded by telling me it was proper for us not only to live, but "morire insieme".

'The latter I hope to avoid—as much of the former as he pleases' (C, I, 15).

Byron was 'vastly happy and childish', chattering with everybody, his Italian lessons interrupted by 'scamperings and eating fruit, and peltings and playings'; he was, in fact, 'at school again'; it was 'too good to last' (C, I, 15-16). From Patras we hear later that 'my ally, Nicolo' is in bed with a fever, the strange term, already applied to the six *'ragazzi'*, forecasting Byron's later protégé, Greece (4 Oct. 1810; LJ, I, 301).

It is almost impossible to see in Byron's account of his life in the Convent the grave and acute author of the Grecian notes to *Childe Harold* (I and II), with all their statesmanlike concern for suffering peoples, which he was composing at this period; and yet the one was basic to the other.[1] This is a perfect example of that boyishness so regularly observed in Byron by Moore, Lady Blessington, Teresa and others (pp. 67, 78); it is also the most vivid example of his love of youth. Here he was at once patron and pupil to a social inferior in a scholastic setting; moreover, a religious context always pleased him; it was probably the happiest moment in his life; and it was probably of Nicolo that he was thinking when he wrote that Greece was 'the only place I was ever contented in' (Trelawny, 15 June 1823; LJ, VI, 224). In his will, made on his return to England, he left £7,000 for Nicolo on his coming of age (LJ, I, 328).

There are other Greek boys in Byron's story. On his return to Greece, or rather Cephalonia, in 1823, Byron was fascinated by the fourteen-year-old son of the Suliote chieftain, Noto Botzaris, especially desiring that he should 'sit down at table with us', though the boy's father forbade it; and afterwards being pleased with his noble appearance and remarking that 'that young spark would hold you and me in utter contempt' for their compunctions in shooting Turks (Kennedy, 244-5). On the voyage to Missolonghi, when in danger from a Turkish frigate in the area, Byron delayed his ship to put ashore a Greek boy, Loukas, whom he had met at Cephalonia and Maurois (III, XXXIV, 389) calls 'a new Edleston': 'I would sooner cut him to pieces, and myself too, than have him taken by those barbarians' (Stanhope, 31 Dec. 1823; Muir, also Hancock, 2 Jan. 1824; LJ, VI, 297, 298-9, 302). Later, when struck by a tempest and expecting to run on the rocks near Missolonghi, Byron's primary concern was for *another* boy, whom he was at pains to reassure, promising to dive with him on his back, a trick Moore notes he had practised at Harrow (Hancock, 13 Jan. 1824; LJ, VI, 304; Moore, LIII, 612,

---

[1] Observe also the research and scholarship of Byron's *Remarks on the Romaic* (composed Athens, Spring, 1811); *Poetical Works*, 1837, 792-7.

note). The attention given to these boys in military despatches at an urgent point in a campaign is worth noting. Loukas was with Byron at Missolonghi. But personal feelings were not necessarily involved. Youth, as such, awakened his response, as when he wrote anxiously to John Cowell at Eton bidding him 'mind his prosody' (Moore, Diary, 11 June 1828; quoted LJ, II, 98, note) and was at pains to solicit his *protection* of a friend's son, suggesting that he take 'some little notice of him' until he found his feet (Cowell, 12 Feb. 1812; LJ, II, 99).

Moore was, as we have seen, baffled by Byron's choosing romantic companionships from his social inferiors. On his first voyage he started in company with three servants: the old retainer Murray, the boy Robert Rushton—the page of *Childe Harold* (I, 13, 3) — and Fletcher. The two former, however, he sent home. From Gibraltar he wrote to Mr. Rushton, saying that Murray and Robert were being returned because he intended to travel through countries 'unsafe particularly for one so young'. He was to use £25 a year for Robert's education, take every care of him, and send him to school; he himself had provided for him, in case of death, in his will; the boy had behaved 'extremely well'. To his own Mother he wrote: 'Pray show the lad kindness, as he is my great favourite.' She was to tell the boy's father the facts, 'who may otherwise think he has behaved ill' (Rushton, 15 Aug.; Mrs. Byron, 13 Aug.; 1809; LJ, I, 242–3). He continued anxious, asking his mother to take care of both old man and boy, urging that Robert be assured his return was wise, and saying: 'Pray take some notice of Robert, who will miss his master; poor boy, he was very unwilling to return.' A PS. adds 'How is Joe Murray?'; and he opens his letter again to give news of Fletcher (19 March, 24 May, 28 June; 1810; LJ, I, 258, 276, 283).

We have a complex of protectiveness, instinctive affection, and consideration for social inferiors. A great deal of Byron is included. As elsewhere, as with Coleridge and his unfinished *Christabel*, Harness and his Cambridge studies, John Cowell and his prosody, we observe the will to education, that is, self-realization, as indeed with Byron's general approach to depressed classes and enslaved nations. After his return to England we find him writing sternly to Robert for insulting a female servant, urging him to attend to his arithmetic and surveying, and asking for *one letter every week,* 'that I may know how you go on'. There followed more academic advice and pressure, enquiry after the boy's health, and assurance of protection and provision in the will of his 'master' and 'friend' (21 Jan.,

73

18 Oct.; 1812; LJ, II, 93-4, 177). Byron's will left him £50 a year and £1,000 on his attaining the age of twenty-five (LJ, I, 328). Later, he was worried at not hearing from Robert, anxious concerning his plans, and eager to know if certain rumours of a proposed marriage were true, in which case he wanted full particulars; if all were satisfactory, 'nothing can be better for your settlement in life, and a proper provision will be made for you' (24 Feb. 1813; LJ, II, 190).

Maurois is right in saying that what Byron could most easily love was 'a certain kind of innocence and youthfulness' (Epilogue, 426); but this love was one with an instinct for protection of more general application. He was nearly as interested in old Murray as in Robert. As early as 22 March 1804 he wrote to Augusta: 'Remember me to poor old Murray; tell him we will see that something is to be done for him, for *while I live he shall never be abandoned in his old age*'; and on 26 March, 'Do not forget to tell me how Murray is' (LJ, I, 21, 24). During dinner, he would give the old man a glass of wine, his expression radiant with cordiality (Moore, VII, 74). He is the 'head of my household'; 'poor honest fellow', he says, and 'I should be a great Brute if I had not provided for him in the manner most congenial to his own feelings and to mine' (Augusta, 14 Dec. 1808; LJ, I, 204). He once noted that Murray was ill, and his Greek servant too (for Demetrius Zograffo, see Moore, XII, 130, note), while his valet had a cough; and how he was administering the doctor's emetic (Augusta, 9 Sept. 1811; LJ, II, 31). He regarded them as his children. To Fletcher, his faithful servant throughout his life, his frequent and amusing references are ubiquitous. Fletcher's own accounts witness his devotion (e.g. on Byron's death, Blaquière, II, 16-21; quoted Spender, App. D and Medwin, App., lxviii; and on his religion, Kennedy, App., 369-75).

We conclude with two final examples of Byron's kindness to his dependants. First, there was the 'witch-like' old 'scare-crow' of a charwoman, Mrs. Mule, whom Byron found at Bennet Street, took with him to the Albany, and finally instated, to his friends' amazement, in his marriage household. Asked why he kept her on, 'The poor old devil was so kind to me,' he said (Moore, XX, 229, note; see also Journal, 27 Feb. 1814; LJ, II, 389-90). Then there was the troublesome Dr. Polidori who attended Byron on his second departure from England in 1816. Once, when he was in tears, Byron followed him to his room. 'Nothing', said Polidori, 'could exceed the gentle kindness of Lord Byron in soothing his mind and restoring him to composure.' Byron nursed him when suffering from a sprained ankle (Moore, XXVII, 318-19). Polidori was endured for a considerable time, until we find Shelley writing on 8 September 1816 that he hoped Hobhouse (whose own opinion of Polidori was uncompromising; Hobhouse, I; VII, 335 and II; VIII, 16) would have by now destroyed whatever 'scruples' the soft-hearted Byron might have felt in dismissing him (C, II, 16). Byron's indulgence to servants and retainers, whom he never could make up his mind to dismiss, was considered by Hoppner as 'culpable' (p. 87). After Polidori's return to England, Byron remained solicitous on hearing he was ill (Murray, 15 Nov. 1817; LJ, IV, 181), and discussed him kindly to Medwin (119-22). His dealings with his various servants show a complex relationship of friend, lover, and master. The recurring note is 'protection'. He was, naturally, unwilling to save Newstead by turning out his tenants in favour of 'monied men' (Hobhouse, 14 Oct. 1811; C, I, 50).

It would be strange if such a man disliked children. Once, when travelling in Italy, he was only roused to interest by 'a crying child' and the awful bread of the local inhabitants, to whom he gave money (Hobhouse, 22 April 1817; C, II, 49). After observing Byron's gift of money to a beautiful child in Switzerland, Moore adds: 'There were, indeed, few things Lord Byron more delighted in than to watch beautiful children at play' (XXVII, 320). He invited a portrait painter from England to paint Allegra and a peasant girl (Murray, 21 March 1821; LJ, V, 262). Earlier we find him arranging with Murray for an illustrated edition of *Childe Harold* with an engraving of 'the pretty little girl you saw the other day' (29 March 1813; LJ, II, 200; see also Lady Melbourne, 5 April 1813; C, I, 145). This was Lady Charlotte Harley, daughter of Lord Oxford, to whom the poem's introductory lines were afterwards addressed:

> Oh! let that eye, which, wild as the Gazelle's,
> Now brightly bold or beautifully shy,
> Wins as it wanders, dazzles where it dwells,
> Glance o'er this page, nor to my verse deny
> That smile for which my breast might vainly sigh
> Could I to thee be ever more than friend:
> This much, dear maid, accord; nor question why
> To one so young my strain I would commend,
> But bid me with my wreath one matchless lily blend.
>
> (*Childe Harold*, Introd.)

Byron was as fascinated by girl-children as was Lewis Carroll; and indeed behind Byron's story, as behind Dante's, lay a childhood passion, at the age of seven, for Mary Duff, on which he once meditated in his Journal, doubting if he had ever been attached since (26 Nov. 1813; LJ, II, 347–8). 'Will I be godfather?' he wrote to Webster on 2 September 1813. 'Yea, verily! I believe it is the only species of parentage I shall ever encounter . . . If it is a *girl*, why not also?' (LJ, II, 259).

In his bachelor days, Byron was by temperament the typical kindly uncle, or godfather, the natural friend of his friends', or relations', children. He liked thinking of sending his god-daughter 'a coral and bells' (Moore, 15 Sept. 1814; LJ, III, 136). He soliloquizes, on 14 November 1813, on another little girl: 'Today Henry Byron called on me with my little Cousin Eliza. She will grow up a beauty and a plague; but, in the mean time, it is the prettiest child! dark eyes and eyelashes, black and long as the wing of a raven. I think she is prettier even than my niece, Georgina,—yet I don't like to think so neither: and, though older, she is not so clever . . . I must get a toy tomorrow for Eliza.' Again, on 16 November, 'Have again forgot a plaything for *ma petite cousine* Eliza; but I must send for it tomorrow. I hope Harry will bring her to me.' Then, with disappointment, on 17 November: 'Harry has not brought *ma petite cousine*. I want to go to the play together;—she has been but once.' All this was written entirely for himself in his personal journal (LJ, II, 314–22). Teresa describes his affection for her little sisters, saying how he loved to caress them (quoted Origo, v, 199). At a party where he met, among others, the Marquis of Buckingham and Richard Wellesley ('a clever man'), he was disgruntled because 'little Henry Fox, a very fine boy, and very promising in mind and manner', went off to bed before he could talk to him: 'I am sure I had rather hear him than all the *savans*' (Journal, 1 Dec. 1813; LJ, II, 365). As with Botzaris (p. 72), Byron was more naturally interested in children than in society. He concludes a letter to Hoppner: 'Pray make my respects to Mrs. H. and take care of your little boy' (28 Oct. 1819; LJ, IV, 367).

The children of the Orient fascinated him. From Prevesa he wrote to his Mother of Hussein Bey and Mahmout Pasha, grandchildren of Ali Pasha: 'They are the prettiest little animals I ever saw . . . Mahmout is ten years old, and hopes to see me again; we are friends without understanding each other . . .' (12 Nov. 1809; LJ, I, 257). He repeated the description to Hodgson: 'His grandson

Mahmout, a little fellow ten years old, with large black eyes as big as pigeon's eggs'—how often *animal*-references accompany these descriptions—'and all the gravity of sixty, asked me what I did travelling so young without a Lala'—that is, tutor (4 July 1810; LJ, I, 287). From Cephalonia, he told Hobhouse of the son of a Suliote chieftain lost in action:

'He is a sturdy little lion's whelp, with an immense head, and neither cries nor laughs like other children; but sits still, and blows out his lips, and snorts as the Highlanders do when they are angry. He already talks of revenging his father's death on the followers of Mahomet according to the good old custom which, of course, his mother patronizes. His organ of combativeness seems considerably developed; and he will doubtless, if he lives, be a credit to the carnage line of business' (6 Oct. 1823; C, II, 280).

The ironic references to 'the good old custom' and 'carnage'—we are reminded of the fierce young Botzaris (p. 72)—are valuable Byronic pointers; so is his naturally switching off from his report to the London Committee to describe this fearsome little boy.

Children roused all Byron's protective instincts. When, at Missolonghi, he had obtained the release of some Turkish prisoners, one little girl, he told Augusta, 'expressed a strong desire to remain with me, or under my care'—how regularly this pattern recurs, with Nicolo, Eustathius, Mahmout, and so many women in Byron's story—and he thought of adopting her. Would Lady Byron take her as a companion to Ada? 'She is very lively and quick, and with great black oriental eyes, and Asiatic features'; he promised financial provision and showed, in his usual manner, anxiety for the child's *education* (23 Feb. 1824; LJ, VI, 331–2). But the girl's mother wished to go too: 'I have not the heart to refuse it'; mother and child ought not to be separated (Kennedy, 10 March 1824; LJ, VI, 348). They were to be provisionally entrusted to Kennedy (Gamba, IV, 183). 'Lord Byron', said Mrs. Kennedy, 'had put us to the test as Christians' and, 'although highly inconvenient, we consented to receive both' (Kennedy, 289, note). There is a touch of humour in Byron's returning Kennedy's attempts at his own theological conversion by this peculiarly Byronic test of *action*. Even at Missolonghi, there was trouble. Millingen reports how Byron had bought her costly dresses and a necklace; and how 'he would then take the little child on his knees, and caress her with all the fondness of a father'. These fine clothes, says Kennedy, made her 'pert and forward'; but, on hearing such reports, he 'sent for the girl and scolded her' (Millingen, quoted Edgcumbe, I, X, 134; Kennedy, 310). After Byron's death, Hato was claimed by her father and said: 'I have lost my adopted father, Lord Byron; now I do not wish to fly from my true father' (Gamba to Kennedy, Kennedy, App., 384).

Hato's story neatly duplicates a central incident in Byron's poetry. In Canto VIII (90-102) of *Don Juan* the hero on the field of battle turns aside to rescue a little Turkish girl, Leila, from two brutal Cossacks. The incident is lovingly handled and the little girl exquisitely realized:

A pure, transparent, pale, yet radiant face,
Like to a lighted alabaster vase.

(96.)

She is—the usual word—his 'protégée'. Whatever the cost, he insists on rescuing her; the child is 'parentless' and therefore, *automatically*, 'mine' (100). In rescuing Hato, as in his Greek campaign as a whole, Byron was living his own past poetry.

After all, Byron was himself, in certain moods, like a child (Teresa, I; II, 79; II; XIII, 279; Blessington, 47, 78, 201); according to Stanhope, a man without 'pedantry' or 'affectation' and 'natural and playful as a boy' (quoted Edgcumbe, I, XVI, 211). He himself defined poets as a species of 'grown children' (Blessington, 325); and to children he was instinctively drawn. Medwin has an interesting note:

'Lord Byron was the best of masters, and was perfectly adored by his servants. His kindness was extended even to their children. He liked them to have their families with them: and I remember one day, as we were entering the hall after our ride, meeting a little boy, of three or four years old, of the coachman's, whom he took up in his arms and presented with a ten-franc piece' (304, note).

As so often, the last word is Teresa's: 'Lord Byron's benevolence also shone forth in his tenderness towards children, in the pleasure he experienced in mingling in their amusements, and in making them presents' (I; IX, 382).

He had two children of his own. Allegra, his natural daughter by Clare Clairmont, he arranged to have with him at Venice, with a nurse (Moore, XXXVI, 422; Webster, 8 Sept. 1818; LJ, IV, 255). A rich lady offered to adopt Allegra, but he refused to relax his paternal claims as a condition (LJ, IV, 325, note; Moore, XXXIV, 401, note). When both father and daughter were ill, he cured the child's fever with bark, and his own with cold water (Murray, 4 Dec. 1819; LJ, IV, 382). His firm repudiation of Clare's interest in the child must be read in the light of his own deep concern for youth, education and religion: 'The Child', he says, 'shall not quit me again to perish of starvation, and green fruit, or be taught to believe that there is no Deity' (Hoppner, 22 April 1820; LJ, V, 15). Again, 'If Clare thinks that she shall ever interfere with the child's morals or education, she mistakes; she never shall. The girl shall be a Christian and a married woman, if possible' (Hoppner, 10 Sept. 1820; LJ, V, 75).

Byron's action in sending Allegra to an Italian convent, where she eventually died, was, with revolution seething (Kinnaird, 26 Feb. 1821; SP, II, 593), sound. Besides, he liked Roman Catholicism, the best and oldest branch of Christianity (Hoppner, 3 April 1821; LJ, V, 264). Shelley, writing to Byron on 16 April 1821, approved of Byron's decision (quoted C, II, 168; see also LJ, V, 263, note; Shelley, 26 April, and Hoppner, 11 May; 1821; LJ, V, 266–7, 279). On 16 July he was even more emphatic: 'I feel more and more strongly the wisdom of your firmness on this subject; and I applaud it the more because I know how weak I should have been in your case, and I see most clearly all the evils that would have sprung from weakness. Allegra's happiness depends upon your perseverance' (quoted C, II, 178–9). In view of Allegra's early death in the Convent, Byron's decisions have been questioned; but he had acted for the best (Drinkwater, V, 309; Edgcumbe, I, II, 22–5).

Byron's blunt manner sometimes masks his feelings. When Shelley first wrote to him of the 'exquisite symmetry' and general loveliness of 'a little being whom we . . . call Alba, or the Dawn' (17 Jan., 23 April; 1817; C, II, 29, 52), and Byron tells Kinnaird that 'Shelley (from Marlow) has written to me about my daughter (the last bastard one), who, it seems, is a great beauty' (13 Jan. 1818; C, II, 65), the contrast in styles is revealing. Later he wrote to Hoppner: 'Allegra is prettier, I think, but as obstinate as a mule, and as ravenous as a Vulture. Health good, to judge by the complexion— temper tolerable, but for vanity and pertinacity. She thinks herself handsome, and will do as she pleases . . .' (31 March 1820; LJ, IV, 428). Moore specifically notes as a peculiarly good example of Byron's favourite perversion of 'imputing to himself faults the most alien to his nature' an instance of his denying absolutely any notion of the 'parental feeling'; while observing the overwhelming impact on him as described by Teresa Guiccioli, of Allegra's death, his reason appearing to be in danger (XXXVI, 422; LJ, VI, 51–2, note; see p. 279).

From his other, legitimate, child, Ada, Byron was separated by his marriage disaster; but she was always in his mind. *Childe Harold III* opens and concludes with an address to her, containing some beautiful and moving stanzas (I, 115–18). When he heard that Lady Byron was to take her on the Continent, a move he considered risky, he was in distraction, demanding that the visit be stopped and planning to have recourse to law (Hanson, 11 Nov. 1816; 25 March 1817; Augusta, 19 Dec. 1816; Hobhouse, 31 March 1817; LJ, IV, 5, 75; SP, II, 378; C, II, 42). Later, he was in continual anxiety about her. He at first withheld his name from *Don Juan* for fear of losing his rights over the child (Murray, 8 Feb. 1822; LJ, VI, 18). Lady Blessington tells us how he liked being told of her portrait's resemblance to himself (5), of his thoughts on her education (315), how he liked to think of her one day reading his works (385), how, if *Don Juan* were likely to offend her, he would write no more of it (386–7; Teresa, I; VII, 305), how he wished to return to England before leaving for Greece to see his wife and child, 'to forgive and be forgiven' and 'embrace Ada' (401). The two, she said, were continually in his thoughts (83); 'there was', she said, 'something tender and beautiful in the deep love' with which Byron turned to his daughter (387). One day, after discussing Ada with Medwin, and suggesting that he could claim her, were that not likely to make her mother unhappy, he said, 'This is Ada's birthday, and might have been the happiest day of my life' (Medwin, 117). 'Byron loved all children,' says Teresa, 'but especially those of Ada's age.' Both at Ravenna and at Pisa he was 'miserable' if he were without news of her: 'a picture of her or a piece of her hair, made it a day of rejoicing' (I; VII, 304). Once when in Cephalonia he saw an infant fall, he dismounted and took it in his arms, saying, 'I cannot bear to look at an English child; I am so reminded of my own, whom I have not seen for a long time' (Kennedy, 264, note). From Cephalonia Gamba wrote to Teresa of Byron's agony at news of Ada's ill-health (14 Oct. 1823; Origo, IX, 364; Teresa, II; XIV, 392; see also Byron's general enquiries to Augusta, 12 Oct. 1823; LJ, VI, 263–4). Among all the pressures and anxieties of his Greek campaign his concern was never relaxed. Stanhope observes how 'passionately fond' of her he was (Edgcumbe, I, XVI, 206). After his seizure at Missolonghi his first fear was for Ada, hoping the disease was not hereditary, and urging Lady Byron to take precautions (Augusta, 23 Feb. 1824; LJ, VI, 332; see also Kennedy, 263). His dying words, according to Fletcher's account, included: 'Oh my poor dear child! My dear Ada! My God, could I but have seen her! Give her my blessing' (Blaquière, II, 16–21; quoted Spender, App. D).

This almost maternal craving appears the more natural when we realize that Byron was, in part, an *effeminate* type, though you would not always think so from his masculine address. Hobhouse regarded him as one would 'a favourite and sometimes froward sister' (*Albania*, I, App., 543). Moore observed in his intuitive ways of thought, 'his caprices, fits of weeping, sudden affections and dislikes', striking traces of 'a feminine cast of character' (LII, 600). Byron's tears are frequently noticed (e.g. at Moore, XLIX, 567; LJ, IV, 267, note; Lady Melbourne to Byron, 31 Jan. 1815; C, I, 297). In the midst of gaiety he would pause, meditate, and his eyes fill with tears (Teresa, quoting both Stanhope and H. Browne; II; II, 35). Lady Blessington also observed a certain effeminacy (3, 112): when saying good-bye to her and Lord Blessington, and leaving, full of presentiments, for Greece, he burst into tears, though quickly covering his emotions with an ironical remark (Moore, LI, 590).

The centre of Byron as man of letters and man of action alike is feminine; more, it is *maternal;* he feels as a mother, whether for children, protégés, or nations. Conrad scorns, yet endures, 'passions worthy of a fool or child' (*The Corsair*, I, 12), and, at the last,

> His mother's softness crept
> To those wild eyes, which, like an infant's, wept.
>
> (III, 22.)

His mature and final heroes, Sardanapalus and Don Juan, are gentle, half-feminine, types; and we may recall the boy-girl Kaled in *Lara*. Parts of *Don Juan* are warmed by a specifically parental emotion, as with the poignant description of the dying child in the wreck:

> The other father had a weaklier child,
> Of a soft cheek and aspect delicate;
> But the boy bore up long, and with a mild
> And patient spirit held aloof his fate;
> Little he said, and now and then he smiled,
> As if to win a part from off the weight
> He saw increasing on his father's heart,
> With the deep, deadly thought, that they must part.
>
> (II, 88.)

In a happier vein, we have the idyll of Juan and Haidée:

> And she bent o'er him, and he lay beneath,
>   Hush'd as the babe upon its mother's breast,
> Droop'd as the willow when no winds can breathe,
>   Lull'd like the depth of ocean when at rest,
> Fair as the crowning rose of the whole wreath,
>   Soft as the sallow cygnet in its nest;
> In short, he was a very pretty fellow,
> Although his woes had turn'd him rather yellow.
>
> (II, 148.)

The concluding couplet marks Byron's half-unwillingness to admit this maternal centre; but neither his life nor his work can be understood without our recognition of it. Again,

> An infant when it gazes on a light,
>   A child the moment when it drains the breast,
> A devotee when soars the Host in sight,
>   An Arab with a stranger for a guest,
> A sailor when the prize has struck in fight,
>   A miser filling his most hoarded chest,
> Feel rapture; but not such true joy are reaping
> As they who watch o'er what they love while sleeping.
>
> (II, 196.)

The emotion is traditionally Christian; it is a twilight, evening, emotion. Stanzas are offered to Hesperus, the evening star:

> Oh, Hesperus! thou bringest all good things—
>   Home to the weary, to the hungry cheer,
> To the young bird the parent's brooding wings,
>   The welcome stall to the o'er-laboured steer;
> Whate'er of peace about our hearthstone clings,
>   Whate'er our household gods protect of dear,
> Are gather'd round us by thy look of rest;
> Thou bring'st the child, too, to the mother's breast.
>
> Soft hour! which wakes the wish and melts the heart
>   Of those who sail the seas, on the first day
> When they from their sweet friends are torn apart;
>   Or fills with love the pilgrim on his way

As the far bell of vesper makes him start,
  Seeming to weep the dying day's decay;
Is this a fancy which our reason scorns?
Ah! surely nothing dies but something mourns!

When Nero perish'd by the justest doom
  Which ever the destroyer yet destroy'd,
Amidst the roar of liberated Rome,
  Of nations freed, and the world overjoy'd,
Some hands unseen strew'd flowers upon his tomb:
  Perhaps the weakness of a heart not void
Of feeling for some kindness done, when power
Had left the wretch an uncorrupted hour.

But I'm digressing: what on earth has Nero,
  Or any such like sovereign buffoons,
To do with the transactions of my hero . . .

(III, 107.)

Again, the swerve to flippancy. This trait he admitted to Lady Blessington, who felt that his natural affections had learned to mask themselves through fear of mockery (Blessington, 161; 44; see also 110, 112, 169, 233, 388; and my pp. 97–8). Byron's prose self certainly feared to express too publicly these too-poignant emotions, which nevertheless often 'filled his poetry'—the phrase is Moore's, writing of Byron's affectionate temperament as the dominating quality of his life—'with the very soul of tenderness' (Moore, VIII, 84). Byron's own tenderness drove him to assert Dante's: 'Why, there is gentleness in Dante beyond all gentleness, when he is tender'(Journal, 29 Jan. 1821; LJ, V, 194). This tenderness it is that dominates the whole treatment of the young lovers Juan and Haidée, felt and loved as 'children' by the poet who wishes they might remain so, with an unsullied and innate delight (Don Juan, IV, 15, 18). Their romance is as another Eden before the Fall (Don Juan, II, 189, 193). These cantos breathe a poetic passion in love with the very youth of its own youthful lovers.

Poetry is the necessary language of this intimate, half-nervous, maternal and protective passion. Poetry is also the language of the Byronic guilt; and the two are intimately related. Of this guilt Cain is the supreme expression. The poem which made so much of England certain that Byron was a kind of fiend levels its charge against our traditional, legalistic, Hell-bound theology, in terms of a little child. Cain and Adah 'tread softly' so as not to wake their 'little Enoch':

CAIN: How lovely he appears! his little cheeks,
       In their pure incarnation, vying with
       The rose leaves strewn beneath them.
ADAH: And his lips, too,
       How beautifully parted! No; you shall not
       Kiss him, at least not now; he will awake soon.
       His hour of mid-day rest is nearly over;
       But it were pity to disturb him till
       'Tis closed.
CAIN: You have said well; I will contain
       My heart till then. He smiles, and sleeps!—Sleep on,
       And smile, thou little, young inheritor—
       Of a world scarce less young: sleep on, and smile!
       Thine are the hours and days when both are cheering
       And innocent! *thou* hast not plucked the fruit—
       Thou know'st not thou art naked! Must the time
       Come thou shalt be amerced for sins unknown,
       Which were not thine nor mine? But now sleep on!
       His cheeks are reddening into deeper smiles,
       And shining lids are trembling o'er his long
       Lashes, dark as the cypress which waves o'er them;
       Half open, from beneath them the clear blue
       Laughs out, although in slumber. He must dream—
       Of what? of Paradise!—Ay! dream of it,
       My disinherited boy! 'Tis but a dream;
       For never more thyself, thy sons, nor fathers,
       Shall walk in that forbidden place of joy!

                                    (III, i.)

In this passage Byron is with Shakespeare, the Shakespeare of Paulina's lines in *The Winter's Tale* (II, iii). Shakespeare's child-poetry is left undeveloped; but this is Byron's peculiar province. More: it is the key and centre to the Byronic problem.

His own clearest self-revelation occurs in *Childe Harold*. His supposed hero (i.e. himself) had learned to love the 'helpless looks' of children, strange though it might seem in one 'imbued with scorn of man'; and this survived all other emotions—'in him this glow'd when all beside had ceased to glow' (III, 54). Even more directly important is a later stanza, addressed specifically to his daughter, Ada:

> To aid thy mind's development, to watch
> Thy dawn of little joys, to sit and see
> Almost thy very growth, to view thee catch
> Knowledge of objects—wonders yet to thee!
> To hold thee lightly on a gentle knee,
> And print on thy soft cheek a parent's kiss—
> This, it should seem, was not reserved for me;
> Yet this was in my nature; as it is,
> I know not what is there, yet something like to this.
>
> (III, 116.)

He baffled himself, like Hamlet, like his own Sardanapalus. What *was* he? Power surged in and through him; but the key to both his personality and his poetry, however it be masked by bitterness and irony, by wit or raillery, remained 'something like to this'; a Christian, mothering care, rising to a Catholic sweetness.

III

We have so far observed Byron's generosity towards men of letters and friends; and next, his more personal and protective interest in youth, dependants, and children; and have insisted that his life revolves round a centre of maternal gentleness. But his instinct as saviour expanded wider, into actions more impersonal and selfless.

Strangers were always struck to find him so different from his dark poetry and frightening reputation. It happened again and again: with Walter Scott (LJ, III, App. IV, 412); Henry Joy and the American, West, who had never met with manners 'more gentle and attractive' (Moore, XXXI, 364–5; XLIX, 562); Lady Blessington (Blessington, 4); Parry (Parry, I, 15); a certain 'gentleman' (Galt, XXVII); 'Miss S', 'Mr. D' (Teresa, II; IV, 65; II; IX, 178); 'Mr. S——' (at Ithaca); and Millingen (Edgcumbe, I, V, 51; VIII, 95). On his arrival at Argostoli in Cephalonia everyone was surprised, his 'pleasing manners' gaining him 'universal esteem' (Gamba, Notes, 288, and I, 46; Kennedy, 3–4; Moore, LII, 595). Kennedy's account bears witness, on page after page, to his sweetness of disposition.

From youth onwards, Byron was innately sympathetic. 'He never', says a person who knew him intimately in the year 1807, 'met with objects of distress without affording them succour'; as a schoolboy, noticing in a shop a woman for whom the price of a Bible was too expensive, he bought it for her (Moore, IV, 45). As early as 6 March 1809 he was writing to his Mother that he had been 'endeavouring to assist' the destitute wife and family of Lord Falkland, 'which, God knows, I cannot do as I could wish, for my own embarrassments and *the many claims upon me from other quarters*' (LJ, I, 216; italics mine). When a young woman author of poor family asked for a subscription, he listened attentively and then, 'as if to divert her thoughts from a subject which could not but be painful to her, began to converse with her in words so fascinating and tones so gentle', that she hardly perceived that he had been writing out a substantial cheque (Galt, App., I; Origo, Pro., 31).[1] When a certain Captain Basil Hall was struck down with fever at Venice, and, after fearing to approach the terrifying hater of Englishmen, was at length forced to do so, Byron was ready to do anything, offering to sit by him and read to him, waiting anxiously over an hour without admittance since the doctor was in attendance, and calling repeatedly, though ineffectually, thereafter (Hall, 31 Aug. 1818; LJ, IV, 252–4 and note); an excellent example of his *nurse-like* instincts (pp. 70, 74, 79). When the house and property of a Venetian shoemaker was burned down, Byron built him a new house and repaired his financial losses (Galt, XXXIII); and something similar happened with a Venetian printer (Origo, Pro., 31). Teresa records an emotional meeting between Byron and an innkeeper whose fortunes he had saved at a crisis, thus earning his undying gratitude (quoted Origo, III, 117). We find him arranging to send home from Ravenna to Trieste 'a poor devil of an English sailor, who had been there sick, sorry, and penniless' from the want of anyone able and willing to assist him (Murray, 12 Aug. 1819; LJ, IV, 343). An Irish woman in Paris having written a letter 'which has moved my entrails', he asked Moore to make enquiries—he always took personal trouble in these matters—about this 'poor creature, ill and solitary', being ready to send money if the case be genuine (Moore, 24 May 1820; V, 30). Before leaving Italy he assisted two destitute young Germans, ejected by the Austrians from Trieste, furnishing them, after carefully testing their veracity, with money and clothes (Bowring, 21 May 1823; LJ, VI, 214; Gamba to Kennedy, Kennedy, App., 381–2). When Kennedy was reluctant to ask Byron's assistance for his wife's girl-school because of 'the many claims' made on his 'generosity', Byron insisted that he was always anxious to hear of such requests

1. Teresa has a full account which appears to refer to this incident: see p. 228.

(Kennedy, 282). His generosity functioned independently of his politics (Moore, XLV, 518), as when he made a gift to the Cardinal for the repair of a church organ at Ravenna (Origo, V, 232). He was continually engaged in such works. Those who knew him were aware of it, if subsequent biographers are not: 'You are great', wrote the Countess Benzoni, 'not only in your head, but in your heart' (Origo, II, 97).

At every turn in his career our various authorities show Byron performing some good and saving action. Of his efforts in the great causes of reform at home and liberation abroad, we shall speak later. Here it is only necessary to remember his support of the oppressed in the House of Lords; his putting his life and purse at the disposal of the Italian Carbonari—'whatever I can do by money, means or person, I will venture freely for their freedom' (Journal, 24 Feb. 1821; V, 208)—and his draining his personal resources to the limit to maintain at his own, personal, cost, the Greek campaign, on which he died.

The greater part of Byron's good works was unspectacular and hidden. 'I am glad', he once wrote to his future wife, Miss Milbanke, 'that you know any "good deed" that I am supposed ever to have blundered upon, simply because it proves that you have not heard me invariably ill-spoken of' (26 Sept. 1813; LJ, III, 401). But she knew better: 'It is not in the great world that Lord Byron's true character must be sought; but ask of those nearest to him—of the unhappy whom he has consoled, of the poor whom he has blessed, of the dependants to whom he is the best of masters' (To Miss Milner, undated, LJ, III, 148, note). Here is an account of Byron's life in Venice, as recorded by the British Resident, R. B. Hoppner:

'. . . Of this I am certain, that I never witnessed greater kindness than in Lord Byron.

'The inmates of his family were all extremely attached to him, and would have endured anything on his account. He was indeed culpably lenient to them; for even when instances occurred of their neglecting their duty, or taking an undue advantage of his good nature, he rather bantered than spoke seriously to them upon it, and could not bring himself to discharge them, even when he had threatened to do so . . .'

He records an example of Byron's leniency to a tradesman who had tricked him, and continues:

'He was also ever ready to assist the distressed, and he was most unostentatious in his charities; for besides considerable sums which he gave away to applicants at his own house, he contributed largely by weekly and monthly allowances to persons whom he had never seen, and who, as the money reached them by other hands, did not even know who was their benefactor' (Moore, XXXV, 418; LJ, IV, 388, note).

It was the same at Ravenna: 'The constant benevolence which he exercised towards the poor of Ravenna being likely, it was feared, to render him dangerously popular among a people unused to charity on so enlarged a scale', steps were taken to expel the Gambas from the city (Moore, XLV, 518). The poor of Ravenna petitioned the Cardinal to prevail upon Byron not to leave them. 'The higher powers', wrote Byron, 'look upon me as the Chief of the Coal-heavers' (Murray, 22 July 1821; LJ, V, 326). We also have Teresa Guiccioli's account, given in a letter to Moore:

'This sort of simple life he led until the fatal day of his departure for Greece, and the few variations he made from it may be said to have arisen solely from the greater or smaller number of occasions which were offered him of doing good, and from the generous actions he was continually performing. Many families (in Ravenna principally) owed to him the few prosperous days they ever enjoyed. His arrival in that town was spoken of as a piece of public good fortune, and his departure as a public calamity; and this is the life which many attempted to asperse as that of a libertine!' (Moore, XLVII, 539; LJ, V, 401, note).

These statements are corroborated by Gamba, who wrote fully to Kennedy from Zante, on 21 May 1824. The letter is printed in Kennedy's volume, Appendix, 375–85. Asked for an account of Byron's religious opinions and acts of charity and beneficence, he said that this would be a long and serious task, 'especially with respect to the second part' (376). His outline runs:

'If we contemplate his acts of charity and beneficence—which, indeed, are the true substance—a volume would not be sufficient for me to narrate only those of which I have been a witness.

'I knew in some cities of Italy, various decent families who had fallen into poverty—with whom he had no relation—to whom he has sent assistance secretly, to the extent of more than two hundred dollars: nor did these people ever learn the name of their benefactor' (380).

After recounting other such examples of Byron's charity, 'In short', he says, 'I could relate many hundreds of such actions.' Had he been spared, 'what did he not desire to do', he asks pathetically, 'for the world—and for his friends?' (382).

Dr. Bruno, Byron's physician at Missolonghi, said that to Byron 'the day seemed sad and gloomy' that was not marked by some generous action (*Westminster Review;* Medwin, App., xxxii); and that such daily exertions sprang from a 'feeling beyond measure for the miserable and the unfortunate'; he was always sending him to attend the townsfolk and gave money for establishing a hospital (Bruno to Kennedy, Kennedy, App., 364). We have, lastly, Fletcher's moving letter on his master's goodness: 'And his charity was always without bounds; for his kind and generous heart could not see nor hear of misery, without a deep sigh, and striving in which way he could serve and soften misery, by his liberal hand, in the most effectual manner. Were I to mention one hundredth part of the most generous acts of charity, it would fill a volume' (19 May 1824; Kennedy, App., 369–70).

Later, in her considered study, Teresa returned to the subject of Byron's benevolent actions. 'Not only', she wrote, 'could Lord Byron never contribute voluntarily to the suffering of a living being, but his pity, his commiseration for the sufferings of his fellow creatures, showed itself all his life in such habitual benevolence, in such boundless generosity, that volumes would be necessary to record his noble deeds' (I; IX, 389). He would send money *secretly* to those in distress. She recalled how at Venice his charity provided especially for the old and infirm with a number of settled pensions. 'Venice', she says, 'watched him as jealously as a miser watches his treasure, and when he left it the honest poor were grieved and the dishonest vexed. Listening to these one might have been led to believe that Lord Byron had by a vow bound himself and his fortune to the service of Venice, and that his departure was a spoliation of their rights.' She quotes Shelley as saying that 'not a quarter of his fortune', but 'the half of it', did he 'expend in alms'; and how in Pisa, in Genoa, and in Greece his purse was ever open to the needy (I; IX, 395–6).

Indeed, when we find Byron commenting bitterly on the mediocre contribution by a man of wealth to the Irish poor, he has, at least, the right to do so (Moore, 12 July 1822; LJ, VI, 96). In spite of his own irony and normal self-masking, he was well aware of what he was doing. Once, struck into self-assertion by his differences with Southey, he stated that he himself, 'in my degree, have done more

real good in any one given year, since I was twenty, than Mr.
Southey in the whole course of his shifting and turncoat existence'
('Byron and Southey', LJ, VI, App. 1, 389). Driven to exasperation
goodness may be allowed, on occasion, to assert itself. Again, once,
after giving money to an old man, he refers both to his record in the
alleviation of human suffering—'I never in my life gave a mistress
so much as I have sometimes given a poor man in honest distress'—
and to those who have persecuted him, thinking that 'when justice
is done to me, it will be when this hand that writes is as cold as the
hearts which have stung me'; and he is soon after (see pp. 171–3)
arranging a pension to save an old woman from manual labour
(Journal, 26 and 29 Jan. 1821; LJ, V, 187, 192). In his *Blackwood's*
Defence he is explicit:

'. . . On the words, "lurking-place", and "selfish and polluted
exile", I have something more to say.—How far the capital city of a
government, which survived the vicissitudes of thirteen hundred
years, and might still have existed but for the treachery of Buonaparte,
and the iniquity of his imitators—a city which was the emporium
of Europe when London and Edinburgh were dens of barbarians—
may be termed a "lurking-place", I leave to those who have seen or
heard of Venice to decide. How far my exile may have been
"polluted", it is not for me to say, because the word is a wide one,
and, with some of its branches, may chance to overshadow the
actions of most men; but that it has been *"selfish"* I deny. If, to the
extent of my means and my power, and my information of their
calamities, to have assisted many miserable beings, reduced by the
decay of the place of their birth, and their consequent loss of substance—if to have never rejected an application which appeared
founded on truth—if to have expended in this manner sums far
out of proportion to my fortune, there and elsewhere, be selfish,
then have I been selfish. To have done such things I do not deem
much; but it is hard indeed to be compelled to recapitulate them in
my own defence, by such accusations as that before me, like a panel
before a jury calling testimonies to his character, or a soldier recording
his services to obtain his discharge. If the person who has made the
charge of "selfishness" wishes to inform himself further on the subject,
he may acquire, not what he would wish to find, but what will
silence and shame him, by applying to the Consul-General of our
nation, resident in the place, who will be in the case either to confirm
or deny what I have asserted.

'I neither make, nor have ever made, pretensions to sanctity of demeanour, nor regularity of conduct; but my means have been expended principally on my own gratification neither now nor heretofore, neither in England nor out of it; and it wants but a word from me, if I thought that word decent or necessary, to call forth the most willing witnesses, and at once witnesses and proofs, in England itself, to show that there are those who have derived not the mere temporary relief of a wretched boon, but the means which led them to immediate happiness and ultimate independence, by my want of that very *"selfishness"*, as grossly as falsely now imputed to my conduct.

'Had I been a selfish man—had I been a grasping man—had I been, in the worldly sense of the word, even a *prudent* man,—I should not be where I now am; I should not have taken the step which was the first that led to the events which have sunk and swoln a gulf between me and mine; but in this respect the truth will one day be made known; in the meantime, as Durande says, in the Cave of Montesinos, "Patience, and shuffle the cards."

'I bitterly feel the ostentation of this statement, the first of the kind I have ever made: I feel the degradation of being compelled to make it; but I also feel its *truth*, and I trust to feel it on my death-bed, should it be my lot to die there. I am not less sensible of the egotism of all this: but, alas! who have made me thus egotistical in my own defence, if not they, who, by perversely persisting in referring fiction to truth, and tracing poetry to life, and regarding characters of imagination as creatures of existence, have made me personally responsible for almost every poetical delineation which fancy and a particular bias of thought, may have tended to produce?' (LJ, IV, App. IX, 476).

Byron seldom spoke out like this on his own behalf. Let us conclude with something more characteristic. A 'poor woman of the name of Yossy', who had published with Murray, writes to Byron for help. He draws Murray's attention to the request, with a grumble:

'Instead of addressing the Bishop or Mr. Wilberforce, she hath recourse to that proscribed, Atheistical, syllogistical, phlogistical person, *mysen,* as they say in Notts. It is strange enough, but the rascaille English, who calumniate me in every direction and on every score, whenever they are in great distress, recur to me for assistance: if I have had one example of this, I have had letters from a thousand, and, as far as is in my power, have tried to repay good for evil, and purchase a shilling's worth of Salvation, as long as my pocket can hold out.

'Now, I am willing to do what I can for this unfortunate person; but her situation and her wishes (not unreasonable, however) require more than can be advanced by one individual like myself; for I have many claims of the same kind just at present, and also some remnants of *debt* to pay in England—God, he knows, the *latter* how reluctantly! Can the "Literary fund" do nothing for her? by your interest, which is great among the pious, I daresay that something might be collected; can you get any of her books published? Suppose you took her as *author* in my place, now vacant among your raga-muffins. She is a moral and pious person, and will shine upon your shelves. But seriously, do what you can for her' (Murray, 31 Oct. 1822; LJ, VI, 132).

He repeated this request in subsequent letters full of other affairs; he does not feel his duty done, and leave it at that; calls on his generosity leave him no rest. His concentration on money during these latter years was the measure of his will to generosity: it is not 'for myself', he says, but rather to leave something to his relations and 'to be able to do good to others to a greater extent' (Kinnaird, 18 Jan. 1823; LJ, VI, 163–4; see also Moore, XXXVI, 420).

Byron's support of Greece was the last flowering of a life dedicated, as the great mass of his political and national poetry witnesses, to the awakening, in men and nations, of their greatest, liberated, selves. But whilst engaged in this high task, he never forgot the humble need for the grand design, never rated the cause above the person. His record at this time of worry, bitterness, responsibility and ill-health was pre-eminently, as we shall see, one of personal goodness to individuals, assisting refugees, protecting enemy captives, saving a thieving soldier, lecturing Hato on her manners, remembering John Hunt in London. With Byron the public action was never distinct from the personal affection and the personal protection. His publisher's royalties were given to Greece in 1823 just as they had been given, ten years before, to Dallas: the new gift is the more spectacular, but the motivating principle is the same. Byron's famous letter to the Greek Government (30 Nov. 1823; LJ, VI, 277; see p. 188) reproving the nation for disunity and urging it to self-realization—as strange a letter as was ever written by an individual to a nation's government—is of-a-piece with his youthful advice to his literary seniors, Scott, Moore and Coleridge, and both are one with his sense of tutorial responsibility for the studies of Harness at Cambridge or Robert Rushton at school. Greece was Byron's new, and last, Edleston; something to be saved, and loved. Byron died lonely, rejected by his own people, but to the end a lover:

> 'Tis time this heart should be unmoved,
> Since others it has ceased to move;
> Yet, though I cannot be beloved,
> Still let me love!

So runs his last poem, *On This Day I Complete my Thirty-sixth Year,* composed at Missolonghi. Among his dying murmurs were thoughts of home and Ada; and also, 'Poor Greece, poor Town, my poor servants'; all were, alike, his children, all contained in his words 'Io lascio qualche cosa di caro nel mondo' (Gamba, VI, 264-5).

Greece was his last protégé, and knew it; like Nicolo (p. 71), his 'ally'. 'All Greece', said the chieftain Botzaris, regarded him (as did little Hato) as their 'father' (Gamba, IV, 172). Turks as well as Greeks had cause to lament the loss of 'the friend of humanity and the protector of the oppressed' (Gamba, VI, 274). 'The poorest citizen' of Missolonghi felt that he had 'lost a friend' (Parry, VI, 137); 'everyone looked upon him as a father and public benefactor' (Millingen; Edgcumbe, I, XIV, 177). At Byron's death Prince Mavrocordato's official proclamation called on Missolonghi, 'where his generosity had been so conspicuously displayed', to honour him, the 'benefactor' (Moore, LVI, 638-9); and Gamba (VI, 267) tells how, when for days the people had been asking continually 'How is my lord?', the town was stunned: 'We did not mourn the loss of the great genius—no, nor that of the supporter of Greece—our first tears were for our father, our patron, our friend.'

IV

It has been our purpose to show that Byron was not envious, that he did not dislike children, and that he was rather more than 'capable' of kindness; that, indeed, he was a man splendid and wonderful in the corresponding virtues.

Our twentieth-century focus is wrong. Byron's most recent biographer, Iris Origo, confuses her scholarly account *The Last Attachment* by some remarkable misjudgments. She is surprised at Teresa's continued faith in Byron even after she had read all Byron's letters and the various accounts; 'but her loyalty and self-assurance were proof against it all', for 'she was certain that *she* knew the truth'

(x, 418). It is our uncompromising contention that she did; more—
that there was nothing whatsoever in what she had read to disturb
her knowledge. Iris Origo makes the fantastic statement that Teresa
and her brother were the only associates 'who took him entirely
seriously—who doggedly, wholeheartedly, and against all evidence,
believed in him'. But against *what* evidence? 'They believed not only
in his noble aspirations and his poetic genius, but in his romantic
attitudes, his kindness, his heroism' (x, 422). If 'romantic attitudes'
means anything at all, it denotes a quality which Byron was conspicuous for repudiating. Of his kindness we have written; of his
heroism, we have yet to write.

Teresa, deeply troubled by the inability of biographers to understand what to her was a patent truth, wished that Hobhouse would
re-establish Byron's goodness before the world: 'Since the last word
on Lord Byron (not as a poet, but as a moral and social being) is
far from having been said, I have always hoped, and still hope, that
it will be said one day by Lord Broughton' (Murray, 2 June 1858;
Origo, x, 417). Now Iris Origo denies that Hobhouse was the man
to do it; 'he was', she says, 'the last man to take Byron's fame seriously,
to consolidate, as Teresa wished, the Byronic legend' (x, 418). Let us
see what Hobhouse had to say on Byron as *a moral and social being*
in a strongly-worded pamphlet written in the middle of the century to lead a plea for the placing of a memorial bust of the poet in
Westminster Abbey:

'Lord Byron had failings—many failings certainly, but he was
untainted with any of the baser vices; and his virtues, his good qualities, were all of the higher order. He was honourable and open in
all his dealings—he was generous and he was kind. He was affected
by the distress, and, rarer still, he was pleased with the prosperity of
others. Tender-hearted he was to a degree not usual with our sex—
and he shrunk, with feminine sensibility, from the sight of cruelty.
He was true-spoken—he was affectionate—he was very brave, if
that be any praise; but his courage was not the result of physical coolness or indifference to danger; on the contrary, he entertained apprehensions and adopted precautions, of which he made no secret, and
was by no means ashamed. His calmness and presence of mind in
the hour of peril were the offspring of reflection and of a fixed resolution to act becomingly and well. He was alive to every indication
of good-feeling in others—a generous or noble sentiment, a trait of
tenderness or devotion, not only in real, but in imaginary characters,

affected him deeply—even to tears. He was, both by his habits and his nature, incapable of any mean compliance, any undue submission towards those who command reverence and exact flattery from men of the highest genius; and it will be the eternal praise of his writings, as it was one of the merits of his conversation, that he threw no lustre on any exploit, however brilliant, any character, however exalted, which had not contributed to the happiness or welfare of mankind.

'Lord Byron was totally free from envy and from jealousy; and, both in public and in private, spoke of the literary merits of his contemporaries in terms which did justice to them and honour to himself. He was well aware of his own great reputation; but he was neither vain-glorious, nor over-bearing; nor attached to his productions even that value which was universally granted to them, and which they will, probably, for ever maintain.

'Of his lesser qualities very little need be said, because his most inveterate detractors have done justice to his powers of pleasing, and to the irresistible charms of his general deportment. There was, indeed, something about him, not to be definitely described, but almost universally felt, which captivated those around him, and impressed them, in spite of occasional distrusts, with an attachment not only friendly but fixed. Part of this fascination may, doubtless, be ascribed to the entire self-abandonment, the incautious, it may be said the dangerous, sincerity of his private conversation; but his very weaknesses were amiable; and, as has been said of a portion of his virtues, were of a feminine character—so that the affection felt for him was as that for a favourite and sometimes froward sister.

'In mixed society Lord Byron was not talkative, neither did he attempt to surprise by pointed or by humorous remarks; but in all companies he held his own, and that too without unbecoming rivalry with his seniors in age and reputation, and without any offensive condescension towards his inferior associates. In more familiar intercourse he was a gay companion and a free, but he never transgressed the bounds of good breeding, even for a moment. Indeed he was, in the best sense of the word, a gentleman' (*Albania*, I, App., 542-3).

We should not, it is true, expect from Hobhouse the philosophical depth of Moore, or the exact insight of Teresa; but, for 'the last man to take Byron's fame seriously' that—and it is part only of a considerable essay—is not so bad. 'God bless him', said Hobhouse, on

Byron's departure from England, 'for a gallant spirit and a kind one' (I; VII, 336).

How comes it, then, that, when all Byron's contemporaries of any standing are essentially in agreement as to his fine qualities, our twentieth-century biographers remain in confusion? It is, indeed, remarkable how much less well they seem to *know* the true Lord Byron than did his contemporaries. They write of a dummy, a thing of sawdust—those others of a man. How has this happened?

There were two main Byrons, woman and man, corresponding —as we shall see later (p. 252)—to Shelley's Maniac and Maddalo. The one was a creature of amazing sympathy and sensibility; the other, as in his epistolary style, caustic, ironic, forceful, slap-dash— but never, even then, cruel; while it needs little literary acumen to feel the generous humour within.

Now it is *all a question of precedence*. We can (1) see Byron as a bold man-of-the-world, a buccaneering adventurer, a Trelawny with a sentimental streak. This is how Harold Nicolson reads Lady Blessington's report (99–103) of Byron's emotion at thought of the devout lady, Mrs. Sheppard, whose prayers were offered on his behalf. Mr. Nicolson regards it as one of the 'stock texts' regularly —though he records no other examples—used by Byron to convince people of his respect for virtue, and adds: 'never assuredly had the Sheppard incident been used with more immediate or more telling effect' (Nicolson, I, 15–16). That is a truly terrible misrepresentation. Byron read Lady Blessington the account (written by Mr. Sheppard) with a voice 'tremulous from emotion' and a deadly 'serious-ness of aspect', saying how he had never before understood the 'beauty of holiness' and that 'the religion that prays and hopes for the erring is the true religion and the only one that would make a convert of me'; his own antipathy to contemporary belief being due to the utter lack of 'Christian charity' in the devout (Blessington, 103). He had thought 'a thousand times' of this good lady praying for him, outcast as he was (106). Now horror at any lack of what might be called 'moral charity', together with its extension in terms of hell and damnation, was absolutely basic to Byron's religious challenge in his greater works; in *Manfred,* in *Cain.* His refusal to accept the traditional, condemnatory, teaching was central. He be-lieved firmly in Christian ethic; but equally firmly rejected doctrines of damnation (Kennedy, 150, App. 376, Gamba's letter; 219–29, 235, 238–43, 259); and when he heard of sympathy being refused 'to an unfortunate person' on grounds of sin, his anger was truly frightening (Blessington, 236–7, 299–300; Teresa, I; IX, 392, see pp. 38, 270). And what of Byron's letter to the lady's husband (Sheppard, 8 Dec. 1821; LJ, V, 488), rating the intercession of a pious woman above 'the united glory of Homer, Caesar and Napoleon'? Lady Blessington (110), Teresa and Hobhouse (pp. 94–5, 235, 269) all observed how deeply Byron was moved at *any* record of true virtue. The reading put forward by Mr. Nicolson makes chaos of Byron's life.

Let us take the alternative. We can (2) see Byron as a person of extreme emotional sensibility, who *both* adopts a show of hard-headed realism as a defence (against just such criticism as Mr. Nicolson's) *and* enlists all the weapons, intellectual and physical, of masculine vigour and prowess—as with his anger just noticed—*in the cause of this central sensibility*. The first Byron, the Byron of twentieth-century commentary, is a fabrication that never existed; the second, the Byron his contemporaries knew, is real.

The originating centre of Byron's emotional life was a compassionate love. In *English Bards and Scotch Reviewers* he wrote:

> The time hath been, when no harsh sound would fall
> From lips that now may seem imbued with gall;
> Nor fools nor follies tempt me to despise
> The meanest thing that crawl'd beneath my eyes.

He remained, however, more soft-hearted than the lines suggest. He admitted once that he had been all his life 'trying to harden' his heart without success; again, 'The fact is, I cannot *keep* my *resentments*, though violent enough in their onset' (Moore; 14 June 1814; 6 March 1822; LJ, III, 92; VI, 35). He was 'the slave of his loving heart' and the pardon of injuries was to him a vital 'necessity' (Teresa, II; X, 194–5; V, 88; see pp. 260, 264–6 below).

The consensus of contemporary opinion regarding this the golden centre of Byron's story is here overpowering. Lady Blessington is in no doubt at all. He was basically one without bitterness, affectionate and loving, though, his best qualities having been rebuffed, he tried, in vain, to hide them (66, 110–11, 129, 194, 201, 385; see my pp. 38, 66–7, 83). 'Byron's heart', she wrote, 'is running to waste for want of being allowed to expend itself on his fellow creatures; it is naturally capacious, and teeming with affection' (284). That, she says, was the true Byron, but it was not always easy to understand him, since he was always ready to mock his own more romantic feelings, which were nevertheless quite patently sincere (47). And we today, with our respect for irony and distrust of flashy emotions, should at least be able to respect him for it. Others say the same. Pigot and Iley asserted his original sensibility: 'never', wrote Iley, did man 'begin life with more of the milk of human kindness' (Moore, IV, 38; Vulliamy, XXI, 302); the Countess Albrizzi said that his heart was governed 'in an extraordinary degree' by sympathy (LJ, IV, App. II, 442); selfishness, writes Ethel Colburn Mayne, was 'totally absent from his nature' (quoted Du Bos, VI, 191); in youth his 'over-expansive sensibility' attracted mockery and forced him to use a mask (Prosper Merimée, quoted Maurois, II, 125). Moore regarded affection as the most striking characteristic of his childhood; it, with a yearning for its adequate return, 'formed the dream and torment of his existence'; and this 'spring of natural tenderness' persisted (Moore, VIII, 84; XXV, 407). 'No one', said a writer in *The London Magazine* at Byron's death, 'ever loved his fellow-man more than Lord Byron' (quoted Vulliamy, XXI, 303). He was, indeed, whatever his strokes of irony, a universal lover: 'Ward—I like Ward. By Mahomet! I begin to think I like every body;—a disposition not to be encouraged; a sort of social gluttony that swallows every thing set before it. But I like Ward' (Journal, 23 Nov. 1813; LJ, II, 334).

To answer one final objection. Granted that Byron's sympathy, generosity and kindliness were, indeed, central, yet how far, we may ask, were they admirable? Sentimentality is ruled out, since no one ever more consistently put his feelings into practice. For the rest, we may turn again to Teresa, who, in her usual precise, almost clairvoyant,[1] manner, makes some helpful distinctions.

Byron, she says, was no careless giver. 'His benevolence' was always linked 'with a sense of order', having nothing in common 'with the capricious munificence of a spendthrift'; he was 'most methodical' in his expenditure, careful to balance his accounts, and unable to sleep unless he were 'on good terms with his friends' and in debt to no one. Moreover, it was charity quite irrespective of return, since he regularly 'preferred to expose himself to ingratitude rather than to forsake the unhappy' (I; IX, 396–8). It was mainly secret. After noting how often Byron 'succoured and restored to the right path' young girls who threw themselves 'at his feet', sending them home 'rescued and enlightened by the counsels of wisdom',

---

1. Teresa claimed to be in communication with Byron's spirit and asserted that 'if she was in doubt about a matter or a date, she would appeal to him' (Origo, X, 415).

she says how such 'noble traits' were known 'almost in spite of himself', since he regularly exercised in a true Christian spirit the Divine precept that 'the left hand shall not know what the right doeth' (I; IX, 393–4). It was the same with his more material bounties. Teresa's chapter 'His generosity a Virtue' opens with a fine eulogy on Byron's goodness, remarking that his generosity was of a kind practised 'without ostentation, habitually, in secret and unknown, with God and our conscience for sole witnesses' (II; IV, 50). It was, too, and her statement is borne out by Byron's letters, a peculiarly 'refined generosity' (II; V, 88), offered with a wonderful tact.[1] But —and this is where her account is so subtle—though possessing all the characteristics of a considered goodness, his benevolence was also impulsive. No excuses, such as his own pecuniary embarrassments or the 'slender merits' of the applicants, weighed in the balance: 'The claim of adversity, as adversity, was a sufficient and sacred one to him, and, to relieve it an imperious impulse' (I; IX, 390). It was a 'kind of universal and habitual charity, which gives without hope of return, which is more occupied with the good of others than with its own, and which is called for only by the instinctive desire to alleviate the sufferings of others' (I; IX, 375). The words 'impulse' and 'instinctive' in these passages raise an important and necessary question: can an instinct qualify as a 'virtue'? Generosity is grouped with his 'passion for Truth' as dividing 'the empire of his soul' (II; IV, 51). It, too, was a passion, as surely as Timon's. She accordingly attempts to strike a balance, saying that 'if his generosity was too instinctive to be termed a virtue, it was yet too admirable to be considered an instinct' and asserts that, though a natural 'quality of his heart', it nevertheless 'elevated and transformed itself often through the exertion of his will into an absolute virtue' (I; IX, 389). She very clearly defines what, in her judgment, constitutes the difference between 'instinct' and 'virtue' (II, IV, 51; V, 89), contending that Byron attained to a self-conquest and a spiritualized generosity out-topping all normal benevolences. Her discussion, however, raises questions and introduces subtleties that must be postponed, and to which we shall return (p. 266).

Our account is now complete. We shall next show how, this

---

1. Compare Lady Blessington's record: 'He is peculiarly compassionate to the poor. I remarked that he rarely, in our rides, passed a mendicant without giving him charity, which was invariably bestowed with gentleness and kindness; this was still more observable if the person was deformed, as if he sympathized with the object' (Blessington, 36).

central sensibility granted, this—to use Shelley's line—'nerve o'er which do creep the else unfelt oppressions of this earth' (*Julian and Maddalo,* 449; see p. 253), Byron enlisted all the arts of vigour and virility in its service.

III

LIFE AGAINST LETTERS

I

DURING a spell of bad weather and revolutionary anxiety Byron wrote: 'It is so far lucky that I have a literary turn; but it is very tiresome not to be able to stir out, in comfort, on any horse but Pegasus, for so many days' (Journal, 12 Jan. 1821; LJ, v, 167). You would think him a retired army-man, dabbling in literature as a hobby.

When young he attached an importance to 'authorship' which he rejected later (Journal, 24 Nov. 1813; LJ, II, 345. See also Elizabeth Pigot, 2 Aug. 1807; Journal, 15 Jan. 1821; LJ, I, 142; v, 175). But as early as 9 March 1807 we find a repudiation in the later manner (Falkner; undated, LJ, I, 124), and again, 'Oh! the misery of doing nothing but make *love, enemies,* and *verses*' (Elizabeth Pigot, 26 Oct. 1807; LJ, I, 146). He felt degraded by the writing world: 'Nothing so fretful, so despicable as a Scribbler; see what *I* am, and what a parcel of Scoundrels I have brought about my ears, and what language I have been obliged to treat them with to deal with them in their own way;—all this comes of Authorship . . .' (Augusta, 2 Sept. 1811; LJ, II, 18). As for the cliques, he could not adopt their *dislikes* (Journal, 5 Dec. 1813; LJ, II, 362) and despised their petty squabbles (Hodgson, 3 Oct. 1810; LJ, I, 299–300), once comparing them to Falstaff's ragamuffins: 'They seem to be an irritable set, and I wish myself well out of it: "I'll not march through Coventry with them, that's flat"' (Journal, 17 March 1814; LJ, II, 402; *I Henry IV,* IV, ii). He never used to know what to say to literary people after praising their last publication (*Detached Thoughts,* Oct. 1821; LJ, v, 435), and was surprised to find Rogers and Moore not priggish as 'poetical persons are apt to be', the one unassuming and the other 'an epitome of all that's delightful', though Sotheby was 'a disagreeable dog, with rhyme written in every feature of his wrinkled physiognomy' (Hobhouse, 9 and 16 Nov. 1811; C, I, 58–60). He told Lady Melbourne:

'as to Madame de Staël, I never go near her; her books are very delightful, but in society I see nothing but a plain woman forcing one to listen, and look at her, with her pen behind her ear, and her mouth full of ink—so much for her' (8 Jan. 1814; C, I, 223).

He instinctively felt himself, with what must have seemed on occasion a maddening superiority, *above* the whole literary field.

He did not feel himself a born poet; it came on him suddenly (Stanhope, quoted Edgcumbe, I, XVI, 209). He admits that, given another chance, he would probably do the same, though if he had a son, he would make him a lawyer, or a pirate (Journal, 17 March 1814; LJ, II, 402). On his early travels he told his Mother 'I have done with authorship' (14 Jan. 1811; LJ, I, 309; see also Drury, 3 May 1810; LJ, I, 265). *Childe Harold's* staggering success changed. his mind not at all, his 'days of authorship' being over (Hodgson, 3 Feb. 1813; LJ, II, 188). He regretted nothing of his 'reign' but its duration and was 'heartily glad to resign' (Journal, 5 Dec. 1813; LJ, II, 360). After the extraordinary success of *The Corsair,* he again determined to stop, saying he had 'done with' such things: 'I have had my day, and there's an end' (Moore, 3 March, 9 April; 1814; LJ, III, 56, 64). The thought recurs quite late (Hobhouse, 8 June 1820: SP, II, 516). He had at one time thought of suppressing all his past work (Moore, XXI, 251). All this was genuine: an amusing rhyme by Lady Byron describes him as 'ashamed to appear like a poet' and talking of finances to conceal his nature (The Marriage Separation; LJ, III, 291). Poetry was a relief, that was all (Journal, 27 Nov. and 6 Dec.; Miss Milbanke, 10 Nov.; 1813; LJ, II, 351, 366, 369; III, 405). He rated geographical and historical accuracy higher than artistic perfection and, without caring 'one lump of sugar' for his poetry, would 'combat lustily' for his correctness of detail in local colour and manners (Murray, 14 Nov.; Clarke, 13 and 15 Dec.; 1813; LJ, II, 283, 308–9; SP, I, 204). His concern for historical accuracy increased. Like many another great writer, he hated 'things *all fiction*', for 'there should always be some foundation of fact for the most airy fabric, and pure invention is but the talent of a liar'; people might say what they pleased of *Marino Faliero* as a play, 'but not so of my costume and dramatic persons, they having been real existences' (Murray, 2 April 1817; 12 Oct. 1820; LJ, IV, 93; V, 95). He took pride in the nautical language of the shipwreck in *Don Juan* and noted that the oriental furniture of Canto III was drawn from observation (Murray, 20 May 1819; 23 Aug. 1821; LJ, IV, 305; V, 346). With him life came before art, though he was, in his own despite, forced on to recognize and exploit his poetic genius.

What he most vigorously rejected was the nostalgic, if shadowy, hero of the early *Childe Harold*. This was, he said, a part of himself only, and even that he would not own to, since 'I would not be such a fellow as I have made my hero for all the world' (Dallas, 31 Oct. 1811; LJ, II, 66). He willed deliberately to surmount this nostalgic, meditative, self, his scorn of his early poetry being exactly placed by this passage. He knew that he had poetry in him, and was glad to have shown the world what he could do in *English Bards and Scotch Reviewers* (Mrs. Byron, 14 Jan. 1811; LJ, I, 309). He might perhaps have been a poet, had he 'gone on and amended'; meanwhile, he liked to think that his temporary celebrity had been wrung from the world 'in the very teeth of all opinions and prejudices' (Moore, 9 April 1814; LJ, III, 64). It was his work's active and social qualities on which he set store. But poetry accomplished little. What did it matter if *Cain was* subversive? 'Who', he asks, 'was ever altered by a poem?' (Murray, 3 Nov. 1821; LJ, V, 470). 'As to defining what a poet *should* be, it is not worth while, for what are *they* worth? What have they done?' (Journal, 31 Jan. 1821; LJ, V, 196). He deplored the tendency to prefer writers to agents, and saw Wordsworth and Southey with all their supposed virtues paling before a single *action* of Voltaire (Journal, 24 Nov. 1813; LJ, II, 345; note to *Don Juan*, V, 147). Since 'no one should be a rhymer who could be anything better', he was annoyed to see Scott, Moore, Campbell and Rogers 'spectators' rather than 'agents and leaders' (Journal, 23 Nov. 1813; LJ, II, 338). The valuation is Shakespearian, and on hearing details of the death of William Windham from one who saw him 'before the fatal operation which sent "that gallant spirit to aspire the skies"' he comments:

'Windham, half his life an active participator in the events of the earth, and one of those who governed nations—*he* regretted,—and dwelt much on that regret, that "he had not entirely devoted himself to literature and science"!!!... What! would he have been a plodder? a metaphysician?—perhaps a rhymer? a scribbler? Such an exchange must have been suggested by illness. But he is gone, and Time "shall not look upon his like again".' (Journal, 24 Nov. 1813; LJ, II, 342–3; *Romeo and Juliet*, III, i; *Hamlet*, I, ii).

The Shakespearian references—Byron's prose and poetry are packed with them—are here organic. Byron's central problem was, as surely as Hamlet's, action. 'Poetry should only occupy the idle,' he said at Cephalonia. 'In more serious affairs it would be ridiculous' (Gamba, I, 48). And yet he knew himself a poet; his life's problem was therefore the problem of *poetic action;* failing that, he oscillated from one to the other. When the Italian revolution failed through dissension and treachery, he wrote to Moore, on 28 April 1821: 'And now let us be literary; a sad falling off, but it is always a consolation. If "Othello's occupation be gone", let us take to the next best; and, if we cannot contribute to make mankind more free and wise, we may amuse ourselves and those who like it' (LJ, V, 272; *Othello*, III, iii).

II

We are not surprised to find Byron taking his athletic exercises seriously. He boxed regularly, enjoying the company of pugilists, Jackson 'the Emperor of Pugilism' and the champion Tom Crib, a 'great man'. 'I like energy—even animal energy—of all kinds; and I have need of both mental and corporeal.' The more 'violent' the fatigue, the better his spirits, with evenings of delightful calm (Journal, 24 and 23 Nov. 1813; 17 March, 10 April; 1814; LJ, II, 345–6, 336, 401, 410–11). He attained considerable proficiency at sword exercise (Kinnaird, 27 Aug. 1819; Moore, 9 June 1820; C, II, 124; LJ, V, 43), and was thoroughly experienced with foil and sabre, fencing regularly, even when his health was failing, at Missolonghi (Gamba, V, 227).

He loved pistol practice and was the best shot on the ship from Gibraltar in 1810; an 'excellent marksman', surpassing his companions (Galt, VIII; Moore, XLIX, 566; Kennedy, 298–9). His skill impressed the mountain tribes under his control at Missolonghi (Gamba, III, 124). He was happy or not according to his success (Medwin, 15; Moore, XLIX, 566). He jots down his results, observing that it was all done 'by *eye* and calculation, for my hand is not steady' (Journal, 21, 23, 26 Jan. 1821; LJ, V, 180–1, 183, 187). His unsteady hand was noted by Medwin (14; also LJ, V, 181, note); by Moore, who reports that he was said to calculate on the vibration (LXIX, 566); and by Parry (IV, 78). He always kept pistols by him by day and night, and Medwin was impressed by their number and quality (14). He loved fire-arms and decorated his room at Missolonghi with various sorts (Parry, IV, 80–1). But his targets were lifeless objects: sticks, bottles, coins, wafers (Journal, 21 Jan. 1821; LJ, V, 180; Galt, VIII; Medwin, 15); candle-flame or pumpkin

(Moore, XXVII, 319; XLV, 523); eggs and chimney-pots (Parry, IV, 78; VII, 155). That he kept his youthful vow is, as we have seen (p. 13), clear from Teresa's statement that he refused to fire at living birds with the Gambas; and only if we consider what overpoweringly strong reasons, amatory, social and political, Byron had for appearing a man of nerve and action to his Italian friends, can we assess properly the moral courage of his refusal. His shaking hand—like his lameness—may be felt as a physical symptom, or symbol, of a general tendency to self-discipline (see p. 265); he told Medwin that he was originally 'the worst shot in the world' (Medwin, 14).

He rode regularly at Venice (Kinnaird, 13 Jan. 1818; C, II, 65) and was ill-at-ease, both at Ravenna and at Missolonghi, whenever weather prevented him (Journal, 12 Jan. 1821; LJ, V, 167; Gamba, V, 227). Medwin opposes certain rumoured criticisms of his horsemanship by insisting that it was 'excellent' and combined 'grace with the security of his seat' (79, note; 13); while Kennedy notes particularly that he was 'a bold and graceful' horseman (Kennedy, 297-8; see also Hobhouse, 30 July 1819; C, II, 117-18). These recorded opinions of two officers in the services may be considered final. When Byron concludes a letter to Moore with 'Excuse haste—I write with my spurs putting on . . . and an Italian Count waiting to accompany me on my ride' (12 Sept. 1821; LJ, V, 252), one senses a significant delight in the interruption.

But of all his athletic attainments he excelled most in swimming. From boyhood onwards it was his primary delight. 'I have been here', he wrote to Moore from Hastings on 3 August 1814, 'renewing my acquaintance with my old friend Ocean; and I find his bosom as pleasant a pillow for an hour in the morning as his daughters of Paphos could be in the twilight' (LJ, III, 117). He was a fine long-distance swimmer. On 11 August 1807, he told Elizabeth Pigot of a swim of three miles from Lambeth (LJ, I, 143), and we have other similar records, the best-known being his swimming of the Hellespont in 1810, a feat in which he was himself deeply, for various reasons, interested (Hodgson, 5 May; Mrs. Byron, 24 May; Drury, 3 May, 17 June; 1810; LJ, I, 270, 275, 263-4, 277; 263, note; also *Lines Written after Swimming from Sestos to Abydos* and *Don Juan*, II, 105). Years later, on 21 February 1821, he sent Murray an account of the exploit with full and professional detail regarding time, currents and choice of direction, continuing with a description of how at Venice in 1818 the Chevalier Mengaldo, Alexander Scott and himself had a friendly contest in which he outswam the others, starting from the Island of the Lido and continuing down the Grand Canal: 'I had been in the water, by my watch, without help or rest, and never touching ground or boat, *four* hours and *twenty minutes*'. He could, he says, have continued for two more, though wearing—as he always did—his trousers. The letter—as he reiterated to Medwin—was not prompted by vanity (he assured Medwin that his Hellespont achievement was equalled by many of the sailors present), but written to disprove certain recent objections to the historicity of Leander's supposed exploit (LJ, v, 246–51; see also Hobhouse, 25 June 1818; C, ii, 84; Medwin, 136–9). As Drinkwater observes (v, 285–90), the incident may be grouped with Byron's remarkable literary output to counter reports of his supposed state at the time of nerveless dissipation (see also Teresa, i; x, 443–4, and Moore, xxxii, 382). Indeed, Byron himself neatly counters a usual biographical misconception in a pithy comment on Hobhouse's aspersions regarding his 'indolence' and 'love of slumber': 'Why,' wrote Byron, 'I do like one or two vices, to be sure; but I can back a horse and fire a pistol "without winking or blinking" like Major Sturgeon; I have fed at times for two months together on *sheer biscuit and water* (without metaphor); I can get over seventy or eighty miles a day *ri*ding post upon (?) of all sorts, and *swim five* at a stretch, taking a *piece* before and after, as at Venice, in 1818, or at least I *could do*, and have done it once, and I never was ten minutes in my life over a *solitary* dinner.' As for being late out of bed nowadays—we must remember that he wrote well into the small hours of the morning—when there was any *occasion* for early rising, he would, he said, be ready—as indeed he was, in Greece (Murray, 9 Nov. 1820; LJ, v, 114). Of Byron's ascetic diet, we shall speak again; in both food and exercise he lived under the self-imposed discipline of a continual training.

Byron's passion for the water approached mania. More—the sea had a strangely soothing, re-creating, effect on him. At Shelley's cremation he mastered his emotion, as he had done earlier by sparring with Robert at his Mother's funeral (Moore, xii, 127–8), by swimming out to his ship (Trelawny, xii; Medwin, 318). Swimming, he told Medwin, was the only exercise he prided himself on, being 'almost amphibious', able to stay for hours in the sea, and coming out 'with a buoyancy of spirits I never feel on any other occasion'; he wonders if he was a Merman in some previous existence (Medwin, 137, 139). His carriage crest was a Mermaid (Moore, 1 June 1818; Kinnaird, 3 May 1820; LJ, iv, 236; SP, ii, 513). This peculiar sympathy cannot be understood in athletic terms alone; rather we should turn to Byron's poetry, in all its variety of realistic description and symbolic overtone the richest sea-poetry in our literature; the poetry of *The Corsair, The Bride of Abydos, Childe Harold,* the early cantos of *Don Juan.*

The Island is a late poem of youthful romance in a South Sea, Melvillian, setting, of idyllic water where one can

> plunge and revel in the rolling surf,
> Then lay our limbs along the tender turf,
> And, wet and shining from the sportive toil,
> Anoint our bodies with the fragrant oil . . .
>
> (II, 2.)

The hero is autobiographically Byronic:

> And who is he? the blue-eyed northern child
> Of isles more known to man, but scarce less wild;
> The fair-hair'd offspring of the Hebrides,
> Where roars the Pentland with its whirling seas;
> Rock'd in his cradle by the roaring wind,
> The tempest-born in body and in mind,
> His young eyes opening on the ocean-foam,
> Had from that moment deem'd the deep his home,
> The giant comrade of his pensive moods,
> The sharer of his craggy solitudes,
> The only Mentor of his youth, where'er
> His bark was borne; the sport of wave and air;
> A careless thing, who placed his choice in chance,
> Nursed by the legends of his land's romance.
>
> (II, 8.)

The poem exults in athletic enjoyment of the water, as in the natives' 'skimming paddles' 'buoyant as wings, and flitting through the spray', the little boats now perching on wave-top and next moment 'dash'd downward in the thundering foam':

> Their art seem'd nature—such the skill to sweep
> The wave of these born playmates of the deep.
>
> (III, 7.)

The story moves to an adventurous escape tunnelling deep beneath the waters:

Young Neuha plunged into the deep, and he
Follow'd: her track beneath her native sea
Was as a native's of the element,
So smoothly, bravely, brilliantly she went,
Leaving a streak of light behind her heel,
Which struck and flash'd like an amphibious steel.
Closely, and scarcely less expert to trace
The depths where divers hold the pearl in chase,
Torquil, the nursling of the northern seas,
Pursued her liquid steps with heart and ease.
Deep—deeper for an instant Neuha led
The way—then upward soar'd—and as she spread
Her arms, and flung the foam from off her locks,
Laugh'd, and the sound was answer'd by the rocks.

(IV, VI.)

But perhaps the most poignant of all Byron's poetic descriptions of this exulting companionship with water occurs in *The Two Foscari*, where the tormented patriot-lover of Venice remembers his athletic skill in happier days. Asked as to his racked limbs, Jacopo Foscari answers:

JACOPO: Limbs! how often have they borne me
Bounding o'er yon blue tide, as I have skimm'd
The gondola along in childish race,
And, masqued as a young gondolier, amidst
My gay competitors, noble as I,
Raced for our pleasure, in the pride of strength;
While the fair populace of crowding beauties,
Plebeian as patrician, cheer'd us on
With dazzling smiles, and wishes audible,
And waving kerchiefs, and applauding hands,
Even to the goal!—How many a time have I
Cloven with arm still lustier, breast more daring,
The wave all roughen'd; with a swimmer's stroke
Flinging the billows back from my drench'd hair,
And laughing from my lip the audacious brine,
Which kiss'd it like a wine-cup, rising o'er
The waves as they arose, and prouder still
The loftier they uplifted me; and oft,
In wantonness of spirit, plunging down
Into their green and glassy gulfs, and making

My way to shells and sea-weed, all unseen
By those above, till they wax'd fearful; then
Returning with my grasp full of such tokens
As show'd that I had search'd the deep: exulting
With a far-dashing stroke, and drawing deep
The long-suspended breath, again I spurn'd
The foam which broke around me, and pursued
My track like a sea-bird.—I was a boy then.

GUARD: Be a man now: there never was more need
Of manhood's strength.

JACOPO: My beautiful, my own,
My only Venice—*this is breath!* Thy breeze,
Thine Adrian sea-breeze, how it fans my face!
Thy very winds feel native to my veins,
And cool them into calmness.

                                                    (I, i.)

In the great sea invocation concluding *Childe Harold,* Byron's own,
personal and boyish, love of it is remembered:

And I have loved thee, Ocean! and my joy
Of youthful sports was on thy breast to be
Borne, like thy bubbles, onward: from a boy
I wanton'd with thy breakers—they to me
Were a delight; and if the freshening sea
Made them a terror—'t was a pleasing fear,
For I was as it were a child of thee,
And trusted to thy billows far and near,
And laid my hand upon thy mane—as I do here.

                                                    (IV, 184.)

Here the sea is a thing of 'eternity' and symbol of divine judgment.
    Naturally enough Byron was led to compose *Heaven and Earth,*
dramatizing the Flood, one of his most striking works, rich with
impressions such as that of

the leviathan
Lord of the shoreless sea and watery world

wondering at his new 'boundlessness of realm' (I, ii); in contrast of
the mountains that 'look eternal' and the fate about to engulf them
when the eagle shall cry vainly to the unanswering seas, and all the
birds who greeted the morning shall, before evening, 'drop their out-

worn pinions on the deep' (I, iii); rising to a climax with even the
sea-birds clustering among the mountains in fear, until:

> The heavens and earth are mingling—God! oh God!
> What have we done? Yet spare!
> Hark! even the forest beasts howl forth their prayer!
> The dragon crawls from out his den,
> To herd, in terror, innocent with men;
> And the birds scream their agony through air.
> Yet, yet, Jehovah! yet withdraw thy rod . . .
>
> (I, iii.)

The poem's power floods equally from Byron's animal-sympathies
and loving awe of the ocean. So, too, with *Cain*. Cain's journey with
Lucifer into timeless and infinite worlds is a *voyage* through 'the
abyss of space' (II, i, direction), first lit by cosmic lights, but later:

> No sun, no moon, no lights innumerable.
> The very blue of the empurpled night
> Fades to a dusky twilight . . .
>
> (II, i.)

It is a new, dark, world of 'enormous liquid plains' and 'floating
moons' (II, i), a realm 'of swimming shadows' and 'mighty phantoms
floating around me', where Cain is enabled by Lucifer's power to
'bathe in regions' of death (II, ii). In this vision of infinity, eternity
and death, Byron's toning is throughout blue and purple, or
shadowy; and his impressions are those of water, of a great ocean,
metaphysically extending his reading of ocean in *Childe Harold* as a
symbol of the eternal:

> CAIN: And yon immeasurable liquid space
> Of glorious azure which floats on beyond us,
> Which looks like water, and which I should deem
> The river which flows out of Paradise
> Past my own dwelling, but that it is bankless
> And boundless, and of an ethereal hue—
> What is it?
>
> LUCIFER: There is still some such on earth,
> Although inferior, and thy children shall
> Dwell near it—'t is the phantasm of an ocean.
>
> CAIN: 'T is like another world; a liquid sun—
> And those inordinate creatures sporting o'er
> Its shining surface?

LUCIFER: Are its inhabitants,
       The past leviathans.
CAIN: And yon immense
       Serpent, which rears his dripping mane . . .
                                              (II, ii.)

But we have quoted enough from these rich and varied stores of
ocean poetry.

Byron's own early love of Venice, 'next to the East, the greenest
island of my imagination', with the 'gloomy gaiety' of its gondolas
(Moore, 17 Nov.; Murray, 25 Nov.; 1816; LJ, IV, 7, 14) was
originally both a sea-love and a poetic love prompted by the reading
of *Othello, The Merchant of Venice* and *Venice Preserved* (*Childe
Harold*, IV, 4, 18). Though he reacted later in disgust (as in his *Ode on
Venice, Marino Faliero*, V, iii; and see Medwin, 78-9), two of his
greater works were composed on Venetian history and all her dis-
advantages were to him compensated for 'by the sight of a single
gondola' (Webster, 8 Sept. 1818; LJ, IV, 256). In terms of the sea,
reality and poetry coalesced. His long account of his Hellespontine
and Venetian swimming was, we may recall, *specifically written to support the cause of legend, or myth*. With Byron poetry must be realistic
and he liked to find myth historical. He was glad to discover local
tradition at Verona supporting the factual basis of *Romeo and Juliet*
(Moore, 7 Nov.; Murray, 25 Nov.; 1816; LJ, III, 386; IV, 13), and
was elsewhere interested in the supposed tomb of Achilles (Mrs.
Byron, 17 April, 28 June; Drury, 3 May; 1810; LJ, I, 262, 280, 265).
Once, with reference to a passage of Campbell's, he noted down:

'Tis false—we *do* care about "the authenticity of the tale of Troy".
I have stood upon that plain *daily*, for more than a month in 1810;
and if anything diminished my pleasure it was that the blackguard
Bryant had impugned its veracity' (Journal, 11 Jan. 1821; LJ, V,
165).

He claimed to venerate Homer 'in the truth of history (in the
material *facts*) and of place'; otherwise it would give him no 'delight'.
Such a passage makes a vivid annotation to his detailed account of
his own swimming of the Hellespont with a view to proving
Leander's exploit possible. His love both of the sea and of Greece,
his will to fuse myth and fact, athleticism and poetry, the fascination
exerted by a legend where physical prowess was pointed to a soft
and amatory objective, above all his own desire to live, not merely

to think, these various fusions, all were symbolized by his swimming of the Hellespont. It was an early expression of that *poetic action* to which his whole life was dedicated: in his invocation at the conclusion of *Childe Harold* the ocean is directly associated with political freedom. Only in such terms shall we understand his statement to Hodgson on 4 July 1810: 'I pleasure myself on this achievement more than I could possibly do on any kind of glory, political, poetical, or rhetorical' (LJ, I, 285).

Such exercises necessitate and inculcate courage; it is as though Byron were forging of himself, with all the temperamental delicacy of a poet, an instrument of action and daring. His courage was regularly observed by his contemporaries and witnessed by his actions. Indeed he feared 'nobody' (Drinkwater, V, 314) and 'nothing' (Maurois, I, XIII, III).

His sea-adventures alone present a remarkable record of risk and danger. He was nearly drowned off Brighton in 1808, boats being sent out (Moore, X, 106, note; Medwin, 138). Hobhouse records as yet more 'perilous' than his imitation of Leander his swimming 'from old Lisbon to Belam Castle' against difficulties of tide, current and wind (Moore, X, 106, note). He welcomed any kind of elemental danger. Countess Albrizzi tells how at Venice during one winter he would row daily to the Armenian monastery and during another to the mainland, however violent the sea (LJ, IV, App. II, 442). He was only just convalescent from a long illness caused by a long swim in the broiling sun, when he rowed for twelve hours on his way from Lerici to Genoa (Hobhouse, 14 Dec. 1822; C, II, 237). When at Cephalonia Trelawny challenged him to swim to the mainland, he immediately agreed, though Trelawny backed out (MacDermott, quoted C, II, 287).[1] During the difficult voyage from Cephalonia to Missolonghi he rashly swam in a rough sea on a wild and cold night, thereby, according to Fletcher, dangerously weakening his constitution (Moore, LIII, 611). He minded neither heat nor cold, and embraced, as freely as Shakespeare's Cassius, tempests by land and sea; of these, and of his dangers on ship-board, we shall speak later. Earthquakes he treated lightly (Augusta, 12, and Duffie, 23, Oct. 1823; LJ, VI, 263, 265). When lost for hours with Hobhouse in the ramifications of a cave his reaction was less fear than an excited laughter (Galt, XVII). His first travels through Albania and Greece were risky enough, the land having been neglected by earlier

1. Trelawny (VI)—if he is referring tò the same incident—has it the other way round!

travellers, with one exception, precisely because of 'the savage characters of the natives' (Drury, 3 May 1810; LJ, I, 264).

Byron feared human or animal ferocity as little as he feared the elements. 'Every day at noon', says Trelawny of the voyage from Italy in 1823, 'he and I jumped overboard in defiance of sharks or weather' (Trelawny, XVIII, 191). The presence of sharks may be questioned; but whether there were any dangerous fishes or not, the argument is unaffected.[1] We have seen (pp. 4–6) how Byron liked fierce animals that frightened his visitors, allowing them a dangerous licence. When his second Italian mistress, Margarita Cogni, whom he called a 'tigress', attacked him with a knife, he scornfully refused protection, 'thinking that I might as well end that way as another'; besides, he 'had been used to savage women and knew their ways'. Indeed, though himself gentle, he liked savage creatures, and in noting that Margarita was 'very devout' and used often to 'cross herself' he was enjoying the paradox that was his own life's heart (Murray, 1 Aug. 1819; LJ, IV, 331, 334).

Long after his more devotional *liaison* with Teresa Guiccioli had, according to local convention, become respectable, the lady's husband, already suspected (Murray, 6 July 1820; V, 47–8) of two assassinations, became dangerous. 'If the man', wrote Byron to Moore on 1 June 1820, 'has me taken off, like Polonius, "say he made a good end"—for a melodrame' (LJ, V, 36; *Hamlet,* IV, v). Again, 'They say here that he will have me taken off, it is the custom.' They 'pop at you from behind trees', or 'put a knife into you' when you are off guard. 'He may do as he pleases,' said Byron, 'I only recommend him not to miss.' He took no precautions, which would be useless, though he carried pistols when riding in the woods. 'A man's life is not worth holding on such a tenure as the fear of such fellows' (Kinnaird, 20 July 1820; SP, II, 520). Iris Origo follows Peter Quennell in observing Byron's 'nervous courage', and suggests that he overestimated the danger (IV, 185); but his letters to Teresa at the time show clearly how she feared for him (18 and 23 July 1820; Origo, V, 195–6). He was shadowed by spies and nearly came to blows with one in the forest (Teresa, 8 Aug. 1820; Origo, V, 209). There were three assassinations in one week (Murray, 22 July 1820; LJ, V, 57). After the revolution, Byron's forest rides caused Teresa, as we shall see (p. 174), an agony of anxiety. Now, though daily

---

1. Byron referred to 'some large fish near us when half across' the Hellespont (in a note to Hobhouse's Journal made on 26 May 1810; LJ, I, 263, note). Galt mentioned the catching of sharks on the boat from Gibraltar in 1809 (VIII).

exposed to risk at the hands of a 'powerful and unprincipled man', Byron asserted that he never slept 'the worse' for it or rode in 'less solitary places', since such dangers were best regarded as one regards the chance of disease (Murray, 29 Sept. 1820; LJ, v, 85). As elsewhere, he drove his cool and fatalistic unconcern to an almost foolhardy extreme. After the Pope had officially pronounced the separation of Count Guiccioli and Teresa, Teresa left her husband and returned to her family. Guiccioli, already dangerous enough, was now forced to pay alimony (Origo, IV, 187 and note), and Byron accordingly had more reason than ever to fear him. Nevertheless, although the Count sent him notice to quit, Byron firmly refused to give up his rooms on the ground floor of the nobleman's palace, living on with extraordinary *sang froid* in the house of the deserted, and dangerous, husband (Origo, v, 192). In such circumstances Byron could display a strangely fatalistic coolness, as in his letter to Kennedy from Missolonghi of 10 March 1824, where, after remarking on the artificers who had left in fright, he added: 'I should like to know *where* our life *is* safe, here or anywhere else?' (LJ, VI, 349). His was no mere courage of fire and excitement; during and after the Italian uprising, he showed, as we shall see, for months on end, an almost unbelievable tenacity.

Though normally refusing to justify himself against slanderous attacks, he was ready to stand up for what he believed his rights on any matter of form. When the Pope's *gens d'armerie* petitioned the Cardinal against his own liveries, 'as resembling too nearly their own lousy uniform', he told Moore on 9 June 1820 that he was preparing his men for a fight. Though himself out of practice, 'I can', he says, 'wink and hold out mine iron,' adding that it made him think of *Romeo and Juliet*—'Now, Gregory, remember thy *swashing* blow' (LJ, v, 42). Such Shakespearian quotations (*Henry V*, II, i; *Romeo and Juliet*, I, i) are used—here as elsewhere—to underline his own half-ironical amusement at such rough and tumble incidents. But, though always well *above* his own 'melodrame', he would not submit to insults. When at Pisa Byron and his friends were involved in trouble with some Italian soldiers, 'his lordship, hearing the order given for their arrest, spurred on his horse, and one of the party did the same; and they succeeded in forcing their way through the soldiers, who flew to their muskets and bayonets, whilst the gate was closed on the rest' (from the deposition signed by those concerned, LJ, VI, App. II, 405; see also Dawkins, 27 March; Scott, 4 May; 1822; LJ, VI, 43, 57; and Medwin, 300–4). After the affair

Byron's life, as previously at Ravenna, was in constant danger and Teresa begged him, in vain, to remain indoors (Teresa, quoted Origo, VII, 305).

Byron's Christian goodness is vivid, but it cohabited with qualities of fire and vigour that clash with the Sermon on the Mount, which indeed expresses views on the proper response to a blow on the cheek directly contravening the code of a Renaissance gentleman. Hence Byron was ready enough to fight a duel, and quite fearless. Hearing that *Blackwood's* was preparing a strong reply to *English Bards and Scotch Reviewers,* he added a postscript, before leaving for the East, to the poem's second edition, lightly commenting (with a reference to *Twelfth Night,* III, iv): 'I suppose I must say of Jeffrey, as Sir Andrew Aguecheek saith, "An I had known he was so cunning of fence, I had seen him damned ere I had fought him."' He has not concealed his authorship and has remained in London ready to answer for his attacks 'in daily expectation of sundry cartels'. 'But alas', he adds, ' "the age of chivalry is over".' This was no idle boast. On his return he was prepared to give Moore satisfaction for an unintended insult, refusing to apologize for 'a charge of falsehood which I never advanced', and being nervous of any arrangement that might compromise his honour (Moore, 27 Oct. 1811; LJ, II, 62–3; Medwin, 175–6).

His challenge to Capt. Cary at Malta was unequivocal, though the matter—as too with Moore—was settled amicably (Cary, 18 Sept. 1809; C, I, 5; 6, note). He was ready to fight duels in connection with Caroline Lamb and Lady Frances Webster, quixotically intending, in the latter instance, not to fire, being himself in the wrong: 'I would not return his shot' (Melbourne, 14 Dec. 1812; 13 Oct. 1813; C, I, 116, 200; Journal, 17 Nov. 1813; LJ, II, 323). After breaking with England, he was continually thinking of returning to challenge Brougham, whom he considered to have wronged him in respect to the marriage separation (Hobhouse, 30 July, 20 Nov.; 1819; 21 Sept. 1820; 26 April 1821; 19 March 1823; C, II, 118, 131, 154, 170, 252). To an insult he responded like lightning. In Italy he had a row on the road 'with a fellow in a carriage', who was 'impudent' to his 'horse', and whom he immediately approached and slapped, giving his name and address, and defying him to the death. The man went to the police, who dismissed his complaint (Moore, 10 July; Murray, 8 July; 1817; LJ, IV, 149, 145). Then there was Lieutenant Rossi, introduced by a certain Hanoverian officer in the Papal troops whom Byron had helped financially. Rossi had sold him a horse which proved unsound. Called a thief, he said that, were it day-light, he would demand satisfaction:

'I then lost my temper: "As for that," I replied, "you shall have it directly,—it will be *mutual* satisfaction, I can assure you. You are a thief, and, as you say, an officer; my pistols are in the next room loaded; take one of the candles, examine, and make your choice of weapons." He replied that *pistols* were *English weapons; he* always fought with the *Sword.* I told him that I was able to accommodate him, having three regimental swords in a drawer near us: and he might take the longest and put himself on guard' (Murray, 29 Aug. 1819; LJ, IV, 350).

But the man ran away, shouting for help, and later complained to the police.

Byron's courage was not limited to instinctive fire; in face of any sort of danger, human or elemental, he was master of an uncanny coolness and steadiness of nerve, to which we shall have occasion to return. Teresa offers us a number of striking examples (II; II, 21–9). Moreover, Byron's courage as a *potential* fighter—potential since his duels luckily failed to mature—was, however, far less emphatic than his courage in actuality as a saviour. Instances abound. As a small boy adventuring in the Highlands with a schoolfellow and meeting a bridge superstitiously supposed dangerous to cross for an only son, he insisted—so the story goes—that the other cross first, since he would leave two parents, himself only one, to mourn (Galt, App., III). Seeing Robert Peel being beaten at Harrow by a bigger boy against whom opposition was useless, Byron asked to divide the punishment (Galt, App., XXI). Whatever be the truth of these early reports, they serve as characterizing pointers. He had a deeply ingrained *instinct* for saving, for protecting. He saved Edleston from drowning (LJ, I, 130–1, note) and, according to Medwin (138), Hobhouse.[1] During a storm in Switzerland he was about to give a sword-stick to a servant to carry, when, fearing it might attract the lightning, he kept it himself (Journal, 22 Sept. 1816; III, 358). On the voyage from Genoa, when the horses broke loose during a storm, he spent the night on deck helping to control them when most of the others were prostrated with sickness (Gamba, I, 11; Moore, LI, 592). When in a severe storm they were in danger from the rocks near Misso-

---

1. Medwin is not sure of the name, but if the incident was that at Brighton in 1808 already noticed (p. 114), it would seem that the man saved was L. Stanhope (see Moore, X, 106, note).

longhi and the sailors themselves gave up all hope, he first made plans to save a boy who could not swim (Hancock, 13 Jan. 1824; LJ, VI, 304; see pp. 72–3), and next proceeded—the incident inevitably recalls St. Paul—to save the ship by his personal skill and exertions (Gamba, II, 86–7). Physical exertion was never spared as when, hearing of a landslide at Cephalonia, he dashed to the scene, and, finding that the victims' comrades had stopped work on account of the danger involved, himself took a spade and led the way, thereby completing the rescue (*Westminster Review*, Medwin, App., xxxii; Galt, App., II; Kennedy—a slightly different version—299–300, note).

A curious incident occurred at Athens in 1810, when Byron at the pistol's point saved a condemned girl from drowning (Moore, 1 Sept.; Journal, 5 Dec.; 1813; LJ, II, 257–8 and note, 361; Medwin, 97–100). On such occasions he was a master of lightning decision and forceful action. So, too, with his attempt to save the local commandant (according to Iris Origo 'an officer of the Cardinal's guard') at Ravenna. Hearing a shot, he called to Tita, the 'bravest' of his people, and broke through soldiers, who threatened them with cocked guns, to find the crowd howling and praying, the doctor not daring to touch the man, everyone afraid of public suspicion or private revenge. Byron, who would 'never be deterred from a duty of humanity by all the assassins of Italy', took the man in, and did his best, though the wound was fatal. A characteristic remark occurs: 'The poor man's wife is not yet aware of his death: they are to break it to her in the morning.' He knew that his action might put him 'in odium with the liberals': he was risking his life to save an enemy (Moore, 9 Dec.; Murray, 9 and 14 Dec.; 1820; LJ, V, 133–40; *Don Juan,* V, 33–9, and notes; Medwin, 31–2; Origo, VI, 243). Byron's humane actions were not merely bold; they were also efficient. When he and Shelley were caught by a squall while sailing in Switzerland, Byron prepared to save his friend, who, though he could not swim, refused assistance with remarkable coolness (Murray, 15 May 1819; LJ, IV, 296–7). Had the boat not righted, it is reasonably certain that either both would have been drowned or both saved. Our idealisms have to choose. Here both men showed an equal courage, but that of the one was practical, of the other suicidal. Shelley was a pacifist and disapproved of duelling. There is a moral in the story.

By his charitable giving Byron was, of course, always saving people, and his Greek Campaign forms, as we shall see, one long essay in the art. But his effectiveness was not limited to the physical and the financial; it was a spiritual, emotional, power. At Montenero the Gambas' cook, in a rowdy battle of knives with Byron's men, ran completely amok, and blockaded the house with murder in his eye, threatening death to whoever dared to come out. Byron and his friends decided that they must not put off their daily ride, so he led the way with what Hunt calls 'his cool tones and an air of voluptuous indolence' (like Sardanapalus); and next the besieger burst into tears, asking Byron to kiss him. All shook hands, repentance and pardon ruled (Hunt, 9–11). As a saviour, Byron was brave, effective, and ready to assist friend or foe alike (as with the commandant); he could also break down emotional barriers, and reconcile. All this we shall find again at Missolonghi. He was a born mediator; and, though theoretically a keen duellist, his primary concern was to *prevent duels.*

Though bold to bravado on matters of honour, he was yet simultaneously reluctant. In the incident of the carriage, he was shocked at himself, 'a quiet man' by nature, for being forced, as his own Sardanapalus is forced, into action (Murray, 8 July 1817; LJ, IV, 146). So, too, after frightening Rossi, 'What else,' said Byron, 'could I do?' The man began it by talking of 'honour' and 'satisfaction' (Murray, 29 Aug. 1819; LJ, IV, 353). On these two occasions the insult was personal to himself. He certainly appeared less uneasy in youth, when, thinking his Mother had been insulted, he would have recourse to 'modern honour' failing redress by 'law': 'Cost what it may, gold or blood, I will pursue to the last the cowardly calumniator of an absent man and a defenceless woman' (Hanson, 4 Aug. 1811; LJ, I, 324). Here and elsewhere (e.g. Taylor, 25 Sept. 1815; LJ, III, 221) we find a balance of 'law' and 'honour': 'Where there is *no law,*' he said in a fiery claim for money owed to him in Italy, 'individuals must then right themselves'; and this he meant to do (Hoppner, 22 April 1820; LJ, IV, 13). Both historically and—like Hamlet—psychologically, Byron existed at a point of balance between rival codes.

It was therefore with a certain reluctance that he—at least in later life—subscribed to the prevailing cult. During the press attacks of 1814 he rather reluctantly considered the possibility of a duel: 'In such cases—at least, in this country—we must act according to usages.' He did not, he said, consider personal feelings at all, but 'any man will and must fight, when necessary—even without a motive' (Moore, 26 Feb. 1814; LJ, III, 51). Those are not the words of the fiery youth whom Hobhouse had once accused of a 'lust for duelling' (Hobhouse, 20 Aug. 1819; C, II, 121), or of the author of the post-script to *English Bards and Scotch Reviewers*. He told Medwin in 1822 that he was now 'tamed', though he had as a young man shown 'some of the blood of my ancestors' (Medwin, 57). But the truth is, from first to last, in this as in other matters, he was probably capable of both approving of, and hating, duels. Though he often meditated on the duty of returning to England to challenge Brougham, he did not in fact do so. Indeed, though believing in the code (Medwin, 14) and continually risking duels, his actual experience was strikingly meagre. Though he had often acted as second, he had only twice been a principal, once against Hobhouse before their friendship (Medwin, 14). Providence appears to have guarded him, as in the Italian Revolution and the Greek Campaign itself he was, or seemed, mysteriously guarded, from engaging in the bloodshed, which, whether of animal or of man, was the prime if paradoxical detesta-tion of his adventurous life. We shall not therefore be surprised to find that he was less interested in fighting duels than in preventing them.

He was once a second to Scrope Davies and another and told Lady Melbourne on 21 August 1813, how, 'having as little desire to make others play the fool as to quarrel myself, with a little manage-ment I made it up between them, as might be done nine times out of ten, if the mediator is not a bully or a butcher' (C, I, 175). The next day (22 Aug.) he wrote to Moore: 'By the bye, I was called in the other day to mediate between two gentlemen bent upon carnage, and—after a long struggle between the natural desire of destroying one's fellow-creatures, and the dislike of seeing men play the fool for nothing—I got one to make an apology, and the other to take it, and left them to live happy ever after' (LJ, II, 248). Though himself daring to foolhardiness, he had a curious instinct for pre-venting others from risking their lives. He was, in fact, not only a born *protector of the weak* but also, by nature, a *mediator between the strong*. His interest in duelling was pre-eminently—as was his interest in war—an interest in avoiding bloodshed; as though mediation were the proper end and function of the duelling which as a code he nevertheless acknowledged:

'I have been called in as Mediator or Second at least twenty times in violent quarrels, and have always contrived to settle the business without compromising the honour of the parties, or lead-

ing them to mortal consequences; and this too sometimes in very
difficult and delicate circumstances, and having to deal with very
hot and haughty Spirits—Irishmen, Gamesters, Guardsmen, Cap-
tains and Cornets of horse, and the like. This was of course in my
youth, when I lived in hot-headed company' (*Detached Thoughts,*
Oct. 1821; LJ, v, 428).

That is one of our key passages for the understanding of Byron.
Notice the reservation 'without compromising the honour of the
parties'. On returning to 'hot-headed company' in Greece he pursued his old, and instinctive, function of mediator; indeed, he went
to Greece primarily to fulfil this self-chosen office.

Byron respected the traditional code whilst in himself somehow
rising above, without actually denying, it. The code itself transcends
the meaner egotism, being a sacrifice of the ego to one's 'honour',
or greater self, even to death. Now Byron was continually aiming
so to transcend all egotisms into a dimension shared by both the
honour-cult at its best and Christian teaching; a dimension of
unselfishness, fair play and straight dealing in general. He pushed
the Renaissance code towards a kind of Christian self-effacement.

He was meticulously fair and open in his own literary attacks. If
Don Juan was to be published anonymously, then the attack on
Southey must be cut out: 'I won't attack the dog so fiercely without
putting my name—*that* is reviewers' work' (Murray, 6 May 1819;
LJ, IV, 294). He cut out his attack on Castlereagh in *Don Juan,*
'which cannot decently appear as I am at too great a distance to
answer the latter, if he wished it, personally'; Southey 'is as great a
coward as he is a renegade', but 'the other villain is at least a brave
one' and should have the opportunity of revenge (Murray, 3 April
1819; LJ, IV, 281–2). Once, when he suspected Southey of spread-
ing a scandal about him, he called him 'a burning liar', adding that
he would 'prove it in ink—or his blood, if I did not believe him
to be too much of a poet to risk it' (Murray, 24 Nov. 1818; LJ, IV,
271–2). But even with Southey he maintained his code of meticu-
lous fairness. When *The Two Foscari* was to be republished with
Byron's attack on him, Southey's answer, which had meanwhile
appeared in the press, must be included: 'This is but fair play; and I
do not desire it out of an affected contempt' (Murray, 8 Feb. 1822;
LJ, VI, 17). Satires against himself he welcomed: 'I should receive it
as the fairest compliment *you* could pay to your good opinion of my
candour, to print and circulate that or any other work, attacking

me in a manly manner, and without any malicious intention, from which, as far as I have seen, I must exonerate this writer . . . Pray publish it; I shall never forgive myself if I think that I have prevented you' (Murray, 12 March 1814; LJ, III, 60; see also Murray, 19 Oct. 1812; 9 Nov. 1820; 29 June 1821; LJ, II, 177; V, 117–18, 315–16).

All his literary dealings witness a keen sense of honour. Whatever his own troubles, he never wished 'to drag others down also' (J. Hunt, 17 March 1823; VI, 173). He regularly showed a fine concern for Murray's interests as a publisher. At the outcry against *Cain* he wrote to Murray on 8 February 1822:

'I can only say, *Me, me, adsum qui feci;* that any proceedings directed against you, I beg, may be transferred to me, who am willing, and *ought,* to endure them all; that if you have lost money by the publication, I will refund any or all of the Copyright; that I desire you will say, that both *you* and *Mr. Gifford* remonstrated against the publication, as also Mr. Hobhouse; that *I* alone occasioned it, and I alone am the person who, either legally or otherwise, should bear the burthen. If they prosecute, I will come to England—that is, if, by meeting it in my own person, I can save yours. Let me know: you shan't suffer for me, if I can help it. Make any use of this letter which you please' (VI, 16).

It was, as we have seen (p. 64), the same when John Hunt was prosecuted for *The Vision of Judgment.* On such occasions (e.g., again, Murray, 24 Aug. 1819; LJ, IV, 348), Byron's concern for others was paramount.

He normally refused to defend himself against calumny. 'At times', he said, 'I can't, and occasionally I won't, defend by explanation; life is not worth having on such terms' (Miss Milbanke, 26 Sept. 1813; LJ, III, 401). During the press attacks of 1814 he told Lady Melbourne, 'Whatever they *can,* they will say; but if stepping across the room would stop them, I would not cross it'; and to Webster, 'I care little for attacks, but I will not submit to *defences*' (18 and 28 Feb. 1814; C, I, 245; LJ, III, 52). At his marriage-crisis he warned Moore not to believe all he heard, adding: 'And don't attempt to defend me. If you succeeded in that, it would be a mortal, or an immortal, offence—who can bear refutation?' (29 Feb. 1816; LJ, III, 266–7). As late as 17 May 1823 he wrote from Missolonghi to an unknown correspondent saying, 'Do *not defend* me—it will never do —you will only make *yourself* enemies' (LJ, VI, 213). At times his consideration for others and hostility to his own interests appears to have attained the status of a 'complex'.

He did, however, sometimes, when severely pressed, speak out, though with shame at being forced to do so, as in his *Blackwood's Defence* (p. 91), and he occasionally took thought of posterity, pre-eminently in the ill-fated *Memoirs*. But in any posthumous publication of his letters he was anxious that nothing appear to hurt 'living feelings or those of survivors' (Murray, 28 Sept. 1821; V, 379). As for the *Memoirs*, he wished Lady Byron to read them, 'that she may have it in her power to mark anything mistaken or mis-stated; as it will probably appear after my extinction, and it would be but fair she should see it—that is to say, herself willing' (Murray, 10 Dec. 1819; LJ, IV, 386; see also Moore, 2 Jan. 1820; LJ, IV, 394). Lady Byron refused, and the *Memoirs* were destroyed. In such transactions he showed an immaculate sense of honour and responsibility. *English Bards and Scotch Reviewers* he repudiated and suppressed (Coleridge, 31 March 1815; LJ, III, 192–3), and made amends for his lines on Carlisle:

> Their praise is hymn'd by loftier harps than mine:
> Yet one I would select from that proud throng,
> Partly because they blend me with his line,
> And partly that I did his sire some wrong. . . .
>   (*Childe Harold*, III, 29.)

The Byronic honour holds a noble, at times a *proud*, humility. Among all the bitternesses of his later life he steadily resisted the temptation to hit back in the manner of his youthful satire. He once (*Childe Harold*, III, 97) defined his personality as 'lightning'. If we want a single word for his *character*, we might choose 'magnanimity'.

It was this largeness of mind or soul that enabled him to over-stand what to most of us are opposites; to love riding and shooting, whilst refusing blood sports; to live passionately and dare death within the Renaissance code whilst labouring to save others from duelling; to exult—since he does exult—in his own bravery, yet exerting it nearly always in a saving cause; to exist as a mediator of all oppositions; to honour warlike heroism, whilst loathing war; and to resent injuries to others whilst, unless driven to an extreme, wel-coming attacks on himself. Such largeness it was, too, that made him so pre-eminently a poet of nations and peoples, rather than a solitary poet of self-induced dream; and it is not strange that he admired, not only the arts of exercise and war, but those of public affairs and statesmanship. To his more public actions we shall now pass, expecting to find in them his characterizing qualities: protection, courage, mediation, magnanimity.

III

'I by no means', wrote Byron to Miss Milbanke, on 10 November 1813, 'rank poetry or poets high in the scale of intellect. This may look like affectation, but it is my real opinion . . . I prefer the talents of action—of war, of the senate, or even of science—to all the speculations of those mere dreamers of another existence (I don't mean religiously, but fancifully) and spectators of this apathy' (LJ, III, 405). The reservation on religion is typical. That we cannot here discuss. We shall now notice briefly Byron's experience in the 'senate'.

He had won praise at Harrow for his promise in declamation. From an early age he admired oratory and statesmanship, as a boy of nineteen writing to Hanson (his family lawyer) on April 2 1807:

'I coincide with you in opinion that the *Poet* yields to the *Orator;* but as nothing can be done in the latter capacity till the Expiration of my *Minority,* the former occupies my present attention, and both *ancients* and *moderns* have declared that the two pursuits are so nearly similar as to require in a great measure the same Talents, and he who excels in the one, would on application succeed in the other. Lyttleton, Glover, and Young (who was a celebrated Preacher and a Bard) are instances of the kind. *Sheridan* and *Fox* also; *these* are *great Names.* I may imitate, I can never equal them' (I, 126).

Byron admired Sheridan as a statesman and loved him as a man; and once, hearing that certain praise of his had drawn tears from the now failing and pathetic orator, he said that he would rather have spoken those words than have written the *Iliad* (Journal, 17 Dec. 1813; LJ, II, 377). In this letter to Hanson we find a blend of youthful modesty and vague discontent. He seems to have started as a somewhat uneasy member of the Whig Club (Hobhouse, 27 Feb. 1808; SP, I, 39). Later, on 15 January 1809, we have a considered and non-committal statement again to Hanson, surprising enough for a young man of twenty-one in its caution, maturity and a certain innate sense of superiority:

'I shall take my seat as soon as circumstances will admit. I have not yet chosen my side in politics, nor shall I hastily commit myself with professions, or pledge my support to any men or measures, but though I shall not run headlong into opposition, I will studiously avoid a connection with ministry. I cannot say that my opinion is strongly in favour of either party; on the one side we have the late underlings of Pitt, possessing all his ill fortune, without his talents; this may render their failure more excusable, but will not diminish the public contempt; on the other, we have the ill-assorted fragments of a worn-out minority . . .

'I shall stand aloof, speak what I think, but not often, nor too soon. I will preserve my independence, if possible, but if involved with a party, I will take care not to be the *last* or *least* in the ranks. As to *patriotism,* the word is obsolete, perhaps improperly so, for all men in the Country are patriots, knowing that their own existence must stand or fall with the Constitution, yet everybody thinks he could alter it for the better, and govern a people, who are in fact easily governed, but always claim the privilege of grumbling. So much for Politics, of which I at present know little and care less; bye and bye, I shall use the senatorial privilege of talking, and indeed in such times, and in such a crew, it must be difficult to hold one's tongue' (LJ, I, 209).

Notice the slight implied by 'talking'. Though he admired true statesmanship, the political *game* from the start repelled him. Whilst on his early travels he wrote to his Mother that he would speak once or twice in the House on his return, but was not ambitious of a Parliamentary career, 'of all things the most degrading and un-thankful'. But he was not cold towards the problems at issue:

'If I could by my own efforts inculcate the truth, that a man is not intended for a despot or a machine, but as an individual of a com-munity, and fit for the society of kings, so long as he does not trespass on the laws or rebel against just governments, I might attempt to found a new Utopia . . .' (Mrs. Byron, 1 July 1810; LJ, I, 284).

'By my own efforts': he was already feeling himself a leader. The 'truth' here suggested is a humanistic, spiritual, fact, independent of period or party; an eternal truth. Byron was not therefore at home with party politics as such. On his first entry into the House of Lords, he deliberately returned the Lord Chancellor's welcome coldly, lest he be considered a party man, meaning to 'have nothing to do with any of them on either side' (Dallas' account; quoted Moore, VIII,

78). It is scarcely surprising that this scornful young nobleman became unpopular with his peers.

On three occasions he did speak in the House of Lords in alignment with the Whigs; and the nature of these occasions was significant. The first concerned the work people of his own home district, Nottingham. Stocking-weavers had been losing employment through the introduction of a new frame that enabled one man to do the work of seven: the incident was a typical forerunner of the Industrial Revolution. Organized bands of workers started to break the new invention; government action was dilatory, but soldiers were eventually called out. A Bill was introduced imposing the death-penalty for the breaking of frames and compelling persons in whose houses frames were broken to act as informers. On the Bill's second reading in the Lords, on 27 February 1812, Byron opposed it.

Before his speech he wrote to Lord Holland, on 25 February, noting that the new invention led to a product 'far inferior in quality, hardly marketable at home, and hurried over with a view to exportation'. But his main reasons for speaking were given in human terms:

'. . . Surely, my Lord, however we may rejoice in any improvement in the arts which may be beneficial to mankind, we must not allow mankind to be sacrificed to improvements in mechanism. The maintenance and well-doing of the industrious poor is an object of greater consequence to the community than the enrichment of a few monopolists by any improvement in the implements of trade, which deprives the workman of his bread, and renders the labourer "unworthy of his hire".

'My own motive for opposing the Bill is founded on its palpable injustice and its certain inefficacy. I have seen the state of these miserable men, and it is a disgrace to a civilized country. Their excesses may be condemned, but cannot be subject of wonder. The effect of the present Bill would be to drive them into actual rebellion. The few words I shall venture to offer on Thursday will be founded upon these opinions formed from my own observations on the spot . . .' (LJ, II, 102-3).

The letter demands attention as evidence that Byron's speech was based on both strong personal conviction and direct personal experience. The speech itself (LJ, II, App. II, 424-30) was a remarkable achievement. Surely no clearer statement was ever later to be made on the evils of the Industrial Revolution; and this was in the year 1812, and Byron twenty-four years old. In reading it we should bear in mind Byron's life-long care and consideration for his own dependants, his liking (pp. 67–75, 232, 256) for the 'lower' classes, his almost neurotic itch towards protection of the weak, and his loathing (pp. 10, 200–2) of capital or corporal punishments.

With a stinging irony he notes how the unenlightened workmen 'in the blindness of their ignorance' had failed to appreciate the beauties of this new invention, in their folly rating themselves above the enrichment of their employers. But this, he says, was not, after all, surprising; and here he made what must have been an extremely bold attack, all but suggesting corruption among the noble audience he was addressing:

'Can you, then, wonder that in times like these, when bankruptcy, convicted fraud, and imputed felony are found in a station not far beneath that of your Lordships, the lowest, though once most useful, portion of the people, should forget their duty in their distresses, and become only less guilty than one of their representatives? But while the exalted offender can find means to baffle the law, new capital punishments must be devised, new snares of death must be spread for the wretched mechanic, who is famished into guilt' (426).

An apt use of Shakespeare serves to make the Government's measures look comic:

'And when at length the detachments arrived at their destination, in all "the pride, pomp, and circumstance of glorious war", they came just in time to witness the mischief which had been done, and ascertain the escape of the perpetrators, to collect the *"spolia opima"* in the fragments of broken frames, and return to their quarters amidst the derision of old women, and the hootings of children' (427; *Othello,* III, iii).

Irony is followed by accusation and that by ridicule. The Governing classes are pilloried again, this time with a reminiscence of *Henry VIII:*

'All this has been transacting within an hundred and thirty miles of London; and yet we, "good easy men, have dreamed full sure our greatness was a-ripening", and have sat down to enjoy our foreign triumphs in the midst of domestic calamity' (428; *Henry VIII,* III, ii).

A neat miniature of England, indeed the civilized world, during the century to follow. What has since been learned by bitter experience, is here neatly hit off in one small sentence. But more important is the simple and sound understanding shown of the true lines of force radiating unseen and unacknowledged beneath the glamour of Regency England:

'But even a mob may be better reduced to reason by a mixture of conciliation and firmness, than by additional irritation and redoubled penalties. Are we aware of our obligations to a mob? It is the mob that labour in your fields and serve in your houses—that man your navy, and recruit your army—that have enabled you to defy all the world, and can also defy you when neglect and calamity have driven them to despair! You may call the people a mob; but do not forget that a mob too often speaks the sentiments of the people. And here I must remark, with what alacrity you are accustomed to fly to the succour of your distressed allies, leaving the distressed of your own country to the care of Providence or—the parish' (428).

It was a salutary, but unheeded, truth; and remained unheeded for generations to come.

The emphasis on 'conciliation and firmness' is intensely and deeply Byronic, since he was the mediator—though paradoxically a mediator with no suggestion of compromise—*par excellence*, in thought and in life. So, too, is the statesmanlike plea for 'temporizing' which follows and makes a neat comment on his own temporizing during his Greek Campaign. Here is the justly famous peroration:

'I have traversed the seat of war in the Peninsula, I have been in some of the most oppressed provinces of Turkey; but never under the most despotic of infidel governments did I behold such squalid wretchedness as I have seen since my return, in the very heart of a Christian country. And what are your remedies? After months of inaction, and months of action worse than inactivity, at length comes forth the grand specific, the never-failing nostrum of all state physicians from the days of Draco till the present time. After feeling the pulse and shaking the head over the patient, prescribing the usual course of warm water and bleeding—the warm water of your mawkish police and the lancets of your military—these convulsions must terminate in death, the sure consummation of the prescriptions of all political Sangrados. Setting aside the palpable injustice and the certain inefficiency of the Bill, are there not capital punishments sufficient in your statutes? Is there not blood enough upon your penal code, that more must be poured forth to ascend to heaven and testify against you? How will you carry the Bill into effect? Can you commit a whole country to their own prisons? Will you erect a gibbet in every field, and hang up men like scarecrows? or will you proceed (as you must to bring this measure into effect) by decimation? place the country under martial law? depopulate and lay waste all around you? and restore Sherwood Forest as an acceptable gift to the crown in its former condition of a royal chase and an asylum for outlaws? Are these the remedies for a starving and desperate populace? Will the famished wretch who has braved your bayonets be appalled by your gibbets? When death is a relief, and the only relief it appears that you will afford him, will he be dragooned into tranquillity? Will that which could not be effected by your grenadiers, be accomplished by your executioners? If you proceed by the forms of law, where is your evidence? Those who have refused to impeach their accomplices when transportation only was the punishment, will hardly be tempted to witness against them when death is the penalty. With all due deference to the noble lords opposite, I think a little investigation, some previous enquiry, would induce even them to change their purpose. That most favourite state measure, so marvellously efficacious in many and recent instances, *temporizing,* would not be without its advantages in this. When a proposal is made to emancipate or relieve, you hesitate, you deliberate for years, you temporize and tamper with the minds of men; but a death-bill must be passed off-hand, without a thought of the consequences' (429; italics mine).

The Bill became, in due course, law (LJ, II, 97, note). Byron's speech was scarcely a party speech; it was more nearly a speech against all parties; a speech in the cause of simple man against all rulers, in any time or place. And yet its spirit was not mystical or otherworldly; nor was it revolutionary. It was a statesman's speech, presenting its case in terms of discipline, control, persuasion, moderation, and 'temporizing', with a closely realized psychology. It represents the will not to anarchy but to a *transformation of government:* it thus points on directly to Byron's lines *On the Repeal of Lord Edward Fitzgerald's Forfeiture* (p. 288); and to his own actions in Greece.

But this was not all. Byron wielded the powers not merely of an orator, but of a poet. There was danger in his pen; and he followed up his speech with *An Ode to the Framers of the Frame Bill,* printed in *The Morning Chronicle,* 2 March 1812 (LJ, II, 97, note). Here are a couple of representative stanzas:

> Those villains, the Weavers, are all grown refractory
> Asking some succour for Charity's sake—
> So hang them in clusters round each manufactory,
> That will at once put an end to *mistake.*

And,

> Men are more easily made than machinery—
> Stockings fetch better prices than lives—
> Gibbets on Sherwood will heighten the scenery,
> Showing how Commerce, how Liberty, thrives.

It is, indeed, easy to understand why London felt ill-at-ease in Byron's presence. Such attacks from extremists were expected, but the ruling powers were here being satirized, treated ironically, laughed at, by a young upstart from their own ranks. So, though Byron clearly had the Tories against him, it is doubtful how far the Whigs were with him: there was quite enough in this speech, and these verses, to make many a Whig plutocrat uneasy. He was attacking not merely a party, but a class; and he set about it, in Professor Pinto's words, 'almost single-handed'.[1] We know what happened later, decade by decade; how the aristocracy was gradually to lose prestige and power, and economic and social forces were let loose to encroach on old authorities, without direction or leadership. Because he saw it all with perfect clarity, because he knew England's aristocracy were not meeting their responsibilities, not because he was a revolutionary—he was not—Byron became first a voice, and next a dangerous incarnation, of the inevitable. There was a *'Mene, Mene, Tekel, Upharsin'* about his presence that was frightening. Failing a complete reversal of governmental procedure London was perfectly right in rejecting Byron: there was nothing else to do. He was the more dangerous—as we shall see—in refusing to align himself with the 'radicals'; it was impossible to place him. Commentators sometimes use the term 'irresponsible' in discussing Byron: the truth is, Byron was, like Hamlet, the one responsible voice in an irresponsible community; and as such rejected.

He spoke next for the Earl of Donoughmore's Motion in sup-

1. See Professor V. de S. Pinto's *Byron and Liberty* (Byron Foundation Lecture, 1944).

port of the Roman Catholic Claims, on 21 April 1812 (LJ, II, App. II, 431–43). Byron was an intensely religious man. 'For the Bible', wrote Gamba, 'he always had a particular respect'; it was always on his table in Greece (Kennedy, App., 378); he read it 'almost daily' (Moore, LII, 600). 'The Deity' was to him an ever-present and impinging reality; but, though himself a deist, his objective sympathies tended strongly away from his Calvinistic upbringing and towards Catholicism.[1] The result was an even more scathing, though perhaps a less balanced, denunciation. He starts mildly:

'It is indeed singular, that we are called together to deliberate, not on the God we adore, for in that we are agreed; not about the king we obey, for to him we are loyal; but how far a difference in the ceremonials of worship, how far believing not too little, but too much (the worst that can be imputed to the Catholics), how far too much devotion to their God may incapacitate our fellow-subjects from effectually serving their king' (431).

Here again he enriches his language with skilfully chosen Shakespearian allusions, noting how the Catholics were at the mercy of every 'pelting petty officer' who might choose to play his 'fantastic tricks before high heaven', to insult his God, and injure his fellow men (433; *Measure for Measure*, II, ii). His love for young people and impulse to education and protection charge with a peculiarly poignant emotion his denunciation of the Protestant Charter Schools and the anti-Catholic catechism forced on the children:

'Allow me to ask our spiritual pastors and masters, is this training up a child in the way which he should go? Is this the religion of the Gospel before the time of Luther? that religion which preaches "Peace on earth, and glory to God"? Is it bringing up infants to be men or devils? Better would it be to send them any where than teach them such doctrines; better send them to those islands in the South Seas, where they might more humanly learn to become cannibals; it would be less disgusting that they were brought up to devour the dead, than persecute the living. Schools do you call them? call them rather dunghills, where the viper of intolerance deposits

---

1. As an example of the misunderstandings current regarding Byron, one may point to the statement of so able a scholar as Professor Basil Willey that Byron was among those who were 'known' to think religion 'all humbug' (*Nineteenth Century Studies*, I, 32). See Fletcher's account (Kennedy, App., 369–75); also Teresa, I; IV.

her young, that when their teeth are cut and their poison is mature, they may issue forth, filthy and venomous, to sting the Catholic' (436).

He quotes Shylock, and, with reference to the prevailing *fear* of Catholicism, *Macbeth:*

'It is impossible to convince these poor creatures that the fire against which they are perpetually warning us and themselves is nothing but an *ignis fatuus* of their own drivelling imaginations. What rhubarb, senna, or what "purgative drug can scour that fancy thence"?' (429; *Macbeth,* V, iii).

The present policy was, he urged, even from the most selfish viewpoint, stupid and short-sighted. Exclusion robbed the nation of valuable talent; the defence of England was entrusted to the Irish militia; the Irish remained faithful when even oppressed classes in England were rising. 'But', he says in a pregnant phrase, one of the finest examples of his many fine examples of political wisdom maturing from the intuition of *energies,* 'till equal energy is imparted throughout by the extension of freedom', the Government cannot enjoy 'the full benefit of the strength' on which they rely; freedom and strength being interdependent, and the granting of freedom accordingly an *investment;* as indeed our own imperial history has, as Byron once practically foretold (see p. 191), shown. He pointed out that England's one successful General—Wellington—was Irish; and yet, had he been a Catholic, his services would never have been available (439–40). The persecution of Catholics was accordingly suicidal. More—it played into the hands of Napoleon: 'It is on the basis of your tyranny Napoleon hopes to build his own' (442–3).

Byron saw the alienation of Ireland as likely to prove a curse on future generations of Englishmen:

'Upon the consequences of your not acceding to the claims of the petitioners, I shall not expatiate; you know them, you will feel them, and your children's children when you are passed away' (441).

In trifling with the rights of Ireland, England was forcing her towards an 'eternal separation'. For, 'What is England without Ireland, and what is Ireland without the Catholics?' (441–2). We have recently seen Byron's prophecy fulfilled.

Next, he proceeded to level against men whom he considered tyrants executing injustice from the seats of highest power, a bitter, sarcastic, humour never found in his letters, journals or poetry:

'And now, my Lords, before I sit down, will his Majesty's ministers permit me to say a few words, not on their merits, for that would be superfluous, but on the degree of estimation in which they are held by the people of these realms? The esteem in which they are held has been boasted of in a triumphant tone on a late occasion within these walls, and a comparison instituted between their conduct and that of (the) noble lords on this side of the House.

'What portion of popularity may have fallen to the share of my noble friends (if such I may presume to call them), I shall not pretend to ascertain; but that of his Majesty's ministers it were vain to deny. It is, to be sure, a little like the wind, "no one knows whence it cometh or whither it goeth"; but they feel it, they enjoy it, they boast of it. Indeed, modest and unostentatious as they are, to what part of the kingdom, even the most remote, can they flee to avoid the triumph which pursues them? If they plunge into the midland counties, there will they be greeted by the manufacturers, with spurned petitions in their hands, and those halters round their necks recently voted in their behalf, imploring blessings on the heads of those who so simply, yet ingeniously, contrived to remove them from their miseries in this to a better world. If they journey on to Scotland, from Glasgow to John o'Groat's, every where will they receive similar marks of approbation. If they take a trip from Portpatrick to Donaghadee, there will they rush at once into the embraces of four Catholic millions, to whom their vote of this night is about to endear them, for ever. When they return to the metropolis . . .' (441–2).

One can imagine what silent, and bitter, hatred that must have stirred in some of Byron's audience; even, perhaps, in some who pretended to congratulate him.

His third and last speech was delivered at the Debate on Major Cartwright's Petition on 1 June 1813 (LJ, II, App. II, 443–5). The political 'rights of this venerable freeman' having been 'violated', Byron called for redress in these words:

'Your Lordships will, I hope, adopt some measure fully to protect and redress him, and not him alone, but the whole body of the people, insulted and aggrieved in his person, by the interposition of an abused civil and unlawful military force between them and their right of petition to their own representatives' (445).

The case is simple and needs little comment.

We do not suggest that Byron was alone in such sympathies. The 'liberty of the subject' was the cause for which such men as Earl Temple,[1] 'Junius' and Wilkes fought strenuously in the preceding century. With the Frame-Breakers, however, Byron was setting himself against the *laissez-faire* of a future liberalism and touching a twentieth-century socialism. As elsewhere, he is pivotal, bestriding the centuries. It was this very largeness that made him appear so dangerous. As we have seen, his attacks were the more deadly in that they came from a nobleman of aristocratic traditions. We should note, too, his conscious or unconscious artistry in choice of occasion. His three subjects were central, involving as they do oppression of the poor, religious conscience and political rights; or the three freedoms, economic, religious and political; and they all grow naturally from his own instinct towards protection, his strong religious sympathies, and his devotion to the cause of liberty.

The first speech was, as a *speech,* reasonably successful, and gained from friends some cordial praise. Byron wrote of it to Hodgson on 5 March 1812:

'I have had many marvellous eulogies repeated to me since, in person and by proxy, from divers persons *ministerial*—yes, *ministerial!* —as well as oppositionists; of them I shall only mention Sir F. Burdett. *He* says it is the best speech by a *lord* since the "*Lord* knows when", probably from a fellow-feeling in the sentiments. Lord H. tells me I shall beat them all if I persevere; and Lord G. remarked that the construction of some of my periods are very like *Burke's*!! And so much for vanity. I spoke very violent sentences with a sort of modest impudence, abused every thing and every body, and put the Lord Chancellor very much out of humour: and if I may believe what I hear, have not lost any character by the experiment. As to my delivery, loud and fluent enough, perhaps a little theatrical. I could not recognize myself or any one else in the newspapers' (LJ, II, 104).

Moore also observes a similarity to 'the poetry of Burke' (XIV, 155); while there is the inevitable comparison in point of irony to Swift. Oratory was an art Byron had long respected. His 'grand patron' at Harrow, Dr. Drury, 'had a great notion that I should turn out an

---

1. See my account of Earl Temple in *The Dynasty of Stowe* (IV, 56–63). The master of Stowe a couple of generations later, the strangely Byronic First Duke of Buckingham and Chandos, was, like Byron, a passionate advocate of Catholic emancipation (V, 73).

Orator, from my fluency, my turbulence, my voice, my copiousness of declamation and my action' (*Detached Thoughts,* Oct. 1821; LJ, v, 453). His immediate, and youthful, satisfaction was natural, and we must beware of supposing the flippant tone of his letter to be incompatible with a deadly earnestness of purpose, since here his most sensitive emotions, those of care and protection, were directly engaged, indeed expanded; and these were, as we have seen, precisely those which he was always most ready to mask by flippancy.

His first success was not developed. His own account is given in *Detached Thoughts* (Oct. 1821). After meditating in his urbane fashion on various orators and doubting the oratorical powers of the English, with Chatham and Burke and perhaps Sheridan as exceptions, he turns to his own experience, noting that his first speech was a success, but how 'dissipation, shyness, haughty and reserved opinions', together with his short stay in England, prevented his continuing. Besides, *Childe Harold* was published directly after and nobody thought about his prose again (LJ, v, 413–15). The truth is, politics disgusted him. On 16 March 1813 he was writing to Augusta:

'My parliamentary schemes are not much to my taste—I spoke twice last Session, and was told it was well enough; but I hate the thing altogether, and have no intention to "strut another hour" on that stage' (LJ, ii, 197; *Macbeth,* v, v).

Again, he was 'sick of parliamentary mummeries', that is, play-acting; though he had 'spoken thrice' he doubted his 'ever becoming an orator'; he had never 'set to it *con amore*' and hated 'all politics' (Journal, 14 and 17 Nov. 1813; LJ, ii, 318, 322). When asked to present a petition for an imprisoned debtor named Baldwin, he wondered why he could not force himself to action, cursing himself as a villain and hypocrite. Had '——'(Augusta?) been with him, she could 'with three words and half a smile' have made him do it; she had always stimulated his senatorial duties, 'particularly'—an interesting phrase—'in the cause of weakness' (Journal, 1 Dec. 1813; LJ, ii, 359). Lord Ernle observes that Byron 'seems to have refused the petition from diffidence', but says that he 'interested himself in the subject and probably induced Lord Holland to take up the question' (LJ, ii, 359, note).

What was the cause of this sudden apathy? Byron's life was full to distraction with love-affairs, friendships, literary work, thoughts of marriage; his self-probing on this occasion occurred at a time of depression and ill-health, when his 'nerves' were gone and he had 'no more charity than a cruet of vinegar' (Journal, 6 Dec. 1813; LJ, II, 366); throughout his life, off and on, he had fears of madness. That he should at such a time have failed to act is not strange; what is strange is his honesty in leaving posterity an account of his failure, with an acute self-questioning and self-accusation.

Byron was being forced from co-operative action into a lonely individualism. He was not at home with his peers, nor they with him; without knowing why he was unable to act through the normal channels. One can in part rationalize the disparity without claiming to pluck out the heart of its mystery: he had known his speeches patronizingly approved on grounds of style—Galt (xxvi) thinks only of this—and utterly neglected in point of substance. They were regarded as a young man's demonstration, and meanwhile starving men were liable to be hanged, Catholics were still oppressed. Byron's hatred of politics became, pretty nearly, a revulsion from all existing systems of government. Parliament was all 'mummeries' and talk, and therefore only one degree better than the despised poetry. Neither side, he said later, roused his interest, 'and as there is no answering without listening, nor listening without patience, I doubt whether I should ever make a debater' (Hobhouse, 17 Oct. 1820; C, II, 158). In his Journal for 16 January 1814 he wrote:

'As for me, by the blessing of indifference, I have simplified my politics into an utter detestation of all existing Governments; and, as it is the shortest and most agreeable and summary feeling imaginable, the first moment of an universal republic would convert me into an advocate for single and uncontradicted despotism. The fact is, riches are power, and poverty is slavery all over the earth, and one sort of establishment is no better nor worse for a *people* than another. I shall adhere to my party, because it would not be honourable to act otherwise; but, as to *opinions,* I don't think politics *worth* an *opinion. Conduct* is another thing:—if you begin with a party, go on with them. I have no consistency, except in politics; and *that* probably arises from my indifference on the subject altogether' (LJ, II, 381).

Others, no doubt, understood all this as well as Byron, though for his time, and for a member of the aristocracy, it was clairvoyant enough. His disgust was maintained. In a letter to Leigh Hunt on 29 January 1816 he saw politics as riddled by corruption and bound for revolution, Parliament as a hospital and the country apathetic (LJ, III, 259). He told Miss Milbanke on 10 November 1813, with a close reference to politics: 'Disgust and perhaps incapacity have rendered me now a mere spectator, but I have occasionally mixed in the active and tumultuous departments of existence, and in these alone my recollection rests with any satisfaction, though not the best parts of it' (LJ, III, 405). He had little in common with either Tories or Whigs, and, as we shall see, hated an irresponsible and subversive radicalism. He was paralysed, like Hamlet; thwarted, like his own Marino Faliero.

He was therefore fighting a lonely battle. He felt himself greater than his contemporaries, yet remained at a loss for an adequate action. He had the will to reform, to teach, to accuse: 'Wherever I find a tyrant or a villain', he wrote to an unnamed correspondent, on 17 May 1823, '*I will mark him*' (LJ, VI, 213). Which recalls Pope's

> Yes, while I live, no rich or noble knave
> Shall walk the world in, credit, to his grave.
> (Horatian Satires, II, i, 119.)

Such was the spirit of the deliberate challenge to society which eventually drove him from England.

The specific and central occasion was his attack on the Prince Regent whom he, with many another, regarded as a renegade to the Whig cause since his accession to power. Byron's verses addressed to Princess Charlotte, who was supposed to have wept at her father's desertion of his friends, ran:

> Weep, daughter of a royal line,
>   A Sire's disgrace, a realm's decay;
> Ah! happy if each tear of thine
>   Could wash a father's fault away!

> Weep—for thy tears are Virtue's tears—
>   Auspicious to these suffering isles;
> And be each drop in future years
>   Repaid thee by thy people's smiles!

Printed anonymously in March 1812 (LJ, II, 135, note), they at first attracted comparatively little attention. Such attacks on royalty were usual enough: the Hunt brothers had been in trouble for a libel on the Prince's defection in *The Examiner* (Moore, XVI, 183).

Soon afterwards the Regent desired that Byron should be presented to him at Cheltenham, and Byron wrote to Lord Holland, on 25 June 1812, that 'our gracious Regent' had 'honoured' him with some conversation and 'professed a predilection for poetry' (LJ, II, 125); and also hastened, as we have seen (p. 53), to let Scott know of his sovereign's admiring approval. Shortly afterwards he wrote, and next published anonymously, *The Waltz* (Murray, 18 Oct. 1812; LJ, II, 176), a poem containing some extremely impolite references to the Prince. Galt calls Byron's behaviour 'something like ingratitude' (xxix); and there is certainly a strange discrepancy between his surprised delight in the Regent's 'tone and taste', which witnessed 'abilities and accomplishments . . . superior to those of any living gentleman' (Scott, 6 July 1812; LJ, II, 134), and *The Waltz*. Byron had the opportunity of favour and advancement; and this he deliberately, almost brutally, rejected. His short piece *The Vault* or *Windsor Poetics* he told Lady Melbourne to hand on to Lord Holland or anyone else, remarking: 'but I suppose you will be *tender,* or *afraid:* you need not mind any *harm* it will do me' (Lady Melbourne, 7 April 1813; C, I, 148). Later we find him wondering how it got about, saying it was 'too *farouche*' for publication, being 'actionable', comparing himself to Juvenal, and feeling it—characteristically—as a duty to bring home to the Prince his failings. He was, or appeared to be, angered at the publication of his *Condolatory Address to Sarah, Countess of Jersey* in *The Champion* (Moore, 12 March, 3 Aug.; 1814; LJ, III, 58, 118–19). The anger was scarcely logical. Byron was playing, deliberately, with fire. He had insisted on reprinting the lines to Princess Charlotte under his own name with *The Corsair,* saying that he cared nothing for the consequences (Murray, 22 Jan. 1814; LJ, III, 17). The press attacks which followed (see LJ, II, App. VII) did not distress him (Journal, 18 Feb. 1814; LJ, II, 382). 'At the beginning of this period,' writes Lord Ernle, 'Byron had suddenly become the idol of society; towards its close his personal popularity almost as rapidly declined before a storm of political vituperation' (LJ, II, preface).

Let us attempt a co-ordination of these strange actions. Long after leaving London Byron held in his mind *two* princes, one a fine gentleman, in his youth 'the prince of princes', with 'fascination in his very bow', 'royalty' written on his brow, 'a finished gentleman from top to toe' (*Don Juan,* XII, 84). Beside this is the more political figure, symbol of all tyranny within kingship 'from Caesar the dreaded to George the despised', a 'gluttonous despot', the 'fourth of the fools and oppressors called George' (*The Irish Avatar,* 1821). Byron probably felt genuinely honoured by the Prince's praise, and as genuinely admired his abilities, but deliberately crushed in himself any responsive emotions. He would not accept poetic sensibility or courtly finesse as excuses for political injustice. Besides, he liked rejecting favours; he did not value fame and was almost pervertedly anxious *not* to 'flatter received opinions' (Journal, 27 Nov. 1813; LJ, II, 351). Again, 'My great comfort is, that the temporary celebrity I have wrung from the world has been in the very teeth of all opinions and prejudices. I have flattered no ruling powers; I have never concealed a single thought that tempted me. They can't say I have truckled to the times, nor to popular topics (as Johnson, or somebody, said of Cleveland), and whatever I have gained has been at the expenditure of as much *personal* favour as possible; for I do believe never was a bard more unpopular, *quoad homo,* than myself. And now I have done' (Moore, 9 April 1814; LJ, III, 65). He never changed. On 18 November 1822, he told Murray: 'It is Madame de Staël who says that "all talent has a propensity to attack the strong". *I* have never flattered—whether it be or be not a proof of talent' (Kinnaird,—Nov. 1822; LJ, VI, 140). He certainly aimed high: 'If they once get to a certain pitch', he wrote of his attackers, 'I shall do something or other probably, and effectual if possible; but I will go to the fountain-head, and not to the muddy little streams that flow from it.' Criticism of his work, good or bad, bored him: 'I have had my day, have done with all that stuff; and must try something new—politics—or rebellion—or Methodism—or gaming' (Lady Melbourne, 18 Feb., 8 April; 1814; C, I, 245, 249). Suggestion of irresponsibility in 'gaming' is exactly related to the thwarted desire for valuable action.

From Byron's standpoint, the Prince's benevolence was accordingly to be resisted. He believed society and politics to be rotten and the Prince a renegade who had betrayed his party. The people, he told Lady Melbourne on 21 September 1813, were sheep and their rulers worthless:

> 'Tis said Indifference marks the present time,
> Then hear the reason—though 'tis told in rhyme—
> A king who *can't,* a Prince of Wales who *don't,*
> Patriots who *shan't,* and Ministers who *won't,*
> What matters who are in or out of place,
> The *Mad,* the *Bad,* the *Useless,* or the *Base?*
>
> (C, I, 182.)

He could not feel the Regent as a representative of true royalty: the opening of Parliament was an absurd 'melodrama' performed by a 'royal Roscius', with reference, probably, not to the Roman but to the boy 'Roscius', Betty, favoured by London playgoers (Lady Melbourne, 26 Nov. 1812; C, I, 110). One can, indeed, sympathize with the Regent. He had thought Moore responsible for the offending lines and discovered Byron's authorship—though why he should be so 'affected' Byron could not understand—'in sorrow rather than anger' (Moore, 10 Feb. 1814; LJ, III, 32). He had, it seems, liked Byron, whose behaviour, as between man and man, was certainly an ingratitude; though between Byron as Promethean 'enlightener of nations' (*Manfred*, III, i) and the corrupt figure-head of a corrupt society there could be no compromise. Himself noble as patron and protector, Byron rejected patronage and refused to act the protégé. If this was pride, he deliberately paid, indeed enforced, the price; his uncompromising behaviour was challenging as Wilkes' or Wilde's. That he was already the most famous poet of England, perhaps of Europe; that society was his for the asking; that, with but a little tact, he might have attained eminence as a statesman—all this was nothing. Instinctively he was rating himself higher; far higher; and that is why he was compared by the Tory journals to—among others—Nero, Apicius, Epicurus, Caligula, Heliogabalus, Henry the Eighth, and the Devil (Medwin, 49). Therefore, whatever we think of his behaviour—and this was, at least by the Byronic code of patron and protégé, the most questionable action in his life—we must recognize that the issues were impersonal. The Prince as man held charm; the Prince as prince was another matter, was indeed, being the highest thing present, Byron's necessary target: 'The Regent', he told Murray on 29 November 1813, 'is the only person on whom I ever expectorated an epigram, or ever should' (LJ, II, 291). He was instinctively led to assist the lowly and attack the great.

But if that were all, Byron would be a comparatively simple phenomenon. Our account of his political thought is not complete. We shall not understand him unless we realize that he loathed the radicals and demagogues as much as he loathed the ruling powers.

After settling in Italy, Byron watched affairs in England with no lessening of concern, and his anxiety at the spread of 'radicalism' at home and at Hobhouse's association with its exponents makes an interesting comment on what might be called his own central position.

'I am', he wrote to Hobhouse on 26 June 1819, 'and have been for *reform* always, but not for the *reformers*. I saw enough of them at

the Hampden Club; Burdett is the only one of them in whose company a gentleman would be seen, unless at a public meeting or in a
public house' (C, II, 115–16). This was no social revulsion; Byron
enjoyed the company of prize-fighters and publicans; but politically
he stood by, and believed in, his class: 'If we must have a tyrant, let
him at least be a gentleman who has been bred to the business, and
let us fall by the axe and not by the butcher's cleaver . . . Lord
George Gordon, and Wilkes, and Burdett, and Horne Tooke, were
all men of education and courteous deportment: so is Hobhouse;
but as for these others, I am convinced that Robespierre was a Child
and Marat a Quaker in comparison of what they would be, could
they throttle their way to power' (Murray, 21 Feb. 1820; LJ, IV,
410–11). His judgment was, as often elsewhere, *personal;* he distrusted
the men, as men. He had always, he told Hobhouse, supported
reform through 'parliament', but not through 'such fellows', who
'make one doubt of the virtue of any principle or politics which can
be embraced by similar ragamuffins'. While admitting 'that revolutions are not to be made with rose water' and that 'some blood may,
and must, be shed', there were limits; and these radicals appeared
to him no better than Jack Cade or Wat Tyler. 'I perceive you talk
Tacitus to them sometimes; what do they make of it?' (29 March
1820; LJ, II, 138).

His most complete statement, written to Hobhouse on 22 April
1820, concerns 'Orator' Hunt who had convoked the meeting
whose dispersal with some loss of life by the Manchester Yeomanry
came to be known as the 'Peterloo massacre':

'I think I have neither been an illiberal man, nor an unsteady
man upon politics; but I think also that if the Manchester yeomanry
had cut down *Hunt only,* they would have done their duty; as it was
they committed murder, both in what they did, and what they did
not do, in butchering the weak instead of *piercing* the wicked; in
assailing the seduced instead of the seducer; in punishing the poor
starving populace instead of that pampered and dinnered blackguard, who is only less contemptible than his predecessor, *Orator
Henley,* because he is more mischievious' (C, II, 143).

Byron realized that many of his friends would be surprised and hurt
by such sentiments; so may certain of my present readers who have
followed with sympathy his support of the oppressed. But on this
issue he remained as uncompromising as in his life-long battle
against oppression:

'What I say thus I say as publicly as you please; if to praise such fellows be the price of popularity, I spit upon it as I would in their faces.'

He again reiterates that he has always stood for 'reform'; but the new word 'radical' troubles him; does it mean 'uprooting'? No 'political events' could change his 'sentiments'; he was protesting, not against 'reform', but against *persons* of whom all that he knew repelled him: 'I should look upon being free with such men as much the same as being in bonds with felons' (C, II, 144). Even freedom, that is, could be bought at too great a price; a hierarchy of values is implied, values of human worth, of culture. Byron's thought descended from a tradition of aristocracy, humanistic and classical learning, and a strong, semi-ethical, sense of what was, and what was not, of ultimate human, and therefore political, worth. Devoted as he was to 'liberty', at the limit he took his stand, as we shall find again, on certain more absolute, if scarcely definable, values. 'Pray don't *mistake me*,' he says; 'it is not against the pure principle of reform that I protest, but against low, designing, dirty levellers, who would pioneer their way to a democratic tyranny' (Hobhouse, 11 May 1820; C, II, 148). The key words are 'pure', 'levellers' and 'tyranny'.

Byron was retracting nothing. On 1 October 1820 he was telling Kinnaird of *Marino Faliero*: 'It is full of republicanism, so will find no favour in Albemarle Street' (C, II, 156); and on 26 October 1820 he was planning, in view of the unsettled state of affairs, to get his investments out of 'the funds'. For himself he cared little, but did not wish his family fortunes sacrificed: 'If I did not abhor your Tory country to a degree of detestation,' he says, he would have returned to settle his own business; 'but I prefer anything almost, to making one of such a people as your present government has made of the present English' (Kinnaird, C, II, 160). It was the Government's *fault* that the radicals were gaining power.

Not only was he as firm as ever on the main issue: he actually thought of returning, should things grow worse, to give active revolutionary assistance. On 17 January 1817, he wrote: 'I think of being in England in the spring. If there is a row, by the sceptre of King Ludd, but I'll be one; and if there is none, and only a continuance of "this meek, piping time of peace"'—well, he would just talk and write in such a way as to terrify the times—'including the newspaper of that name' (Moore, LJ, IV, 48; *Richard III,* I, I). On 24 February 1817, he was considering his return as demanded by trouble at home, and directly envisaged—with a mock reference to the hurly-burly of servants in *Romeo and Juliet*—fighting (Kinnaird, C, II, 37). 'Till a great blow be struck, the present system will only conduct Castlereagh to his object'; if anything serious was to be done, in which his own 'insignificance can add an o to the number', he would come (Hobhouse, 12 Dec. 1818; C, II, 95–6). He deplored his idle life, and wanted action. Though his old fighting desires had subsided, he would not altogether mind a 'revolutionary commission'; the patriots should have a full account of Lady Noel's property; and what colours for the uniform? He must look up his broadsword exercise (Hobhouse, 20 Aug.; Kinnaird, 27 Aug.; 1819; C, II, 121, 124). His references to fighting, here and elsewhere, are nearly always ironic or accompanied by a—usually comic—Shakespearian reference (e.g. references to Pistol, Nym, or the servants in *Romeo and Juliet*). Though as early as 27 December 1812 he had told Lady Melbourne that the country 'wants a little "civil buffeting" to bring some of us to our senses' (C, I, 122), he half knew that his sensibilities would be disgusted by actual civil, or any other, warring. On 3 October 1819 he wrote to Hobhouse: 'I feel no love for the soil after the treatment I received before leaving it for the last time, but I do not hate it enough to wish to take a part in its calamities, as on either side harm must be done before good can accrue; revolutions are not to be made with rosewater. My taste for revolution is abated, with my other passions' (LJ, IV, 358).

On 2 January 1820, he wrote anxiously to Augusta about the family finances. Even members of government, he had heard, were transferring investments abroad. If 'the funds' were to go, and the country come to civil warfare, he would join in. He writes in a mood of bitterness and disillusion, explaining that he would wish to finish his days 'in quiet', and how he dreaded the unleashing of his pent-up passions in such scenes as were likely to ensue: 'If you but knew how I despise and abhor all these men, and all these things, you would easily suppose how reluctantly I contemplate being called upon to act with or against any of the parties' (LJ, IV, 397). His sympathies, or rather his antipathies, were horribly divided, not only by his love of action so paradoxically combined with his loathing of slaughter, but also by his equal hatred of both Tory government and Radical demagogue: 'No one can be more sick of, or indifferent to, politics than I am . . . but if the time comes when a part must be taken one way or the other, I shall pause before I lend myself to the views of such ruffians, although I cannot

but approve of a Constitutional amelioration of long abuses'
(Murray, 21 Feb. 1820; LJ, IV, 410). Liberation was never easy;
just as the Greeks, slaves for five centuries, would be unfit for freedom, so with the class-war: 'There is no tyrant like a slave' (Fragment, *The Present State of Greece*, 1824; LJ, VI, App. VIII, 441).

Byron's only positive hope appeared to be what he called a
'republic'. In his Journal for 18 February 1814, he had written
with a characteristic realism: 'The greater the equality, the more
impartially evil is distributed, and becomes lighter by the division
among so many—therefore, a Republic!' (LJ, II, 384). In *Detached
Thoughts* (Oct. 1821) he comments: 'There is nothing left for Mankind but a Republic, and I think that there are hopes of such. The
two Americas (South and North) have it; Spain and Portugal
approach it; all thirst for it. Oh Washington!' (LJ, V, 462). The
perfectly balanced state was envisaged in *Marino Faliero:*

> Condensing in a fair free commonwealth
> Not rash equality but equal rights,
> Proportioned like the columns to the temple,
> Giving and taking strength reciprocal . . .
>
> (III, ii.)

There was to be no 'rash equality'. Byron's natural desire was to
preserve the constitution and the aristocracy if possible; but he
feared it might not be possible. In a note appended to *The Two
Foscari* (11 Dec. 1821), he saw revolution as at once deplorable and
unavoidable:

'I look upon such as inevitable, though no revolutionist: I wish
to see the English constitution restored, and not destroyed. Born an
aristocrat, and naturally one by temper, with the greater part of my
present property in the funds, what have *I* to gain by a revolution?
Perhaps I have more to lose in every way than Mr. Southey, with all
his places and presents for panegyrics and abuse into the bargain.
But that a revolution is inevitable, I repeat. The government may
exult over the repression of petty tumults; these are but the receding
waves repulsed and broken for a moment on the shore, while the
great tide is still rolling on and gaining ground with every breaker'
(LJ, VI, App. I, 388).

There was no pleasure in the thought. Medwin reminds us that
the early poems in *Hours of Idleness* show how Byron prided himself
on his ancestry, recalling that at Harrow he 'prevented the school-

room from being burnt during a rebellion, by pointing out to the boys the names of their fathers and grandfathers on the walls' (Medwin, 68). He was never, like Wordsworth, a simple revolutionary. Both principles were in him *together* from start to finish. He blamed the aristocracy for not fulfilling their responsibilities; but they remained to him an aristocracy. They deserved to fall; and it troubled him.

Our various strands are tightly woven in one rather remarkable letter to Hobhouse on 12 October 1821:

'Your infamous government will drive all honest men into the necessity of reversing it. I see nothing left for it but a republic *now;* an opinion which I have held aloof as long as it would let me. *Come* it must. *They* do not see this, but all this driving will do it, it may not be in ten or twenty years, but it is inevitable, and I am sorry for it.

It might take time, as in other countries, but:

'I am so persuaded that an English one is inevitable that I am moving Heaven and Earth (that is to say Douglas Kinnaird, and Medea's trustee) to get me out of the funds. I would give all I have to see the country *fairly free,* but till I know that *giving* or rather *losing* it, *would free* it, you will excuse my natural anxiety for my temporal affairs.

'Still I can't approve of the ways of the radicals; they seem such very low imitations of the Jacobins. I do not allude to you, and Burdett, but to the Major, and to Hunt of Bristol, and little Waddington, etc. etc.

'If I came home (which I never shall) I should take a *decided* part in politics, with pen and person; and (if I could revive my English) in the House; but am not yet quite sure *what* part, except that it would *not* be in favour of these abominable tyrants.

'I certainly lean towards a republic. All history and experience is in its favour, even the French; for they butchered thousands of citizens at first, yet *more* were killed in any one of the great battles, than ever perished by a democratical proscription.

'America is a model of force, and freedom, and moderation; (in spite of) all the coarseness and rudeness of its people' (C, II, 203).

That is, were he to act, which he will not, his action would be a decided action, though exactly what he cannot say. Could baffled confusion go further? We cannot even be quite certain whom he means by 'abominable tyrants'. And yet it is doubtful if any contemporary so unerringly detected the true lines of force, nor so exactly balanced past tradition and future necessity. It was because he saw so clearly that, like Hamlet, he could not act. That same comprehensive thinking which made him both so rich a poet and also, as we have seen, a natural mediator, here appears in a negative form; but no clear positive is envisaged.

Let us attempt to construct the positive aim, or aims, which Byron himself could, in his day, scarcely be expected to formulate. What did he really stand for? There are two answers, in terms of (i) the political philosophy of the Whig statesman, Edmund Burke, and (ii) human personality as distinct from political parties.

Byron's opinions, being at once liberal and aristocratic, lay in the Whig tradition. In offering his services to the new constitutional government of Naples he wrote that 'as a member of the English House of Peers, he would be a traitor to the principles which placed the reigning family of England on the throne, if he were not grateful for the noble lesson so lately given both to people and to kings' by the Neapolitans (trans. from the Italian, Moore, XL, 468). Though opposing the foreign policy of England, says Medwin, he was 'no revolutionist', but rather wished to see our constitution spread 'over the world' (Medwin, 339). Both Parry and Kennedy reported him as refusing to align himself with 'radicals' and 'levellers'; he told Parry that he was devoted to the British Constitution and would uphold the cause of its 'ancient and honourable aristocracy' with his life (Parry, VIII, 174; IX, 205, 211-14). What he wanted was to expose 'the errors and vices of the great' with a view to their 'amendment' (Kennedy, 250-5). As with Milton,[1] it was always a traditional (pp. 170, 177) liberty he felt threatened; and he knew that constant watchfulness was needed to preserve it from insidious encroachments (Parry, VIII, 174-5; see pp. 194, 178).

Burke regarded the English constitution as an organic whole, with its past, present and future converging under the concept 'eternity' and man and God directly interacting within the political order. If you blend Burke's *On Conciliation with the Colonies* with his *Reflections on the Revolution in France,* you have a neat correspondence to Byron's comprehensive political outlook, as expressed pre-eminently in the poetry, where alone the eternal categories receive their due; which is natural, since poetry is, regularly, the language of the eternal dimension. Let us glance at the central symbolic episode of Byron's greatest political work, *Marino Faliero,* where the Doge, on

1. See my *Chariot of Wrath,* II.

the brink of revolution, is struck by remembrance of the mighty, ancestral, dead both within the aisles of the Church of San Giovanni e San Paolo and overstanding the action in the Equestrian Statue. The Doge, a sovereign bent on aligning himself with a plebeian revolution against the aristocracy, meditates:

> Yes, proud city!
> Thou must be cleansed of the black blood which makes thee
> A lazar-house of tyranny: the task
> Is forced upon me, I have sought it not;
> And therefore was I punish'd, seeing this
> Patrician pestilence spread on and on,
> Until at length it smote me in my slumbers,
> And I am tainted, and must wash away
> The plague spots in the healing wave. Tall fane!
> Where sleep my fathers, whose dim statues shadow
> The floor which doth divide us from the dead,
> Where all the pregnant hearts of our bold blood,
> Moulder'd into a mite of ashes, hold
> In one shrunk heap what once made many heroes,
> When what is now a handful shook the earth—
> Fane of the tutelar saints who guard our house!
> Vault where two Doges rest—my sires! who died
> The one of toil, the other in the field,
> With a long race of other lineal chiefs
> And sages, whose great labours, wounds, and state
> I have inherited—let the graves gape,
> Till all thine aisles be peopled with the dead,
> And pour them from thy portals to gaze on me!
> I call them up, and them and thee to witness
> What it hath been which put me to this task—
> Their pure high blood, their blazon-roll of glories,
> Their mighty name dishonour'd all *in* me,
> Not *by* me, but by the ungrateful nobles
> We fought to make our equals, not our lords . . .   (III, i.)

Israel Bertuccio, the conspirator, enters, and the Doge is struck by disgust at both his association with such a companion and the proposed deed. Bertuccio has insisted that 'we' are not traitors:

DOGE: *We—We!*—no matter—you have earn'd the right
      To talk of *us*.—But to the point.—If this

Attempt succeeds, and Venice, render'd free
And flourishing, when we are in our graves,
Conducts her generations to our tombs,
And makes her children with their little hands
Strew flowers o'er her deliverers' ashes, then
The consequence will sanctify the deed,
And we shall be like the two Bruti in
The annals of hereafter; but if not,
If we should fail, employing bloody means
And secret plot, although to a good end,
Still we are traitors, honest Israel;—thou
No less than he who was thy sovereign
Six hours ago, and now thy brother rebel.

BERT: 'Tis not the moment to consider thus,
Else I could answer.—Let us to the meeting,
Or we may be observed in lingering here.

DOGE: We *are* observed, and have been.

BERT: We observed!
Let me discover—and this steel—

DOGE: Put up;
Here are no human witnesses: look there—
What see you?

BERT: Only a tall warrior's statue
Bestriding a proud steed, in the dim light
Of the dull moon.

DOGE: That warrior was the sire
Of my sire's fathers, and that statue was
Decreed to him by the twice rescued city:—
Think you that he looks down on us or no?

BERT: My lord, these are mere fantasies; there are
No eyes in marble.

DOGE: But there are in Death.
I tell thee, man, there is a spirit in
Such things that acts and sees, unseen, though felt;
And, if there be a spell to stir the dead,
'Tis in such deeds as we are now upon.
Deem'st thou the souls of such a race as mine
Can rest, when he, their last descendant chief,
Stands plotting on the brink of their pure graves
With stung plebeians?

149

BERT: It had been as well
  To have pondered this before—ere you embark'd
  In our great enterprise.—Do you repent?
DOGE: No—but I *feel,* and shall do to the last . . .

                                             (III, i.)

The close relation of this passage and indeed the whole play to Byron's distrust alike of aristocrat and plebeian, will be clear.

Observe the disgust at 'bloody means' and secrecy, together with the ironic realism of the thought that the conspirators' spiritual status may seem to be determined by the event. The words apply poignantly to Byron's own engagements at Ravenna. There is also the *mystique* of the past, as important to Byron as the pressure of futurity. He never for long forgets 'the dead but sceptred sovereigns who still rule our spirits from their urns' (*Manfred,* III, iv), even though, as with Nimrod and Semiramis in the central dream episode of *Sardanapalus* (IV, i)—a great scene to be balanced against the incident just quoted from *Marino Faliero*—they may be impregnated with evil. Byron's poetic work is perhaps even more heavily weighted with the concept 'eternity' than with 'freedom', though indeed, as is rendered explicit in the invocation to Ocean in *Childe Harold,* the two converge:

  The armaments which thunderstrike the walls
  Of rock-built cities, bidding nations quake,
  And monarchs tremble in their capitals,
  The oak leviathans, whose huge ribs make
  Their clay creator the vain title take
  Of lord of thee, and arbiter of war—
  These are thy toys, and, as the snowy flake,
  They melt into thy yeast of waves, which mar
Alike the Armada's pride or spoils of Trafalgar.

  Thy shores are empires, changed in all save thee—
  Assyria, Greece, Rome, Carthage, what are they?
  Thy waters wash'd them power while they were free,
  And many a tyrant since; their shores obey
  The stranger, slave, or savage; their decay
  Has dried up realms to deserts:—not so thou,
  Unchangeable, save to thy wild waves' play,
  Time writes no wrinkle on thine azure brow:
Such as creation's dawn beheld, thou rollest now.

Thou glorious mirror, where the Almighty's form
Glasses itself in tempests; in all time,
Calm or convulsed, in breeze, or gale, or storm,
Icing the pole, or in the torrid clime
Dark-heaving—boundless, endless, and sublime,
The image of eternity, the throne
Of the Invisible; even from out thy slime
The monsters of the deep are made; each zone
Obeys thee; thou goest forth, dread, fathomless, alone.

(IV, 181–3.)

Throughout *The Prophecy of Dante* the theme of political liberty is weighed down, loaded, with an icy, eternal, condemnation, deploring servitude and willing freedom; there is no final distinction; the two concepts coalesce, are indeed to be identified. Nor, of course, is Byron's sense of tradition to be limited to his own country. He feels, thinks, acts, as a European. His sense of Greece and Rome as the ancestors of modern Europe is witnessed by passage after passage, as with the ghosts of ancient Rome in *The Deformed Transformed,* which 'flit along the eternal city's rampart'—memories of Sulla, Cato, Caesar—threatening the approaches of the Bourbon tyrant (I, ii). One has only to turn the pages of *Childe Harold,* especially the fourth canto, or of *The Prophecy of Dante,* to feel the past, especially the past of Rome, ancient or medieval, imperial or Catholic, as an impinging, and often denouncing, present. For an exact commentary we may turn to Burke's statement from his *Reflections on the Revolution in France:*

'As the ends of such a partnership cannot be obtained in many generations, it becomes a partnership not only between those who are living, but between those who are living, those who are dead, and those who are to be born. Each contract of each particular state is but a clause in the great primeval contract of eternal society, linking the lower with the higher natures, connecting the visible world, according to a fixed compact sanctioned by the inviolable oath which holds all physical and all moral natures, each in their appointed place.'

Both Burke and Byron show a blending of traditional piety and liberal principle; both feel an eternal reality impinging from above to shadow all political and national transactions.

Such poetic and comprehensive thinking many find difficult;

but without it we cannot understand Byron. You find it everywhere —in his simultaneous loathing of militarism and respect to the arts of war; his admiration of the leader as leader together with his horror of tyranny. His eye was fixed throughout on a single, dramatic and inclusive, positive; he is never confused, though he may appear so. The only satisfying definition is through drama, where the opposites are constituent to a dynamic whole in contact with the eternal; and this was his final literary statement. For the rest, he was in the central tradition of British political theory, descending directly from the Whigs of the Eighteenth Century. And yet he is not to be considered a 'party' man; he reflected both principles, conservative and liberal; but this is exactly what the Whigs during the eighteenth century had done, and that is why they remained in power so long. They had for a while housed the essential sovereignty of Britain in continual tension with the Hanoverian king. Byron's attitude to George III in *The Vision of Judgment* was uncompromising: the Crown had not then, as it has since, become itself the symbol of the very sovereignty, or eternity, Byron stands for. In an age of increasing disruption, he kept something of the old synthesis alive.

Nevertheless, the synthesis *was* crumbling, and that is why he was forced to reject all parties. Two vital considerations remained in terms of personality rather than parties: first, the rights of individual persons (e.g. the stocking-weavers), however lowly; and, second, the need of personal action by a leader great enough to act, or symbolize, the wanted, unnameable, solution. The constitutional monarchy of Britain today precisely symbolizes, if shadowily, this dual necessity, the royal person functioning as a symbolic reflection of every humblest member of the community. It was therefore with something of a prophetic insight that Byron attacked the Regent for not providing, in his own person, the needed synthesis. He was at once a fine gentleman and a political fiasco; and so were the out-dated and irresponsible nobility, whether Whigs or Tories; and since his own political judgment functioned always in terms of concrete, human, actuality, he could not fail to recognize that the extremists, however justified in theory, were, *as persons*, inadequate, dangerous and detestable. With Byron personal need and personal worth alike took precedence over political theory. A person might therefore conceivably do, or be, or at least symbolize, what politics could not.

And that is why Byron idolized Napoleon.

IV

Napoleon stood for action rather than talk, and Byron admired action. As a boy, he had once meant to organize a troup called 'Byron's blacks' (Moore, IV, 46). He admitted that revolutions, battles, *'aventures'* of any sort, roused him and that he envied 'certain adventurers' more than Mahomet (Journal, 22 Nov. 1813; LJ, II, 329). He considered joining the forces in Portugal in 1809 and again in 1811 and 1813 (Mrs. Byron, 11 Aug. 1809; Hodgson, 29 June 1811; Moore, 13 July 1813; LJ, I, 241, 316; II, 231; also Hobhouse, 19 June 1811; C, I, 36). Such thoughts were desultory. More organic was his closely related admiration of Napoleon. In his Journal for 17 November 1813 we have:

'Ever since I defended my bust of him at Harrow against the rascally time-servers, when the war broke out in 1803, he has been a *Héros de Roman* of mine—on the Continent; I don't want him here' (II, 323).

That neatly defines his attitude. It was an *imaginative,* youthful, admiration, related to the revolutionary principle, but not necessarily anti-British or unpatriotic. So much being granted, we can follow his fascinated attention.

Napoleon, the down-thrower of effete dynasties, symbolized the possibility of strong, liberal and creative action. As Moore put it in a letter to Byron, 'we owe a great debt of gratitude to this thunder-storm of a fellow for clearing the air of all the old legitimate fogeys' (quoted LJ, II, 323, note). Byron wished him success 'were it only to choke the *Morning Post'*. He deplored his 'flights, leaving of armies etc. etc.' If he were to be beaten by 'men', well and good; but not 'by three stupid, legitimate-old-dynasty boobies of regular-bred sovereigns'(Moore, 5 Sept.; Journal, 17 Nov.; 1813; LJ, II, 261, 324). He saw Napoleon as, apart from all politics, *greater* than his opponents. Besides, England had no business on the Continent: 'He has my best wishes to manure the fields of France with an in-vading army. I hate invaders of all countries, and have no patience with the cowardly cry of exultation over him, at whose name you all turned whiter than the Snow to which (under Providence and that special favourite of Heaven, Prince Regency) you are indebted for your triumphs' (Murray, 22 Jan. 1814; LJ, III, 17). In his Journal for 18 February 1814, his anxiety and sense of impotence directs a Shakespearian reminiscence against his own inaction:

'Napoleon!—this week will decide his fate. All seems against him; but I believe and hope he will win—at least, beat back the invaders. What right have we to prescribe sovereigns to France? Oh for a Republic! "Brutus, thou sleepest". Hobhouse abounds in continental anecdotes of this extraordinary man; all in favour of his intellect and courage, but against his *bonhommie*. No wonder—how should he, who knows mankind well, do other than despise and abhor them?' (LJ, ii, 383; *Julius Caesar*, ii, i).

On 27 February 1814 he records: 'Buonaparte is not yet beaten, but has rebutted Blücher and repiqued Schwartzenburg. This it is to have a head. If he again wins, *Vae Victis!*' (LJ, ii, 390). He has his 'fine print of Napoleon' framed: 'the Emperor becomes his robes as if he had been hatched in them' (Journal, 6 March 1814; LJ, ii, 393). But disaster follows. 'If Wellington', he wrote on 8 April 1814 to Lady Melbourne, 'or one hero had beaten another, it would be nothing; but to be worried by brutes, and conquered by recruiting serjeants—why, there is not a *character* amongst them' (C, i, 250). This strangely *personal* and *dramatic* valuation is vitally important; while the high rating of Wellington, later his *bête noire*, is interesting. The next day he recorded a soliloquy of impassioned bitterness at Napoleon's abdication and retreat to Elba. He was 'utterly bewildered and confounded' at the great man's willingness to *outlive* such a disgrace: 'I don't know—but I think *I*, even *I* (an insect compared with this creature), have set my life on casts not a millionth part of this man's.' He begins to believe that 'this imperial diamond hath a flaw in it', but nevertheless 'won't give him up even now', though everyone else does (Journal, 9 April 1814; LJ, ii, 409). The following day, 10 April, he composed his bitter *Ode to Napoleon*, and finally, on 19 April, in utter disgust, closed his Journal, tearing out its remaining leaves, writing 'that the Bourbons are restored', and concluding: 'To be sure, I have long despised myself and man, but I never spat in the face of my species before—"O fool! I shall go mad"' (Journal, 19 April 1814; LJ, ii, 412; *King Lear*, ii, iv): a conclusion of high pressure, thickly loaded with Shakespearian quotations. At Napoleon's death he recalled that 'his overthrow, from the beginning, was a blow on the head to me' (Moore, 2 Aug. 1821; LJ, v, 336).

Byron was bitterly angered at thought of Napoleon choosing to survive his shame and ekeing out a miserable existence at Elba, or, later, St. Helena, considering that a spectacular, Shakespearian, suicide would have been nobler. Both the *Ode to Napoleon* and *The Age of Bronze* define this disgust. He did, however, warm to his sudden return into the European arena in 1815: 'It is impossible', he wrote to Moore, 'not to be dazzled and overwhelmed by his character and career' (27 March 1815; III, 188). Again, the judgment is more personal than political. Though the idol again fell, Byron would not respect Wellington. The plain of Waterloo was not much to him after Marathon and Troy, Chaeronea and Plataea: 'Perhaps there is something of prejudice in this, but I detest the cause, etc., the victors and the victory, including Blücher and the Bourbons' (Hobhouse, 16 May 1816; C, II, 6). Wellington was merely a breaker of heads; 'the best of cut-throats' (Murray, 18 Nov. 1820; LJ, V, 119; *Don Juan*, IX, 4; *Macbeth*, III, iv), who took vast sums of money as a reward (*Don Juan*, VIII, 49; IX, 1–8). The Peace of Vienna he saw as an iniquitous reinstatement of dynastic tyrannies (*Don Juan*, IX, 5). He grew to hate Castlereagh and Wellington and all their doings.

Byron envisaged a supreme good of which liberty was an aspect and with which the old dynastic orders were felt as incompatible. He had always hated tyrants, and could level strong indictments even against the more reputable examples, such as Julius Caesar, whom he felt to have crushed his own essential humanity:

> Had Caesar known but Cleopatra's kiss,
> Rome had been free, the world had not been his.
> And what have Caesar's deeds and Caesar's fame
> Done for the earth? We feel them in our shame:
> The gory sanction of his glory stains
> The rust which tyrants cherish on our chains.
> Though Glory, Nature, Reason, Freedom, bid
> Roused millions do what single Brutus did—
> Sweep these mere mock-birds of the despot's song
> From the tall bough where they have perch'd so long—
> Still are we hawk'd at by such mousing owls,
> And take for falcons those ignoble fowls,
> When but a word of freedom would dispel
> These bugbears, as their terrors show too well.
>
> (*The Island*, II, 13; *Macbeth*, II, iv.)

The reference to Cleopatra, Byron's whole life and work considered, is extremely important. The thought is that of *Childe Harold:*

> Ah monarchs could ye taste the mirth ye mar,
> Not in the toils of glory would ye fret,
> The hoarse, dull drum would sleep, and Man be happy yet.
>
> (I, 47.)

Or of *Don Juan*—

> What icebergs in the hearts of mighty men
> With self-love in the centre as their pole . . .
>
> (XIV, 102.)

It is as though he diagnoses tyranny as caused by some crushing of the warmer emotions, and his Sardanapalus, as enlightened ruler, is necessarily characterized by a certain erotic laxity. Here we are close to the heart of the Byronic challenge.

There is no doubt as to Byron's loathing of 'tyranny'. The only question was, who is or is not a 'tyrant'? Everything depends on the way power is exercised. Thus Napoleon and Wellington were to be judged by their fruits. As a great revolutionary power Napoleon had the opportunity of proving such a benefactor as man had never known. *The Age of Bronze* deplores the result:

> Alas! Why must the same Atlantic wave
> Which wafted freedom gird a tyrant's grave—
> The king of kings, and yet of slaves the slave,
> Who burst the chains of millions to renew
> The very fetters which his arm broke through,
> And crushed the rights of Europe's and his own,
> To flit between a dungeon and a throne?
>
> (V.)

Wellington had a similar chance:

> Never had mortal man such opportunity,
> Except Napoleon, or abused it more.
>
> (*Don Juan*, IX, 9.)

The one was broken, the other used his advantage to forge new fetters (*Don Juan*, IX, 1–13; XII, 20). Without blaming Wellington or Castlereagh—what has blame to do with these impossibly complex matters?—we can see Byron's view as, finally, justified. The old dynasties *have* since fallen. Whatever may be said on the other side, the Congress of Vienna, while professing to serve the rights, freedom and independence of nations, nevertheless inaugurated a lengthy period of reaction and revolution throughout Europe. As with the Industrial Revolution and the class-wars to come, we can say that Byron has been, in fact, proved right; intuitively, he saw the precipice, or precipices, ahead.

But what of Napoleon's warring? Did he not too invade? Was he not as much a 'butcher' as Wellington? How can Byron, the detester of war, approve of either? 'Politics!' he wrote to Hunt on 1 June 1815. 'The barking of the war-dogs for their carrion has sickened me of them for the present' (LJ, III, 201); in politics we hear 'nothing but the yell for war' (Moore, 12 June 1815; LJ, III, 205). The anger is against 'politics' as well as war; the war was ill-conceived, unnecessary, and therefore wrong, so that Pitt, who, unlike Wellington, received no reward, was to be 'renowned for ruining Great Britain gratis' (*Don Juan*, IX, 8). Slaughter was, in itself, to Byron hateful and war 'a brain-spattering, windpipe-slitting art' *unless* its cause be 'sanctified'; and this is precisely why Wellington was merely 'the best of cut-throats' (*Don Juan*, IX, 4; *Macbeth*, III, iv). Therefore when Byron cries 'Oh, bloody and most bootless Waterloo!' (*Age of Bronze*, V), the field is considered bloody because it was bootless: in which there is perhaps more common sense than exact logic.

It is, however, also true that the warrior as such could have, to Byron, a certain rather insecure appeal countering his loathing of war. On 7 July 1815 he told Moore that 'every hope of a republic' was over; that 'we must go on under the old system'; that he was 'sick at heart of politics and slaughters'; that he thought little of Blücher; but of Wellington—'He *is* a man—the Scipio of our Hannibal' (LJ, III, 208). Notice the classic, legendary, reference. Byron was willing to accord Wellington an hero's halo won in his own right as warrior, and allowed thereafter provided he did not sully his heroism by ignoble action:

> You *did great* things: but not being *great* in mind
> Have left *undone* the *greatest*—and mankind
> (*Don Juan*, IX, 10.)

The man 'great in mind' should *either* use his power for human good, *or*, failing that, end dramatically; the alternative being allowed, since this heroism, this being-the-victor, is a personal, poetic, value, a greatness, not subject to ethical criticism. 'Commend me to the Romans, or Macbeth, or Richard III,' he wrote, disgusted at Napoleon's survival of disaster. A 'thorough mind', he said—

observe again the word 'mind'—should go out 'with harness on its back', like Macbeth; or, we might add, Brutus, who bore 'too great a mind' ever to go 'bound' to Rome (Lady Melbourne, 12 Jan. 1814; C, I, 231; *Macbeth*, V, v; *Julius Caesar*, V, i). In a letter answered by Hunt on 2 April 1814 (LJ, App. V, III, 416), Byron had apparently again made the comparison with Macbeth and Richard III. Though wicked, they remained great; but Napoleon roused Byron's anger by not having ended with a dramatic, Shakespearian, death in battle, or suicide. 'Napoleon', he told Medwin, 'was his own antithesis . . . He was a glorious tyrant after all. Look at his public works. Compare his face, even on his coins, with those of the other sovereigns of Europe. I blame the manner of his death: he shewed that he possessed much of the Italian character in consenting to live. There he lost himself in his dramatic character, in my estimation. He was master of his own destiny; of *that*, at least, his enemies could not deprive him. He should have gone off the stage like a hero: it was expected of him' (Medwin, 223). 'Master of his own destiny': the thought is that of 'Cassius from bondage will deliver Cassius' (*Julius Caesar*, I, iii). This poetic, dramatic, greatness clearly cannot be defined in ethical terms. In Shakespeare we recognize, without being able to place, it. Byron was, accordingly, driven back on a poetic definition, as when he saw Europe as having destroyed the Lion, or Eagle (Napoleon is an eagle regularly, as in *Napoleon's Farewell* and *The Age of Bronze*), only to be destroyed by wolves (*Childe Harold*, III, 18, 19); a contrast also suggested by his line in *The Irish Avatar*—'From Caesar the dreaded to George the despised'. There is here an important valuation; but it is not an ethical valuation.

As always with Byron, the problem was poetic; he was always searching for that in life which might properly correspond to great poetry. We have already seen how, and why, his own swimming of the Hellespont held a peculiarly rare, and symbolic, importance to him; and it was to be the same with his rides in the Ravenna forest (pp. 113–14, 175). In poetry opposites coalesce. In poetry he could indulge his admiration for the matador together with his sympathy for the bull; or his response to 'battle's magnificently stern array' together with his revulsion at carnage (*Childe Harold*, I, 72–80; III, 28). For a while Byron had glimpsed in Napoleon a fusion of these incompatibles; that is, of power and goodness; but the glimpse proved false. His goodness, clearly, could be questioned, while his claim to personal greatness irrespective of good and evil was forfeited by his failing to end dramatically. That such greatness can exist within the dramatic or poetic dimension in dissociation from goodness may appear the less irrational when we remember that great virtue cannot come from a small man. Napoleon had at first appeared to possess the necessary stature; and to the dramatic imagination the stature in itself exerts authority.

Byron half felt that he himself had been created on such a scale, though the requisite actions eluded him. His sympathy with Napoleon accordingly survived the burning scorn of his *Ode* and *Age of Bronze*. Stendhal recorded Byron as remarking that he and Napoleon both signed their names 'N. B.' (Noel Byron), though he both hints and falsifies a truth in saying that Byron was 'jealous' of Napoleon (LJ, III, App. VIII, 439). Byron was mildly amused at being compared to Napoleon as one of 'the two greatest examples of human vanity in the present age' (Murray, 4 Dec. 1821; LJ, V, 486); he was 'delighted' to know that his belief in 'presages' was shared by Napoleon (Countess Albrizzi, quoted LJ, IV, App. II, 442); Gamba remarks how interested he was in anything pertaining to Napoleon (I, 15). That Napoleon was an intimate, personal, possession is clear from such a phrase as 'I mean his favourite—his Buonaparte' (*Detached Thoughts*, Oct. 1821; V, 434). He told Medwin that his sister had sent him the 'valuable present' of a lock of Napoleon's hair 'which is of a beautiful black' (Medwin, 288). When parting from Lord and Lady Blessington, 'he took a pin from his breast containing a small cameo of Napoleon', which, he said, 'had long been his companion', and gave it to Lady Blessington. But 'the next day he asked for it back' (Moore, LI, 590; Lady Blessington, 2 June 1823; LJ, VI, 221). Whatever his failures, Napoleon lived on in Byron's mind as a symbol and inspiration. In certain great stanzas of *Childe Harold* (III, 36–45), which we shall discuss later (pp. 239–40), he all but equates the Napoleonic with his own, Promethean and poetic, genius.

We may accordingly distinguish two Napoleons: (i) the symbolic, talismanic figure of personal and dramatic power; and (ii) the real, the historic, man. Byron's first indignation at his idol's fall reflected his recognition that the superman was a figment of his own creation. In his *Ode* he asserts that had the hero only died 'as honour dies' (XI), man would still have been left with an ideal, a potentiality, a dream of human greatness and therefore of racial purpose; but the idol was shown to have 'feet of clay' (III). The *Ode* witnesses a personal, almost an ugly, revulsion—'All evil spirit as thou art' (IX);

and again, 'It is but a bastard devil at last' (Lady Melbourne, 12 Jan. 1814; C, I, 231). Byron saw Napoleon's fall as a warning, and indeed learned to attune his own tumultuous energies and sense of power to an un-Napoleonic patience. More, he learned somehow to fuse his strong will to saving action with his innate loathing of slaughter; to preserve, as a golden star within him, his schoolboy's 'Buonaparte' without sacrifice of his own maternal and protective sensibility. What he instinctively searched for was action, not copying Napoleon, *but springing direct from that poetic dimension in which Napoleon was, or was felt to be, symbolic.* Sometimes, as in *The Age of Bronze* (VIII), he turned to Washington and Bolivar as types of true heroism; and yet they scarcely acted on him so potently; it was somehow too easy to rationalize their goodness; they lacked something of the dark magic, the personal radiations, of the hero; almost, one is tempted to say, they lacked evil. What was wanted was highest virtue and power in Nietzsche's sense, involving less politics than personality. Napoleon, at once conquering liberator and captive tyrant, darkly symbolized and yet horribly falsified a dimension in which the crushing opposites of power and love, of slaughter and saintliness, of evil and good, man and God, were harmonized. That dimension once glimpsed, it was hard, impossible almost, to turn back. Byron had to be either nothing or greater than Napoleon. Yet he had seen Napoleon's miserable, because undramatic, non-tragic, uneternal, end; and what was wanted was a heroism not merely transcending political parties and all opposites of authority and liberty, of war and peace, of evil and good, but a heroism independent of success or failure; a heroism blending life and death; a tragic heroism. For only in closest relation to that eternity so weighty in Burke's political thinking and Byron's own poetry, that eternity which *is* the dimension explored by *greatest* poetry, can these opposites, on our plane, be harmonized.

I shall next show how Byron's later actions fulfilled these conditions. A warning is, however, necessary: if the result is to the superficial eye a little less spectacular than one expects, we shall not be the first who have found it so.

IV

POETIC ACTION

I

THE daring and large conceptions seething in Byron sufficiently explain the fear he instilled into his country. France denied him a passage through her territory (Maurois, II, XXV, 257): indeed, he seems never to have visited France (C, II, 166, note). He travelled through Switzerland and made his home in Italy.

He was by nature cosmopolitan. As early as 18 November 1808, he told Hanson that he wished to travel in order to study 'India and Asiatic policy and manners', meaning 'to take a wider field than is customary with travellers'. If he returned, his judgment would be 'more mature' and he could enter politics (LJ, I, 199). His projects had also included Iceland (Pigot, 11 Aug. 1807; LJ, I, 143), but he finally confined his ambition to the Mediterranean. He left England without regret and with little wish to re-visit anything there but his Mother and Newstead (Mrs. Byron, 22 June 1809; LJ, I, 225). On his travels he took pleasure in peoples of various nationalities, noting that he had been talking to French, Italians, Germans, Danes, Greeks, Turks, Americans, and was learning, without forgetting England, to judge of other countries and other manners. When he saw the superiority of England, he was pleased, and where he found her inferior, enlightened (Mrs. Byron, 14 Jan. 1811; LJ, I, 309). He was so much 'a citizen of the world' that the delightful shores of the Archipelago would always be a home to him (Mrs. Byron, 28 Feb. 1811; LJ, I, 310). He was interested in distinctions of national character and liked German women better than Austrian statesmen (Murray, 31 Aug. 1820; Journal, 12 Jan. 1821; LJ, V, 68, 172). Though he read and composed French with more ease and pleasure than Italian, which he calls 'a heavy language to read in *prose*', yet his 'foreign speech is Italian' and he was temperamentally more attuned to the Italian than to the French way of life (Kinnaird, 9 March 1821; C, II, 167; see also Rogers, 3 March 1818 and *Detached Thoughts;* LJ, IV, 209; V, 436). After his return from his first travels he delighted in foreign touches, often signing his name in Greek and sprinkling his letters with Italian phrases. His later poetry was deeply influenced by the Italian. He once spoke of writing his greatest work in it (Murray, 6 April 1819; LJ, IV, 284).

When he referred to 'my Italians' (Moore, 17 Sept. 1821; LJ, V, 364) it was more than a phrase; and his devotion to Greece was no sudden thought, as his early notes to *Childe Harold,* as well as the poetry, show. He was, as a man and as a poet, cosmopolitan and international, though with a tendency to favour southern countries. His ability to fall into the ways and passions of foreign peoples has probably been matched by no other poet on record; in the Tales, *Childe Harold, Don Juan.* His self-identification with Greece from youth onwards needs no emphasis. His grip of Italian history is witnessed by *The Prophecy of Dante* and the plays; of Spanish, by *The Age of Bronze.* He never sentimentalized the countries concerned. His poetry regularly attacks, willing that decadence and slavery be replaced by memory of great traditions and nobility of action. We are to review Byron's *actions* for both Italy and Greece; but, in passing, we may first draw attention to the remarkable passage in *The Age of Bronze* on Spain, the third of the three Southern countries which so moved his imagination. It is a late poem, written after the Congress of Verona, the theme of our passage being the attempt at domination of Spain by the new—or old—France established by Wellington and Castlereagh. The ease and resource of it are amazing, cramming into one verse paragraph the history of Spain, rousing her with her own war-cry and reminders of her legendary hero, noting characteristics of her various peoples and provinces, and rising with a swift crescendo of couplets to level this comprehensive yet lightning intuition at the present crisis:

> But not alone within the hoariest clime
> Where Freedom dates her birth with that of Time,
> And not alone where, plunged in night, a crowd
> Of Incas darken to a dubious cloud,
> The dawn revives: renown'd, romantic Spain
> Holds back the invader from her soil again.
> Not now the Roman tribe nor Punic horde
> Demand her fields as lists to prove the sword;
> Not now the Vandal or the Visigoth
> Pollute the plains, alike abhorring both;
> Nor old Pelayo on his mountain rears

The warlike fathers of a thousand years.
That seed is sown and reap'd, as oft the Moor
Sighs to remember on his dusky shore.
Long in the peasant's song or poet's page
Has dwelt the memory of Abencerrage;
The Zegri, and the captive victors, flung
Back to the barbarous realm from whence they sprung.
But these are gone—their faith, their swords, their sway,
Yet left more anti-christian foes than they;
The bigot monarch, and the butcher priest,
The Inquisition, with her burning feast,
The faith's red 'auto', fed with human fuel,
While sate the catholic Moloch, calmly cruel,
Enjoying, with inexorable eye,
That fiery festival of agony!
The stern or feeble sovereign, one or both
By turns; the haughtiness whose pride was sloth;
The long degenerate noble; the debased
Hidalgo, and the peasant less disgraced,
But more degraded; the unpeopled realm;
The once proud navy which forgot the helm;
The once impervious phalanx disarray'd;
The idle forge that form'd Toledo's blade;
The foreign wealth that flow'd on ev'ry shore,
Save hers who earn'd it with the natives' gore;
The very language which might vie with Rome's,
And once was known to nations like their homes,
Neglected or forgotten:—such was Spain;
But such she is not, nor shall be again.
These worst, these *home* invaders, felt and feel
The new Numantine soul of old Castile.
Up! up again! undaunted Tauridor!
The bull of Phalaris renews his roar;
Mount, chivalrous Hidalgo! not in vain
Revive the cry:—'Iago! and close Spain!'
Yes, close her with your armed bosoms round,
And form the barrier which Napoleon found—
The exterminating war, the desert plain,
The streets without a tenant, save the slain;
The wild sierra, with its wilder troop
Of vulture-plumed guerrillas, on the stoop

For their incessant prey; the desperate wall
Of Saragossa, mightiest in her fall;
The man nerved to a spirit, and the maid
Waving her more than Amazonian blade;
The knife of Arragon, Toledo's steel;
The famous lance of chivalrous Castile:
The unerring rifle of the Catalan;
The Andalusian courser in the van;
The torch to make a Moscow of Madrid;
And in each heart the spirit of the Cid:—
Such have been, such shall be, such are. Advance,
And win—not Spain! but thine own freedom, France!
(*The Age of Bronze,* VII.)

That is characteristically Byronic; characteristic both of his historic
equipment and complete loss of self, as man or Englishman, in
objective interest in the fortunes of other nations. He never acted for
Spain; for Italy and Greece he did; but with Byron there is no great
difference. His life, his poetry, his prose, all make a single statement,
urging individuals and peoples to be worthy of, indeed to be, their
greatest selves.

Byron felt, passionately, that the spirit of man was in bondage.
On the threshold of a new era, he saw the old dynasties as moribund,
while nevertheless resenting their attempts at self-perpetuation and his
own country's bolstering up of their effete dignities. Liberty was to
him, as in his *Sonnet on Chillon,* a spiritualized concept. His attempts
at opposition at home had, certainly, failed, but something might yet
be done in Europe. Given an opportunity, he was ready for action.
As early as 1813 he had thought of going to Holland with Ward
'to be in at the Revolution' and 'listen to the shout of a free Dutch-
man' (Journal, 23 and 26 Nov. 1813; LJ, II, 340, 349). From youth
upwards the cause of national liberation was an obsession, almost a
mania. After leaving England, he was actively engaged in the cause
of liberation, first in Italy and next in Greece:

When a man hath no freedom to fight for at home,
    Let him combat for that of his neighbours;
Let him think of the glories of Greece and of Rome,
    And get knock'd on the head for his labours.

So he wrote to Moore on 5 November 1820 (LJ, V, III). His own
neatest statement is reported by Medwin, who met him in 1821:

'Perhaps, if I had never travelled—never left my own country young—my views would have been more limited. They extend to the good of mankind in general—of the world at large. Perhaps the prostrate situation of Portugal and Spain—the tyranny of the Turks in Greece—the oppressions of the Austrian Government of Venice —the mental debasement of the Papal States (not to mention Ireland) —tended to inspire me with a love of liberty. No Italian could have rejoiced more than I, to have seen a Constitution established on this side the Alps. I felt for Romagna as if she had been my own country, and would have risked my life and fortune for her, as I may yet for the Greeks. I am become a citizen of the world' (Medwin, 282).

Medwin aptly quotes from *Don Juan:*

And I will war, at least in words (and—should
My chance so happen—deeds), with all who war
With Thought;—and of Thought's foes by far most rude
Tyrants and sycophants have been and are.
I know not who may conquer: if I could
Have such a prescience, it should be no bar
To this my plain, sworn, downright detestation
Of every despotism in every nation.

(IX, 24.)

'Thought' is involved. Tyranny shackles the mind, or spirit, of the race, and therefore the providential plan. The war for liberty was a poetic war, a modern crusade. Such was the context for Byron's actions in Italy and in Greece.

When in his prefatory address to Hobhouse prefixed to *Childe Harold IV* Byron wrote in bold praise of Italy and her longing after the 'immortality of independence', we can observe how closely related in his thinking were such concepts as 'freedom' and 'eternity'. He contrasts the lamenting songs of Roman labourers with the exultation 'over the carnage of Mont St. Jean, and the betrayal of Genoa, of Italy, of France, and of the world' by an England itself now enduring 'a permanent army and a suspended Habeas Corpus'. For what the English had done abroad he saw retribution waiting; he believed that the Italian states had been better off under Napoleon, and he was, according to G. M. Trevelyan, right: 'Napoleon, not very tenderly, but most effectually, raised his mother Italy, still but half-conscious, out of the death-trance of two centuries.' The 'medieval laws' of 'decadent tyrants' were replaced by the *Code Napoléon* and education was modernized (*English Songs of Italian Freedom,* 1911; Int., xi–xii).

All this Byron had seen reversed. When a new and free constitution was, on 1 October 1820, set up in Naples,[1] he accordingly welcomed it with enthusiasm, offering his services and a sum of money. His letter, translated from the Italian, is given by Moore. In it Byron acknowledged that his offer was 'small in itself', 'as must always be that presented from an individual to a nation', and continued (writing in the third person):

'His distance from the frontier, and the feeling of his personal incapacity to contribute efficaciously to the service of the nation, prevents him from proposing himself as worthy of the lowest commission for which experience and talent might be requisite. But if, as a mere volunteer, his presence were not a burden to whomsoever he might serve under, he would repair to whatever place the Neapolitan Government might point out, there to obey the orders and participate in the dangers of his commanding officer, without any other motive than that of sharing the destiny of a brave nation, defending itself against the self-called Holy Alliance, which but combines the vice of hypocrisy with despotism' (Moore, XL, 468).

Here already we sense that purity of purpose, that humility before the demands of a great cause, which Byron showed later, on a yet greater scale, in Greece.

At Ravenna Byron directly identified himself with the Carbonari movement in attempt to throw off the Austrian yoke. The 'Spanish business', he told Murray and Kinnaird, had started a 'ferment' throughout Italy; and he meant to stay, and perhaps help, which was preferable to the 'Anglo-fashion' of talk merely (16 and 14 April; see also Hobhouse, 22 April; 1820; LJ, v, 8; C, II, 141, 144). He himself cared for the Italians as a nation more than for any other people, but he realized that they lacked 'union' and 'principle', and that success was dubious. The general atmosphere he characterized as one of unrest, with occasional assassinations. 'The Cardinal', he wrote, 'is at his wits' end; it is true that he had not far to go' (Murray, 16 April and 22 July; 1820; LJ, v, 10, 57). His life at Ravenna was a centre of numerous political, amatory and poetical tensions and calls on his time, attention and energy: 'None of your *damned proofs* now *recollect;* print, paste, plaster and destroy—but don't let me have any of your cursed printer's trash to pore over' (Murray, 22 Aug.

1. For an account of the new Neapolitan Government, see Origo, v, 225–6.

1820; LJ, v, 66). Not that he loved poetry the less, but that he loved action, of this essentially poetic kind, more. Of his recently completed *Marino Faliero* he wrote, '*I have "put my Soul* into the tragedy" (as you *if* it); but you know there are damned souls as well as tragedies' (Murray, 31 Aug. 1820; LJ, v, 67). The theme of *Marino Faliero* was revolution; Byron's life and art were converging.

He rapidly assumed a certain leadership among the nondescript revolutionaries at Ravenna, calling, according to Teresa (Origo, v, 205), 'for less talk and quicker action, for a concerted plan'. The Byron of Cephalonia and Missolonghi was being foreshadowed. He was urged on by his 'love of liberty in general and of Italy in particular' (Hobhouse, 21 Sept. 1820; C, II, 153). He enjoyed the title of a 'Capo', or chief (Murray, 4 Sept. 1821; V, 358). The plot, he told Kinnaird, was 'as pretty a plot as Hotspur's' (*1 Henry IV;* II, iii), but the sudden desertion of Bologna—Origo, v, 223—had plunged everything into confusion, both sides 'watching each other like hunting leopards'. With a characteristic irony he saw God's 'image' about to be defaced once again by war, and recalled what the English were like 'when we were burning the frames and sometimes the manufactories'. Meanwhile there was risk from the authorities. If the Austrians censored his letters, they would discover how he hated and detested them, 'and all they can do in their temporary wickedness', which must inevitably sooner or later meet punishment (Kinnaird, 1 Oct. and 22 Nov.; 1820; C, II, 156, 163–4). To Murray he wrote on 23 November 1820, saying that the Austrians would eventually pay for their tyranny, though it might not be very soon, since the Italians had 'no union nor consistency among themselves'; but he supposed Providence would get tired of their oppressors at last, and show that God was not an Austrian (LJ, v, 129). Exactly such a want of 'union' and 'consistency' he was to find later in Greece: his patterns repeat themselves.

Byron's cool courage during these months was remarkable. He had been watched continually by the police, at Ravenna and elsewhere (Origo, III, 103–4; V, 232; VI, 253, 256). He was already a suspected man when he definitely threw in his lot with the Carbonari (Origo, v, 203). The risks whether of arrest and legal punishment (Origo, VI, 242), or, more likely, of sudden assassination (pp. 115, 119), were extreme. With a callous disregard he insulted the authorities in his letters, joined the Carbonari, and rode freely in the forest.

As the crisis approached his Journal records his various activities.

On 7 January 1821 Count Pietro Gamba had told him that the Patriots, who had heard that the Government was about to strike, were arming. What was Byron's advice? He had urged them to fight, had offered his house as a defensible position, and himself and his as defenders, and suggested lending Gamba his pistols. Left alone he did not go to bed, but stayed up, soliloquizing: 'Expect to hear the drum and the musquetry momently (for they swear to resist, and are right)—but I hear nothing, as yet, save the plash of the rain and the gusts of the wind.' He has mended the fire, prepared the arms, and is turning over a book or two. The house, he thinks, could be defended for twenty-four hours (LJ, v, 157–8). On 8 January, he was advising further on matters of strategy, sending off his corrections to Bacon's *Apophthegms* (p. 21), and wondering if the Italians would prove good fighters (LJ, v, 159–61). At this time of tension and unease his Journal shows him turning from one to another of his multiple interests—his love for Teresa, his voluminous reading, abstruse matters of learning, his animals, correcting his own, and others', literary works, hearing and discussing music. There was cause for anxiety. He had no official position nor moral backing from friends at home. Such an undertaking by a lonely and foreign adventurer was dubiously respectable and success, as he knew, unlikely. Typically he nerved himself with a Shakespearian quotation: if the Austrians march,—'Let them—"They come like sacrifices in their trim", the hounds of Hell!' (LJ, v, 163; *1 Henry IV*, iv, i). He analyses, in a speech compact of strong meanings to which we shall refer again, his own, quixotic, intentions:

'Heard some music. At nine the usual visitors—news, *war*, or rumours of war. Consulted with P. G. etc., etc. They mean to *insur-rect* here, and are to honour me with a call thereupon. I shall not fall back; though I don't think them in force or heart sufficient to make much of it. But, *onward!*—it is now the time to act, and what signifies *self*, if a single spark of that which would be worthy of the past can be bequeathed unquenchedly to the future? It is not one man, nor a million, but the *spirit* of liberty which must be spread. The waves which dash upon the shore are, one by one, broken, but yet the *ocean* conquers, nevertheless. It overwhelms the Armada, it wears the rock, and, if the Neptunians are to be believed, it has not only destroyed, but made a world. In like manner, whatever the sacrifice of individuals, the great cause will gather strength, sweep down what is rugged and fertilize (for *sea-weed* is *manure*) what is cultivable. And so, the mere selfish calculation ought never to be made on such occasions; and, at present, it shall not be computed by me. I was never a good arithmetician and shall not commence now' (9 Jan. 1821; LJ, v, 163).

The thoughts are characteristic. But here is something even more peculiarly Byronic. On 12 January we find him worrying about the enemy. He had already ruminated on the cruelties likely to be perpetrated by *both* sides; now he remembers the good qualities of the German people; and, while hating the Austrians as oppressors, he would be 'sorry', he says, '*to find deeds correspondent to my hate, for I abhor cruelty more than I abhor the Austrians*' (italics mine); he was never savage except 'on impulse' (LJ, v, 172). Such sensitiveness on active service is rare; we shall find more of it.

On 23 January he was hearing of nothing but war: 'the cry is still, They come' (*Macbeth*, v, v). The Carbonari, who have no proper plan, infuriate him: some have gone off on a shooting party involving 'small shot, water-hen and waste of powder', and the prospects of a muster are poor (LJ, v, 183–4). Again, on 26 January, he grumbles at their 'buffooning' expedition and complains of his choice of associates, while comforting himself with thoughts of Holland and Spain, America and England, Greece and Xerxes. Riding in the Forest, he came across and planned to 'examine' an old peasant woman (p. 90). On 29 January he interviewed her, decided that she was taxing her strength by labour, arranged her a pension, and read Schlegel (LJ, v, 187–93). Two days later he was complaining that he found serious composition on the brink of a volcano hard and wondering if it were merely laziness (LJ, v, 195). During this time of tension and hourly expectation of sudden action or summary arrest, he wrote his long first defence of Pope, the poet of peace (completed 10 Feb. 1821; LJ, v, 201: The Bowles Controversy, LJ, v, App. III). On 15 February he was finishing the first act of *Sardanapalus* (LJ, v, 202). Nowhere is his remarkable power of diverse yet simultaneous activity and interest more vividly apparent. He could hold violent excitement and a serene calm in balance, and often appears, like a dramatist or an actor, to be living in a dimension well above, though including, his own most pressing and immediate engagements.[1]

1. Compare the calm of his letters on a wide range of subjects during, and in the months following, his marriage disasters and expulsion from England. See p. 63, note.

On 16 February Pietro Gamba sent to his house certain arms which Byron had purchased at the revolutionaries' request for a rising that should have taken place ten days ago. They had 'asked me to purchase some arms for a certain few of our ragamuffins', but the rising was prevented by the 'Barbarians' marching sooner than expected. Orders having now been issued stating punishments for those concealing arms, the arms were—it is the kind of thing everybody did with Byron—without warning and during his absence—dumped in *his* house. He noted the risk to himself and his servants with remarkable coolness, observing that he had originally supplied them at *their* request and his own 'peril and expense', and that now he was to be made responsible (LJ, v, 202–3; see also Origo, vi, 250 and Medwin, 29). On 18 February we read:

'Today I have had no communication with my Carbonari cronies; but, in the mean time, my lower apartments are full of their bayonets, fusils, cartridges, and what not. I suppose that they consider me as a depôt, to be sacrificed, in case of accidents. It is no great matter, supposing that Italy could be liberated, who or what is sacrificed. It is a grand object—the very *poetry* of politics. Only think—a free Italy!!! Why, there has been nothing like it since the days of Augustus' (LJ, v, 205).

'The very *poetry* of politics.' Such a phrase was indeed needed to keep his faith burning in face of the behaviour of his associates.

There followed the ignominious collapse. Bologna had already failed. Next, the new Neapolitan Government itself proved renegade. Bitterly Byron observed that he always knew it would be bungled. Even so, he advised his associates to rise immediately rather than await arrest. Though the cause was lost and his own safety depended on lying low, he remained firm:

'Whatever I can do, by money, means, or person, I will venture freely for their freedom; and have so repeated to them (some of the Chiefs here) half an hour ago. I have two thousand five hundred scudi, better than five hundred pounds, in the house, which I offered to begin with' (24 Feb. 1821; LJ, v, 208).

Byron was not deterred, in Italy or in Greece, by either unworthiness or ingratitude. His eye was fixed on the cause and that alone, irrespective of success or failure. But the Carbonari were discouraged, and the revolution at an end. On 27 February Byron was sending off more material for the Bowles Controversy to Murray, and was given two bunches of violets by the old peasant woman he had assisted (LJ, v, 210). Here his Journal of 4 January to 27 February 1821 stops. All was ready for helping the Patriots, his drawers 'full of their proclamations' and the lower rooms of hidden weapons. The Journal was discontinued in momentary expectation of war—and because the paper book was filled up (*My Dictionary*, 1 May 1821; LJ, v, 403). 'The whole country was ready' (Hodgson, 12 May 1821; LJ, v, 283).

Though the revolution had failed, Byron's loathing of the 'infamous oppression' of the 'German-Austrian scoundrels' (Murray, 16 Feb. 1821; LJ, v, 245) was not relaxed. While his recurring scorn of all human endeavour was only too clearly corroborated, he mastered his annoyance at such 'treachery and disunion' (Murray, 26 April 1821; LJ, v, 270) and tried, as later in Greece, to make allowances for human weakness; and, while execrating the Neapolitans, refused to blame the Italian people as a whole.

And he remained at Ravenna. Though publicly denounced as 'the Chief of the Liberals' and threatened with assassination, this, he adds, 'shall never silence nor bully my opinions' (Hoppner, 25 May 1821; LJ, v, 297). A paper was posted in the market-place putting a price on his head (LJ, v, 355, note). Both sides clearly knew him as a man, indeed *the* man, of consequence. He was watched by the police, followed by spies, his letters opened, every movement observed; at Bologna, Ravenna and, later, Pisa. The Papal police were, however, 'so much in awe of the great Lord that they did not dare to approach him' (Origo, III, 103–4; v, 232; VI, 256). Something more than Byron's status as an English peer is needed to explain this extraordinary official diffidence.

He was not idle, but remained assiduous on behalf of his revolutionary associates (Duchess of Devonshire, 15 Feb. [July?] 1821; LJ, v, 237; Origo, VI, 259, and—correcting the date—Notes, 506). On 23 July he told Hoppner that a thousand people had been arrested, and banished or imprisoned; that they would have done the same by him if they had dared; and that his motive for remaining was to serve those who had been exiled (LJ, v, 327–8). Teresa considered that he ran a thousand dangers by staying (LJ, v, 328, note). Such was Byron's care for the various 'poor proscribed exiles', which left him 'no time or patience' for writing his preface to the volume containing *Sardanapalus* and *The Two Foscari* (Murray, 30 July 1821; LJ, v, 330). The claims of man took precedence over those of literature.

Meanwhile, he maintained the initiative. Had he shown any signs of fear, the authorities would probably have, directly or indirectly, struck; but he did not. Even after he had persuaded Teresa to leave, he remained a solitary pillar of the revolution, refusing to budge, and keeping up his normal routine of forest rides. He seems, indeed, to have promised Teresa to take a 'safer route'; but the hour of those evening rides, which she expected would lead to his assassination, remained a daily nightmare to her (quoted Origo; Teresa to Byron, 11 Aug. 1821; Origo, VI, 261, 269 and note): 'By the love you have felt for me—by all that you hold dearest on earth, swear to me to keep your vow, *never, never to go riding* in the Forest !!!' (Teresa to Byron, 25 July 1821; Origo, VI, 261). Though she implored him to join her, Byron stayed on at Ravenna, riding, teaching his steward Lega Zambelli to swim, bathing (Teresa, 4 Sept. 1821; Origo, VI, 279, 282). And during October, in his lonely apartments in Count Guiccioli's Palazzo, he penned his *Detached Thoughts*, so suave and urbane, that one would think them composed by a retired statesman, or cleric, in some rural retreat.

Byron's utter lack of respect for power as such was here, as in England, emphatic. He was 'conscious of no fault' and would go at his 'own good time' (Alborghetti, 28 July; see also 15 Aug. 1821; Origo, VI, 254, 271). His own pithy summing up of his general behaviour and attitude was excellently reported by Medwin. The 'proscription' was immense, numerous suspects being exiled and their property confiscated:

'They knew that this must eventually drive me out of the country. I did not follow them immediately: I was not to be bullied' (Medwin, 29–30).

Had sufficient proof been available, he would have been arrested, but he had received 'a very high degree without passing through the intermediate ranks', and evidence was lacking. However—

'Shortly after the plot was discovered, I received several anonymous letters, advising me to discontinue my forest rides; but I entertained no apprehensions of treachery, and was more on horseback than ever. I never stir out without being well armed, and sleep with pistols. They knew that I never missed my aim; perhaps this saved me' (Medwin, 30–1).

Perhaps it did; but more probably what saved him was something

easier to recognize than define. Anyway, the assassins remained
behind their bushes.

The Ravenna forest held for Byron strong poetic associations. 'I
was never tired', he told Medwin, 'of my rides in the pine-forest: it
breathes of the *Decameron;* it is poetical ground. Francesca lived, and
Dante was exiled and died, at Ravenna. There is something inspiring
in such an air' (Medwin, 28). The forest he called 'Boccaccio's
pinery' and he was living within fifty yards of Dante's tomb (Hobhouse, 30 July 1819; C, II, 117–19). A lovely stanza of *Don Juan*
tells how 'Boccaccio's lore' and 'Dryden's lay' made the Ravenna
forest at twilight 'haunted ground' to him (III, 105). His courage on
these evening rides enjoyed poetic support.

II

In Byron a bulldog, Churchillian, pugnacity cohabited with a
detestation of bloodshed or any sort of cruelty. 'Politics!' he wrote in
1815. 'The barking of the war-dogs for their carrion has sickened me
of them for the present'; he was 'sick at heart of politics and slaughters'
(Hunt, 1 June; Moore, 7 July; 1815; LJ, III, 201, 208). Once, hearing
of the deaths of a dentist and a hairdresser, he remarked that they 'were
both as much superior to Wellington in rational greatness, as he who
preserves the hair and the teeth is preferable to the "bloody, blustering
booby" who gains a name by breaking heads and knocking out
grinders' (Murray, 18 Nov. 1820; LJ, V, 119). With this we may
group the war satire in *Don Juan:*

> The drying up a single tear has more
> Of honest fame than shedding seas of gore
>
> (VIII, 3.)

—which condenses masses of his most important poetry from *Childe
Harold* to *Don Juan* and *Sardanapalus.*

He was not, however, a pacifist; he believed in the warrior-
values, given a pure cause (*Don Juan,* IX, 4); and such was the cause
of liberation. 'With these things and these fellows', he wrote, 'it is
necessary, in the present clash of philosophy and tyranny, to throw
away the scabbard. I know it is against fearful odds; but the battle
must be fought; and it will be eventually for the good of mankind,
whatever it may be for the individual who risks himself' (Moore,
8 Aug. 1822; LJ, VI, 101). Note the phrase '*present* clash': the contrast of 'philosophy' and 'tyranny'; and the limiting of expectation to

a long-range success. War and force were bad; but at this moment in history Byron was convinced that resistance was justifiable.

What, we may ask, *is* this 'philosophy'? It is both related to, and distinguished from, 'poetry'. On the failure of the Italian attempt Byron wrote to Moore, saying: 'And now let us be literary . . . If "Othello's occupation be gone", let us take to the next best; and, if we cannot contribute to make mankind more free and wise, we may amuse ourselves and those who like it' (Moore, 28 April 1821; LJ, v, 272; *Othello,* III, iii). Poetry was akin to the greater reality, it was the 'next best'; but that greater reality itself involved not merely freedom, but *wisdom;* more, there was the impulse (which we have already met in Byron's dealings with individuals) to make mankind better, nobler, wiser. This essentially creative purpose is a kind of art, though with mankind rather than ink and paper for its materials.[1] Byron distinguished this grand-scale and poetic education or ministry from the lighter kinds of written poetry by using terms such as 'philosophy' and 'wise', which are nevertheless to be closely related to the *greatest* poetry, as Byron argued in the Bowles Controversy: e.g. 'He who can reconcile poetry with truth and wisdom is the only true *"poet"* in its real sense, *"the maker", "the creator"* ', (LJ, v, App. III, 559): such wisdom relates also, variously, to the concepts of 'liberty', or 'freedom', and *also* 'eternity' and even 'immortality' (as in the associations of *Childe Harold,* IV, 182–3 and the *Sonnet on Chillon;* and the phrase 'the immortality of independence', Prefatory Address, *Childe Harold,* IV). No concepts are wholly satisfying. But tyranny must certainly be opposed to the death: 'I should almost regret that my own affairs went well, when those of nations are in peril. If the interests of mankind could be essentially bettered (particularly of these oppressed Italians), I should not so much mind my own "sma peculiar". God grant us all better times or more philosophy!' (Journal, 11 Jan. 1821; LJ, v, 165). 'Philosophy' again; and yet the Italian revolution was also 'the very *poetry* of politics' (Journal, 18 Feb. 1821; LJ, v, 205): that is, poetry in Aristotle's 'more philosophical' sense; the *logos* of the human spirit, whose suppression Milton denounced in the *Areopagitica.* On John Hunt's trial for the publication of Byron's *Vision of Judgment* Byron wrote: 'Mr. K. is providing

---

1. Compare St. Paul's vision of his pupils as a living poetry written not with 'ink' or on 'tablets of stone' but 'with the spirit of the living God' engraved on human 'hearts' (2 *Corinthians,* III, 3); and also Nietzsche's 'My burning will to create driveth me ever and again unto man as the mallet is driven unto the stone' (*Thus Spake Zarathustra,* II, 2).

you with the best counsel, and seeing the question at least *fairly* tried
—it is an important one in a general point of view, or there is an end
of history' (J. Hunt, 8 Jan. 1823; LJ, VI, 159). 'History' presupposes
human significance; and without justice in this matter—he does not
say without reckless freedom—history is gone and public life purpose-
less. Byron's is a crusade against all 'tyrants and sycophants' who war
with 'thought'; 'thought' here suggesting the essence of human advance (*Don Juan*, IX, 24; p. 167). His own poetic warfare was part
of this, civic, battle: 'They hate me,' he wrote with reference to *Cain*,
'and I detest them, I mean your present public, but they shall not
interrupt the march of my mind, nor prevent me from telling the
tyrants who are attempting to trample on all thought that their
thrones will yet be rocked to their foundation' (Kinnaird, 2 May;
C, II, 222). Byron's revolutionary activities were closely related to
his own poetry; they were poetry in action.

He admitted himself to be by nature a 'philosopher' rather than a
soldier (Hobhouse, 7 April 1823; C, II, 254; Augusta, 12 Oct.
1823; LJ, VI, 260; p. 184); but despite his philosopher's temperament
and imaginative sensibility, he had trained himself from youth, had
nerves of steel, and would not falter. He saw, or felt, man's spirit
being broken. He believed *both* the heritage of the past *and* the hopes
of the future, indeed, the inmost fires of life, of the providential plan,
to be at stake: the 'spirit of liberty' was as a 'spark' from the past to
be 'bequeathed unquenchedly to the future' (Journal, 9 Jan. 1821;
LJ, V, 163; p. 170). This is the Promethean, the divine, spark, beyond price; the 'eternal spirit of the chainless mind' of his *Sonnet on
Chillon*. He told Medwin that he would be glad to think that he had
'added a spark to the flame' (Medwin, 284), and wrote in a letter
addressed to Lady Byron:

'You neither know nor dream of the consequences of this war.
It is a war of *men* with monarchs, and will spread like a spark on the
dry, rank grass of the vegetable desert. What it is with you and your
English, you do not know, for ye sleep. What it is with us here, I
know, for it is before and around and within us' (1 March 1821;
LJ, V, 383).

'The king-times', he had written, 'are fast finishing. There will be
blood shed like water, and tears like mist; but the peoples will conquer in the end. I shall not live to see it, but I foresee it' (Journal,
13 Jan. 1821; LJ, V, 173). If men remained slaves, it was their own
fault. Already England, France, Spain, Portugal, America, Switzer-

land had won freedom; men would prove victorious over 'systems', tyranny falls if resisted (*Detached Thoughts*, Oct. 1821; LJ, v, 451).

And yet it all appeared sometimes merely a poetic fantasy. The Fourth Canto of *Childe Harold*, he told Medwin, was looked at by the Italians 'in a political light'. 'They indulged', he said, 'in my dream of liberty, and the resurrection of Italy. Alas! it was only a dream!' (Medwin, 194). Indeed, both in Italy and in Greece Byron's actions were doubly poetic. Not only was liberty itself a poetic, Promethean, cause, but these two nations were together fountain-heads, in poetry, politics and religion, of our Western culture. The depth of Byron's feeling for Italy as 'mother of arts' and 'parent of our religion' (*Childe Harold*, IV, 47) and his sympathy for her people's long enslavement are witnessed by his poetry; by *Childe Harold* (IV), *The Deformed Transformed* and the Venetian plays, *The Ode on Venice, The Lament of Tasso*, and pre-eminently by *The Prophecy of Dante*. 'I don't wonder', said Byron, 'at the enthusiasm of the Italians about Dante. He is the poet of liberty. Persecution, exile, the dread of a foreign grave, could not shake his principles' (Medwin, 195). Byron loved Ravenna for its Dantesque associations. He felt liberation not merely as a removal of restrictions, but rather as the preservation of some great traditional (p. 147) good, which yet demanded perpetual struggle, century by century:

> Yet, Freedom! yet thy banner, torn, but flying,
> Streams like the thunder-storm *against* the wind . . .
> (*Childe Harold*, IV, 98.)

The test was severe, and in certain moods Byron all but despaired of Europe.

When that happened, he dreamed of America, the land of liberty. He actually planned to emigrate to the new world, north or south, but preferably south, to the land of Bolivar or Washington, and wild but noble freedom. But he did not go; nor was it, strictly, within his proper destiny to go. He was as much the poet of tradition and culture as the prophet of liberation, and a land without traditions was not within his pattern.

Byron's actions in Italy were only superficially ineffective; they proved, as he half foresaw (p. 170), creative. To put it bluntly, Byron turned out to be right and England wrong. 'The day was coming', wrote Trevelyan, when England would be 'on the right side'; and that day 'was prepared by the zeal with which Byron took up the Italian cause', his influence proving powerful at home. He was indeed the first Englishman 'who saw, in these dark days, that the Italians had a cause and a purpose of their own' (*English Songs of Italian Freedom*, Int., xvi–xviii). There was, from the creative view, no failure; Byron's Italian fame lived after him; as in Greece later, he left a legend, a creative myth, to work silently beyond his own life's span. To his Greek adventure we shall now pass, observing a direct continuation in descent from his Italian experience. Two developments of peculiar interest should be watched. One is Byron's solicitude for the enemy, which, slightly suggested in Italy (pp. 119, 171), was to be a major theme in Greece. The other is this. In Italy he had learned a lesson of primary importance, which he never forgot in Greece: that is, that the fight for national liberation by a people themselves lacking unity must be futile. His Italian experience formed a perfect rehearsal, as it were, for the drama to follow.

III

A few months after the Italian fiasco, Byron, on 4 June 1821, wrote to Moore: 'The Greeks! What think you? They are my old acquaintances—but what to think I know not' (LJ, V, 306).

Byron's early *Childe Harold* had done much to create the occasion. 'He had been the poet of Greece—more than any other man he had turned the attention of Europe on Modern Greece. By his eloquent and spirit-stirring strains, he had himself powerfully co-operated in raising the enthusiasm of regeneration which now reigns in Greece' (*Westminster Review,* Medwin, App., lxxxviii). Harold Nicolson (III, 48–9) likewise emphasizes the predominating part played by Byron's early poetry, echoing through England, France, Germany and Russia, in preparing the European mind for the Greek War of Independence which broke out in the spring of 1821. Meanwhile Byron himself had been otherwise engaged; now Greece swims back into focus.

Byron's approach was from the start closely realistic. There was no romantic glamour about it. He told Lady Blessington that the adventure was conforming to the usual pattern of an original enthusiasm followed by doubt and anxiety (Blessington, 318–19).[1] He knew Greece to be in a state of confusion amounting to civil war and foreigners to be suspect (Hobhouse, 11 Sept. 1823; C, II,

1. Compare: 'If ever I laughed with the laughter of the creative lightning, that is followed by the long thunder of the deed, growling but obedient' (*Thus Spake Zarathustra,* III, 16).

276; Gamba, I, 34). Teresa Guiccioli emphasizes his inward struggle before leaving (Moore, LI, 590); at the last moment, he confessed that he would *like* to turn back (C, II, 272, note), and according to Barry persisted only through a sense of 'duty and honour' (Moore, LI, 592). After all, he expected never to return (Gamba, I, 12; Moore, LI, 592; Lady Blessington, *The Idler in Italy,* quoted Origo, VIII, 339; Medwin, 103; Millingen, quoted Nicolson, XI, 263). 'He came', said Tricoupi in his Funeral Oration, 'according to the testimony of those who were intimate with him, with a determination to die in Greece and for Greece' (quoted Edgcumbe, I, XV, 186; see p. 217). But not for a romantic Greece. He always knew that the Greeks were not necessarily descended from the ancients (note 11 to *Childe Harold,* II, 73), and told Parry that they were 'a mixed race, of various tribes' (Parry, VIII, 171). The Greeks, he knew, were split by factions and intrigues, and he was soon to be writing: 'Now I will take care that it *is* for the public cause; otherwise, I will not advance a *para*' (Barry, 25 Oct. 1823; LJ, VI, 268). Again, 'Some of their bankers tried to make me pay interest for *my own money* in my *own possession,* which I came to spend, for their cause too!' (Kinnaird, 29 Oct. 1823; C, II, 284). St. Paul's statement that 'there is no difference between a Jew and a Greek' disposed him 'to credit all the rest of the dicta of that powerful Apostle' (Barry, 29 Oct. 1823; LJ, VI, 271; Kennedy, 248). But he was ready to make allowances for a country rendered backward by centuries of tyranny (Journal, 28 Dec. 1823; LJ, VI, 246-7). He told Kennedy at Cephalonia—and this corroborates Barry—that he was reluctantly forced on by 'public duty' and 'what was expected of him'. Admittedly he loved the cause of the Greeks, liberty, but could not help knowing—as he had known when writing his note to *Childe Harold,* II, 74—that the Turks were as good and in some ways better. On Kennedy's superficial remark that he was then acting as the slave of circumstances and opinion, Byron, with a Shakespearian[1] understanding of human motive and action, answered: 'It is true. There is a chain which binds us all, high and low, and our inclination and will must bend to the circumstances of our situation.' He would at least attempt to allay animosities and encourage unity, and then, if need be, retire (Kennedy, 246-8). Mr. S—— (p. 275) at Ithaca reported him as saying that he expected roguery and imposition, and was going precisely in order to discover, and if possible remedy, such evils; and that in a good cause one must not look too closely at the people

1. See my *Principles of Shakespearian Production,* Pelican Books, 1949, III, 105, note.

concerned, 'or, God knows, we shall seldom do much good in this world' (Edgcumbe, I, V, 49).

Galt was annoyed—as was Trelawny—by Byron's delaying at Cephalonia to study the general situation and the various parties soliciting his alliance and money, at a time when his friends at home 'longed in vain to hear of that blaze of heroism by which they anticipated that his appearance in the field would be distinguished'. He admits that the sending of such dull things—clearly of no entertainment value—as medical supplies (Bowring, 12 May 1823; LJ, VI, 207) was important, 'but there was too much consideration in all that he did' and too little of that 'heroic enthusiasm with which the admirers of his poetry imagined he was kindled' (XLII). Later we hear that, after one of the many crises at Missolonghi, 'Lord Byron's undisciplined spirit could ill brook delay' (XLV). It is hard to please the biographers.

Galt's comments are worth quoting, since we are still far from clear as to what Byron was doing. Mr. Harold Nicolson sees him at Cephalonia adopting 'a non-committal, if somewhat languid, attitude' (VI, 136), while Hobhouse and Kinnaird (at home) were growing impatient:

'They did not realize that he was clutching at these potent justifications for delay mainly because he flinched from the responsibilities which he visualized so clearly; mainly because he was acutely, torturingly, diffident. The temptation to remain in Cephalonia was indeed all but invincible: he had proclaimed himself a man of action; from the moment he landed in Greece this pretension would, he knew too well, be pitifully exposed. At Metaxata he could be generous, be acute, be prudent; at Missolonghi he would have to *control*. And so he lingered there, hoping that something would emerge to strengthen him; hoping that something would emerge to keep him there for ever; hoping, predominantly, that the Committee would send out someone else. If only it could be Napier! ... And in the meantime he could at least place his fortune at their disposal. No strength of character, no dominance, was required for that' (VII, 155).

Surely there is something wrong here. When did Byron ever 'flinch' from responsibility? Or 'proclaim' himself a man of action? Is the unloading of one's 'fortune' for an ideal no test of 'character'? As for Byron's ability to 'control', his 'dominance', to this we shall return. Harold Nicolson himself tells us that Edward Blacquière had advised Byron not to act until he had studied the rival parties (IV, 83); and quotes Dr. Millingen's statement that 'much credit' was certainly due to him for his studied caution (VII, 156). In his Preface Mr. Nicolson says that Byron's sojourn at Missolonghi was 'a succession of humiliating failures', though he admits the emergence in him of 'a superb physical courage' against the background of his 'diffidence, irresolution, perplexity, and fear': 'Lord Byron accomplished nothing at Missolonghi except his own suicide; but by that single act of heroism he secured the liberation of Greece. Had Byron, as he was urged, deserted the Hellenic cause in February 1824, there would, I feel convinced, have been no Navarino. The whole history of South-Eastern Europe would have developed differently.' That is exactly what Trevelyan said of Byron's effect in Italy (p. 178; see also p. 226, and Maurois, III, XXXV, 429). But if such successes be 'humiliating' failures, where are we? What of the New Testament?

I shall proceed to argue that Byron's heroism was far from simple; that his courage, *moral* as well as 'physical', was remarkable; and that he acted throughout, here as in Italy, with full awareness of what he was doing, with slight expectations of any spectacular success, and with perfect consistency; and that all this was an expression in action of the noblest assertions of his own poetry. His actions can only be assessed in terms such as Moore's:

'Like many other such contests between right and might, it was a cause destined, all felt, to be successful, but at its own ripe hour;—a cause which individuals might keep alive, but which events, wholly independent of them, alone could accomplish, and which, after the hearts, and hopes, and lives of all its bravest defenders had been wasted upon it, would at last to other hands, and even to other means than those contemplated by its first champions, owe its completion' (LII, 597).

This, he next says, is how Byron saw it. He expected no immediate success: 'He but looked upon himself—to use a favourite illustration of his own—as one of the many waves that must break and die upon the shore before the tide they help to advance can reach its full mark.' Moore was paraphrasing Byron's Journal for 9 January 1821; LJ, V, 163 (see pp. 170–1; also pp. 172, 175–8).

Such a purpose is strange; it implies, as it were, a tragic understanding, is indeed a tragic purpose. It is deeply poetic and creative, but to be, provisionally, distinguished from written poetry. Shown some Homeric sites at Ithaca, Byron said, according to Trelawny, that he had not come to Greece to 'scribble more nonsense'; wished he had never written a line; and would show the world that he could do 'something better' (Trelawny, XIX). But it was clearly something essentially poetic, something greater, not less, than poetry at which he aimed. In reading Col. Stanhope's assertion, 'There was nothing that he detested more than to be thought merely a great poet' (Edgcumbe, I, XVI, 209), we should put the accent on 'merely'. Besides, he had no ambition to shine as a conqueror. Much of his best work turns on hatred of war and cruelty to animals (pp. 13–15); and if, as Moore suggests, he now feared that his connection with poetry might romanticize his action and render it less useful, if he was willing to exchange his poetic fame for 'an equivalent renown as philanthropist and liberator' (Moore, LI, 593), we must recognize that his was no normal ambition, but rather the self-sacrifical impulse of a Socrates, or a Gandhi.

Though repudiating poetry, Byron did, according to Lady Blessington, call the whole adventure a 'scrape' caused by his 'poetical temperament' (Blessington, 317). He was right. After all, his early poetry had prepared the stage. The truth is, poetry and life were now converging. His poetic genius from the first had, as Galt puts it, 'dwelt not with airy fancies, but had its power and dominion amidst the living and the local of the actual world' (XXX). Moreover, his poetic interest in historical exactitude and realism grew steadily stronger, his poetry simultaneously becoming more thoroughly an expression of his whole self—the heroes of *Childe Harold* and the Tales were aspects only (p. 105)—till we find him asserting that he would have acted exactly as did the Doge in *Marino Faliero* (Murray, 27 Jan. 1821; V, 232). *Sardanapalus* offers a remarkable self-portrait. Meanwhile his life, always dramatic, had aspired with increasing exactitude to poetic, in his terminology philosophic (pp. 176–7), action. In the Greek Campaign, as surely as in *Sardanapalus,* life and art coalesced: his life's central purpose was compacted in both.

His later poetry is simple, lucid and pure, and his critical canons severe and classical. Now for an individual to put such poetry, the fruit of a life's drive towards uttermost sincerity involving a continual rejection of the false, the meretricious, and the spurious, into action on a world-wide scale was, admittedly, hard. Gamba notes how averse Byron was 'to every appearance of ostentation and charlatanism' (II, 59): himself neither a 'fanatic' nor a 'blind enthusiast' (I, 33), he purposed to deliver Greece from 'the hymns and elegies of fanatics and enthusiasts' into the hands of statesmen (v, 212). His own task he approached in purity of heart and humility of mind.

From the start (as before to the Neapolitan Government) he had said that he 'could not pretend to anything in a military capacity' and had not the 'presumption of the philosopher of Ephesus who lectured before Hannibal on the art of war'. What an individual foreigner might do, perhaps as a 'reporter', he would do, 'here' (i.e. Italy) 'or elsewhere' (i.e. in Greece), 'by correspondence or otherwise'. He was ready to follow 'any directions', and, 'what is more to the purpose, to contribute my own share to the expense'; but he had 'no wish either to shine or to appear officious' (Hobhouse, 7 April 1823; C, II, 254–6). That is the spirit in which he pledged himself to service. He would serve the Committee in London, 'as humbly as they please' (Kinnaird, 19 April 1823; C, II, 259). Here, as before (p. 168), he asserted his willingness to collaborate or serve *in any way whatsoever,* and to obey instructions even if against his own 'opinions' (Bowring, 12 May 1823; LJ, VI, 210). From Cephalonia, on 9 September 1823, he told Col. Napier that he knew it was 'a fool's errand from the outset', while doubting his own capacity for the kind of 'bear-taming' the mountain chieftains required, and thinking a more 'military man' would do better. But he liked the cause and would stick to it (LJ, VI, 257). Later he re-emphasized the need of a *'military* man' and urged that Col. Napier should take over the command (Hobhouse, 16 Oct., 14 Sept.; Bowring, 10 Dec.; 1823; C, II, 282, 277; LJ, VI, 282). Gamba (II, 96) asserts uncompromisingly that he had no pretensions to the military ability which Mr. Nicolson suggests that he claimed; while the type of glory Galt had in mind seems not to have occurred to him.

So we have a lonely poet-philosopher half-unwillingly dedicated to the 'bear-taming' of a chaotic and faction-torn country and the conquest of its foes; a poet-pacifist in the field; paradoxes abound. 'Oh Plato,' he wrote to Augusta, quoting Julian the Apostate with reference to the intriguing Greeks, 'what a task for a philosopher!' (12 Oct. 1823; LJ, VI, 260). Nevertheless, the poet-philosopher-pacifist was a man of cool and prolonged courage, with nerves of steel and a flair for lightning action; and he was, as Harold Nicolson tells us, eventually, at the cost of his life, successful; and successful in precisely the manner that he had himself foreseen. How, then, was it done?

In studying Byron's Greek Campaign we study Renaissance

poetry, with all its balancing of opposites, its heroic and yet Christian valuations, its humanity and creative potency, in action; and it would be hard to find a parallel. Moore (LII, 598) neatly lists his considered purposes, which we may briefly characterize as: (i) to give; (ii) to unite; (iii) to humanize.

Byron freely put his money at the service of the cause. From the start, and throughout, he was determined to do the thing 'handsomely': 'Let the Greeks but succeed, and I don't care for myself' (Kinnaird, 21 Feb. 1824; C, II, 289). He characteristically began by arranging for a supply of medical stores to be purchased and conveyed at his own expense (Hobhouse, 28 May; Kinnaird, 8 June; 1823; C, II, 261–2). Soon after we find him pouring out his fortune for Greece. He advanced £4,000 to mobilize the Greek fleet whose delay was one of the causes of his stay at Cephalonia (Bowring, 7 and 13 Dec.; Kinnaird, 23 Dec.; 1823; LJ, VI, 281–2, 286; Gamba, I, 52) and the Greek Government pressed him for more (Hancock, 17 Jan. 1824; LJ, VI, 309). At Missolonghi he financed the papers of the liberation (Gamba, II, 103). The 'primates' of Missolonghi were always pestering him for funds (Gamba, IV, 192, 196–7). When presented with the citizenship of the town, the honour involved him in more sacrifices, including the charge of fortifications (Gamba, V, 231–2). Parry (II, 40) says that he was spending about 2,000 dollars (= £400) a week in rations alone. Nor were these donations the outpourings of an inexhaustible fortune. From the start Byron's means and 'credit' were being strained with his target of £9,000 (Hobhouse, 17 April; Kinnaird, 16 June; Bowring, 7 July; 1823; C, II, 257, 264; LJ, VI, 228). He had to draw 'most formidably' on future assets:

'To say the truth, I do not grudge it now the fellows have begun to fight *again*—and still more welcome shall they be if they will go on. But they have had, or are to have, some four thousand pounds (besides some private extraordinaries for widows, orphans, refugees, and rascals of all descriptions) of mine at one "swoop"; and it is to be expected the next will be at least as much more. And how can I refuse it if they *will* fight?—and especially if I should happen ever to be in their company? I therefore request and require that you should apprise my trusty and trust-worthy trustee and banker, and crown and sheet-anchor, Douglas Kinnaird the Honourable, that he prepare all monies of mine, including the purchase money of Rochdale manor and mine income for the year ensuing, A.D. 1824, to answer, or anticipate, any orders or drafts of mine for the good cause, in good and lawful money of Great Britain, etc., etc. May you live a thousand years! which is nine hundred and ninety-nine longer than the Spanish Cortes' Constitution' (Bowring, 13 Dec. 1823; LJ, VI, 286; *Macbeth*, IV, iii).

He later told Kinnaird it was now 'in for a penny, in for a pound'; his four thousand pounds had 'got the squadron to sea'; the total account was approaching £11,000; he was maintaining 'nearly the whole machine' at his own cost; and now, even if his advances were repaid, he would devote them to the cause (Kinnaird, 23 Dec. 1823; 21 Feb., 30 March; 1824; C, II, 285, 289; LJ, VI, 329, 363). He implored Hobhouse to get Kinnaird to stretch his credits 'to the uttermost': 'Never mind *me*, so that the *cause goes on;* if that is well, all is well'(27 Dec. 1823; C, II, 286). Lord Byron, wrote Gamba, 'contributed from his own purse more than the whole government put together' (II, 96). His use of his wealth was magnanimous, uncompromising and well-directed.

The money was to come not only from his Rochdale[1] proceeds and Government Funds (Kinnaird, 21 Feb. 1824; C, II, 288), but also from royalties; and his hard bargaining with Murray since leaving England is now seen in perspective. His desire for money had never been selfish, but flowered from thought of his relatives and the general will to do 'good' (Kinnaird, 18 Jan. 1823; LJ, VI, 164). Byron hoped that high terms might be arranged for the last cantos of *Don Juan,* so that those, with his other assets, might be ready for use (Hobhouse, 17 April 1823; and see Kinnaird, 21 Feb. 1824; C, II, 257, 289). On 23 December 1823, just before leaving Cephalonia for Missolonghi, he wrote to Kinnaird hoping to get £200 or £300 for *Werner:* 'For £300 I can maintain in Greece, at more than the *fullest* pay of the Provisional Government, rations included, one hundred armed men for *three months*' (LJ, VI, 287). The despised poetry thus helped to finance this peculiarly poetic campaign, Byron's mental battle with society proving at last valid in terms of hard cash and military action. On the brink of a new age, he knew that money rivalled 'knowledge', or philosophy, as the true 'power' (Moore, 6 Feb. 1822; LJ, VI, 11). It was 'the sinews of war' (Kinnaird, 21 Feb. 1824; C, II, 289); and the desired

---

1. For the selling of Byron's Rochdale estate, see LJ, VI, 307, note; also Hobhouse, 17 April and 27 Dec.; Barry, 11 Dec.; 1823; Kinnaird, 30 March 1824; C, II, 257, 286; LJ, VI, 284, 363.

loan from London would be, internally and otherwise, no less than 'the salvation of Greece' (Gamba, I, 52).

Next, Byron laboured to unite the Greeks. Poetry, and especially dramatic poetry, is by its nature the unifier, the resolver of oppositions; and Byron, we may remember, himself compact of opposites, was also by nature and by practice the mediator (pp. 120–2). He *liked* mediating. Once at Missolonghi, after typically and of set purpose reporting to its object, in the presence of both, Parry's criticism of Prince Mavrocordato, he next proceeded, how it is hard to imagine, to reconcile the two angry men (Parry, VII, 160–2). He appears to have prided himself peculiarly on this power which his duelling acquaintances found so valuable; and perhaps that is why Galt, after asserting that such plans as Byron's to reconcile the Greek, or indeed any, factions must imply a human ignorance incredible in such a man, concludes that he was suffering from 'vanity' (XLII). If so, it was vanity of an extremely scarce and highly desirable sort.

At Cephalonia there were problems enough. Rather than involve the Ionian government[1] in an embarrassment, Byron for a while lived on his ship (Moore, LII, 595), moving later to the village Metaxata. Whilst on the island he was wooed simultaneously by rival emissaries from Colocotronis, Mavrocordato, Odysseus, Petro Bey; from Missolonghi, Anotolikon, Salamis, Gastouni, and 'the islands'; from Crete and Southern Albania and Mount Athos (Nicolson, VII, 145). To Byron it was a heavy business. 'I did not come here to join a faction, but a nation', he wrote, and it 'will require much circumspection'; other foreign helpers were leaving in disgust but, after the shackles of four centuries, one must hope that 'time and better treatment' will alter things (Journal, 28 Sept. 1823; LJ, VI, 246–7). 'No less than three parties', he told Hobhouse, 'and one conspiracy going on amongst them at this moment'; a civil war was possible; they were all trying to enlist him, but he had refused to recognize anyone but the Government, 'without reference to the *persons*' composing it, avoiding all 'private preferences of individuals'. He did not, however, despond, though the Greeks clearly needed a 'police force' for themselves as much as an 'army' for the enemy. Himself a 'peaceable man', he had, he says, kept his patience, though it was nearing exhaustion (Hobhouse, 27 Sept., 6 Oct.; 1823; C, II, 277–80). When he offered 1,000 dollars a month for the succour of Missolonghi, the government

1. For the 'United States of the Ionian Islands' under British protection, see Nicolson, VI, 114.

suspiciously hinted at other uses for the money; government and opposition each warned him against the other; he determined not to let go a penny except for the cause, while asserting his will to reconciliation (Barry, 25 Oct. 1823; LJ, VI, 268). Again, 'If I can but succeed in reconciling the two parties (and I have left no stone unturned there*for*) it will be something' (Kinnaird, 23 Dec. 1823; C, II, 286).

At Cephalonia Kennedy warned him that his 'name' and 'money' would inevitably drag him into public life and repellent scenes. What was needed was a 'sort of Buonaparte' who would 'compel obedience by awe and terror', rather than a soft-hearted man like Byron. Byron, says Kennedy (who took all Byron's answers at their face value), replied humbly that he knew well how his 'weak side' would be discovered and preyed on, until he was squeezed dry (Kennedy, 215–16). But the reference to Napoleon would have stirred him; not to emulate the master at his game, but to pit his own, different, poetic, mastery against the odds. He knew his Christian weakness; he knew the boy Botzaris would despise his humanity (p. 72); and that a poet-philosopher was scarcely the person for such 'bears' (p. 184). Nevertheless, he remained rocklike. If he found he could do no good 'in allaying the animosities' and restoring 'unanimity', he would come back (Kennedy, 247). His main purpose was clear.

Such is the context for his remarkable 'public letter to the general government of Greece'. Since he had been declared the official representative of the English and German Committees (i.e. of the European interest generally), a letter was judged proper. On 30 November 1823 he wrote from Cephalonia, saying that without union all hopes of a loan would be vain and Europe write off Greece as incapable of self-government:

'Allow me to add, once for all—I desire the well-being of Greece, and nothing else; I will do all I can to secure it; but I cannot consent, I never will consent, that the English public, or English individuals, should be deceived as to the real state of Greek affairs. The rest, Gentlemen, depends on you. You have fought gloriously; act honourably towards your fellow-citizens and the world; and it will then no more be said, as has been repeated for two thousand years with the Roman historians, that Philopoemen was the last of the Grecians. Let not calumny itself (and it is difficult, I own, to guard against it in so arduous a struggle) compare the patriot Greek, when resting from his labours, to the Turkish Pasha, whom his victories have exterminated' (LJ, VI, 278).

In another letter to Prince Mavrocordato, on 2 December 1823, he urged that Greece had three choices: liberty, European dependence, and Turkish slavery. 'If she is desirous of the fate of Walachia and the Crimea, she may obtain it tomorrow; if of that of Italy, the day after; but if she wishes to become truly Greece, free and independent, she must resolve today, or she will never again have the opportunity' (LJ, VI, 279).

These letters alone suffice to discredit the complaint concerning Byron's delay at Cephalonia. Had he not learned in Italy the folly of national action without national unity? Gamba's letters to Teresa, written from the seat of action, emphasize the difficulties being faced: delay was dictated by 'the most profound policy' (26-9 Nov.; see also 8 Oct.; 1823; Origo, IX, 369, 362). Byron was not idle, but rather kept busy by a stream of visitors soliciting his personal attention (Teresa, 29 Nov. 1823; postscript to Gamba's letter; Origo, IX, 370). From these visitors he was gaining invaluable information on which, when the time came, to act.

At one time he planned to approach the central government in person, hoping, with his old confidence as mediator, that his influence on the spot might produce 'a general reconciliation' (Gamba, I, 51); and when he arrived at Missolonghi, it was felt that his presence alone was preventing civil war (Gamba, II, 90-1). His position was delicate and difficult, but his chosen part of reconciler would, says Gamba, be 'the most glorious that a stranger could attempt to perform'. Intrigues were alien to his character; but 'now it was that we all saw the advantage derived from his protracted residence in the Ionian Islands'; he and the Greeks had got to know each other, and his influence accordingly grown (Gamba, II, 93). That is true. When the chieftain Sessini asked him to settle his differences with the Government, Byron consented to act as mediator, though with a characteristic caution demanding the surrender of a fortress as proof of sincerity (Gamba, V, 205-6; see also *Westminster Review*, Medwin, App., lvi). A Greek partisan Parucca, who had been formerly engaged to thwart the Greek deputies sent to London, later asked Byron 'to assist in bringing about an union of all parties'. Byron's answer was noble, courteous and judicial; if, without prejudicing his obligation to the centre, he could serve any purpose 'either as a mediator, or, if necessary, as a hostage', he was willing to do so (Gamba, V, 207-9). The powerful Colocotronis and his followers, while suggesting terms of agreement with the Government, 'wished his Lordship to come into the Morea, and were willing to submit themselves to his judgment' (Gamba, v, 217–18). Gamba's testimony witnesses that Byron's considered technique—cut short by his death—was basically sound; and that Galt's and Kennedy's fears as to the impossibility of peaceful reconciliation were not. Byron himself played, with far more success than could reasonably be expected, his part of 'bear-tamer'; he had done so, from youth, with his pet beasts (pp. 4–5). He could do it because, in the depths, he liked them; even liked, whilst deploring all cruel deeds, their ferocity; just as he could reconcile duellers through his very acceptance of duelling.

He was not, however, only concerned with patching up quarrels. In working for 'the peaceful submission of the factions' he planned to organize a 'national party' able to resist the foe; but he also aimed by strengthening the 'legislative body' to 'lay the foundations' of those institutions which might 'confirm the freedom and independence of Greece'. 'This', says Gamba, 'was the aim of Lord Byron: *to this were directed all his actions*'; and he was about to succeed when he died (Gamba, II, 94–5; italics mine). Nor was his interest confined to long-range politics in dissociation from economics. He felt that a 'strong national Government' could only succeed if 'means were found to put into circulation the great natural resources of the country'. For that the Loan was needed, and meanwhile he tried to rouse a 'public spirit' and organize the 'requisite government'. *'The enterprise against Lepanto, and all the other occupations on which we saw him intent at Missolonghi, were only of a secondary interest, although momentous in themselves, and tended only to his great object'* (Gamba, II, 96–7; italics mine).

Byron was working in the tradition of his own poetry, so deeply witnessing, from the early *Childe Harold* to the late *Age of Bronze*, the consistent will to make of nations free people worthy of freedom; the will to *raise* each with regard to its own highest traditions; the will to make of them—as of individuals (pp. 53–74)—the best that it was in them to be. He was therefore out less to conquer Turks than to *remake* Greece. Without that, he saw conquest as scarcely possible and dubiously desirable. No solution to anything could exist, to him, on the purely Napoleonic plane. Poetry, it has been said, exists not to save souls, but to make them worth saving; translate this into statesmanship, and you have Byron's idea.

Shortly before his death, on 11 March 1824, he discussed with

Gamba the prospects of the Greeks. Unity seemed near; the approach of danger was likely to help; his own confidence, shown by enlisting their fellow-countrymen as his personal guards—a typical stroke of human understanding and leadership—had borne fruit. If only the Greek deputies to London had moved sooner, all might have been well. He considered the height to which Greece might rise, from the sphere of poetics and fanaticism to that of practical politics, whilst observing with a hard-headed realism that the European situation, the selfish interests and rivalries of the great nations, was in her favour. He remarked that her soil was good for crops. He saw a 'vacuum' to be filled at this corner of the world, with Greece rising as Turkey declined. He had hopes of Canning, and thought England, 'no longer infected with the mania of adding to her colonies', might soon realize that *her true interests are inseparably con-nected with the independence of those nations who have shown themselves worthy of emancipation*' (Gamba, v, 211–14; italics mine).

There was heroism in Byron's adventure, but the heroism was no less than the diplomatic ability and statesmanlike, and even— as, in our last quotation—prophetic, wisdom shown. When it was known that an English nobleman of fame and wealth had arrived at Cephalonia, every means, direct and indirect, were employed to solicit his attention and tap his bank-balance. 'He occupied him-self', says Gamba, 'in discovering the truth, hidden as it was under these intrigues, and amused himself in confronting the agents of the different factions' (Gamba, I, 39). Often Byron appears, like a dramatist, to be *above* the parties surrounding him (see pp. 171, 197).

His incisive penetration of human sincerity, so evident in his work and emphasized by Lady Blessington and Teresa (61; 11; XIII, 281, 294; see pp. 268–9), made him a natural diplomatist. His primary difficulty, says Moore, was to distinguish what was real from what was 'merely apparent' in the political situation (LII, 596). Count Delladecima told Kennedy that Byron throughout 'shewed a profound, cool, and deliberate judgment', together with patience, sound political wisdom, and sympathy; which he thought surprising enough in one whom you would expect to be 'full of imaginary and fanciful schemes' and 'fickle and changeable in his judgment'. On the subject of the regeneration and independence of Greece, Byron was, of all people he had met, the most sensitive and wise (Kennedy, 305). The Count need not have been surprised: from youth up-wards, as in the early notes to *Childe Harold,* Byron's judgments of peoples and nations showed the gravity and acumen of an experienced statesman. In such matters there was in him 'not a tinge of the unsubstantial or speculative' (Moore, LIV, 620). On 24 May 1824, Blacquière wrote that all Byron's letters on the Greek question had been deeply judicious and diplomatically tactful, showing a most thorough knowledge of the people (Edgcumbe, I, XVI, 199). Of his final decision to identify himself with Mavrocordato, Harold Nicolson observes that 'the subsequent history of the Greek War of Independence proves the wisdom of this decision' (X, 244). The 'coolness, foresight and self-possession' noted by Moore (LII, 596) must accordingly be contrasted with the flashy expectations of superficial admirers. Byron was known by his contemporaries to be, potentially, a national and international power demanding respect; society had been stunned by his impact; England, France and Italy had, in turn, feared his presence. London wanted to hear of him leading a cavalry charge to victory; instead, there was little news-value in what he did—who could possibly regard the saving of Turkish prisoners as of any real importance?—and, as Nicolson says, apparent, though surely not 'humiliating', failure. In the New Testament likewise we find expectancy of strong action similarly, and for much the same reasons, disappointed; but in both instances the creative result in its own good time matures. How today does Byron's careful diagnosis of Greece's conditions and prospects, and his will on every front to regeneration, conciliation and synthesis, compare with Kennedy's demand for a Napoleon, ruthlessly suppressing disorder? Or the suggestion that he should arbitrate between the military chieftain Colocotronis and Prince Mavrocordato, not as 'a simple mediator' but 'avec une main de fer'? (Westminster Review, Medwin, App., xxxvi—a good account). How could a newly-arrived stranger, however extraordinary his powers and prowess, have immediately set about bloodily uniting a divided nation as a preliminary to forcing it to fight an external war for its own sake? Col. Napier told Trelawny that no less than two European regiments and a portable gallows could do any good (Trelawny, XXII). By his personal exertions Byron, in the three months allowed him before his death, all but succeeded without either. More, his actions, no less than his words to Gamba, serve to define the long-range policy at its best of Great Britain during the centuries to follow. In answering Trelawny's complaints regarding Byron's stay at Cephalonia—'Had I gone sooner', wrote Byron, 'they would have forced me into one party or other' (Bowring, 7 Dec. 1823; LJ, VI, 282)—Drinkwater exactly defines the nature of his approach throughout: 'It was in fact the careful rhythm of a real statesmanship that was quite beyond Trelawny's intelligence' (VI, 369).[1]

Naturally therefore Byron was deceived by no catchwords of 'liberty' and 'freedom'. We have seen what he thought of extreme radicalism at home. As he told Parry (IX, 204), he was neither a 'leveller' nor an 'infidel'. He was consequently brought into conflict with Col. Stanhope, a man of extreme libertarian tenets and a child-like faith in reason, print and propaganda, concerning the *Greek Chronicle*. Byron, who was in part financing the paper, wished it to avoid personal attacks which in an unsettled society with no proper laws would only lead to assassinations and feuds; and also unnecessary insults to the great powers which might be in a position to influence the destiny of Greece; but Stanhope, who believed in the invincibility of reason, urged the value of an 'unlimited liberty' (Gamba, II, 102–3). He claimed that little more was needed than the reading of Bentham throughout Greece; the literature once distributed, he said, 'conviction follows' (Stanhope to Bowring, 24 June 1823; Edgcumbe, I, IX, 108); while forgetting, as Harold Nicolson neatly observes (X, 240), that most of the Greek public could not read. Once accused by Stanhope after a fiery argument of being an enemy to freedom, Byron asked where, without his money, 'would your Greek newspaper be?'—and concluded with the trenchant: 'Judge of me by my actions, not by my words' (Gamba, III, 140). He certainly admired Stanhope, as he did the Hunt brothers, for his integrity and sincerity, but he could also write ironically of the Swiss Dr. Meyer, to whom Stanhope gave the editorship of the *Chronicle,* as a 'petty tyrant' like 'most demagogues' enjoying 'the freedom to exercise an unlimited discretion' (Barff, 19 March 1824; LJ, VI, 355). When a number of the *Chronicle* appeared attacking monarchy in general and the Austrian despotism in particular, Byron suppressed the issue; but the prospectus of the new *Greek Telegraph* definitely served, according to Millingen, to damage the interests of Greece with the Ionian (i.e. the British) Government and the Austrian States (LJ, VI, 355, note; Edgcumbe, I, IX, 112–14; Nicolson, X, 240–1). Byron did what he could to modify Stanhope's policy, significantly choosing as a motto for the *Telegraph* Homer's 'When man falls into slavery he loses the half of every virtue' (Gamba, V, 211).

Byron was himself concentrating less on liberty than on right,

1. For a neat treatment of Byron's problems in face of the factions, see the *Westminster Review* account given in the Appendix to Medwin's *Conversations.*

justice and acts of humanity; and also, throughout, on common sense. When a conflict arose between the Greeks of Missolonghi and Captain Yorke of the *Alacrity* concerning a breach of international law in the taking of an Ionian ship, he appeared, to Stanhope's disgust, as a supporter of British interest. He aimed both to do his duty by the law and also to save the Greeks from trouble with England, since he knew that the British Government would not give way (Gamba, III, 135–9; Parry, X, 233). Captain Yorke demanded reparation; Mavrocordato's reluctant promise to pay within eight days was refused; so was Byron's offer to advance the sum, though he managed to pay it surreptitiously through a Greek official (Gamba, III, 139). As elsewhere, he functioned as both mediator and source of wealth, as—to quote Mrs. Shelley's ungainly but telling word (p. 66)—everyone's 'prop'.

Meanwhile he risked appearing reactionary to some of his hotheaded companions. He knew the Greeks were wild and uncivilized, and that 'time' was necessary for their proper self-government: 'It will take', he said, 'a century to come to change their character' (Parry, VIII, 183; and see 172–3). He saw men like Stanhope as hopelessly astray: 'He is like all political jobbers, who mistake the accessories of civilization for its cause; they think if they only hoist the colours of freedom, they will immediately transform a crazy water-logged bark into a proud man-of-war' (Parry, IX, 190). But the *imposing* of a system was as bad as the encouragement of anarchy: 'We who come here to fight for Greece have no right to meddle with its internal affairs or dictate to the people or government' (Parry, VIII, 181); again, 'I came here to serve the Greeks on their own conditions and in their own way' (Parry, VIII, 181, note). If Greece be liberated he would 'leave the Greeks to settle their government as they like' (Parry, VIII, 184). Greece must choose for herself; but it must *be* Greece, not a faction, that chooses. Any sound order must be an organic growth. 'There is no abstract form of government which we can call good. I won't say with Pope, "Whate'er is best administer'd is best"; but I will say, that every government derives its efficiency as well as its power from the people.' It must not be the prerogative of a single class; moreover, true freedom demands effort; it cannot flourish without continual watchfulness to 'prevent both individual and general encroachment' (Parry, VIII, 174–5). Therefore, though he himself would defend England's 'ancient and honourable aristocracy' with his life, he did not necessarily recommend her constitution to another country, suggesting as a better model for Greece the new system of America (Parry, VIII, 174). He advised, however, against any alignment with revolutionary movements elsewhere in Europe lest she risk the enmity of 'one of the two great parties that at present divide the civilized world'. Instead, he would officially define the present contest as one 'between barbarism and civilization', or as between 'Islamism' and 'Christianity'; or again, as a struggle on behalf of the nation which gave Europe its science and art (Gamba, V, 210; Parry, VIII, 170); a struggle, we may say, for the European tradition.

Throughout these discussions as reported by Gamba and Parry Byron's political and cultural insight appears truly impressive. Neither in thought nor in action would he take the easy, the spectacular, partisan, course; in both he remained balanced, comprehensive and holistic. He worked creatively, poetically, dramatically, in terms not of any negative but of a supreme positive compounded of opposing negations; and such creative, poetic, positives—as St. Paul, Milton, Nietzsche and many another great prophet have found—are always far harder to define than the lesser contraries in isolation; and yet harder to put into practice. Parry aptly observed that Byron's general aims, his creative planning, for Greece were impossibly high and demanded, as Moore also observed (LII, 597; p. 182), a succession of wise men for their completion. Immediate success was unlikely: Byron's statesmanship was essentially a long-range and creative statesmanship. Nevertheless, the 'chimerical' nature of his 'poetical mind' was, says Parry, however ambitious it might seem, superior to the lower, rationalistic, approach. He adopted 'a much more likely method to succeed than those who drew up constitutions and codes for Greece' (V, 130–1). That is, when direct military action was not in question, poetic (i.e. creative) planning and action were superior to a rationalist propaganda.

It must not, however, be supposed that Byron's thoughts were limited to such long-range creative plans. He was in Greece to fight, and knew it. He could even say, when irritated at the supplies (e.g. bugles and mathematical instruments) sent out by the London Committee, 'we must conquer first and plan afterwards' (Bowring, 26 Dec. 1823; LJ, VI, 293). 'It is odd enough', he once remarked, 'that Stanhope, the soldier, is all for writing down the Turks; and I, the writer, am all for fighting them down' (Gamba, III, 138). His letters show military grip and gusto (e.g. Kinnaird, 23 Dec. 1823; C, II, 285). He willed to remove 'discord' precisely because he was not satisfied with the 'petite guerre' of local defences and trivial captures, but aimed rather at a full-scale 'offensive' (Bowring, 10 Dec. 1823; LJ, VI, 283). At Missolonghi he planned the attack on Lepanto, though here again, according to Gamba, he regarded the chief advantage of the enterprise as the employment of idle soldiers and the attainment of mutual confidence. 'The chieftains appeared very eager to undertake this enterprise under the orders of Lord Byron; and Mavrocordato was persuaded that their irregular troops would more willingly obey him than any Greek, or any other foreigner.' Byron, says Gamba, did not claim military skill, but had the necessary courage and energy to control 'undisciplined forces'; and also the money. 'The peril, the difficulty and the sacrifices' would all be his; and so he undertook the command (Gamba, II, 95–6). 'The garrison consisted of 500 Turks, and a considerable number of Albanians,' the latter being, it was said, willing to surrender on receiving their arrears of pay, amounting to 23,000 dollars (*Westminster Review,* Medwin, App., lvii). Byron's comment on the Government's offer of the command ran: 'Though my desires are as far as my deserts upon this occasion, I do not decline it, being willing to do as I am bidden; and as I pay a considerable part of the clans, I may as well see what they are likely to do for their money; besides, I am tired of hearing nothing but talk' (Jan. 1824; *Westminster Review,* Medwin, App., lviii). However, the unruly behaviour of the intractable Suliotes 'put an end to the enterprise'; they preferred a target of more 'booty' and less 'stone walls'. Byron admitted that he seemed to have lost 'time, money, patience and health', but said that he was 'prepared for it'; he expected no 'path of roses', and was ready for 'deception and calumny and ingratitude'. Though weakening, he refused to leave the feverous Missolonghi for his health; he had not come for 'tranquillity', and had been 'neither undeceived nor discouraged'. The Lepanto enterprise was *secondary;* his primary aim was to test the soldiers, and that point had been attained. Now more waiting was necessary. He started forthwith to fortify Missolonghi—Kennedy (306) tells us that these fortifications made at Byron's expense were later of great value—and initiated a training course for regular troops under European officers (Gamba, IV, 191–4). If a large body of regulars could not be created, the number was to be made up by 'undisciplined forces', so that he 'could take the field with them in the spring', a nucleus of regulars serving as a pattern. Artillery was reorganized and exercised (Gamba, IV, 195–7). Byron's great object throughout was to prepare for use of the London Loan by 'internal organization and arrangements for offensive warfare'; and when, on 22 March, news of the Loan being granted came through, he advised the Government through Mavrocordato to mobilize the fleet (Gamba, v, 225).

But what of Byron's loathing of war as expressed in *Childe Harold, Don Juan* and *Sardanapalus?* We have seen him as an enthusiastic marksman who consistently, at the risk of ridicule (p. 107), refused living targets; as a man of honour fiery to resent a slight, who yet never actually seems to have avenged one; as a duellist whose duelling appears to have been confined to the mediation of others' quarrels. Though he regularly went armed and kept pistols by him at night, there seems to be no record whatever of his ever having drawn human blood. His regular practice was that of pacifier, or peace-maker; and yet for the peace-maker, as opposed to the pacifist, the battlefield is, after all, the best possible, indeed the only proper, place. In Byron, personifying as he does the best traditions of classic and Renaissance poetry, admiration of military prowess was joined to detestation of war. War itself he never rejected absolutely; not, that is, in a pure cause (*Don Juan,* IX, 4); a cause on behalf of the human essence, of, we might suggest, peace itself, properly understood. He therefore wars poetically; he, the pacifier, so regularly *above* and containing any opposition, wars on both sides at once. As drama contains and transcends its own opposites, so Byron acts, as near as may be, dramatically, overstanding, not only the Greek factions, but the whole conflict, like a Colossus. He loved Turkish history from youth (p. 19; Gamba, III, 149). His notes to *Childe Harold (II)* witness his general respect for the Turks (p. 180), whom he rated as high as the Greeks, or higher (Kennedy, 246), having a great respect for their military efficiency (Medwin, 285–6), though he could also call them 'barbarians' for their cruelty (Stanhope, 31 Dec. 1823; LJ, VI, 297). Moreover, he certainly *was* the soft-hearted man Kennedy feared would prove incapable; he knew well that the boy Botzaris would scorn his squeamishness (Kennedy, 245); but he was also the rock-like and astute diplomatist and leader, whom no factions could mould and no incompetence or treachery discourage. What was the result in practice of these unusual combinations?

Byron had already showed a concern for the possible sufferings of his Austrian foes (p. 171). At Ravenna he had done his best for the dying commandant (p. 119), and was ready to use his influence with the revolutionaries on such enemy officers' behalf (Murray, 14 Dec. 1820; LJ, V, 139). Now, when first setting out

for Greece, one of his *primary* purposes was the alleviation of all
unnecessary suffering on *both* sides and, in general, the *humanizing
of the war*. One may well doubt if such has ever, before or since,
been a declared and central purpose of a prospective commander.

From the start he continued his life-long policy of relieving
distress. Whilst at Cephalonia, he thought of going personally to
Constantinople to redeem some Greek captives whom he had promised their families in Genoa to help, but was dissuaded from the
attempt (Kennedy, 296). Gamba describes how at Ithaca his 'generous disposition' assisted a number of—in Byron's words—'widows,
orphans, refugees, and rascals of all descriptions' (Bowring, 13 Dec.
1823; LJ, VI, 286) and in particular rehabilitated one family, giving
them a house at Cephalonia and a monthly allowance (Gamba, I,
28, 45; see also Kennedy, 303; Moore, LII, 595–6; Journal, 28 Sept.;
Capt. Knox, 26 Aug.; Hobhouse, 11 Sept.; 1823; LJ, VI, 244–5,
256; C, II, 275). 'Knowing and relieving the distressed', said Millingen, 'were with him simultaneous actions' (Edgcumbe, I, X, 135).
Even when he dismissed his factious and maddening Suliotes, he
continued to support their families (Gamba, IV, 171; see also V, 203).
But even more striking was his consideration for enemy sufferers.
'If I go there', he had written to Hobhouse on 17 April 1823, 'I
shall do my best to civilize their mode of treating their prisoners;
and could I only save a single life, whether Turk or Greek, I should
live "mihi carior", and I trust not less so to my friends' (C, II, 258).
'The first measures which his Lordship attempted after his arrival'—
that is, at Missolonghi—says Galt, 'were to mitigate the ferocity with
which the war was carried on; one of the objects, as he explained to
my friend who visited him at Genoa, which induced him to embark
in the cause' (XLIV). 'One of his first objects', wrote Gamba to
Kennedy, on 21 May 1824, 'was to inspire both parties with more
humane sentiments' (Kennedy, App., 383; Galt, XLIV). Soon after
his arrival at Missolonghi he seized, as Gamba says, 'the first opportunity' of advancing this, one of his 'principal objects', by rescuing
and taking to his own house a captured Turk (Gamba, III, 107);
and later, in return for the kind treatment of Gamba and others of
Byron's friends who had fallen into Turkish hands on the voyage,
sent this Turk with three more to Yussuf Pasha, writing, on 23
January 1824, that, though no conditions were suggested, he hoped
that his action might be reciprocated by an equivalent consideration
to Greek prisoners, 'since the horrors of war are sufficiently great in
themselves, without being aggravated by wanton cruelties on either

side' (LJ, vi, 313). Later, he sent over twenty prisoners, long held at Missolonghi without 'means of support and the consolations of their home', to the English Consul at Prevesa, with the words: 'Coming to Greece, one of my principal objects was to alleviate as much as possible the miseries incident to a warfare so cruel as the present. When the dictates of humanity are in question, I know no difference between Turks and Greeks. It is enough that those who want assistance are men, in order to claim the pity and protection of the meanest pretender to humane feelings' (Mayer, undated, LJ, vi, 328; Gamba, iv, 181; Kinnaird, 21 Feb. 1824; C, ii, 289). This was done shortly after his epileptic seizure. When complexities and disasters were crowding round him, Gamba, on 24 February, told Kennedy that 'My lord employs all his influence to inspire the Greeks with more Christian and humane sentiments even towards their enemies' (Kennedy, App., 354). When at last a chance of action presented itself with the stranding of a Turkish brig, he thought immediately—at the cost, clearly, of both hampering and alienating his soldiers—of the enemy, promising a reward for every Turk captured alive (Gamba, iv, 186). 'His Lordship,' says Parry, 'with that active attention to humanity which characterized all his proceedings in Greece, gave me strict injunctions, should any prisoners be taken, to endeavour to save their lives' (Parry, iii, 53–4). Parry also describes the saving of twenty-four prisoners, mostly women and children, presumably those already mentioned. They were brought before Byron, who was seated Oriental-fashion on a cushion. 'After a short time it was evident that what Lord Byron was hearing affected his feelings; his countenance changed, his colour went and came, and I thought he was ready to weep.' He tried to hide his emotion by talking to the interpreter; but when the women came in turn, with their children, to kiss his hand and invoke a blessing on him for his protection, uncontrollable emotion forced him to turn away (Parry, vii, 163–4). Too easily, says Parry, we forget the 'generosity' that strove to relieve every 'want' and 'woe' in turn, and the 'humanity' which made him 'sacrifice time and money and ease to soothe the sorrows of the unhappy prisoners' (Parry, x, 261). Of Byron's care for the little Turkish prisoner, Hato, we have already (pp. 77–8) written. His command was, indeed, characterized by an emotional regard for the enemy surely unique in military history.

Such actions were liable to reduce Byron's influence over the wild tribes under his control. He had arrived among them with an extraordinary reputation, and was using up capital of greatest importance. Harshness is understood and often admired; such mercy is rarely understood and likely to raise suspicion. In allegiance to his own instincts, and in direct descent from the moral courage of his refusal to shoot living game with the Gambas (p. 107), Byron took, successfully, these risks, pursuing one undeviating course mapped from the start. He was thus a fighter both in and above the fight; a commander who cares, father-like, for the enemy; one who would rather fight mercifully than fight successfully.

Equally significant was Byron's humane treatment of those directly or indirectly under his command, as with the six British artificers who said they had never bargained for the turbulent atmosphere of Missolonghi, and insisted on leaving. Byron, to whom their demand for absolute safety must have been maddening, arranged for their passage home, while giving orders for an allowance 'to purchase them some little extras as comforts', adding with exquisite understanding and chivalry, 'as they are quite out of their element' (Barff, 21 Feb.; Murray, 25 Feb.; Moore, 4 March; Kennedy, 4 and 10 March; 1824; LJ, VI, 327, 334, 338, 339, 349; Gamba, IV, 194; Parry, III, 64–7; IV, 69).

Our last example is perhaps the most important of all. All Byron is in it. He had always hated severe punishments. Once, meditating on an execution, he said that he would not attend unless there were a chance of saving the victim, adding: 'It is detestable to take life in that way, unless it be to preserve two lives' (*Detached Thoughts,* Oct. 1821; LJ, V, 439). He did not wish offenders against himself punished (Murray, 9 Dec. 1816; LJ, IV, 21); and we may recall his instructions to Hoppner regarding a man whom he had helped, but who had subsequently robbed him: 'If he is in prison, let him out; if he is not, put him in for a week' (Hoppner's Account; LJ, IV, 388–9, note). Such personal sentiments, as sentiments, are not unusual, but they fail before the harsh and impersonal necessities of government. Now Byron at Missolonghi held—mainly by force of his own personality—supreme power, pretty nearly, in his turbulent little community, and at once proceeded to show that such humane sentiments could be practised.

His dislike of corporal punishment rings in his writing off Stanhope's educational schemes as a plan 'for whipping little boys in the newest and most approved mode' (Parry, IX, 189). So, when a Greek soldier was convicted of theft and the German officers urged that he should be flogged, a procedure not within the French military code officially followed by the Greek legislature, the punishment was 'flatly opposed' by Lord Byron, who declared that, as far as he was concerned, 'no barbarous usages, *however adopted even by some civilized people*' (i.e. by the British, etc; italics mine), 'should be introduced into Greece'; especially as 'such a mode of punishment would disgust rather than reform'. A reformative punishment was eventually devised aiming at rousing the thief's sense of disgrace, whilst suiting military discipline; 'but it required not only all Lord Byron's eloquence, but his authority, to prevail upon our Germans to accede to it'. Such an example of 'severity tempered by a humane spirit' produced an excellent effect on soldiers and townsfolk alike; but it led to more trouble. High words that evening passed between three Englishmen, two of them officers, cards were exchanged, and two duels arranged for the morning. After an exhausting day Byron, whose own health was now rapidly failing, heard of this new trouble late at night, had them promptly arrested, and, after considerable difficulty, prevailed on them, in his old manner, to shake hands. Such an example from English officers would have been disgraceful indeed in a community already only too fractious (Gamba, v, 228–30).

Byron's actions on this occasion showed clearly that his general will to persuasion held no weakness, that Kennedy's Napoleon and Napier's 'portable gallows' were rejected on principle. He had merely to let the punishment go ahead; an example was certainly needed in his fierce and fractious community. Instead, he showed a superb moral courage, acting strongly, dictatorially and unpopularly, in the cause of a softness and a humanity that must have appeared to the Prussian officers an inexplicable weakness. Notice Byron's (i) insistence on respect to a high compulsion of honour and justice, here the exact observance of the French Code; (ii) his will, once again, to re-create, not demolish, the person (or nation), to preserve and nurture the subject's self-respect; (iii) his being ahead of his time (as with his speeches in the Lords, his support of the Italian *risorgimento,* and his later poetry, *Cain* and *Don Juan,* regarded *then* as devilish, but approved now), since severe floggings were normal in the services of 'civilized countries'; (iv) his resulting unpopularity and the raising of evil passions in others; and (v) his final function as mediator and peace-maker. These are, with variations, usual Byronic patterns. He was himself gratified by his success, telling Kinnaird on 30 March, and Barff on 3 April, noting the arrest of a Prussian officer, and saying that anger was high, 'but I stuck to my intent' (1824; LJ, VI, 364, 369). As with his joint hatred and acceptance of war, this was no other-worldly idealism— the man *was* punished—but rather an interpenetration of social necessity by an individual sensibility.

IV

At Missolonghi we watch an individual pitting his best wisdom and conscience against the inertia of custom and the mass of governmental brutality, whether in peace or in war. He was opposing all those evils which the individual deplores but the man as a social creature agrees to; at once facing and redeeming the antagonism of Christian ethic and human justice dramatized in *Measure for Measure*. He was acting as an individual in matters usually left to committees and communities.

We have already (pp. 136–8) found Byron sick of politics; that is, of group-action; and consequently driven back on his admiration for the man of personal power, Napoleon. Parry says that his political antipathies never sprang from dislike of any particular system, but rather from actual and *personal* experiences of 'injustice, cruelty, and oppression'; and that he specifically dissociated himself from 'theory' (Parry, IX, 211). He neither attacked nor wholeheartedly supported any theory; but rejected nearly all systems *in practice*. We have seen (p. 194) how he quoted, and was not far from subscribing to, Pope's

> For Forms of Government let fools contest;
> Whate'er is best administer'd is best
> > (*Essay on Man*, III, 303.)

Such 'administering' must be a highly personal matter; and so we find Byron injecting, time and again, his own personal, and that is poetic, powers into the harsh world of communal action, of politics: he would, as a man, master Leviathan. He once saw himself as an individual 'playing at Nations' rather than gaming, racing, or dining out (Kinnaird, 23 Dec. 1823; C, II, 286). He, and others, were aware of his essentially lonely battle. 'If I fall', he had written to Hodgson as early as 25 September 1811, 'I shall fall gloriously, fighting against a host' (LJ, II, 47). From the start of the Greek adventure he was willing to do all that an 'individual' could (Hobhouse, 7 April; Kinnaird, 8 June; 1823; C, II, 254, 263). Again, 'In the meantime, I stand paymaster, and what not; and lucky it is, that from the nature of the warfare and of the country, the resources even of an individual can be of a partial and temporary service' (Kinnaird, 23 Dec. 1823; C, II, 285). 'How seldom', wrote Gamba, could it have happened that 'an independent and disinterested stranger' exercised 'so beneficent and powerful an influence for the salvation of an oppressed people' (II, 93–4).

Now since it was all an intensely personal, poetic, matter, since the way, the doing, was, as suggested by Pope, at least as important as the thing done; and since, too, the rationalization of Byron's actions, abounding as they do in poetic paradox, was extremely hard; it is accordingly necessary to scrutinize not merely his deeds, but the *spirit* of his approach. The poetic analogy is here close; in poetry the style or manner often appears to take precedence over, indeed to *be,* the thing said; so, too, in Byron's actions, the end appears to be subservient to the means. In examining his personality in action, we find it characterized by (i) self-discipline, (ii) patience, and (iii) courage.

He approached his task in deadly earnest. 'From this time forward', writes the Editor of *Correspondence,* 'there is little of the banter and recklessness which characterize his earlier letters' (C, II, 248). 'He carefully avoided every appearance of ostentation, and had a great dread of being taken for a searcher after adventures' (Gamba, I, 35–6; also II, 59). He had no desire to 'shine', wishing to contribute 'without *éclat*' (Hobhouse, 7 April; Earl of Blessington, 23 April; 1823; C, II, 255; LJ, VI, 196). He showed remarkable self-discipline. Though for years he had written late into the morning and risen late in the day, he now, regularly, rose early (Moore, LII, 599; Gamba, I, 45). He had practised abstinence in food often enough, and now of set purpose and on principle limited himself, even when his health was failing, to the rations of a Suliote soldier. He 'submitted', says Parry, who describes his daily routine for us, 'to live on the coarsest and meanest fare', being ready, 'like some general of old Rome, to share the privations of the meanest soldier' (Parry, IV, 79; Gamba, IV, 177; also I, 45–6, IV, 197). In Ithaca he risked positively harmful food with a view to conditioning himself for active service (Mr. S——, quoted Edgcumbe, I, V, 54; see p. 275). He also accustomed himself to cold (Hancock, 7 Feb. 1824; LJ, VI, 318). His own quarters were miserable; he died in what Harold Nicolson calls a 'dark and squalid' room (XI, 254). He was always ready, as we shall see (p. 210), to show a lead by engaging in manual labour. 'Here again', writes Parry, with reference to the

training of the European officers, 'he set an admirable example':
he 'submitted to be drilled with them', and went himself through
all the exercises (IV, 80). 'I should be perfectly ready', he said—and
had said as much from the start, here as in Italy—'to serve as a
common soldier, under any body, if it be thought of any good to
the cause' (Gamba, IV, 162). Parry might be speaking of our own
time when he suggests that 'the people of England, who have been
amused by the records of some trifling peculiarities of Lord Byron,
little know to what privations and sacrifices he submitted to from
the cause of the Greeks'; beyond all ideals of pen and theory, he
gave, by his own submission and endurance, such proofs of devotion
'as no other man in this age and country has given' (Parry, II, 36;
IV, 79–80).

His self-control was noteworthy: he deliberately laboured to
acquire a prudence beyond his past attainment (Gamba, I, 35).
His bearing was remarkable for both prudence and—though his
temperament found it hard (Edgcumbe, I, VIII, 94)—patience. Here
are some of the trials he had to endure. The disorderly Suliote
soldiers who had originally wished him to direct them (Bowring,
7 Dec.; Journal, 17 Dec.; 1823; LJ, VI, 251, 282) and whose
bravery he respected, proved impossible. They were not only fractious, but also dishonest, their pay-roll being made out three times
their real strength to increase the revenue of their chief (Gamba, IV,
165–6). When Byron was planning the attack on Lepanto, one of
them, a spy of Colocotronis and a man whose family Byron had
previously assisted, intrigued to upset the scheme, with the result
that out of three or four hundred soldiers they demanded com-
missioned rank, with pay, for one hundred and fifty, including
two generals. The Suliotes were so completely unreliable that the
Lepanto scheme was discontinued (Gamba, IV, 167–73). Half an
hour after Byron's seizure, an alarm was raised of a Suliote insurrection, originating from two drunken Germans who broke into his
room (Gamba, IV, 178–9). A week later a German or Swedish
officer, Sasse, was killed while supporting an Hungarian guard in
resisting a Suliote soldier, who was accordingly arrested but had
to be released to avoid a general mutiny (Gamba, IV, 188–90).
Then there were the six artificers who insisted on leaving (p. 200).
Next, Byron had to order the arrest of a Russian of whose dangerous
behaviour a complaint had been lodged by a Greek, and on the
man's denying the accusation Byron's justice, patience and will to
a balanced handling of affairs are witnessed by the length and care

of his letter to this, private, soldier (Gamba, VI, 234–6; Edgcumbe—who comments on Byron's extraordinary consideration—I, XIII, 159). On 3 April a threatening force arrived from Karaiskaki demanding vengeance for an injury, and proceeded to arrest two leading citizens of Missolonghi, the town being thrown into tumult and the simultaneous appearance of the Turkish fleet, together with other information, suggesting treachery. Byron's personal guard declared itself unwilling to oppose their countrymen. Though he managed to intimidate the rebels and save the hostages, he was, to his deep disappointment, unable to leave for the important conference at Salona (Gamba, VI, 236–41; Millingen, quoted Edgcumbe, XIII, 161). A spy, whose confession proved Karaiskaki's guilt, was next discovered in Byron's own house (Gamba, VI, 241–2; Nicolson, X, 243).

That Byron's post of responsibility was by no means a sinecure is driven home by his own remark that 'between Suliote chiefs, German barons, English volunteers, and adventurers of all nations, we are likely to form as goodly an allied army as ever quarrelled beneath the same banner' (Hancock, 7 Feb. 1824; LJ, VI, 318). There were continual animosities and much danger of duelling, especially among the Germans, who were also violently hostile both on the occasion of the flogging incident and also on Parry's promotion as major of artillery, one of them utterly refusing to serve under him (Gamba, V, 205; IV, 161–2; Parry, II, 30–2; see also IV, 71). There were three mutinies owing to the badness of the bread (Barff, 26 March 1824, LJ, VI, 360).

Here is a series of headings from Gamba's fourth chapter: 'Intrigues with the Moriote chiefs—Difficulties with the Suliotes—Lord Byron attacked by a convulsive fit—Alarm at the Seraglio—Lord Byron releases twenty-four Turkish prisoners—Destruction of a Turkish brig—Captain Sasse killed by a Suliote'. Or, as Byron himself put it to Parry: 'In one week, I have been in a fit; the troops mutinied; the Turkish brig burned; Sasse killed; an earthquake; thunder, lightning, and torrents of rain—such a week I never witnessed' (Parry, IX, 193; see also Murray, 25 Feb. 1823; Moore, 4 March 1824; LJ, VI, 334, 338). But this particular week was scarcely exceptional, since most of the others had their quota of similar disturbances. 'We have had', wrote Byron to Kinnaird on 30 March, 1824, 'strange weather and strange incidents—natural, moral, physical, martial and political' (LJ, VI, 363).

There were few Byron could trust. Rumours, such as those that had tracked him in England, were set going by the factions that he was himself a Turk in disguise plotting the ruin of Greece (Gamba, IV, 168). Moore follows Parry in seeing him as an essentially lonely man at Missolonghi, without companions (Moore, LVI, 634; Parry, II, 27). He had differences with Col. Stanhope (p. 193); and also with Gamba, inveighing bitterly against his rash expenditure (Hancock, 13 and 19 Jan. 1824; LJ, VI, 306, 310–11, and note; Nicolson, X, 238–40; Kennedy, 309–10). According to Harold Nicolson, only the Italian servant, Tita, and the boy Loukas remained, on one occasion, in favour (X, 238–40). It is likely enough that during March 1824 Byron was often 'no easy master' (Nicolson, X, 238–40). He was, or felt himself, poorly treated by the London Committee whom he regarded as inefficient and even suspected of deceit, and who at first appeared to be using him as a decoy and only gradually grew to trust his abilities (Trelawny, XIX; Parry, V, 106; IX, 187; Nicolson, IV, 80; VI, 120). The Congreve rockets, from which so much had been expected, proved a chimera (Gamba, IV, 157). The continual demands on his money, so pressing throughout his life, were now exorbitant and maddening: 'the Greeks seemed to think he was a mine from which they could extract gold at their pleasure' (Parry, III, 50–1; IV, 95).

That Byron's seizure was directly caused by these anxieties is suggested by his own Journal (15 Feb. 1824; LJ, VI, 323–4; also Parry, V, 106–7). Gamba gives them as the main cause, in conjunction with his meagre diet; he promised Kennedy to eat more (Gamba, IV, 177; and quoted Origo, IX, 378; Kennedy, 4 March 1824; LJ, VI, 339). He was met, says Moore, with 'every possible variety of obstruction and distraction that rapacity, turbulence and treachery could throw in his way' (LVI, 634). He had to master a community of 'great indolence and total disorganization' (Gamba, I, 39). As he once said of Leigh Hunt (Moore, 2 April 1823; LJ, VI, 182)—how the Byronic patterns repeat themselves—he was being faced with the maddening problem of trying to help what made no proper effort to help itself.

Such was the test of Byron's patience, involving his waiting at Cephalonia for the situation to clear, his long wait for the Greek fleet, the delay of the Greek deputies to London, the waiting at Missolonghi for news of the Loan; irritations which were reinforced by the intransigence of the political factions, the demands on his money, the fractious Suliotes and quarrelling Europeans, the intrigues and treachery, the stupidities and cowardices, the distrust at home and child-like and wearing reliance on him alone by every one at home and in Greece, the impossible weather, the sirocco, rain and wind, thunder and earthquakes, the inaction, his epileptic seizure, the scare of plague and inroads of fever. Providence, indeed, appeared intent on raining every possible annoyance, human and elemental, on his head: indeed we can, with Moore, 'half regret that he should have been great at such a cost' (LVI, 634). It was nevertheless under such conditions that he won the hearts of everyone by his care, patience, justice and magnanimity. At Cephalonia he was, however busy, accessible to the dullest visitors (Moore, LII, 599). No individual, as such, was ever unimportant to him; and at Missolonghi, where petitions and demands 'never left him a moment's peace at any hour of the day', he bore all, says Gamba, 'with great patience'. It was 'impossible to do justice to the coolness and magnanimity which he displayed on every trying occasion' (Gamba, IV, 173; II, 88; IV, 176). Whilst thinking himself detested and neglected at home and betrayed in Greece, and steadily dying of epilepsy and fever, he yet added to his difficulties, directly after his seizure, by rescuing the Turkish prisoners at Missolonghi and writing letters on their behalf (Gamba, IV, 180–3, and see p. 199); and by offering a reward for every prisoner saved alive from the Turkish brig (p. 199). He found time to insist on humane punishment for a thief (p. 201); to act as agent for the Bible Society in distributing Kennedy's tracts and a number of Greek Testaments (Kennedy, 4 and 10 March 1824; LJ, VI, 339, 348–9, and note); to lecture the little Turkish girl Hato on her manners, to make plans for her and her mother (pp. 77–8); and to write for comforts on the voyage home (p. 200) for the frightened workmen.

To pass from 'self-discipline' and 'patience', to 'courage'. Byron's was not, says Mr. Vulliamy, a 'spectacular' heroism; he himself might not have looked on it as heroism at all; but he showed himself nevertheless a man of 'sublime courage' (XVI, 239). When in danger from a Turkish frigate on the way to Missolonghi, 'his Lordship', said the sailors, 'conducted himself with admirable coolness' (Stanhope to Bowring, 5 Jan. 1824; LJ, VI, 305, note). We have seen how during a violent tempest he saved the ship from running on the rocks when the crew itself had despaired (Gamba, II, 86–7). Missolonghi itself was clearly a death-trap, situated, as Trelawny notes, by a 'dismal swamp' (Trelawny, XXI). There was considerable sickness among the Europeans. Everyone was ill, even Parry, 'a sort of hard-working Hercules' (Kinnaird, 30 March 1824; LJ, VI, 363; Parry, VI,

135–6). On 13 March 1824 'the greatest alarm prevailed in the town' through a scare of plague (Gamba, v, 215–17). Byron, who expected to die in Greece, often said to Gamba, 'Others may do as they please—they may go—but I stay here, *that is certain.*' 'No, Tita,' he once said to his faithful Italian, 'I shall never go back from Greece —either the Turks, or the Greeks, or the climate will prevent that' (Gamba, III, 128). 'I shall *stick* by the cause', he told Sidney Osborne, 'as long as a man of honour can, without sparing *purse* and (I hope, if need be) *person*' (9 Feb. 1824; LJ, VI, 322). When begged to visit Athens for health, rest and relief, he replied that he did not come out for 'tranquillity' (Gamba, IV, 193). After his seizure, letters from Zante and Cephalonia implored him to move, but he replied: 'I cannot quit Greece while there is a chance of my being of (even *supposed*) utility: there is a stake worth millions such as I am, and while I can stand at all, I must stand by the cause'; as for the Greeks, 'allowance must be made for them by all reasonable people' (Barff, 10 March 1824; LJ, VI, 344). Entreaties were clearly of no use, 'for in proportion as Byron thought his position more perilous, he the more resolved upon remaining where he was' (Gamba, v, 204). Meanwhile the rain descended in torrents, and between the floods on the land side and the sirocco from the sea, Missolonghi was now a 'pestilential prison' (Moore, LVI, 635). On 4 March 1824, he told Kennedy in an important letter that it was proper he should remain in Greece; that he had already prevented confusion growing worse; that, should he become, or be deemed, superfluous, he would be ready to retire; but in the interim he must not consider personal consequences. 'The rest is in the hands of Providence—as indeed are all things' (LJ, VI, 338).

As for his courageous actions during these three and a half months at Missolonghi—and one can hardly believe that little more than three months are in question—they are written on every page of every contemporary record. He had the instincts of a soldier and his title of *Archistrategos* both amused and thrilled him with the prospect of peril (Gamba, III, 115–16). Twice—once just after his seizure— he was only with difficulty persuaded not to lead an attack in person (Gamba, III, 124; IV, 184). When on his first rescue of a Turk the piratical captors fiercely demanded of him their prize, he drove them from him with great personal risk at the pistol's point (Gamba, III, 109–10; Gamba to Kennedy, Kennedy, App., 383). Directly after this incident, he deliberately (Nicolson, IX, 199) followed up, as though to brand forcibly into his allies his own merciful intentions, by freeing three more. Once, soon after his arrival, when there was great tumult with play of steel and fire-arms over a Customs quarrel involving the sum of $2\frac{1}{2}$d., 'my lord ran into the midst of the combatants, and contrived to quiet them' (Gamba, III, 108). He lived for weeks as the pivotal person in a community of primed pistols and flashing ataghans without showing a quiver of personal fear. When, whilst in bed after his first seizure, 'faint with over-bleeding' and his 'whole nervous system completely shaken', certain wild Suliotes dashed into his room brandishing weapons and making demands, he suddenly appeared to recover, and 'the more the Suliotes raged, the more his calm courage triumphed'. 'The scene', says Stanhope, 'was truly sublime' (Stanhope, quoted Edgcumbe, I, XVI, 209).[1] His efforts to master his illness were 'described as gigantic' (*Westminster Review*; Medwin, App., lxi). He risked, and incurred, fever after getting wet through rather than show an unsoldierly concern (Gamba, VI, 249). The many earthquakes at Cephalonia worried him no more than the terrific thunderstorms, by land and sea, which punctuate his life's story; and towards the end, among the other Byronic pleasantries of the period, was a mock-earthquake staged to frighten—and, in effect, infuriate—Parry (Gamba, V, 204-5; Parry, VII, 153-5). Byron was naturally playful at times of danger (Gamba, notes, VII, 302); 'a more undaunted man in the hour of peril never breathed' (Gamba, IV, 177). 'Personal fear', says Millingen, 'never entered his mind' (Edgcumbe, I, XIII, 161). 'Lord Byron's mental and personal courage', wrote Stanhope simply, 'was unlike that of other men' (quoted Edgcumbe, I, XVI, 207). In Greece, as throughout his life, his moral courage was the equal of his physical courage; and his cool endurance of risk over a period of months, here as in Italy, the equal of his impulsive fire.

The achievement was an achievement of personal understanding, sympathy, openness, example and leadership. The burly Parry, nervous on his arrival, found Byron 'so kind, so cheering, so friendly' in his reception, that he was quickly at his ease (Parry, I, 15). Byron's frank and open honesty and loathing of hypocrisy bore fruit. When an intriguer attempted to poison his relations with Mavrocordato, he faced the Prince directly with the reports and all was quickly cleared up (Parry, V, 105). On another occasion he dispelled the suspicions of a Greek dignitary by his easy and open manner (Gamba, notes, VII, 302). He was thus able to dispel unnecessary

---

1. Gamba refers to two *Germans* breaking into his room (IV, 178-9; see p. 204 above).

suspicions and fears. The technique was probably both instinctive and conscious. Parry regarded Byron's immediate reporting to Mavrocordato of his own criticisms as a neat way of teaching *both* certain salutary lessons (Parry, VII, 162). Byron understood his people. He knew how to avoid hurting local susceptibilities and superstitions (Moore, LII, 595). He also knew how to impress. The Greeks were deeply impressed by his markmanship (Gamba, III, 124–5). He was regarded by the townsfolk as alone able to control the turbulent Suliotes (Gamba, III, 111); and this he could do because, as with the fierce little barbarian boy and the young Botzaris (pp. 77, 72), he half loved their ferocity, just as he had always loved, and could therefore control, his fierce beasts. Once when in full Colonel's uniform he summoned the chieftains and made them promise to restore order, the 'dignity' and 'prudence' of his bearing won Parry's admiration (Parry, III, 63). He ran the considerable risk of appointing the dangerous Suliotes as his personal guard, and told Gamba that he intended to use them against Lepanto in order to gain their confidence by showing his, even though it was waning. 'Above all,' he added, 'these semibarbarians should never entertain the least suspicion of your personal courage' (Gamba, III, 115). On that principle he worked throughout. When the whole town was in terror from Karaiskaki's attack, he rode out, with his full entourage, into the country to 'reassure the panic-stricken populace' (Nicolson, X, 243); calculating also, we may suppose, the effect on the attackers. The incident recalls the great moment in *Sardanapalus,* a play compacted of the noblest Byronic virtues, when the king, warned that he would be recognized by the revolutionaries, answers: 'I go forth to be recognized' (III, i). When before the attack on Lepanto Byron was urged to nurse and augment his prestige by acting above and at a distance, he replied, with the instinct of a true leader, that such influence was better acquired by his sparing 'neither sacrifices, fatigues, nor dangers' (Gamba, III, 134–5). He was always ready to lead by example, as when he himself seized a spade to rescue the men buried in the land-slide at Cephalonia and by his example saved their lives (p. 119). When some Missolonghi workmen refused to unload certain perishable stores on a Holy Day, he set to himself, and started the others (Gamba, IV, 156). We have seen how he refused regularly to take personal advantage of his position as chief. He worked continually by example, and among the reported words of his last delirium was the cry: 'Forwards—forwards—courage —follow my example—don't be afraid' (Gamba, VI, 261).

Whilst never sparing himself, he was considerate of others. On his deathbed, 'with that kind consideration for those about him which was one of the great sources of their lasting attachment to him', he said to Fletcher: 'I am afraid you and Tita will be ill with sitting up night and day' (Moore, LVI, 637; Fletcher's Account; Medwin, App., lxxii). Servants loved him for the care so evident throughout his letters from youth onwards. At his death Tita wrote that in Byron 'he had lost a father rather than a master', while 'expatiating upon the indulgence with which he had always treated his domestics, and the care he expressed for their comfort and welfare'; and Fletcher, overpowered at the disaster, writes: 'He was more to me than a father' (Moore, LVI, 639). The devotion Byron inspired was not strange. Millingen tells us that his conduct to the poor and the distressed of Missolonghi, made him the 'idol' of the townsfolk, who looked upon him as a 'father' (Edgcumbe, I, IX, 105; I, XIV, 177). At Missolonghi it was reported 'that the day seemed sad and gloomy to him when he had not employed himself in some generous exertion' (*Westminster Review;* Medwin, App., xxxii). In his turn, he enjoyed, lover-like, a response from his many protégés; and when a simple Greek countrywoman offered him a gift of cheese and honey on his return from a ride, he remarked, according to Parry—'I have felt more pleasure this day, and at this circumstance, than for a long time past' (Parry, VII, 166).

There was, as it were, a romantic, lover's, contact, radiation, from Byron to any individual wanting his help; an expansive love, for mankind. And this roused a corresponding devotion in return: 'No man ever lived', said Hobhouse at Byron's death, 'who had such devoted friends. His power of attaching those about him to his person was such as no one I ever knew possessed' (Drinkwater, II, 132; no ref.). The records speak with one voice: 'Such was the attachment, mingled with a sort of reverence and enthusiasm, with which he inspired those around him, that there was not one of us who would not, for his sake, have willingly encountered any danger in the world' (Gamba, V, 267). Parry's respect for Byron 'gave him something of that power over my mind which the late Emperor Napoleon is said to have had over his soldiers' (Parry, II, 24).

Such comments help to explain the remarkable success attained. Proud mountain chieftains were willing to serve under him as under no one else, believing that their wild troops would obey him more readily than any Greek, both Draco and Botzaris offering on separate occasions to act under 'his lordship' as a common soldier, though refusing subordination to a Suliote (Gamba, II, 95–6; III, 144–5; IV, 172). We have already (pp. 189–90) seen how the factions were becoming more amenable, the powerful Colocotronis, Sessini and Parucca all soliciting Byron's mediation. He died before complete success was possible, but 'much good' was done in inculcating submission to the central Government (*Westminster Review;* Medwin, App., lv). He was about to succeed in stabilizing the Government when he died (Gamba, II, 95). In Western Greece Prince Mavrocordato recognized his value. 'So far', wrote Byron, 21 February 1824, to Kinnaird, 'I have succeeded in supporting the Government of *Western* Greece for the present, which would otherwise have been dissolved' (C, II, 288). 'Nobody knows,' said Mavrocordato at his death, 'except perhaps myself, the loss Greece has suffered. Her safety even depended on his continuing in existence. His presence here has checked intrigues which will now have uncontrolled sway.' He saw him as the protector of Missolonghi (Parry, VI, 137–8). Gamba says that, had he lived, it was likely that the general government of the country would have been placed in his hands (notes, IX, 304). But Parry clearly asserts that Byron himself had no political ambitions. Certain insinuations that he aimed at making himself king of Greece were totally 'unfounded'. With his money and reputation, he could certainly have established an invincible army; 'the whole of the Suliotes were completely at his beck'; all this he knew, but never wished to hold political power. 'I came', he said, 'to serve the Greeks on their own conditions and in their own way' (Parry, VIII, 179–81, note). At every turn, we find evidence of Byron's growing prestige; at every turn he exerted a selfless, saving and guiding power. Karaiskaki's treacherous betrayal and attack on Missolonghi synchronizing with the appearance of the Turkish fleet (p. 205) failed, says Iris Origo, 'largely owing to Byron's energy and common-sense' (IX, 382). Even in the lesser matters—if such they be —of his humane actions, his influence was effective. Everyone seems to have been impressed by his precepts and actions. The author of the *Westminster Review* account lays considerable emphasis on the value of Byron's praiseworthy example (Medwin, App., lii, liv). The two pirates who had angrily claimed their captured Turk became his rivals in benevolence, returning to apologize with the assurance that they had only been fearful for the captive's welfare (Gamba, III, 112–13). At every instant, it is what Byron *is* and *does* that radiates power and example: Blacquière emphasized the powers of his *personal* influence (Edgcumbe, I, XIV, 176–8). Lord Sidney

Osborne said that 'no one unacquainted with the circumstances of the case could have any idea of the difficulties he had overcome. He had reconciled the contending parties and had given a character of humanity and civilization to the warfare in which they were engaged' (Edgcumbe, quoting Hobhouse, I, XVI, 201–2).

Byron's leadership affected Englishmen too. On 24 January 1824, Col. Napier had been so 'fired' by his example that he 'determined to throw up' his appointment in Cephalonia with a view to serving in Greece (Nicolson, VI, 117). Even more important was the effect on London. Money poured in for the Loan (Hobhouse to Byron, 23 Feb. 1824; C, II, 294). A man 'with £8,000 per annum' turned back from Corfu on hearing of Byron's death; while others were flocking to devote their fortunes less to the Greek than to the Byronic cause (Trelawny, quoted Gamba, V, 282, note; Parry, X, 252–3). During these few months, the War of Independence *was* Byron; and his plan, if success were won, to charter a schooner and sail to America to gain recognition of the Federation was, as Parry urged and in despite of Galt's ridicule (Galt, XLVI), perfectly sound: 'Nothing, I think, within the power of an individual to accomplish could be better conceived' (Parry, VIII, 184–5).

Byron's accomplishment has scarcely received its due. Moore observed the 'thanklessness' which 'too often waits on disinterested actions'; and noted the insidious growth of ungenerous and taunting criticisms. What more, he asked, could have been done by a single man in a task wherein 'all the great powers of Europe' had, in the six succeeding years, failed? He reminds us that Byron himself knew perfectly well that no spectacular success was possible; that 'individuals' were as nothing in the slow accomplishment of the great purpose (pp. 170–1). His various measures, the reconciliations, the humane precepts of his 'example', his preparation for the Loan, his well-devised and valuable fortifications, his diplomatic avoidance of collision with the Ionian Government and the courts of Europe; all were 'seeds' sown for a future harvest (LV, 631). Given the background of violence, treachery, confusion, ineptitude and distrust, Byron did, as a lonely newcomer of merely poetic fame, achieve marvels. Considering the time taken for communications, and how greatly success depended on dispatch, it is difficult to see how, in a little over three months, a greater result was conceivable. Besides, as Moore says, the nature of his essentially poetic achievement must finally be assessed in terms of its long-range, creative, action:

'But it would be unjust to close even here the bright catalogue of his services. It is, after all, *not* with the span of mortal life that the good achieved by a name immortal ends. The charm acts into the future—it is an auxiliary for all time' (LV, 631).

Here, as in Italy, his name became a talisman, working to deflect the history of Europe.

The story possesses, as it were, a poetic aura; and, like any work of art, tends to reveal, as time passes, surprising contemporary significances. Byron's statement that Britain's true interest lay in the freedom of nations rather than in imperial possession (Gamba, v, 214; p. 191) sounds modern enough. Gamba remarks that the heterogeneous crowd of 'English, Scotch, Irish, Americans, Germans, Swiss, Belgians, Russians, Swedes, Danes, Hungarians and Italians'—in addition to Greeks and other Levantines—embattled under Byron against the Turks, made of it all 'a sort of crusade in miniature' (IV, 201). The Christian, the crusading, element in the campaign seems, indeed, to have been felt strongly by the Greeks themselves; and in Byron's own final definition of it—in spite of his liberal sympathies—as a conflict of Christianity and Hellenism against paganism (p. 195), we can feel overtones that apply to Europe today. Not only was Byron's own life's poetry in the cause of European liberation compacted and enacted in those few months at Missolonghi, but the widest general significances are contained, involving the European tradition, the power of England abroad, the opposing rights of revolution and authority, of education and force. There is little left out. At Missolonghi there was lived something of universal meaning.

There was also something eternal about it, which may again be related to Byron's peculiarly poetic technique, his rating of the means, or style, as equal to, or above, the end: 'I know not', he writes, 'whether it be true that "Honesty is the best policy", but it is the only kind that I am disposed to practise or to sanction' (Barry, 25 Oct. 1823; LJ, VI, 269). He had, as it were, a vertical allegiance. In a strangely independent spirit of assurance and generosity he maintained his direction. As Drinkwater observes, the whole business was, at the time, not greatly important at home; comparatively few, at first anyway, were interested; Byron could expect little advantage; the splendour the occasion has since gathered is the splendour he gave it; and of that he himself could know nothing. On 10 March

1823, he had told John Hunt that he was 'the most unpopular man in England' (LJ, VI, 171); and on 17 March, he referred again to the hostility accorded his works. 'Time and Truth', he said, might remove it; but he did not wish to drag others down with him, though alone he minded, comparatively, little: 'Every publication of mine has latterly failed; I am not discouraged by this, because writing and composition are habits of my mind, with which Success and Publication are objects of remoter reference—*not causes, but effects, like those of any other pursuit*' (LJ, VI, 173). *Exactly the same can be said of his Greek expedition.* There, too, he acted according to a central instinct; an instinct of liberality, generosity, self-sacrifice; something you find throughout his life, and which burns in his own poetic diction; one could call it, in the finest sense, nobility. It was, moreover, an inward devotion, independent of success or failure, hard to define outside religious terminology; a devotion to some eternal dimension such as is the origin and purpose of all artistic creation and religious enquiry. Byron was, indeed, the 'pilgrim of eternity'. No other English poetry is so heavily weighted with the concept 'eternity' as his, while his prose thinking is equally solemn in reverence to 'the Deity', or 'Providence'. He did what he did without over-valuing the profit and the loss; all that, as he told Kennedy, 'is in the hands of Providence, as indeed are all things' (4 March 1824; LJ, VI, 339). Among his last struggling words, in answer to Fletcher's 'Not our will, but God's be done' were, 'Yes, not mine be done . . .' (Fletcher's account; Medwin, App., lxxiv; Spender, App. D, 315). We shall not understand these actions whilst we confine ourselves to a horizontal, a humanistic, view. The selflessness and creative power displayed were too strange for that; it was all, somehow, done differently, and for other reasons.

But neither was it independent of the temporal order. It was an act in history, and for history. Its greatness was recognized by those best qualified to judge, those who had *felt* the powers radiated. By Byron himself they were, necessarily, treated lightly: 'Mavrocordato's letter says that my presence will "electrify the troops", so I am going over to "electrify" the Suliotes' (Hobhouse, 27 Dec. 1823; C, II, 286). His poetry had gone before him; indeed, had half created the cause; and adulation and expectation were high. His reception at Missolonghi suggested 'a triumph' (Millingen, quoted LJ, 305, note); 'the coming of a Messiah' (Stanhope to Bowring, 31 Dec. 1823; LJ, VI, 296, note); a delivering 'angel' (Gamba to Teresa, 8 Jan. 1824; Origo, IX, 374). These expectations were never falsified. More—

even the phlegmatic Hobhouse was forced into a semi-apocalyptic style, writing, in the hour of success on 15 March 1824, 'I can assure you here that the Greeks look upon your Avatar as a perfect god-send; one of them said to me in so many words, *"It is Providence who sent that man to our help"* '; and again, he calls Greece the one bright spot in a darkened Europe, adding, 'Your present endeavour is certainly the most glorious ever undertaken by man . . . Go on and prosper' (C, II, 297, 299). These words arrived too late; Byron never read them, never realized fully his own success. The atmosphere of *apparent* failure in which he died inevitably recalls the New Testament. The manner of his death, its visible defeat and inward triumph, with its circle of simple yet loving followers, Gamba, Parry, Fletcher, Tita, Loukas and Lyon, suggests, indeed, the greatest of comparisons. No production 'within the range of *mere human composition*', wrote Moore, was so deeply moving, *all the circumstances considered,* as Byron's poem at Missolonghi on his completing his thirty-sixth year (LIV, 615; italics mine). The accounts of Gamba and Parry read like the accounts, simple yet authentic—and authentic because so simple —of disciples. Instead of 'Christ is risen' on Easter Day the townsfolk were all asking, 'How is Lord Byron?' (Funeral Oration, Tricoupi, Medwin, App., xci; Edgcumbe, I, xv, 185; Galt, XLVIII). The name of 'Christ' was seldom, comparatively, on Byron's lips, or in his writings; but among his dying words Parry includes, 'Ah, Christi' (Parry, V, 127). At the moment of his death there broke, says Parry— a burly realist if ever there was one—'one of the most awful thunderstorms I ever witnessed'; and the 'superstitious' Greeks, regarding it as 'the signal of his doom', cried to each other, 'The great man is gone' (Parry, V, 128, note; Moore, LVI, 638).

By those who knew him, Byron's greatness was quickly recognized. Officers who had known him at Cephalonia were astonished at their sense of loss, acknowledging 'that their regard was not measured by the time they had known him, but by *his superior worth*' (Kennedy, Int., ix; italics mine). At his death, our various authorities vie with each other in adulation. Was his sacrifice not 'the most generous and beneficent action which could be undertaken by a Christian'? (Gamba to Kennedy, Kennedy, App., 382). 'England has lost her brightest genius, Greece her noblest friend,' said Stanhope (Moore, LVI, 639). Those who gazed on his dead body saw there 'the hope of a whole nation and the admiration of the civilized world' (Millingen; Nicolson, XI, 268). This was, said Trelawny, 'no private grief'; adding, 'The world has lost its greatest man, I my best friend'

(Trelawny to Stanhope, Moore, LVI, 639). 'Thus died George Lord Byron,' wrote Parry, 'the truest and greatest poet England has lately given birth to, the warmest hearted of her philanthropists, the least selfish of her patriots, and unquestionably the most distinguished member of her nobility' (Parry, V, 128); distinguished, not alone by birth, but rather because his name was likely to be echoed 'among the watchwords of Liberty from age to age' (Moore, LIV, 619).

Most impressive of all, however, was the Funeral Oration spoken by the young Spiridion Tricoupi. Had Byron, he said, remained at home, he might with his financial assistance alone have saved Greece: 'But if this was sufficient for us, it was not so for Lord Byron'; he was one *destined by nature to uphold the rights of man whenever he saw them trampled upon'*; one born in a free and enlightened country, and early taught, by his reading of the ancients, *'not only what man is, but what he ought to be, and what he may be'*; and so offered his wealth, his judgment, and his sword for the cause. His poetic greatness was justly acclaimed; as a poet, 'he was born for all Europe and for all ages'. The fight for liberty in Greece was a *new* phenomenon, in that an oppressed nation, by its own efforts, was throwing off a tyrannic yoke: 'Such is the extraordinary time in which we live. My friends, the insurrection of Greece is not an epoch of our nation alone; it is an epoch of all nations: *it is a phenomenon which stands alone in the political history of nations.'* With this cause, Byron had identified himself; and it is recalled with pride that his dying words coupled Greece with the name of his own daughter. To her Tricoupi sent a message, telling her how a whole nation was inconsolable, how all ecclesiastical, civil and military honours had attended her father's last rites, blessed by the benedictions of the Archbishop, Bishop and 'all our Clergy'. Chieftains bore the bier, thousands of soldiers, armed against 'the implacable enemy of Christ', swearing never to forget this sacrifice, 'and never to allow the spot where his heart is placed to be trampled upon by barbarous and tyrannical feet'. He concluded: 'Thousands of Christian voices were in a moment heard, and the temple of the Almighty resounded with supplications and prayers that his venerated remains might be safely conveyed to his native land, and that his soul might rest where the righteous alone find rest' (Funeral Oration, Tricoupi, Medwin, App., xci–xcix; Edgcumbe, I, xv, 185–90; italics mine).

That Byron's remains were refused a place in Westminster Abbey would not have troubled him. 'I should prefer', he had told the Earl of Blessington, 'a grey Greek stone over me to Westminster

Abbey' (23 April 1823; LJ, VI, 196); and when death was near, 'Lay me in the first corner without pomp or nonsense' (Millingen, Nicolson, XI, 263). Nevertheless the impact on England was powerful enough. Drinkwater follows Parry (Parry, VI, 136–7) in observing that friends and enemies alike were aware 'of something almost cataclysmic having happened'. 'Nobody', he writes, 'could remember anything like this public sensation being caused by the death of a poet . . . it might be a national calamity or a national blessing, but in any case it was national' (VII, 386).

It was more than national. It was, in a way, even more than a Christian event, since all pacifisms, all rejections of the temporal order, were excluded. It was political and national, without ceasing to be Christian; not only militant, but military. Here revolution and authority, Church and State, God and Caesar, tradition and prophecy, converged; the Sermon on the Mount was all but lived on the battlefield. The unity cannot be thought; it can only be lived, or dramatized. It has been lived once only and dramatized once only, and both by Byron.

NOTE ON THE GREEK WAR OF INDEPENDENCE

Our understanding of the underlying and determining forces of the Greek Campaign, and of Byron's actions in particular, is assisted by a valuable article in *The Times Literary Supplement*, 2 June 1950, on the second edition of Y. Makriyiannis' *Apomnimonévmata* (edited by Y. Vlakhoyiannis).

In Makriyiannis' autobiographical account of the war as he saw it we have not only the origins of modern Greek prose, but a remarkable and revealing story:

'The seeds of this growth, now more than a century old, are for this reason themselves worth examination, and there could be no better introduction than a study of the first outstanding individual prose-writer of modern Greece, a hero and narrator of the War of Independence, who was both too naïve and too discerning to succumb to the pretentious shams which were the fashion among his fellow countrymen at the time' (333).

It is our purpose to show that the integrity here indicated bears an important relation to Byron.

Makriyiannis was born, in or about 1797, into an 'adventurous' world of oppression and confusion, the oppressors including both

Turks and 'medieval adventurers such as Ali Pasha', the Greeks, whose national consciousness was yet 'in embryo', taking whatever advantages they could of either. There had been, indeed, a 'nascent' 'resistance movement' as early as 1797, ranging from brigandage to considered and provincial action (333), but the confusions were appalling: 'So confused were the times that when Makriyiannis was first initiated into the Greek revolutionary conspiracy . . . Ali Pasha was looked upon by the Greek plotters as an ally'; and 'It says much for Makriyiannis' good sense and patriotism (an emotion which he was one of the first Greeks to feel with deep understanding) that he thought twice before accepting his initiation' (334).

Not dissimilarly Byron may be said to have 'thought twice' on more than one occasion before enlisting his name for the various claimants to his support. In both, as our quotation hints, such caution was dictated by both 'good sense' and a 'patriotism' of a kind unknown to the average Greek at that period.

The revolution broke out into open warfare in 1821. But it was scarcely a clear-cut war. Makriyiannis preferred Turkish doctors for his wounds and observed a host of faults in his fellow-countrymen, his account here exactly corroborating the judgments of Byron:

'He writes as candidly and un-selfconsciously of the virtues as of the monstrous cruelties of the Turks and Albanians. His bitterest castigations are against his fellow-countrymen, whose conduct he represents as a far more formidable obstacle to their own independence than anything that the Turks could do. After the Greeks themselves, the next lowest position in Makriyiannis' scale of contempt belongs to the Great Powers. "The English wanted to make us English," he says, "the Russians Russians and the French Frenchmen." Of the three, he thought England behaved the worst, apparently because His Majesty's Government was afraid of Greece becoming a rival sea-power. The names of Codrington and Byron never figure in Makriyiannis' long narrative from one end to the other' (334).

Such an omission is strange. We appear to be faced by an example of unconscious plagiarism not unlike that to be observed with reference to Shelley (pp. 258–9). The similarity between Byron and Makriyiannis in point of judgment was, of course, in part forced by the same facts impinging on two men of vision and integrity; but it is likely that the semi-illiterate Greek—for so he was—could not so vividly have struck out his considered account without the example, the symbolic action as well as the declared purposes, of Byron, whose impact had ignited a host of conscious values in Greece previously dormant. Even were his settled opinions known to antedate Byron's actions of 1823 and 1824, we may remember that the early *Childe Harold*, with its notes, had already done much (p. 179) to arouse a patriotic consciousness throughout Greece.

Like Byron, Makriyiannis was shocked at the unnecessary complicating of what to him was 'a simple issue' by a quite unbelievable want of simple comradeship among his compatriots. After recounting an incident where Greeks left Greeks with appalling callousness to their death, he says: 'That is what quarrels do, that is what division does, these are the results that civil war brings again and again. And now too our comrades watch us from afar when we are in danger; and the one eyes the other . . .' (334). After reading such a passage, surely the most adverse critic of Byron's technique at Cephalonia must admit the wisdom of his emphasis on the need for national unity. Makriyiannis' most bitter complaints, 'the passionate scorn of a man who never had the least doubt of his duty', complaints growing from a life dedicated to Greece—he fought strenuously from 1821 to 1827—regard precisely those faults which Byron intuitively diagnosed, and against which he levelled all his powers of persuasion and statesmanship.

Makriyiannis' patriotism lay in exact descent from Byron's early *Childe Harold*: 'Being a Greek then meant for him a passionate devotion to two things: his country's past and his country's future. These two devotions, the natural scholar's and the natural statesman's, found a rare and indissoluble union in the single character that Makriyiannis remained beneath his quick, dynamic, exterior.' Like Byron, he delighted to set the great names of Greek history, Themistocles, Leonidas, Alexander, beside those of Napoleon and the Czar of Russia.

'And what has the name of the Greeks done for you, you nobles of Europe, you learned, you rich? All the learned men of the ancient Greeks, the ancestors of all humanity, Lycurgus and Plato and Socrates and Aristides and Themistocles and Leonidas and Thrasybulus and Demosthenes, and the rest of the fathers of humanity in general, laboured and tortured themselves night and day with virtue, with sincerity, with pure enthusiasm to enlighten humanity and to raise it up in virtue and light, nobility and patriotism. All these great men of the world have been living so many centuries below, in a dark place, weeping and tormented by the many hardships that their unhappy country is suffering in division. Lose these and their country Greece is lost too, its name wiped out. These men did not look to lay up vain treasures for an hour, they looked to enlighten the world with everlasting light. They clad men in virtue, they stripped them of ill conduct; and thus they thought for all humanity and they were teachers of truth' (334).

Here, we are told, was his 'whole faith in a single paragraph'. And it is pure Byron, every phrase of it.

We are not, of course, primarily concerned to make out a case of 'debt' or 'obligation' in the literary sense. But it is worth noting that this typical and typifying personality of the Greek Cause followed in thought the tradition started by *Childe Harold* and corroborated by his own bitter experience the exact wisdom of Byron's approach to the problems of Greece in 1823 and 1824.

Like the Byron of *The Curse of Minerva* and the Notes to *Childe Harold*, he set value on works of ancient art and dreaded the thought of their removal to Europe. When some soldiers were about to sell two fine statues to some Europeans he urged, 'Even if they offer you ten thousand dollars, you must not let these things go out of our country. These are what we fought for' (334). That was to him 'one half' of the Greek cause; the other half involved what he called 'Laws': 'He was as far ahead of his time in the sovereign importance he attached to a Constitution for Greece as he was in his clear insight into the potential value of ancient tradition as a unifying symbol' (334). We are reminded of Byron's conversations with Gamba and Parry.

Makriyiannis' book was written between 1829 and 1850. The writer of our article rates it high as a first-hand account by a central personality of the war in question; as a transition document in the history of written Greek, replacing the conventional and lifeless classic style with a new, non-literary, use of direct and naïve speech from the vernacular; and also as a work of literary vitality in its own right. But with Makriyiannis and his book we are only indirectly concerned. What I wish to insist is that, after an hundred years, an authoritative article is found praising such a figure for having proved 'upon his pulses', point by point, the deep truth—which need not be limited to Greece—of the Byronic gospel.

V

THE NEW PROMETHEUS

I

BYRON'S challenge can be defined as the impact of a person on politics; perhaps as a triumph of personality over politics. We have seen (pp. 24-5) how, in running over the battle-fields of Epaminondas, Miltiades, Themistocles, Leonidas, Hannibal, Caesar and Napoleon, he wondered how it was that, though they all sprang so readily to mind, those of Alcibiades were less easily remembered: 'Yet upon the whole', he adds, 'it may be doubted, whether there be a name of Antiquity, which comes down with such a general charm as that of *Alcibiades*. Why? I cannot answer: who can?' (*Detached Thoughts*, Oct. 1821; V, 461). Scott annotated this passage with the suggestion that Alcibiades' romantic personality, in which voluptuousness alternated with 'the very opposite extreme', appealed to Byron as a self-portrait, adding: 'Was he who selected Alcibiades from the great names of antiquity quite sincere when he proclaimed Washington his modern hero? Had Napoleon been a *gentleman*, I suspect he would have been the man' (LJ, IV, 77-8, note). The illogical fascination exerted on Byron by Napoleon certainly did, in spite of his many violent repudiations, surpass his *reasoned* admiration of a Washington or Bolivar. Those stood for leadership in goodness, liberation and wisdom; but he did not carry the pictures of any of *them* as a talisman. He confessed to Lady Blessington that his denunciations of Napoleon were as the denunciations of a lover who could not tolerate blemishes in his idol (Blessington, 202). What Byron admired or loved in him was a certain greatness, not merely a goodness; a personal magnetism, or aura, indefinable in intellectual terms. Conversely he distrusted Henley and Henry Hunt, since he believed no theory—theory as such never appealed to him (p. 194)—was safe with such *persons* (pp. 141-7). He could, in jocular mood, feel them as subhuman: 'My monkey, too, has been playing such tricks about the room as Mr. Hunt at his meetings' (Hobhouse, 22 April 1820; C, II, 145). Therefore, in some strange, personal, way, Napoleon, however tyrannic, lifts mankind; Hunt and Henley, however justified, drag man down. Finally, in his own policy and statesmanship, all his actions matured from personal judgment and personal feeling. His consideration for suffering individuals sprang from an instinctive concentration on persons, on the 'thou', on—at the limit—love's magic; wherein there was somehow no great difference between his stalwart allies and the frightened artificers. When his aid was needed he made no political or religious—nor indeed any other—distinctions (Moore, XLV, 518); he only provisionally distinguished friend from foe, brave man from coward. Moore tells us that in company he never spoke to a group, but always to his neighbour (XXXV, 414), and Shelley said that he was only *in earnest* when talking to one person (Trelawny, V). His sole obedience was to the 'thou', the poetic, the eternal, dimension, in which every man was 'fit for the society of kings' (p. 126); and in this dimension Napoleon existed pre-eminently as a great power; and yet not as the greatest, the Promethean, power, which, as we shall presently argue, Byron himself was to incarnate. And it was as a personality, as a legendary, a poetic power, in Italy, in Greece, throughout Europe, that Byron's greatest, his eternal, contribution lies. 'As a myth', writes Bertrand Russell, 'his importance, especially on the Continent, was enormous' (*History of Western Philosophy,* 1946, XXIII, 780).

Our problem is accordingly no simple problem of wisdom and goodness alone. As with Alcibiades and Napoleon, certain more imaginative categories were involved. That peculiar lustre, or aura, which we have observed settling on the hero, the great man, cannot with any finality be distinguished from the lustre enjoyed by an aristocracy, and pre-eminently by royalty, at any time or place. A royal house may be founded by a great conqueror, Alexander or Napoleon, the belief in an hereditary transmission of magical power being an attempt to capture, to bottle and preserve, what is in essence mysterious, occasional and fleeting. Now, though strong in repudiation of the royal houses of Europe, Byron himself sprang from the aristocracy. His self-assertion—if such it were—may be related both to (i) his sense of inward power and rectitude as man of wisdom and enlightenment; and (ii) his sense of noble descent, together, perhaps, with knowledge of his own personal fascination. These correspond, roughly, to our previous distinction (p. 160) of the rationally good leader from the magical personality. Both are needed, and Byron's awareness of both in himself made his position unique.

In spite of his normal humility—'in all good faith', writes Du

Bos, 'he was always surprised, even scandalized, by both his literary and his amorous conquests' (v, 133)—Byron was genuinely interested in his title. Lady Blessington observes his 'taste' and 'prejudices' in favour of aristocracy, and attributes to him an 'aristocratic pride' (68, 392-4). Though he lived at a period of transition which saw the falling of an age-old valuation, and indeed was, as a revolutionary aristocrat, fated (like his own Doge in *Marino Faliero*) to live out this transition in person, there remained in him (as in all matters of 'honour') a firm sense of responsibility to his own rank. On his visit to Turkey in 1810 he engaged in an argument as to his proper position relative to the British ambassador in a Turkish ceremonial, and was not content till ruled wrong by an acknowledged authority, when his forthright retraction serves as a model for all such disagree-ments: 'On all occasions of this kind, one of the parties must be wrong—at present it has fallen to my lot; your authorities (particu-larly the *German*) are too many for me' (Adair, 4 July 1810; C, I, 9). How often have Byron's biographers, who have not been slow to seize upon the incident, observed its characteristic conclusion?

Some relevant remarks are offered by Stendhal, who met Byron in Milan, and observed in him 'pride of birth', jealousy of Napoleon and respect for the dandy, Beau Brummell (LJ, III, App. VIII, 439-40). Byron knew his own powers, while lacking utterly—we still do —any system of thought in which his stature could be placed. He therefore attempted to relate it to various established forms or persons, such as those mentioned by Stendhal. But they were quite inadequate.

It seems that the graces of society appealed to his imagination, whilst failing to satisfy him in practice. 'At the best of times', he told Lady Melbourne on 21 September 1813, he was a 'miserable beau' (C, I, 182). Again, 'I wonder', he wrote on 18 February 1814, 'for what purpose dandies . . . were ordained—and kings—and fel-lows of colleges—and women of "a certain age"—and many men of any age—and myself, most of all!' (LJ, II, 384). On page after page of the Blessington conversations he is recorded as inveighing against the superficialities of London society. Lady Blessington says that he had no 'small change' for such intercourse, since 'his gold is in ingots' (49). Parties bored and irritated him (Journal, 20 and 22 March 1814; LJ, II, 402, 405; *Don Juan*, XIV, 15-18; Blessington, 51, 123, 209-12). Once he told Lady Blessington how he used to writhe in agony, levelling Shakespearian curses against the 'well-dressed automatons' who 'threw a spell' over his faculties, forcing him to his chamber in doubt of his own 'sanity' and 'identity'. 'Such', he said, 'was the overpowering effect produced on me by exclusive society in London' (Blessington, 374). The key-word is 'exclusive'. Brilliant talk, such as Madame de Staël's, was 'glittering nonsense' (Journal, 18 Feb. 1814; LJ, II, 384; Blessington, 123, 375). But, though mixed society grated on him, he apparently felt more at his ease with 'the Dandies'. 'I liked the Dandies,' he wrote in later life; 'they were always very civil to *me* . . . The truth is, that, though I gave up the business early, I had a tinge of Dandyism in my minority, and probably retained enough of it to conciliate the great ones at four and twenty' (*Detached Thoughts*, Oct. 1821; see also Earl of Blessington, 5 April 1823; LJ, V, 423; VI, 189). A certain affinity was natural in view of Byron's rating of the arts of life above those of the pen. All social functions are attempts to dramatize, to poeticize, life, whilst tending to inculcate those excellences so highly valued by Castiglione of gentility and grace, culminating in the dance. Dandyism is written into much of *Don Juan*, and Juan's dancing, with its *unostentatious* excellence (*Don Juan*, XIV, 38–40), a characterizing expression. At its best dandyism was no vulgar flamboyance, and what Byron admired most in Brummell was 'a certain exquisite propriety' (LJ, II, 126, note). The cult can even be said to have had philosophical and moral implications; and where these are involved, Byron's recorded behaviour may serve to suggest the level on which he was thinking.

When the young poetess whom Teresa called Miss S. (see p. 86) sought in trepidation the great man's assistance, she was not only struck—as indeed was everyone—by his kindliness in place of the gloom and severity she expected, but was in addition peculiarly aware of his whole *ensemble* of graces, his 'beautiful expression', 'graceful' manners, 'exquisite' hands, and wonderful 'tone of voice':

'All that formed such an assemblage of seductive qualities, that never before or since have I remarked any man who could be compared to him. What particularly struck me was the serene gentle dignity of his manner' (II; IV, 66).

Moore's first impressions of Byron were precisely similar, including 'the nobleness of his air, his beauty, the gentleness of his voice and manners, and—what was naturally not the least attraction—his marked kindness to myself' (XIII, 145; LJ, II, 67, note). Now Miss S. goes on to speak of his 'varied and delightful' conversation, 'the purity of his English', his 'refined pronunciation', which all offered a complete contrast 'even with the most distinguished men I had had the good fortune to meet' (69). Nor was all this a preliminary to exchanges of love, though she herself was quite spelled by his magic. Her account was set down especially to show how he acted as a *father,* speaking with 'so much right reason, goodness, and judgment far above his age, that one remained enthralled' (63); and how his whole behaviour, over a number of visits, was calculated, with consummate tact, to serve her interests whilst preserving her from any harm, even though he clearly endured a great struggle (70) with himself to remain unmoved by her presence. In old age she remembered him as 'good and generous'; 'never in all my long years have I seen a man *worthy to be compared to him*'; in no 'other human being' had she ever come across so 'rare' an 'assemblage' of 'great and beautiful qualities'; and that is why his memory 'lives in my heart like a brilliant star' (61, 63).

In Byron's Greek Campaign, it was the way, the means, not merely the purposed end, to which we called attention; and in the smaller interchanges of life, especially in giving, in charity, the way is everything. Tact, Byron told Lady Blessington, should be added to the virtues, since it is 'the real panacea of life' (178). He himself never passed a beggar without a contribution 'invariably bestowed with gentleness and kindness', particularly when the object of his charity was 'deformed' (Blessington, 36). Teresa tells us that his humour was in exquisite taste, how he never mocked involuntary defects, of mind or body (II; XIII, 286–8); while his generosity was always a 'refined generosity' (Teresa, II; V, 88). That is what dandyism became in Byron; a goodness not merely moral, but what the Greeks would have designated in terms of the word 'kalos', or beautiful. It must be understood in depth.

And here we may perhaps approach on a deeper than the usual level his 'Napoleonic carriage' (Hobhouse, I; VII, 334), his bed with its motto 'Crede Byron' surmounted by baronial coronets, and all those horses' trappings and 'tawdry' liveries which, according to Lady Blessington, he pointed to as 'rich and handsome' (Blessington, 264). Lady Blessington quite failed to understand such—in her judgment—ill-considered showiness. She was staggered by the contrast between these 'appendages of rank' and his own 'extremely simple' 'mode of life' (95). Himself independent and even ignorant of the 'elegancies and comforts' of refinement, he was nevertheless imaginatively attracted by expensive furniture and plate, though always refusing to waste money on them, being glad that he had no such tastes (263–4). She remained baffled, calling it all 'extraordinary', and adding 'but everything in him is contradictory and extraordinary' (95). We can, however, clarify these contradictions. The 'tawdry' effects she disliked were merely the expressions of his private world: he was not conscious of the tawdriness, since it was the idea, not the show, that mattered. But he was never really at home with them. They served rather insecurely as symbols and poetic possibilities, but the reality remained alien; it was the same with social life in general, with the aristocracy, with Napoleon, with kings. He accepted and believed in them up to a point; but they falsified his demands.

Byron's tendency to show himself, at one time a beau, regularly a lord and, finally, *in his own way*, a Napoleon, were all aspects of his will to self-dramatization and the incarnation of poetry; since all these, on different levels, held poetry. Nor was this all. Once, in a letter to Lady Melbourne, he wrote: 'Buonaparte has lost all his allies but *me* and the King of Wirtemberg. Do you remember Wolsey, "I and my King"? No matter, my alliance is quite as useful as that of Bavaria' (4 Nov. 1813; C, I, 214). Byron was interested in the damning *hubris* of Wolsey's phrase *Ego et Rex Meus* in *Henry VIII* (III, ii), and refers to it elsewhere (Hobhouse, 11 Nov. 1818; C, II, 89; Bowles Controversy, LJ, V, App. III, 568). He half felt himself a *rival* to the sovereigns he attacked. His Father, who was descended from the Normans, gave him a nobleman's rank; but through his Mother he believed that he had a yet greater, indeed a royal, ancestry.[1] Moore tells us how Mrs. Byron had dreams of his greatness, and was devoted to the fortunes of his early poetry; how she impelled him from the depths, from childhood, to his destiny, so that he could once again be compared with Napoleon, as one whose eminence was derived from a maternal impulse (XII, 128). Mrs. Byron was proud of her Gordon and Stuart descent and emphasized its superiority over her husband's ancestry (Moore, XII, 128). Now Byron was likewise interested. On leaving England he had sent Ada a gift: 'The ring is of no lapidary value, but it contains the hair of a King and of an ancestor, and I wish it to be preserved to Miss Byron' (Lady Byron, — April 1816; III, 281). In writing to Lady Melbourne on 7 April 1813 he was explicit:

'Your letters are delightful, particularly the parts *not* about Caroline, but *Carolus*. I wish he had exchanged heads with your Regent *Log* with all my heart, or that they were *stitched together;* what an

1. My discussion of Byron's grounds for this belief must be postponed.

admirable Janus of a fool and a knave. I take C (i.e. Charles the First) to be the greatest *king* (that is, villain) that ever lived. Our family got a peerage, and lost everything else for the Stuarts, and my mother was their lineal descendant (from James 2nd of *Scotland's* daughter); all the bad blood in my own composition I derive from those bastards of Banquo' (C, I, 147).

Charles is here a knave, the Regent a fool. But the Stuart king is not despised; the suggested exchange of heads underlines an admiration, though the swift return to 'knave' is Byronically forced. In his pregnant fashion Byron in one statement attributes greatness and villainy to King Charles. It is a greatness which *is* villainy, since kings are—for the immediate purpose—repudiated, but the greatness is there; and the Shakespearian quotation, ironically handled, completes the blazing enigma by raising it to the poetic dimension. We cannot say how much this sense of royal blood drawn from a line of kings who at least *were* kings meant to him; he may even have felt that he had a distant right to the throne. As for the 'bad blood', that may be grouped with his statement to Lady Blessington that the 'violent paroxysms of rage' to which he was subject from childhood derived from his Mother (Blessington, 127). Here is another relevant passage, written in an outburst of anger against Southey:

'What is there in such a man to "envy"? Whoever envied the envious? Is it his birth, his name, his fame, or his virtues, that I am to "envy"? I was born of the aristocracy, which he abhorred; and am sprung, by my mother, from the kings who preceded those whom he has hired himself to sing' (*Blackwood's* Defence; LJ, IV, App. IX, 483).

To the last he remembered his ancestry. It was something to which he tried, deliberately, to adjust himself, urging himself to 'awake', to 'think through whom' his 'life-blood' traced its descent (*On This Day I Complete My Thirty Sixth Year*). The valuation is Shakespearian, at once royal and poetic; the relation of poetry to royalty being exact.[1]

Granted, then, the knowledge of his own natural powers, together with his supposed blood-relationship to the magical radiations of royalty, Byron's behaviour assumes a new coherence. His turmoil

---

1. See my own working out of this relation in *The Olive and the Sword* and *Christ and Nietzsche;* and also my commentary on the royal boys in *Cymbeline* in *The Crown of Life.*

of soul during the years of his political challenge; his, and others', recognition of a similarity to Napoleon; the danger of his presence, like Hamlet's, all but challenging the Hanoverian usurper; all this is newly clear, at least as it took vague form in his own imagination. But, this granted, his record remains striking in point of democratic sympathy and a quite amazing humility. He appears to have rigidly distinguished his own, lesser, despised and slighted 'ego' from his other, greater, self as aristocrat or genius, rather as St. Paul distinguished himself from the 'Christ' (i.e. the 'anointed one') within. Moreover, whatever power, wealth, or greatness were his, were always at the disposal of the weak, the humble and the oppressed. He saw through the falsities of our social order whereby what were merely 'errors' in the rich became at once 'crimes' in the poor (Blessington, 328). He valued his title in part because it allowed him to associate the more freely with the low (Blessington, 372–3); 'he always admitted into his affections those who possessed fitting qualities of head or soul, without any consideration of their birth' (Teresa, II; XI, 201). In every man, however obscure, he recognized, as we have seen (p. 126), a being 'fit for the society of kings'.

Therefore, though he was an aristocrat by birth and would defend our 'ancient and honourable aristocracy' with his life (p. 147); though he could deplore the necessity, as he saw it, of revolution and the probability of a 'republic', sometimes, it is true, hailed, but elsewhere felt as only a second-best to the English constitution (pp. 145–7); though he was troubled to see the 'march of intellect' accompanied by a general reduction of eminence and distinction to 'the level of a decent mediocrity' (Blessington, 228); yet he never forgot the masses, and their rights, as men. When Parry told him of a plan to educate the workers in England, after asserting that the scheme should be guided *by* the workers (with fears lest they be 'duped'), and that they themselves should reap the benefits of their labours, he concluded by remarking that in this way the masses would learn to judge rightly of England's political system, and her nobility survive for ages to come; that is, the tradition would remain intact. He deplored the secession of America, which had left them with no traditions, no 'history'; nothing, that is, to look up to (Parry, IX, 204–14). Clearly, what Byron demanded was a *responsible and benevolent aristocracy,* or leader; a man, or men, of power and education able and anxious to assist, educate and raise—as he himself spent his life assisting, educating and raising—those below. His personal tragedy was forced by his agonized knowledge that nothing

of the sort was being done. Poverty, he told Parry, was to be preferred to 'the heartless unmeaning dissipation of the higher orders' at
home. 'I am thankful', he remarked, 'that I am now entirely clear
of this, and my resolution to remain clear of it for the rest of my life
shall be immutable' (Parry, IX, 205–6). He saw only too clearly that
few 'specimens' remained of 'the pure English patrician breed'
(Blessington, 54). The aristocracy and throne of England had failed
in leadership; and what, in Byron's day, was left? Aristocracy without talent he scorned. 'He seemed to think', wrote Lady Blessington
(160)—and one wonders how far she realized the profound implications of the conception—*that the bays of the author ought to be entwined
with a coronet to render either valuable*' (italics mine). Rank, as Byron
understood, or tried to understand, it, held spiritual radiations and a
spiritual responsibility.[1]

On 14 July 1824 the poet John Clare witnessed the effect of
Byron's funeral *cortège* on the common people of London, and later
described how clearly they felt his 'merits' and 'power'. 'The common
people' of any country, he says, are, in their instinctive feelings, prophetic; they are 'the veins and arteries that feed and quicken the
heart of living fame' (*John Clare*, J. W. and Annie Tibble, 1932; XI,
226). Their instinct was right, since in Byron the humblest had lost a
potential friend, a potential lover. So, 'they felt by a natural impulse
that the mighty was fallen, and they moved in saddened silence'.
Such heart-felt and simple reverence was of more worth than the
official honours of Church and State: 'It is said that Byron is not to
have a monument in Westminster Abbey. To him it is no injury.
Time is his monument, on whose scroll the name of Byron shall be
legible when the walls and tombs of Westminster Abbey shall have
mingled with the refuse of ruins, and the sun, as in scorn, be left
free again to smile upon the earth so long darkened with the
pompous shadows of bigotry and intolerance' (XI, 227).

II

At each step Byron appears to have been conscious of what he
was doing. He felt his life as a destiny, or a pattern, and tried to
adjust himself to that pattern. So we find him writing to his Mother
from Harrow in 1804, after being angered by certain slights from the
authorities:

1. Compare Byron's insistence on nobility as a necessary constituent to the best
poetry in the Bowles Controversy (LJ, V, App. III, 591–2).

'But thank God they may call me a Blackguard, but they can never make me one. If Dr. Drury can bring one boy or any one else to say that I have committed a dishonourable action, and to prove it, I am content. But otherwise I am stigmatized without a cause, and I disdain and despise the malicious efforts of him and his Brother' (SP, I, 9).

Feeling that he has been reproached for the 'narrowness' of his 'fortune', he continues:

'But, however, the way *to riches, to greatness,* lies before me. I can, I will, cut myself a path through the world or perish in the attempt. Others have begun life with nothing and ended greatly. And shall I, who have a competent if not a large fortune, remain idle? No, I will carve myself the passage to Grandeur, but never with Dishonour. These, Madam, are my intentions' (SP, I, 10).

Such was his occasional bitterness and will to self-assertion. From youth his lameness had troubled him and may be felt as acting on him as, according to *The Deformed Transformed* (I, I), it acted on Timur Leng. Slights, loneliness, his Mother's passions, his rather doubtful family fortune, all stimulated the boy's sense of innate power.

But his ambition was, as his letter shows, conditioned by honour and ethic. A good definition occurs in his early lines, dated 1806, to the Rev. J. T. Becher (used by the lynx-eyed Teresa, II; IX, 159), who had advised him to 'mix more with society'. He admits the wisdom of such advice, while saying that his temperament forbids him to 'descend' to a world which he 'despises', though 'ambition' may later prompt him to 'distinguish' his 'birth' in 'senate' or 'camp', and continues:

> The fire in the cavern of Etna conceal'd
>   Still mantles unseen in its secret recess;
> At length, in a volume terrific reveal'd,
>   No torrent can quench it, no bounds can repress.
>
> Oh! thus, the desire in my bosom for fame
>   Bids me live but to hope for posterity's praise.
> Could I soar with the phoenix on pinions of flame,
>   With him I would wish to expire in the blaze.
>
> For the life of a Fox, of a Chatham the death,
>   What censure, what danger, what woe would I brave!
> Their lives did not end when they yielded their breath;
>   Their glory illumines the gloom of their grave.

Yet why should I mingle in Fashion's full herd?
Why crouch to her leaders, or cringe to her rules?
Why bend to the proud, or applaud the absurd?
Why search for delight in the friendship of fools?

He has, he says, experienced love and friendship, and knows how
the one may prove bitter, the other false. As for wealth and title,

To me what is wealth?—It may pass in an hour,
If tyrants prevail, or if Fortune should frown:
To me what is title?—the phantom of power;
To me what is fashion?—I seek but renown.

Deceit is a stranger as yet to my soul:
I still am unpractised to varnish the truth:
Then why should I live in a hateful control?
Why waste upon folly the days of my youth?

This early poem does much to interpret Byron's later life; in it his
dominant interests lie beautifully exposed. Note especially his im-
agery of flame, so exactly forecasting the Prometheus-symbolisms we
are shortly to discuss; and the claim to 'truth'. Devotion to Truth,
'with all the qualities flowing from it', was to be, as Teresa tells us,
'the master-passion' of his mind (II; XV, 400).

Byron's reverence of fame was not self-centred: any trait of genuine
virtue or courage, any record of generosity, patriotism, or sacrifice
moved him deeply (Teresa, II; XIII, 295-6; Hobhouse and Lady
Blessington, my pp. 94-5, 97, 269). Byron's actions in Italy and
Greece were the direct result of living in himself the good he most
respected in the great names of history. His ambitions were, from an
early age, of the noblest kind. Consider again his statement to his
Mother on 1 July 1810:

'If I could by my own efforts inculcate the truth, that a man is
not intended for a despot or a machine, but as an individual of a
community, and fit for the society of kings, so long as he does not
trespass on the laws or rebel against just governments, I might
attempt to found a new Utopia . . .' (LJ, I, 284).

We are pointed not merely to what is good, but to what *is*: man *is*
already a person, or personality, with a purpose, and certain ways of
life thwart Providence ('intended'). 'Community' is used as a cor-
rective to the mechanical inter-relation of 'despot' and 'machine'.
Man is thus innately royal; kings are not lowered, but man raised;

law and order are respected and rebellion, unless forced, repudiated. Something very like the constitutional, that is the communal, monarchy of Britain today is suggested. If it be a 'Utopia', it is a sane one. Byron felt himself called on to lead the way to it.

Byron's loathing of tyranny was instinctive: 'It makes my blood boil to see the thing' (*Detached Thoughts*, Oct. 1821; LJ, v, 451). He was clearly, as Tricoupi's Funeral Oration emphasized, one 'destined by nature to uphold the rights of man whenever he saw them trampled upon'; and one with a clear sight of 'not only what man is, but what he ought to be and what he may be' (p. 217); these last phrases, properly understood, exactly reflecting, with a shift from metaphysics to ethics, our previous quotation, since both equally suggest a compelling necessity. But the weight of opposition was heavy. Here is another early miniature, written to Hodgson on 25 September 1811, with reference to certain national statements in the early *Childe Harold*:

'It would not answer for me to give way, now; as I was forced into bitterness at the beginning, I will go through to the last. *Vae Victis!* If I fall, I shall fall gloriously, fighting against a host' (LJ, II, 47).

But at first it seemed that little or nothing could be accomplished; and meanwhile he saw oppression everywhere; politics as rotten, England as treacherous, Europe ruined, and man's destiny compromised. The passionate republicanism of our next quotation, from the Journal of 23 November 1813, is the result of these confusions impinging on his will to leadership:

'If I had any views in this country, they would probably be parliamentary. But I have no ambition; at least, if any, it would be *aut Caesar aut nihil*. My hopes are limited to the arrangement of my affairs, and settling either in Italy or the East (rather the last), and drinking deep of the languages and literature of both. Past events have unnerved me; and all I can now do is to make life an amusement, and look on while others play. After all, even the highest game of crowns and sceptres, what is it? *Vide* Napoleon's last twelvemonth. It has completely upset my system of fatalism. I thought, if crushed, he would have fallen, when *fractus illabitur orbis*, and not have been pared away to gradual insignificance; that all this was not a mere *jeu* of the gods, but a prelude to greater changes and mightier events. But men never advance beyond a certain point; and here we

are, retrograding, to the dull, stupid old system—balance of Europe
—poising straws upon kings' noses, instead of wringing them off!
Give me a republic, or a despotism of one, rather than the mixed
government of one, two, three. A republic!—look in the history of
the Earth—Rome, Greece, Venice, France, Holland, America, our
short (*eheu!*) Commonwealth, and compare it with what they did
under masters. The Asiatics are not qualified to be republicans, but
they have the liberty of demolishing despots, which is the next thing
to it. To be the first man—not the Dictator—not the Sulla, but the
Washington or the Aristides—the leader in talent and truth—is next
to the Divinity! Franklin, Penn, and, next to these, either Brutus or
Cassius—even Mirabeau—or St. Just. I shall never be any thing,
or rather always be nothing. The most I can hope is, that some will
say, "He might, perhaps, if he would."

12 midnight.

'Here are two confounded proofs from the printer. I have looked
at the one, but for the soul of me, I can't look over that *Giaour* again
—at least, just now, and at this hour—and yet there is no moon'
(LJ, II, 338).

In the phraseology of his 1810 statement, Byron could not regard
England's as a 'just government', and was accordingly forced back
on thought of a leader 'in talent and truth'; but his recognition of such
a leader, at least for Europe, in Napoleon had been falsified by the
event.

He seems to have felt personally responsible. He had in 1810
known the compulsion to inculcate political truth by his 'own
efforts' (p. 126), and now imagines people saying, 'He might, perhaps, if he would.' When soliloquizing on Napoleon in his 1814
Journal, he had quoted against himself 'Brutus, thou sleepest' (p.154).
He varied between excessive ambition, '*Aut Caesar aut nihil*' (i.e.
'either Caesar or nothing'), and excessive humility, once (p. 154)
seeing himself as 'an insect' compared with Napoleon. Then again,
he who had so long despised himself, was finally disgusted with the
whole species for *falsifying their destiny as men* by the failure of Napoleon and restoration of the Bourbons (Journal, 19 April 1814; LJ,
II, 412; pp. 154, 159–60). He once considered Sulla 'as the greatest
character in History, for laying down his power at the moment when
it was "too great to keep or to resign", and thus despising them all'
(*My Dictionary*, May 1821; LJ, V, 404). Such scorn, even his *self-*
scorn, was itself an assumption of superiority; and his statement to

237

Lady Melbourne that he did not envy the Prince his regency (15 Jan. 1814; C, I, 235–6) was perhaps a half-truth only. He felt himself a natural leader, and yet remained as baffled as Hamlet. Moore rightly notes his diffidence and distrust of his poetic genius (VIII, 83); and yet he could also uncompromisingly refer—after leaving England—to his genius and the 'march of my mind' (Kinnaird, 2 May 1822; C, II, 223); and once (*Don Juan*, XI, 55–6) asserted, in contradiction of his early self-criticisms, that he, formerly 'the grand Napoleon of the realms of rhyme', would now reign as monarch or not at all. We have seen already (p. 159) how closely Byron associated himself with Napoleon; and his association, or affinity, was recognized by others. Gamba said that no one better understood the character and genius of Napoleon (I, 15–16); Parry said that he exerted 'something of that power over my mind' which Napoleon is said to have radiated (II, 24); and to Stanhope he was 'this extraordinary person, whom everybody was as anxious to see, and to know, as if he had been a Napoleon, the conqueror of the world' (Edgcumbe, I, XVI, 211). There was clearly something overpoweringly Napoleonic about him. Lady Blessington leaves us in no doubt that in conversation at least he could assert his own genius, whilst strongly denouncing a society that was repelled by, and jealous of, anything beyond mediocrity (see pp. 38–9, 250). The confusions, which are the natural confusions of genius here raised to an exceptional pitch, multiply. Pride, inferiority and shyness were all mixed in him as early as 1807 (Moore, IV, 43; and see XXI, 250–1). Byron's whole statement on both poetry and politics, his ambition for superlative leadership and liberating action, his respect for great men and hatred of official tyrants, his own self-despisal which was at once diffidence, scorn, and attack, are all vividly, if enigmatically, defined in one of his blazingly compact and multifacial miniatures, when, disgusted at being compared to Scott, the monarch (p. 53) of letters, he comments: 'Even if I had my choice, I would rather be the Earl of Warwick than all the *kings* he ever made' (Journal, 17 Nov. 1813; LJ, II, 322); of which the various poetic and political suggestions can be read in almost as many ways as there are words.

Only in so far as we realize how near Byron was in thought at least to claiming Napoleonic stature, can we properly understand his fury at the ignominy of Napoleon's fall, rising to 'it is but a bastard devil at last' (Lady Melbourne, 12 Jan. 1814; C, I, 231) and 'all Evil Spirit as thou art' (*Ode to Napoleon*, IX). Napoleon had satisfied his demand for human greatness. Byron had wanted Napoleon to be and do what he saw no clear way of being and doing himself. Had Napoleon only died 'as honour dies', mankind might yet have hoped for another such to arise and 'shame the world' (*Ode*, XI); that is, shame man with his own littleness, whilst giving future generations something to *look up to,* and aim at. But now humanity had been taught for all time not to submit to the spell of

> Those Pagod things of sabre sway
> With fronts of brass, and feet of clay.
>
> (III.)

The superman remained unincarnated and human creation without meaning or justification. That is why in the great passage of his Journal he wrote: 'To be sure, I have long despised myself and man, but I never spat in the face of my species before' (19 April 1814; LJ, II, 412). In Napoleon the whole 'species' fell. This was not the voice of jealousy; it derived rather from a craving to find something *greater than himself* to absolve him from the appalling duty of facing his own powers.

Napoleon's fate stood now as a living warning against all such fantasies. Though in a mood of self-denigration Byron could see himself as merely an 'insect' compared to Napoleon (p. 154), he could also feel himself as a potential leader:

> But who would soar the solar height
> To set in such a starless night?
>
> (*Ode to Napoleon,* XI.)

Henceforth he was a stern critic of all 'Napoleonic' actions. More, he tended to see them as comic. 'The laughing devils', he told Lady Blessington, who was surprised at his refusal to romanticize his approaching Greek expedition, *would* return and 'make a mockery of everything', since 'with me there is, as Napoleon said, but one step between the sublime and the ridiculous' (Blessington, 319). In *Childe Harold* (III, 36–45) he presents a remarkable diagnosis of Napoleon, whilst turning a searching light on his own half-formulated and self-mocked ambitions. He sees Napoleon as 'the greatest, not the worst, of men', swerving from the heights to pettiness, 'extreme in all things', and unable to find the middle path; one who thundered terror over the earth, at once conqueror and captive; flattered by Fame till he became a 'god' unto himself; a paradox, uncertain whether 'more or less than man'; crushing empires, but unable to command himself, and thus tempting fate. Though philosophic

in captivity, his life remains a torment, its soul's fire thirsting evermore for 'high adventure':

> This makes the madmen who have made men mad
> By their contagion; Conquerors and Kings,
> Founders of sects and systems, to whom add
> Sophists, Bards, Statesmen, all unquiet things
> Who stir too strongly the soul's secret springs,
> And are themselves the fools to those they fool;
> Envied, yet how unenviable! what stings
> Are theirs! One breast laid upon were a school
> Which would unteach mankind the lust to shine or rule.
>
> (III, 43.)

The diagnosis is throughout a self-diagnosis:

> He who surpasses or subdues mankind
> Must look down on the hate of those below.
>
> (III, 45.)

Which may serve as a text for genius, in any time or place. More,
its very aptitude for such a text defines the relation between 'surpassing' and 'subduing'. The imaginative genius is a Napoleon of the
mind or soul, and the hatred aroused is the natural reaction to a
tyrannic and mastering power.

Simple definition fails before Byron's mixture, almost identity,
of pride and humility, his own confusion as to whether his ambition
or his inaction be the greater cause for self-despisal. And yet, at the
base, was, as he knew, a superlative virtue. *Manfred* is a study of a
Faust-like figure who yet appears *simultaneously greater and inferior,
better and worse* than other men (as Napoleon was invoked as 'more
or less than man' at *Childe Harold,* III, 38); one who is known for
'deeds of good and ill, extreme in both' (II, ii). Manfred *feels* superior:

> For if the beings, of whom I was one—
> Hating to be so—cross'd me in my path,
> I felt myself degraded back to them,
> And was all clay again.
>
> (II, ii.)

And yet he suffers from an agony of remorse, a dark sense of loneliness and evil, and the bitterness of failure:

MANFRED: Ay—father! I have had those earthly visions,
        And noble aspirations in my youth,

> To make my own the mind of other men,
> The enlightener of nations; and to rise
> I knew not whither—it might be to fall;
> But fall, even as the mountain-cataract,
> Which, having leapt from its more dazzling height
> Even in the foaming strength of its abyss
> (Which casts up misty columns that become
> Clouds raining from the re-ascended skies)
> Lies low but mighty still.—But this is past,
> My thoughts mistook themselves.

ABBOT: And wherefore so?

MANFRED: I could not tame my nature down; for he
> Must serve who fain would sway; and soothe, and sue,
> And watch all time, and pry into all place,
> And be a living lie, who would become
> A mighty thing amongst the mean, and such
> The mass are; I disdain'd to mingle with
> A herd, though to be leader—and of wolves.
> The lion is alone, and so am I.   (III, i.)

That is certainly true of Byron. He, like Manfred 'the enlightener of nations', had refused to extend his poetic fame by meeting the Regent's advances. He fell—or rose—by a Promethean pride.

To Byron's imaginative eye the archetypal figure of Prometheus was associated with his dreams of human advance. Of the three Greek tragedies he most enjoyed in youth, one was the *Prometheus* of Aeschylus of which he was 'passionately fond' (Murray, 12 Oct. 1817; IV, 174), some lines of which, translated at Harrow, appear among the early poems. The myth was, necessarily, cogent to the romantic imagination; Shelley wrote a major work on it, and Hobhouse records his reading of Aeschylus' play in 1814: 'I finished yesterday the *Prometheus* of Aeschylus. Went to the play with Byron, to his box . . .' (10 March 1814; I; V, 94). Prometheus opposed tyranny in the cause of human advance; he is the fire-bringer and fore-thinker, nourishing the divine spark in man and looking to his great futurity. It is accordingly important that Byron saw Napoleon's *survival* of failure as a failure to assume Promethean stature:

> Or, like the thief of fire from heaven,
> Wilt thou withstand the shock?
> And share with him, the unforgiven,
> His vulture and his rock!

Fordoom'd by God—by man accurst,
And that last act, though not thy worst,
    The very Fiend's arch mock;
He in his fall preserved his pride,
And, if a mortal, had as proudly died!
                            (*Ode to Napoleon,* XVI.)

Again, in the (much later) *Age of Bronze,* Prometheus is invoked to
pronounce the moral of St. Helena:

Hear! hear Prometheus from his rock appeal
To earth, air, ocean, all that felt or feel
His power and glory, all who yet shall hear
A name eternal as the rolling year.
                                        (v.)

Prometheus is the archetypal and therefore 'eternal' principle of
human liberation and advance. And this is the moral:

A single step into the right had made
This man the Washington of worlds betray'd:
A single step into the wrong has given
His name a doubt to all the winds of heaven;
The reed of Fortune, and of thrones the rod,
Of Fame the Moloch or the demigod;
His country's Caesar, Europe's Hannibal,
Without their decent dignity of fall.
Yet Vanity herself had better taught
A surer path even to the fame he sought,
By pointing out on history's fruitless page
Ten thousand conquerors for a single sage.
                                        (v.)

Franklin, Washington, Bolivar are contrasted—must Europe have
none such? There is, I think, an unacknowledged hint that Napoleon is, or might have been, a greater than those, had not 'France got
drunk with blood to vomit crime' (*Childe Harold,* IV, 97). Napoleon
was one

Who burst the chains of millions to renew
The very fetters which his arm broke through . . .
                            (*The Age of Bronze,* v.)

Such was the enigmatic hero, half-god, half-devil, denounced by the 'eternal' Prometheus.

The great task of Byron's life was to subdue, or rather raise, the Napoleonic to the Promethean. Manfred was, like the Napoleon of *Childe Harold,* compounded of

> Light and darkness,
> And mind and dust, and passions and pure thoughts
> Mix'd, and contending without end or order.
>
> (III, i.)

And yet he was one born to be the 'enlightener of nations' (p. 241). He was accordingly Promethean:

> Slaves, scoff not at my will!
> The mind, the spirit, the Promethean spark,
> The lightning of my being is as bright,
> Pervading, and far-darting as your own.
>
> (I, i.)

Byron laboured throughout for the 'Promethean spark' in man. The spirit of liberty was such a 'spark'; it would spread like a 'spark' in dry grass (Lady Byron, 1 March 1821, LJ, v, 383); death would be nothing 'if a single spark of that which would be worthy of the past can be bequeathed unquenchedly to the future' (Journal, 9 Jan. 1821; LJ, v, 163); death's beauty is itself a 'spark' gleaming from life's 'heavenly birth' (*The Giaour*). 'I should be glad', Byron told Medwin who had praised certain lines on Greece, 'to think I have added a spark to the flame' (Medwin, 284). 'He is a sworn foe', wrote Lady Blessington, 'to Materialism, tracing every defect to which we are subject to the infirmities entailed on us by the prison of clay in which the heavenly spark is confined' (Blessington, 105). The divine essence was in question in all Byron's political thinking and the true leader one who (i) alleviates, like his own Sardanapalus, human misery, and (ii) nurtures, like Prometheus, the divine fire. It was mainly because Napoleon, through his personal magnetism, ful-filled *in part* the second condition that Byron went so far towards forgiving him his failures in both.

The true Prometheus, however, must act more gently. In 1816, the year of his rejection by London, Byron composed his poem *Prometheus:*

> Thy Godlike crime was to be kind.
> To render with thy precepts less

> The sum of human wretchedness,
> And strengthen man with his own mind . . .
>
> (III.)

There (with 'mind' as the divine 'spark') the two conditions are balanced. We may recall Byron's will to be a 'leader in talent and truth' (p. 237) and his many associations of 'philosophy' (pp. 175–7) with his chosen direction as 'enlightener of nations' (*Manfred*, III, i; p. 241). Such a Prometheus is 'kind', a universal lover. He will be a poet, but not necessarily a poet in writing; he will be rather an incarnation of poetry. In *The Prophecy of Dante* Byron defined again this Prometheus, outlining one aspect of his own lonely self in repudiation of poetic fame:

> Many are poets who have never penn'd,
>> Their inspiration, and perchance the best:
>> They felt, and loved, and died, but would not lend
>
> Their thoughts to meaner beings; they compress'd
>> The god within them, and rejoin'd the stars
>> Unlaurel'd upon earth, but far more bless'd
>
> Than those who are degraded by the jars
>> Of passion, and their frailties linked to fame,
>> Conquerors of high renown, but full of scars.
>
> Many are poets but without the name,
>> For what is poetry but to create
>> From overfeeling good or ill; and aim
>
> At an eternal life beyond our fate,
>> And be the new Prometheus of new men,
>> Bestowing fire from Heaven, and then, too late,
>
> Finding the pleasure given repaid with pain,
>> And vultures to the heart of the bestower,
>> Who, having lavish'd his high gift in vain,
>
> Lies chain'd to his lone rock by the sea-shore?
>> So be it: we can bear.—But thus all they
>> Whose intellect is an o'ermastering power
>
> Which still recoils from its encumbering clay
>> Or lightens it to spirit, whatsoe'er
>> The form which their creations may essay,
>
> Are bards . . .
>
> (IV.)

That is an excellent self-portrait. It contains two selves; the lonely, superior, ascetic Byron, independent of fame, self-dedicated and self-renowned, an ideal which helps to explain many of his peculiar repudiations; but also it defines the poet, the Promethean liberator and advancer of man, 'the new Prometheus of new men', which Byron became, striving for man's mental liberation in opposition to a society 'without one spark of intellectual fire' (*The Curse of Minerva*); opposed by inertia and 'custom's falsest scale', with

> Opinion an omnipotence—whose veil
> Mantles the earth with darkness, until right
> And wrong are accidents, and men grow pale
> Lest their own judgments should become too bright,
> And their free thoughts be crimes, and earth have too
> much light.
>
> (*Childe Harold*, IV, 93.)

The 'ambrosial sin' of young love's first freedom is equated with Prometheus' fiery theft (*Don Juan*, I, 127). Such positive powers remain basic to all education; and when, hearing from Parry of the school for artisans (see p. 232 above), Byron remarked, 'It gives me pleasure to think what a mass of natural intellect this will call into action' (Parry, IV, 205), '*natural* intellect' suggests the potential mind-fire whose stifling or ignition depends on social assistance. Or, even, on the reviewers. 'Poor fellow,' he wrote of Keats, 'his was an untoward fate', and continued:

> 'Tis strange the mind, that fiery particle,
> Should let itself be snuff'd out by an article.
>
> (*Don Juan*, XI, 60.)

And yet there is, too, a magic power in the poet's words that can survive death:

> But words are things, and a small drop of ink,
> Falling, like dew, upon a thought, produces
> That which makes thousands, perhaps millions, think.
>
> (*Don Juan*, III, 88.)

That is, in Byron's view, the business of poetry, of all writing; he feels it not merely as enjoyment, nor, normally, as strictly prophetic, but rather as, pre-eminently, mental fire.

He was instinctively, from first to last, the educator (Index A, IV), and that is why he was so interested in the workers' education.

Byron's Promethean survey was wide, even encroaching on recent scientific advances. Once when discussing steam, air-travel and the possibility of voyages to the moon, he instinctively equated such advances with the myth of Prometheus (Medwin, 227–8). His views on medical science, in which, he said, he had as little faith as Napoleon, were ahead of his time, laying emphasis on the 'idiosyncrasies' of different persons, on temperament and psychology, and the dangers of over-dieting, which he asserted to be the cause of 'more than half our maladies', through putting 'too much oil into the lamp' till it 'blazes and burns out' instead of burning 'brightly and steadily' (Blessington, 367). If Byron's thoughts and feelings justify the Countess Albrizzi's rating of them as 'more stupendous and un-measured' than those of a Napoleon (LJ, IV, App. II, 442), that is precisely because Byron's intellect was Promethean rather than Napoleonic. He instinctively associated himself with Prometheus. 'They might as well', he wrote to Moore of *Marino Faliero* on 20 January 1821, 'act the *Prometheus* of Aeschylus. I speak of course humbly and with the greatest sense of the distance of time and merit between the two performances' (LJ, V, 229). Once, in a context that suggests a reference to himself, he described a poet as one 'whose works have raised our thoughts above this sphere of common every-day existence, and who, Prometheus-like, has stolen fire from Heaven to animate the children of clay' (Blessington, 184). Again, when suffering from a chill and bilious attack after a rash adventure in the water, on being asked by Trelawny how he felt, 'Feel!' he replied. 'Why just as that damned obstreperous fellow felt chained to a rock, the vultures gnawing my midriff, and my vitals, too' (Trelawny, XIV). Notice the half-ironic characterization of Prometheus as 'damned obstreperous'. The implications go deeper than you would think; for Byron felt himself opposed by mighty powers, by tyrannic powers, like Prometheus, or Satan. 'In all he wrote at this fatal period of his life', says Teresa, 'one perceives the wide gaping wound, which is however endured with the strength of a Titan' (II; II, 32). 'His attacks on the world', wrote Lady Blessington, 'are like the war of the Titans against the Gods—the weapons he aims fall back on himself' (304). In his *History of Western Philosophy*, Bertrand Russell devotes a section to Byron (XXIII, 774–80) in which he differentiates the aristocratic rebel from others with more obvious reasons for revolt as one fighting for something greater than personal success. 'It may be that love of power is the underground source of their discontent, but in their conscious thought there is criticism of the government of the world, which, when it goes deep enough, takes the form of Titanic cosmic self-assertion or, in those who retain some superstition, of Satanism. Both are to be found in Byron' (775). That Byron saw the great man as 'a Titan at war with himself' (777) is correct enough, but the inmost cause of Byron's pain must be observed. Like his own Prometheus and Sardanapalus, Byron endured with a peculiar sensitivity a clear sight of man's 'sufferings', and an attendant sense in himself of endurance under an 'inexorable Heaven' and 'the ruling principle of Hate' (*Prometheus*, I, II). From childhood he bitterly regarded his lameness as 'a signal mark of the injustice of Providence' (Blessington, 128). It was the same with his later hero, in *Cain;* and hence, as Russell notes, Titanic assertion and Satanism converged.

Byron was himself tortured by those 'antithetically mixed' qualities he attributed to Napoleon, 'one moment of the mightiest', and the next miserably small, 'a god unto thyself', yet doubtful whether 'more or less than man' (*Childe Harold*, III, 36–8). He seems to have felt evil, or at least cursed; and his rejection by society, with the accompanying charges of unholy crime, can have done little to remove the superstition. 'From his boyhood', wrote Edgcumbe, Byron 'always believed that there was a blood-curse on him' (II, 293). 'Always' may be an exaggeration, but certainly Manfred suffers from some 'half-maddening sin' associated with the shedding of blood (II; i, ii). Byron's early Calvinist up-bringing helped to inculcate a sense of guilt and predestined damnation. From his boyhood he was an Ishmael (Miss Milbanke, 26 Sept.; Journal, 22 Nov.; 1813; LJ, III, 402; II, 330). Manfred is a lonely soul, a thing apart (II, ii). Byron's *poetic* being appears to have felt itself opposed not merely by the Tories and London society, but by Providence; the reservation being necessary, since his prose thinking and conversation kept on happier—if awestruck—terms with 'the Deity'. The darker poetry drives to the limit an implanted tendency; and it is this struggle with the *lesser* deities, or devils, of damnation that is dramatized in *Manfred*, where the hero is *both greater and inferior* in relation to what Nietzsche called 'the herd'; while in *Cain* the whole pattern is elucidated in terms of Old Testament myth, with the hero indeed guilty, but guilty *by reason of his loving gentleness to the animal creation*, and so condemned. Such an attribution of positive significance to Cain is important. We find it again in Ibsen's *Emperor and Galilean*, in direct Byronic descent.

Highest virtue is, and must be, anti-social; more, it *plays with fire*, like Prometheus, and is therefore as near the Satanic as the Divine. The Divine, as it were, becomes Satanic under opposition, and may begin to endure the *fiery* guilt of the great 'scorpion' passage in *The Giaour*. In his *Monody on the Death of Sheridan*, written shortly after his own disaster, every word 'direct from my heart' (Blessington, 241), Byron vividly described how those 'who track the steps of glory to the grave' tend instinctively to persecute greatness, how they

> Watch every fault that daring Genius owes
> Half to the ardour which its birth bestows,
> Distort the truth, accumulate the lie,
> And pile the pyramid of Calumny!

Even the greatest are thus worn down, however strongly charged with Promethean fire:

> If such may be the ills which men assail,
> What marvel if at last the mightiest fail?
> Breasts to whom all the strength of feeling's given
> Bear hearts electric charged with fire from Heaven,
> Black with the rude collision, inly torn,
> By clouds surrounded, and on whirlwinds borne,
> Driven o'er the lowering atmosphere that nurst
> Thoughts which have turn'd to thunder—scorch,
>   and burst.

Compare the '*electric* thought' of *Lara* (xxvi), the *electric* chain and 'lightning of the mind' of *Childe Harold* (IV, 23–4; and see 41, 88), and ideas that 'lighten through the frame' in *The Waltz*. The *Monody* here tells the truth less of Sheridan than of Byron, and so, the voice softening—the lines were written for the stage—the address continues

> But far from us and from our mimic scene
> Such things should be—if such have ever been;
> Ours be the gentler wish, the kinder task,
> To give the tribute Glory need not ask . . .

Sometimes, however, genius may be *forced* to ask, to assert its rights. Byron saw himself as 'lightning' in *Manfred* (p. 243). Again:

> Could I embody and unbosom now
> That which is most within me—could I wreak
> My thoughts upon expression, and thus throw
> Soul, heart, mind, passions, feelings, strong or weak,

All that I would have sought, and all I seek,
Bear, know, feel, and yet breathe—into *one* word,
And that one word were Lightning, I would speak;
But as it is, I live and die unheard,
With a most voiceless thought, sheathing it as a sword.
(*Childe Harold*, III, 97.)

And when the time came he levelled his lonely curse on mankind
in the exact manner of Aeschylus'—and his own (in his poem of
that name)—Prometheus, calling the elements to witness his
complaint:

And thou, who never yet of human wrong
Left the unbalanced scale, great Nemesis!
Here, where the ancient paid thee homage long—
Thou who didst call the Furies from the abyss,
And round Orestes bade them howl and hiss
For that unnatural retribution—just,
Had it but been from hands less near—in this
Thy former realm, I call thee from the dust!
Dost thou not hear my heart?—Awake! thou shalt, and must.

It is not that I may not have incurr'd
For my ancestral faults or mine the wound
I bleed withal, and, had it been conferr'd
With a just weapon, it had flow'd unbound;
But now my blood shall not sink in the ground;
To thee I do devote it—*thou* shalt take
The vengeance, which shall yet be sought and found,
Which if *I* have not taken for the sake—
But let that pass—I sleep, but thou shalt yet awake.

And if my voice break forth, 'tis not that now
I shrink from what is suffer'd: let him speak
Who hath beheld decline upon my brow,
Or seen my mind's convulsion leave it weak;
But in this page a record will I seek.
Not in the air shall these my words disperse,
Though I be ashes; a far hour shall wreak
The deep prophetic fulness of this verse,
And pile on human heads the mountain of my curse!

That curse shall be Forgiveness.—Have I not—
Hear me, my mother Earth! behold it, Heaven!

Have I not had to wrestle with my lot?
Have I not suffer'd things to be forgiven?
Have I not had my brain sear'd, my heart riven,
Hopes sapp'd, name blighted, Life's life lied away?
And only not to desperation driven
Because not altogether of such clay
As rots into the souls of those whom I survey.

(*Childe Harold,* IV, 132–5.)

These are the stanzas which Hobhouse tried to make Byron suppress (note to Hobhouse, 5 March 1818; C, II, 69), and which, as we shall see, infuriated Shelley. Teresa defends them (II; II, 31).

Though in both prose and poetry he was normally averse from laying direct claim to his own powers, yet the Blessington conversations show how bitterly Byron realized that he had been persecuted not for his faults, but for his greatness (p. 38); that a certain 'superiority' caused him to be 'assailed by all the falsehoods that malice could invent or slander publish' (276); that his powers excited the 'malice' of his 'calumniators', his fame itself acting as the 'blaze' of his own 'funeral pile' (382); that, while 'mediocrity' was regularly acclaimed (173–4, 276), while wealth might be pardoned if liberally handled, beauty forgiven if 'accompanied by folly', and 'talent' tolerated if not 'of a very superior order', 'genius' could 'hope for no mercy' (124–6):

He who surpasses or subdues mankind
Must look down on the hate of those below

(*Childe Harold,* III, 45.)

Such hatred is increased by the knowledge that its object remains untouched (Blessington, 383). That such was the nature of the attacks on Byron is clear enough. To understand these Promethean stanzas one must therefore be willing to believe that Teresa may have been exactly right when she tells us that the English aristocracy were furious with Byron 'for revealing their weaknesses and upbraiding their pretensions' (I; I, 50); and that, during the crisis of 1816, an unnamed person called on him suggesting that the campaign of lies would be stopped if he changed his political opinions (I; Int., 40; note). The editor John Scott later admitted to Byron 'that he, and others, had been greatly misled; and that some pains, and rather extraordinary means, had been taken to excite them' (LJ, V, App. III, 576; see also Teresa, II; V, 87). Byron knew himself the victim of deliberate calumny; and it is generally agreed that such was, in the main, what happened; that, as Teresa puts it, 'the first cause of the unjust verdicts passed upon him lay in the bad passions stirred up by his success, by the independent language he used, and his contempt for a thousand national prejudices' (II; VI, 96). But there was more in it than literature, or even politics. Whether or not persecution tends, as Teresa suggests, to oppress 'all greatness and all virtues' (II; VI, 104), Byron's story certainly supports the thesis. What he told Lady Blessington of Napoleon is yet truer of himself: 'This was the rock on which Napoleon foundered; he had so often wounded the *amour propre* of others, that they were glad to hurl him from the eminence that made him appear a giant and those around him pigmies'. From the other side, the discrepancy is defined by his admission that he felt in London 'cabin'd, cribb'd, confined', like 'a Tiger in too small a cage' (Blessington, 336–7; *Macbeth*, III, iv).[1] He was consequently rejected rather as a bird of strange plumage is set upon by those more normally accommodated. And if it appear almost unbelievable that intelligent and upright people should descend to irrational and dishonest behaviour merely because they are faced by a power beyond their comprehension, we can offer a vivid example with, as its subject, a person of unimpeachable intelligence and integrity: Percy Bysshe Shelley.

Shelley saw Byron at Venice in August and September of 1818 and set down a poetic record of their meeting in *Julian and Maddalo,* composed in the same year. In his Preface he describes Maddalo, supposed a Venetian nobleman:

'He is a person of the most consummate genius, and capable, if he would direct his energies to such an end, of becoming the redeemer of his degraded country. But it is his weakness to be proud: he derives, from a comparison of his own extraordinary mind with the dwarfish intellects that surround him, an intense apprehension of the nothingness of human life. His passions and his powers are incomparably greater than those of other men; and, instead of the latter having been employed in curbing the former, they have mutually lent each other strength. His ambition preys upon itself, for want of objects which it can consider worthy of exertion. I say that Maddalo is proud, because I can find no other word to express the concentred and impatient feelings which consume him; but it is on his own hopes and affections only that he seems to trample, for in

1. The Blessington *Conversations* are, like the letters, sprinkled with Shakespearian quotations (e.g. also at 228, 317).

social life no human being can be more gentle, patient, and unassuming than Maddalo. He is cheerful, frank, and witty. His more
serious conversation is a sort of intoxication; men are held by it as
by a spell.'

In discussion of the cosmic mystery, Julian (= Shelley) argues
against that 'despondency' or seemingly perverted view of human
nature which Lady Blessington continually deplored:

> but pride
> Made my companion take the darker side.
> The sense that he was greater than his kind
> Had struck, methinks, his eagle spirit blind
> By gazing on its own exceeding light.
>
> (48.)

The poem next describes a visit to a madhouse, where there lives a
stranger who had gone mad, and whom Maddalo had supplied
with books, flower-vases and musical instruments:

> Nay, this was kind of you—he had no claim,
> As the world says—'None, but the very same
> Which I on all mankind were I as he
> Fallen to such deep reverse . . .'
>
> (262.)

The words suggest Byron's personal benevolences; but the Maniac
also reflects those 'affections' on which Shelley's Preface, in the
manner of the Blessington *Conversations* (pp. 38, 83), sees him as
'trampling'. Two persons, as in Disraeli's *Venetia*, are thus used to
cover the Byronic complexity, their association being pointed by the
name 'Maddalo'. The Maniac, like Maddalo in the Preface, was
proud in a peculiar way:

> There are some by nature proud,
> Who, patient in all else, demand but this—
> To love and be beloved with gentleness;
> And being scorned, what wonder if they die
> Some living death?
>
> (206.)

That is exactly true, as we have seen (pp. 66–7, 93, 96–8; especially
Blessington, 169) of Byron.

The Maniac has hitherto been vaguely and far from satisfactorily equated with Shelley himself, as in Dr. Newman Ivey White's discussion in his *Shelley* (II; XX, and notes). But that does not fit the text. He is one who sympathized with 'the Stranger's tear', who 'loved and pitied all things', responding to woes of which others were oblivious; who wept with the poor and the imprisoned, himself a lonely

> nerve o'er which do creep
> The else unfelt oppressions of this earth.
>
> (442.)

He is said to be deeply grieved by oppression and cant, but nevertheless a humorist (237–44). He tells his story, and it is Byron's. It asserts devotion to 'truth' (348) and implacable opposition to tyranny (363). It recounts (383–510) a hideous reversal in love (= the marriage disaster), whilst denying (408–11) the 'pride' with which Lady Byron had repeatedly charged him (LJ, III, 300, 311, 313; and see my p. 275). It includes appropriate thoughts of his 'spirit's mate' (= Augusta, 337) and his child (= Ada, 484). We have his loss of 'friends and fortune' (535). He suffers agonies recalling *Manfred* (382–97), but is used to represent *a side of Byron* that rejects scorn, hate, ambition, revenge or avarice as anodynes (355, 366–8). He insists, moreover, that he forgives (500–1) in spite of everything, exactly following the Byron of *Childe Harold IV*, which Byron discussed with Shelley on his first visit,[1] and Shelley is known to have read aloud on the second (White, II; XX, 34, 39); and so we are told that 'the wild language of his grief' was 'such as in measure is called poetry' (541). Shelley, who half thought Byron mad (p. 255), explicitly stated that the Maniac was an idealized 'painting from nature' (White, II; XX, 43; Notes, 559). The intention is surely transparent.

In his *Lines Written Among the Euganean Hills*, composed during October 1818, Shelley sees Venice as redeemed from utter degradation in slavery by having afforded Byron an asylum:

> That a tempest-cleaving Swan
> Of the songs of Albion,
> Driven from his ancestral streams
> By the might of evil dreams,
> Found a nest in thee; and Ocean

---

1. Dr. White says that in August 'Byron was full of his wounded feelings and of the fourth canto of *Childe Harold's Pilgrimage* which he was then writing' (II; XX, 34). He had, however, completed it well before Shelley's visit.

Welcomed him with such emotion
That its joy grew his, and sprung
From his lips like music flung
O'er a mighty thunder-fit
Chastening terror . . .

(174.)

'Music' refers to the great invocation to Ocean at the conclusion to
Childe Harold succeeding the 'thunder-fit' of the Promethean stanzas.
But what of the 'might of evil dreams'? Shelley was aware of a pro-
fundity in Byron at once authentic and, since fearful, a kind of
'evil'. This is clearer in an important sonnet of the same (White,
II, XX, 50–3) group:

Lift not the painted veil which those who live
Call Life: though unreal shapes be pictured there,
And it but mimic all we would believe
With colours idly spread,—behind, lurk Fear
And Hope, twin Destinies; who ever weave
Their shadows o'er the chasm, sightless and drear.

Here Shelley has passed to Maddalo's side in his argument with
Julian; he confesses that life's superficial appearance is a cheat.
Behind, lie Fear and Hope; that is, (i) something terrible and yet
also (ii) the *one real hope for humanity;* Satan and Prometheus; or
Satan-Prometheus. Shelley likewise regarded the basis of *Julian and
Maddalo* as something 'dreadful or beautiful' (White, Notes to XX;
II; 559). Byron personified this dual mystery, had penetrated this
dimension; and our sonnet accordingly continues, with more remin-
ders of Shelley's preface, Maddalo and the Maniac:

I knew one who had lifted it—he sought,
For his lost heart was tender, things to love,
But found them not, alas! nor was there aught
The world contains, the which he could approve.
Through the unheeding many he did move,
A splendour among shadows, a bright blot
Upon this gloomy scene, a Spirit that strove
For truth, and like the Preacher found it not.

I cannot agree with Dr. White that Shelley is here writing of himself. Every line is corroborated in Teresa's study; the tenderness, the
craving to expend himself in love (cp. Blessington, 284; p. 97), the
uncompromising and world-damning idealism, the unique splen-

dour, the ruling passion of 'truth', in all its forms, which she coupled with generosity as the two qualities 'dividing the empire of his soul' (Teresa, II; IV, 51; 'Love of Truth', xv). But see how, with all this admitted, Shelley yet, with a poet's honesty in paradox, calls him at once 'a splendour among shadows' and 'a bright blot upon this gloomy scene'. The unique excellence is disturbing, it spoils the picture. And Shelley means it. A fragment *To Byron* (also 1818) runs:

> O mighty mind, in whose deep stream this age
> Shakes like a reed in the unheeding storm,
> Why dost thou curb not thine own sacred rage?

There, compactly, is what happened in London: Byron fell on his contemporaries like an elemental force. His impact shook the age; and Shelley, with others, was disturbed.

His perturbation was genuine. He used to say that at this period he had formed a 'far higher' estimation of Byron's 'powers' than ever before (Moore, XXXII, 382). And yet, after his third visit to Byron (LJ, IV, 259, note), he was writing to Peacock on 22 December 1818: 'I entirely agree with what you say about *Childe Harold*. The spirit in which it is written is, if insane, the most wicked and mischievous insanity that ever was given forth. It is a kind of obstinate and self-willed folly in which he hardens himself. I remonstrated with him in vain on the tone of mind from which such a view of things alone arises . . .' (LJ, IV, 259, note). He next proceeded to imply that these denunciatory stanzas sprang from Byron's disgust at his Venetian associates, whereas they were obviously motivated by the London calumnies that precipitated his exile. Shelley admitted the greatness of the address to Ocean, and acknowledged that Byron showed 'a certain degree of candour while you talk to him', but added that 'it does not outlast your departure', and concludes: 'No, I do not doubt, and for his sake, I ought to hope, that his present career must end soon in some violent circumstance.' The style witnesses a certain unease: 'violent circumstance' is a vile phrase. Shelley was in the painful position of having to reject with his prose thinking what his poetic genius had already recognized as something of superlative, if baffling, greatness. We must beware of underrating his difficulties. One has only to let the thunder of those stanzas roll through the mind *without putting up any mental defences* to feel vaguely what powers Byron's presence must, on occasion, have radiated.

But were these powers in any ultimate sense evil? Fear and Hope, wrote Shelley, were the inhabitants of that unseen world Byron had penetrated. Fear is not necessarily evil. In religious experience the fear of God may be the threshold of wisdom. 'So alien to your soul is the great', wrote Nietzsche, 'that the Superman would seem to you *terrible* in his goodness . . . I divine that ye would call my Superman the devil' (*Thus Spake Zarathustra* II, 21). What if those Venetian women, to Shelley 'perhaps the most contemptible of all who exist under the moon—the most ignorant, the most disgusting, the most bigoted'; in a city where even 'the countesses smell so strongly of garlic, that an ordinary Englishman cannot approach them'; what if Byron's association with 'the lowest sort of these women', and with 'wretches who seem almost to have lost the gait and physiognomy of man' (LJ, IV, 260, note), were—whatever the vices indulged or pretended—*a necessary part of his goodness*? His Venetian experience was nothing new; at the most an exaggeration of an implanted tendency. He consorted regularly with the lowest in society. He told Lady Blessington how in London he would rush from an assembly of grand names to find relief—'are you not shocked?' he asked—in a 'cider-cellar', where he found more food for speculation than in the 'vapid circles of glittering dullness'; and how he was abused for dining at Tom Cribb's (Blessington, 372–4). After his break with London society, he inevitably plunged deep in revulsion, balancing Manfred's 'I plunged amidst mankind' (II, ii). Women of all sorts loved him to distraction. The poor of city after city, both 'honest' and 'dishonest'(Teresa, I; IX, 395), looked on him as a father (pp. 88–9). Besides, do we not find the saints of Christendom taking an almost perverted delight in contact with the dregs of humanity? Was not Christ himself blamed for consorting with the lowest of the low? Did not *his* critics, like Byron's, see him as allied with Satanic powers? And, in conclusion, can one conceive of Byron writing of *any* human beings whatsoever, except the self-righteous, the hypocrites, the tyrants and time-servers, in the vein of Shelley's letter? Lady Blessington observed his kindliness to beggars, especially when deformed (p. 229; see also Stanhope, quoted Edgcumbe, I; XVI, 206). Teresa tells that his humour was never directed against any 'involuntary defect', physical or mental; how his 'favourite beggar' at Ravenna limped; and how when everyone, including 'the kind Shelley', was making fun of Taaffe, the Dante enthusiast, Byron, recognizing his *sincerity*, alone took up his cause (Teresa, II; XIII, 286–9; p. 58 above). Finally, we may gather something of the nature of Byron's experience from Shelley's letter: 'He says he disapproves, but he endures.'

And there is more to say. In her *Shelley and the Unromantics,* Olwen Ward Campbell admitted that Shelley was 'much influenced' by Byron (II, 23); that he 'drew material, and, if not inspiration, *impulse*' from Byron's works (II, 34); that his powers were 'immensely stimulated' by—among other stimulants—'friendship with Byron' (V, 140). 'At this time', she writes of the autumn of 1818, 'Byron meant much to him' (VIII, 233). But exactly how much, no one has, it seems, realized. During the summer he wrote that he was unable to compose; 'and within a few months of this lament', says Miss Campbell, 'he has composed *Julian and Maddalo, The Lines Written Among the Euganean Hills,* and the first act of *Prometheus Unbound*' (V, 161). She attributes this renewal of inspiration to his reading of Greek. But he had meanwhile visited Byron at Venice; of the three works named, one is specifically about Byron; the other contains the eulogy already quoted and, being concerned largely with Venetian slavery in the manner of Byron's *Ode on Venice,* may be called strictly Byronic in theme. There remains the first act of *Prometheus Unbound.*

Shelley wrote of the labour his *Prometheus* caused him, and regarded it 'the most perfect of my productions', claiming it to be 'original', without any real resemblance to the Greek. 'But where his idea for it originated', writes Miss Campbell, 'he does not tell us.' Shelley named the Italian climate as an inspiration, but it must, she says, 'have had one other parent', which she takes, rather weakly, to be Aeschylus (VII, 197–8). Weakly, since Aeschylus is, of course, *behind* the drama: Shelley only meant that his work was not directly and inherently derivative. The unnamed parent was, very clearly, Byron. Shelley's preface admits his work's relation to both Milton and contemporary writers with a phraseology ('lightning') exactly suggesting Byron. The drama itself contains Byronic elements, as in Jupiter's description of man's soul as an 'unextinguished fire' which 'burns towards heaven' and hurls up 'insurrection' (*Prometheus Unbound,* III, i). It recalls both Byron's *Prometheus* and *Manfred:* in his association 'with earthquakes and storms as well as with wars and tyrannies and individual crime' (Campbell, VII, 205), Jupiter is a precise duplication of Arimanes (*Manfred,* II; iii, iv). The ethical complexities of *Manfred* are in Shelley replaced by the black and white opposition of a bad Jupiter against a good Prometheus, with a final dissolution of *drama*—I am casting no aspersions on Shelley's poetry throughout—in an un-Byronic lyric mysticism written after his immediate influence had waned. But Byron's influence is certainly evident elsewhere. 'This first act', wrote Miss Campbell, 'is not only in itself perhaps the most wonderful part of the poem, but it contains practically the whole dramatic development of the play' (VII, 213): more, it is probably more humanly conceived, more rounded and weighty, than anything else in Shelley. Let us glance at the key incident.

The hero demands to hear again his age-old, Aeschylean, curse. A Phantasm, symbolizing the darker, more bitter, side of man's Promethean, or Byronic, challenge, rises to speak it, and is described in lines which suggest strongly one aspect of Byron:

> I see the curse on gestures proud and cold,
> And looks of firm defiance, and calm hate,
> And such despair as mocks itself with smiles.   (I, i.)

This is, at least if we read 'bitterness' for 'hate', almost exactly how Shelley in *Julian and Maddalo* and Lady Blessington, in commentary after commentary (e.g. at her book's conclusion), saw Byron. The curse is next spoken, only to be deliberately withdrawn by its original speaker:

PROMETHEUS: Were these my words, O Parent?
THE EARTH: They were thine.
PROMETHEUS: It doth repent me: words are quick and vain,
          Grief for a while is blind, and so was mine.
          I wish no living thing to suffer pain.

                                        (I, i.)

That holds the very accent of Byron in 1818. Indeed, we find here not only a reminder of the Maniac's forgiveness in *Julian and Maddalo*,[1] but also *an exact dramatization of the curse crowned by forgiveness* in the Promethean stanzas of *Childe Harold*.

During the autumn of 1818 Shelley was seething with impressions of Byron. We now suggest that the noble opening of the *Prometheus Unbound*, composed in the early autumn (White, Notes to XX; II, 557), was a transcription of those very Promethean stanzas which Shelley shortly afterwards condemned to Peacock with an irrational fury. What had happened? That Shelley had apparently

---

1. Dr. White has already observed (Notes to XX; II, 560) a similarity in the technique of split personalities (with Maniac = Shelley). But note that the under-self in the one poem corresponds to the controlling self of the other.

seen more of Byron's Venetian life and been shocked by it scarcely covers the problem. There is a simpler solution to this, and to all other Byronic enigmas; and only in so far as we accept it shall we understand the various ramifications of Byron's extraordinary relationship to his environment. Shelley and others (To Byron, 16 April; Shelley, 26 April; 1821; Murray, 6 April 1819; C, II, 169; LJ, V, 268; IV, 283-4) implored him to house his genius in a great poem of traditional sort. But he was instinctively impelled to aim at something higher; in him literature had taken on flesh and blood, poetry had become indecently and threateningly alive; and that is why everyone was always offering him advice, trying to get the Djinn back into the bottle. In these Promethean stanzas Byron had, as never before, spoken out in person, thrown off the mask, and come before his public as a confessed Titan. I suggest that Shelley was mostly deeply disturbed, and, purposely or instinctively, proceeded as quickly as possible to bottle up the dreaded substance once more in his own magnificent and highly respectable fiction: that, and that only, was its proper home. After all, our culture has no place for the reality. This Byron knew, and instinctively took pains to disguise himself. Hence that Sir Percy Blakeney air of foppish indolence that went so far to deceive Trelawny and infuriate Hunt.

So these Promethean stanzas which Shelley denounced as 'mischievous insanity' had nevertheless been at work within himself to mature in a scene which for human realization and dramatic weight out-topped his normal accomplishment, the supposedly wicked lines forcing him to write above himself and compose his masterpiece; and something similar has happened with European literature as a whole. Though critic after critic has tried to dispose of Byron, his fertilizing value for our greater European minds has been prodigious. And he has not yet come into his own:

> But I have lived, and have not lived in vain:
> My mind may lose its force, my blood its fire,
> And my frame perish, even in conquering pain;
> But there is that within me which shall tire
> Torture and Time, and breathe when I expire;
> Something unearthly, which they deem not of,
> Like the remember'd tone of a mute lyre,
> Shall on their soften'd spirits sink, and move
> In hearts all rocky now the late remorse of love.
>
> (*Childe Harold*, IV, 137.)

Notice, as in his lines on Sheridan and his curse of 'forgiveness', how this Titanic indictment is, at each turn, *softened;* all the most tumultuous energies in Byron's life and verse are thus regularly subdued to that prevailing sweetness in whose cause they were originally aroused. A Timon in stature, he was nevertheless one, in Teresa's words, in whose soul 'rancour could never live' (I, VI, 279; see also p. 97); and those 'expressions of indignation' which have been attributed to anger belong really 'to his disinterested, heroic, generous nature' (II; VII, 143). Of Byron's Timon-like, personal, anger, we cannot here treat. Meanwhile we may suggest that Teresa's words remain, his whole life's story and total output considered, basically true.

'Something unearthly'. Until we face that 'something' we shall never make sense of Byron's life or work, nor of the various authorities that knew him and have left their all but unanimous impressions. 'It is only', wrote Augustine Birrell in *William Hazlitt,* 'by reading the lives and letters of his astonished contemporaries and immediate successors that you are able to form some estimation of the power of Byron' (quoted Lovelace, I, 6, note). Two 'illustrious' writers quoted by Teresa (I; IX, 401) regarded Byron's death as a sort of cosmic disaster. Byron himself felt that he housed superlative powers:

'If I live ten years longer you will see, however, that it is not over with me—I don't mean in literature, for that is nothing; and it may seem odd enough to say, I do not think it my vocation. But you will see that I shall do something or other—the times and fortune permitting—that, "like the cosmogony or creation of the world, will puzzle the philosophers of all ages". But I doubt whether my constitution will hold out. I have, at intervals, ex*or*cised it most devilishly' (Moore, 28 Feb. 1817; LJ, IV, 62).

What, after all, if he was right?

Teresa saw Byron as a being having attained 'perfection', and for that reason removed from earth by a death suited to his virtues (I; II, 81). Whether or not we agree, we can see Byron's death as the perfect completion to an interesting pattern of events. His first youthful journey introduced him to Europe, and pre-eminently to Greece. Returning to England, he was in, but not of, the society and politics of his day (*Manfred,* II, ii). He next plunged back to Italy, to the heart of European history, celebrating the past, whether of Venice, as in his *Ode* and the plays, or Rome, as in *Childe Harold* (IV, 78–82),

The Prophecy of Dante (IV) and *The Deformed Transformed* (I, ii; II, i),
with strong feeling for the 'eternal city' (II, i, 5) as the centre of
Western civilization. And last, he returned again to Greece, to the
yet earlier origins, to the home of that Prometheus-myth itself which
kindles the tormented history of Europe. And, as we watch Byron
at Missolonghi taking part in the fight for liberation for which his
own early verses had set the stage, we may suggest that there he did,
more nearly than any other on record, live out and in himself har-
monize the most agonizing dualisms of Western civilization. Thinking of those few months before his death, we can address to him his
own words to the Titan:

> But, baffled as thou wert, from high,
> Still in thy patient energy,
> In the endurance and repulse
>   Of thine impenetrable Spirit,
> Which Earth and Heaven could not convulse,
>   A mighty lesson we inherit:
> Thou art a symbol and a sign
>   To Mortals of their fate and force;
> Like thee, Man is in part divine,
>   A troubled stream from a pure source . . .

That is the self-imposed ideal to which he laboured to attune his life,
with an indefinable yet assured trust in that 'firm will' and 'deep'
knowledge

> Which even in torture can descry
> Its own concenter'd recompense,
> Triumphant where it dares defy,
> And making Death a Victory.
>
> (Prometheus, III.)

'Dares' suggests that the defiance acts strictly within the limits of a
noble cause; and, considering Byron's last rock-like endurance for
human good, under every trial that humankind and human frailty,
nature and the elements, Providence itself, could level at him, we
may call his own sacrifice, in the noblest sense, Promethean.

His supreme positive intuition was perhaps never more perfectly
expressed than in his lines to the Apollo Belvedere:

> Or view the Lord of the unerring bow,
> The God of life, and poesy, and light—
> The Sun in human limbs array'd, and brow

All radiant from his triumph in the fight;
The shaft hath just been shot—the arrow bright
With an immortal's vengeance; in his eye
And nostril beautiful disdain, and might
And majesty, flash their full lightnings by,
Developing in that one glance the Deity.

(*Childe Harold*, IV, 161.)

It is a 'delicate form' such as might be dreamed by one longing for 'a deathless lover from above', only to be 'maddened by that vision'; it speaks to the mind 'in its most unearthly mood', when 'each conception was a heavenly guest', 'a ray of immortality'. Such blazing intuitions are a torment until housed, returned, as it were, to Heaven, in art:

And if it be Prometheus stole from Heaven
The fire which we endure, it was repaid
By him to whom the energy was given
Which this poetic marble hath array'd
With an eternal glory . . .

(*Childe Harold*, IV, 163.)

The description is, in part (as are the descriptions so often of Don Juan), a self-description; Byron is, to use Shelley's words (p. 252), 'gazing on his own exceeding light'. And indeed, he 'repaid' the Promethean flame to Heaven not alone by words, by art, but preeminently by his life, and death; and the statue he moulded of its fire was, quite simply, himself.

III

Byron was a living incarnation of a synthesis to be later expounded by others, and in particular by Ibsen, in *Emperor and Galilean*, and by Nietzsche.[1] Provisionally, we can say that they demand a new blending of the Christian and the pagan in both psychology and politics. They appear, too, as were both Milton and Byron, to be unable to align themselves with any particular parties. It was at one time Dante's aim to make and lead a *third* party, beyond Guelphs and Ghibellines. The tendency recurs, this itch towards a *third* term, as in Ibsen's 'third empire' and Whitman's statement in *Democratic Vistas* that from the 'mass-man' and the

1. The Byronic ancestry of these I hope to discuss shortly in a study of Ibsen.

individual 'a greater product, a *third,* will arise'. A central difficulty to be faced is that of harmonizing the democratic conscience with the aristocratic valuations, though the word 'aristocratic', by derivation merely signifying the 'power of the best', need not be limited to an hereditary system. But it would be a gross error to regard Byron as a precursor of modern dictatorship, as we know it; though in these matters it is true that the best and the worst—as he himself found with Napoleon—lie disconcertingly close. His major actions point towards what might be called a blend of poetic wisdom and communal life; and if this implies a new ruling caste, or aristocracy, that is, a new 'best' to guide and lead, we need not necessarily fear the conception. He himself was not given to theory; what he did was, in his own life, to demonstrate the nature of true leadership and good government. His demonstration was throughout characterized by what he once named as his central principles, 'a strong love of liberty and a detestation of cant' (Blessington, 390), which in practice became an insistence on real as opposed to specious liberty, involving education and the aim to rouse the best self-hood of person or nation, with a corresponding abhorrence of all tyrannies except that tyranny of truth itself which Milton proclaimed in the *Areopagitica.* Teresa asserts that the 'empire' of his 'soul' was divided between the 'passion for truth' and 'generosity' (pp. 45–6). So we have, as another allegiance: generosity, forgiveness, humane actions, humility, self-criticism and self-discipline, his letters and actions alike witnessing his ever-strengthening control of the Napoleon in himself and, finally, as we shall see, his rejection of all claims to superlative status.

His blend of humility and pride was extraordinary. At one of those testing moments when, as Drinkwater puts it, he was 'attacked with almost unexampled venom and injustice' (x, 257–8), he wrote to Lady Melbourne, on 21 February 1814:

'As for the *world,* I neither know nor enquire into its notions. You can bear me witness that few ever courted it or flattered its opinions less. If it turns, or has turned, against me, I cannot blame it. My heart is not in it, and my head better without it' (C, 1, 247).

The words are a simple statement of fact, of an existent discrepancy. And with it goes a profound metaphysical humility. In March he was writing to her:

'Prosecute? Oh no. I am a great friend of the liberty of the press, even at the expense of myself. Besides, do I not deserve all this? and am I not in reality much worse than they make me? They shall not break my heart or my spirit, personally or paragraphically; but if the man, whoever he is, were delivered bound hand and foot into my hands, I would cut the cords—though, if he turned out a gentleman, I might cut his throat instead. But that is to oblige the world and its regulation, and not myself' (C, I, 247).

Byron was referring to the compulsions of a gentleman's 'honour'; while the slightly inapposite phrase 'cut his throat' (cp. Lady Melbourne, 13 Oct. 1813; C, I, 200) makes an ironic comment on the brutalities of the prevailing code, as when he calls Wellington as professional soldier a 'cut-throat' (*Don Juan*, IX, 4). His own pride, if pride it be, was one with a profound humility due to his clear sense of human, and therefore his own, littleness and inadequacy; so that in the depths he knew himself far worse than any slanderous detractions could make him. 'That *relative superiority*', wrote Teresa, 'which he felt in himself left him *perfectly modest*, for he knew it was subject to other relations that showed it to him in extreme littleness: that is to say, the relation of the finite with the aspiration towards the infinite' (II; III, 48). This was the cause of that 'positive necessity of calumniating' or 'persecuting' himself (II; VI, 97; and see my pp. 41–5, 51, 63, 136–7) so emphasized by Moore and others: 'He placed his ideal standard too high' (II; VI, 105). Lady Blessington (e.g. at 44, 117–20, 293, 318, 320–1) offers many subtle comments on this trait, her profoundest explanation corroborating Teresa's in seeing him as so fond of tracing thought to its origins that he insisted on full responsibility for all darker 'motives and feelings' which existed fleetingly in the 'shadow' world of his mind, so that he 'detects in himself what is little, whilst failing to credit himself with what is great' (321, 35). He himself attributed this self-persecution to his detestation of cant (Blessington, 118; see also 14–15; 316, 389–90), and said that 'self-examination' helped to reconcile him to all the 'incongruities' of human nature and make him 'more lenient to faults' that his 'tongue' censured, but that his 'heart pardons from the consciousness of its own weakness' (330–1). From such humility forgiveness followed logically, and the more readily from his innate generosity, which, as Teresa (I; IX, 389) so exactly puts it, if 'too instinctive to be called a virtue', was yet 'too admirable to be considered as an instinct'.

But after the slanders of 1816 and the crash of Byron's marriage, forgiveness—as his more violent *epistolary* outbursts witness—was not easy, and the moral will certainly engaged also. Nevertheless, as Teresa tells us, the 'quality of his heart' finally 'elevated and transformed itself through the exertion of his will into an absolute virtue' (1; IX, 389). Let us try to elucidate her meaning.

Teresa emphasizes in general his record of self-discipline deriving from 'the desire and resolution of making *matter* subservient to the *spirit*' (1; X, 448). He deliberately starved himself to lend power to his mind (Blessington, 48, 138) and subdue his passions (Journal, 17 Nov. 1813; LJ, II, 328; Blessington, 337, 367; Teresa, quoting Dallas, 1; X, 450). All our authorities emphasize what Teresa calls, with reference to food and personal comfort in general, the 'Pythagorean abstinence which he had laid down as the rule of his life' (1; III, 129). Trelawny had seen nothing like this 'self-restraint' and 'resolution', in a man always 'hungry' who would eventually eat 'like a famished dog'; he respected the nobility of Byron's 'motive', and said that 'by starving his body' he 'kept his brains clear' (VI). Parry tells us that he was more a 'mental being' than anyone he had met, sustaining himself on 'thought' rather than on 'food' (Parry, V, 107). Whilst travelling he was disgusted at others' complaints, his own instincts being monastic (Teresa, 1; X, 449); he called Fletcher's grumbles on their early travels the result of a 'hog's eye' view (Trelawny, XVIII); while his travelling companion Hobhouse accused Byron in turn of a 'brutal indifference' (Murray, 9 Nov. 1820; LJ, V, 115). The Countess Albrizzi, noting the violence of his athletic exercises, said that his body and spirit alike were bended to his inclinations (LJ, IV, App. II, 442); and Moore observed the 'task-like perseverance' which he brought to these pursuits (LVII, 646). He fenced to dominate 'matter' and give sway to the 'ethereal' part of his nature (Journal, 10 April 1814; LJ, II, 410). 'He never gave over struggling against himself,' wrote Teresa, 'seeking to acquire dominion over his faculties and passions, intellectually by hard study, and materially by the strictest regime' (II; VII, 144). Whatever we know, or think we know, about his various sexual encounters, which were more complex than is usually supposed, we must face the evidence, already (pp. 42–3) cited, of Hobhouse, Moore and others, together with Teresa's sharp summing up: 'Lord Byron had no vices' (II; VI, 113; see p. 41). Such statements supplement the fervent puritanism of *Marino Faliero*. Sexual passion was, anyway, not Byron's danger; indeed, it was a refuge and a safeguard. His real temptations were rather akin to the Napoleonic ambition; or what the theologians call 'spiritual pride', including pride at his own humility; and to resentment at the vindictive and poisonous rancour roused in others by his own superior abilities. This last was the hardest test of all. Teresa, who knew him intimately during the years of greatest temptation, draws a helpful distinction between instinctive generosity and a yet greater quality more deserving of the 'sacred' name of 'virtue', while directly attributing to Byron what she calls this 'highest triumph of moral strength'; a virtue which not only succeeds in overcoming 'appetite', or instinct, but forgets 'the most just resentments', forgives, returns good for evil, and finally 'constitutes the very heroism of Christian charity' (II; IV, 51; V, 72).

Among those who attacked Byron in 1816, few can have pained him more than John Scott, who had been his schoolfellow at Aberdeen—and to Byron such an association was vitally important —and was later editor of *The Champion*. Hobhouse describes his execrable behaviour in the publication of Byron's two poems *Fare Thee Well* and *A Sketch* (Hobhouse, II; XV, 331–2). Now Scott later, in chastened mood 'bowed in grief by the loss of his son' and himself experiencing 'the bitterness of a domestic privation' (the words are Byron's), visited Byron in Italy, confessing 'that he and others had been greatly misled, and that some pains, and rather extraordinary means, had been taken to excite them'. Byron's welcome was generous and his attitude summed in the almost superhuman charity of his remark to Scott that the moment of his own disaster had been 'too tempting for many friends and for all enemies!' On Scott's death he commented: 'Peace be with him!—and may all such other faults as are inevitable to humanity be as readily forgiven him, as the little injury which he had done to one who respected his talents and regrets his loss' (Bowles Controversy, LJ, V, App. III, 576; see also LJ, V, 266, note; and Teresa, II; V, 86–8). He contributed (Murray, 21 April 1821; LJ, V, 265) to a subscription raised by Murray for the assistance of Scott's family, preferring, with what Teresa calls his 'refined generosity', to leave the action anonymous to avoid an indelicacy (Teresa, II; V, 88). He was still feeling bitterly his position as social outcast when he so wholeheartedly forgave one who had helped to hound him from England; and one must beware of underrating the self-conquest involved, even though, as Teresa puts it, 'the pardon of injuries was . . . a habit with him, a necessity, his sole vengeance, even when such conduct might appear superhuman' (II; X, 195).

He consistently and of set purpose refused to answer his enemies.

'Byron', wrote Drinkwater, 'could be deadly in assault; but in his own defence he was, with the one exception that he regretted, silent' (IV, 258). He had every incitement to hit back: his later works were received with hostility or coldness even by his friends. Murray, Moore, Hobhouse, Kinnaird all disapproved of *Don Juan*. He was rapidly becoming a literary as well as a social Ishmael. And he *felt* it; his reiterated desire for letters from home alone shows how heavily the exile, at times, bore down on him. Nevertheless, on 24 September 1821, he specifically told Murray to avoid sending him reviews lest attacks tempted him back to satire:

'. . . if I took you all in hand, it would not be difficult to cut you up like gourds. I did as much by as powerful people at nineteen years old, and I know little as yet, at three and thirty, which should prevent me from making all your ribs Gridirons for your hearts, if such were my propensity. But it is *not*' (LJ, V, 374).

In a lecture containing some good comments on Byron, Herbert Hensley Henson, Bishop of Durham, after asserting that Byron's 'judgment was ever the slave of his resentments', and that 'the violence of his feelings found such easy expression in his verse that he wrote for the mere pleasure of writing', supports his statement by quoting this very passage as an example, whilst *omitting the concluding sentence:* 'But it is *not*' (*Byron,* The Rede Lecture, Cambridge, 1924; 31–2). That is typical of the dishonesty, conscious or otherwise, that has tracked Byronic biography. Again, Bishop Henson blames Byron for his attack on Carlisle, whilst preserving silence on his noble apology (*Childe Harold,* III, 29).

Throughout his life Byron sternly repudiated and suppressed his youthful satire (*English Bards and Scotch Reviewers*), which he called, in a note containing a number of most cauterizing criticisms of his own individual attacks (e.g. on Wordsworth; see p. 53), 'this miserable record of misplaced anger and indiscriminate acrimony' (see Moore, VIII, 81; also XV, 161–2; also Coleridge, 31 March 1815; LJ, III, 192). And yet was it, after all, so primed with rancour? His own preface to the second edition correctly described it as, in the main, impersonal and even *moral* in conception and aim. 'My object', he wrote—and his attitude elsewhere (see pp. 53–62) argues his sincerity—'is not to prove that I can write well, but, if possible, to make others write better'; and he proceeded to pay compliments to the 'real talents' of those pilloried. For the rest, we should remember the author's age and bitter sense of injustice at the harsh treatment of his early verses, 'the first flower and perfume', as Teresa rightly called them, of a soul 'devoted to friendship and other generous emotions' (Teresa, II; IX, 161; see also XIV, 307–8); that is, those 'fresh unworldly feelings' Moore likewise observed (XL, 468). Byron was fighting on behalf of his own first idealism; in the cause of 'the heart of man' at the age of 'eighteen', which he still regarded as the key to human existence in 1823 (Blessington, 345; see pp. 67, 74, 83). As so often thereafter, the Byronic energy was first enlisted in service to a gentleness, a love, a humility; and in *that* cause it could, when it chose, be slaughterous.

Byron's mature satire is fundamentally kind. In *Don Juan* this is, as the poet himself reminds us (e.g. at IV, 98–9; XI, 63; XIII, 89 and XVI, 3), clear enough. Here it is more to the point to glance briefly at certain accounts of Byron's conversation given by Lady Blessington and Teresa.

Lady Blessington continually refers to his satiric thrusts, while leaving us in no doubt as to his basic kindliness (110, 154, 176, 193, 201, 321, 343). It was all a 'natural flippancy', with no 'premeditation or bitterness'; nevertheless, one felt nervous of his sallies, 'though in half an hour he would put himself to personal inconvenience to render a kindness to the person so shown up' (59). He was so 'acute' an observer that nothing escaped him, 'all the shades of selfishness and vanity' being 'exposed to his searching glance' (61). At any sign of 'vanity', 'selfishness' or 'mundane sentiments', we are told, 'every arrow in the armoury of ridicule is let fly, and there is no shield sufficiently powerful to withstand them' (111). This ridicule could be simultaneously merry and devastating:

'Friend and foe alike come under its cutting point; and the laugh which accompanies each sally, as a deadly incision is made in some vulnerable quarter, so little accords with the wound inflicted, that it is as though one were struck down by summer lightning while admiring its brilliant play' (127).

The laugh was *genuinely kindly*. Whatever malice there might appear in the result, there was none, we are told, in the feeling which dictated it. Besides, he was equally ready to observe virtues, and at the worst somehow never left an unfavourable impression of those concerned (246–7). These various descriptions suggest something highly paradoxical, abnormal and rather frightening. Teresa observes the almost 'supernatural perspicacity' with which Lord Byron 'penetrated into the arcana of souls' (II; XIII, 294). Her description is vivid:

'His delight with intimates was to bring out strongly their defects, as well as their qualities and merits, by dint of jests, clever innuendo, and charming sallies of humour. The promptitude with which he discovered the slightest weakness, the faintest symptom of exaggeration or affectation, can hardly be credited. It might almost be said that the persons on whom he bestowed affection became *transparent* for him, that he dived into their thoughts and feelings. It was this state of mind especially that gave rise to those sallies of wit which formed such a striking feature of his intelligence. Then his conversation really became quite dazzling. In his glowing language all objects assumed unforeseen and picturesque aspects. New and striking thoughts followed from him in rapid succession, and the flame of his genius lighted up as if winged with wild fire. Those who have not known him at these moments can form no idea of what it was from his works . . . But in this gay exercise of his faculties, which was to him a real enjoyment, in all his sallies or even in his railleries, not one iota of malice could be traced' (II; XIII, 281).

We have already observed Teresa's statement that his wit was never directed against any limitations of mind or body (p. 256), and how he respected Taaffe's sincerity (p. 58). His targets were, indeed, always some variety of 'the vice he most abhorred—hypocrisy' (II; XIII, 294). He declared that he could sooner pardon 'crimes', since they derived from the passions, than the vices of selfishness and conceit (Blessington, 61). From these sallies his friends were not exempt. Indeed, they appear to have been his main objectives, and our simplest comment is the self-diagnosis of Nietzsche's Zarathustra: 'He loveth his enemies; this art knoweth he better than any that ever I saw; but he taketh vengeance therefor on his friends' (*Thus Spake Zarathustra*, IV, 15). Nietzsche's prophet on page after page recalls Byron.[1]

These lighter excursions, however, did not involve Byron's weightier emotions: 'flippancy' ceased at what Lady Blessington calls a '*tête-à-tête*' (23); and when any genuine goodness was in question and he was assured of its sincerity, all the dormant 'affections of his nature' were excited (110). He never made light of others' 'distress' or 'misfortune', which at once roused all his instincts of

---

1. Compare Mr. Herbert Read's valuable statement: 'My own view is that Byron was in some sense beyond good and evil, one of Nietzsche's "free spirits" ' (*Byron*, British Council, 1950).

alleviation (111). Any uncharitableness towards real suffering, however deserved, raised his wrath. Once, when someone was refusing to pity a wrong-doer on the grounds that his troubles were his own fault, 'I shall never forget', she says, 'the expression of Byron's face; it glowed with indignation.' Such a man, he urged, was *twice* to be pitied; the lack of charity among moral people infuriated him; he himself claimed always to 'pity the guilty and respect the unfortunate' (236–7; see also Teresa, I; IX, 392–3; and pp. 38, 96–7 above).

We have established Byron's humility, will to forgiveness and kindliness; while *the darker passages of his private letters merely serve to underline the force of those passions he was controlling*. His ambitions were gradually softened, without losing their force. In his youth, he told Lady Blessington, it had seemed to him that Galt had not sufficient respect towards 'my sublime self', either as a 'peer' or as an 'author'; but all that had passed (Blessington, 249). He who had once asserted '*aut Caesar aut nihil*' (p. 236) offered to serve for Italy and for Greece in any capacity, however obscure, being not anxious to 'shine', since he had seen through the falsities and worthlessness of fame (Blessington, 279; see also pp. 168, 183–4). The Journals and Blessington conversations alone corroborate Teresa's assertion of his remorseless self-probing and self-criticism (II; VII, 144); and when he engaged himself in Greece he had become master of a humility and patience of extraordinary sweetness and purity. But he was also tempered, like steel; and was ready not to demonstrate by ink but rather, as we have seen, to *incarnate* the thing to which his whole life had been pointing and which went far to solve his—and our—riddles. But this incarnation, being an incarnation of what are, in humanity's present stage, pretty nearly incompatibles, demanded, necessarily, death. On 24 January 1824, he penned at Missolonghi the following lines (from *On This Day I Complete my Thirty-Sixth Year*):

> Awake! (not Greece—she *is* awake!)
>   Awake, my spirit! Think through *whom*
> Thy life-blood tracks its parent lake,
>   And then strike home!
>
> Tread those reviving passions down,
>   Unworthy manhood!—unto thee
> Indifferent should the smile or frown
>   Of beauty be.

If thou regrett'st thy youth, *why live?*
The land of honourable death
Is here:—up to the field, and give
Away thy breath!

Seek out—less often sought than found—
A soldier's grave, for thee the best;
Then look around, and choose thy ground,
And take thy rest.

Each single word in that last stanza is weighted with exact meaning. 'The sadnesses of great souls', writes Teresa, 'are unspeakable, almost superhuman. They are beyond the scales where we would weigh them. But we know that he understood and tasted the bitterness of this chalice, without drawing back, without failing to drain it to the last' (II; v, 94). The sacrifice was deliberate.

IV

Byron left an expanded record of his final choice in a late, and uncompleted, work, *The Deformed Transformed*. We should always be ready to enlist, with due caution, Byron's poetry in our study of the man, *especially of the man-as-genius*, or, again, of Byron-as-Prometheus; for of this greater self his poetry is, regularly, the language. This granted, *The Deformed Transformed* is peculiarly revealing.

The hero, who suffers from a deformity, is, as Byron himself observed (Blessington, 129), autobiographically conceived, suffering from a deformity and rendered miserable, as was Byron as a child, by his own Mother's scorn, on one occasion, of his misfortune. Following the *Faust* pattern, Arnold, the hero, is offered by the Stranger—a kind of Mephistopheles—the chance of changing his form; and various choices from the ancient world pass before him. They are, in turn, Julius Caesar, suggesting Byron's Napoleonic ambitions ('*aut Caesar aut nihil*', etc); Alcibiades, who so fascinated Byron (pp. 25, 225), suggesting personal magnetism and charm (Napoleon, Brummell); Socrates, ugly but symbolizing wisdom, to be related to Byron's ascetic propensities and his continual use of 'philosopher' and the concept 'wise' to define his political intuitions (see pp. 175–7); Antony, the great lover, to be associated with Byron's love affairs, and in especial the claims of Teresa which he had to break when leaving for Greece; and last, two most interesting figures, Demetrius Poliorcetes and Achilles.

Demetrius Poliorcetes was a Macedonian conqueror welcomed by Athens as a liberator and accorded *divine honours:*

> Who is this?
> Who truly looketh like a demigod,
> Blooming and bright, with golden hair, and stature,
> If not more high than mortal, yet immortal
> In all that nameless bearing of his limbs,
> Which he wears as the sun his rays—a something
> Which shines from him, and yet is but the flashing
> Emanation of a thing more glorious still.
> Was *he e'er human only?* (I, i.)

Who, asks Arnold, was 'this glory of mankind' (I, i)? The figure reflects Byron's intuition of his own fine looks and spiritual power; something for which he had no name, but which we might, after Nietzsche, call 'superman'. *This shape Arnold deliberately rejects.* The choice falls on Achilles.

Achilles is here used as a personification of: (i) many of Byron's favourite imaginative emphases from boyhood of sea and river, remorse and pity, tears, and soft, here raised to the dignity of wedded and 'sanction'd', love; all his gentler and idealistic—and they were, as Moore, Teresa and Lady Blessington all insist, his central—qualities; the world, we may say, of *Sardanapalus;* and (ii) the spirit of Greece, his earliest and latest love among the nations. The stranger offers to 'animate the ideal marble', that is, revive the ancient beauty of Greece, and Arnold, seeing the result, makes his choice:

ARNOLD: Content! I will fix here
STRANGER: I must commend
            Your choice. The god-like son of the sea-goddess,
            The unshorn boy of Peleus, with his locks
            As beautiful and clear as the amber waves
            Of rich Pactolus, roll'd o'er sands of gold,
            Soften'd by intervening crystal, and
            Rippled like flowing waters by the wind,
            All vow'd to Sperchius as they were—behold them!
            And *him*—as he stood by Polixena,
            With sanction'd and with soften'd love, before
            The altar, gazing on his Trojan bride,

With some remorse within for Hector slain
And Priam weeping, mingled with deep passion
For the sweet downcast virgin, whose young hand
Trembled in *his* who slew her brother. So
He stood i' the temple! Look upon him as
Greece looked her last upon her best, the instant
Ere Paris' arrow flew.

ARNOLD: I gaze upon him
As if I were his soul, whose form shall soon
Envelope mine.   (I, i.)

There follows a strange dialogue. Asked if he would assume
Achilles' giant *stature,* Arnold says that he will. But here the
Stranger offers a valuable warning:

Thou shalt be indulged
If such be thy desire; and yet, by being
A little less removed from present men
In figure, thou canst sway them more; for all
Would rise against thee now, as if to hunt
A new-found mammoth . . .   (I, i.)

Byron had himself suffered from precisely such a 'hunt'. He had
himself known and most bitterly *felt*—as his *Monody on the Death of
Sheridan* and the Blessington conversations (pp. 38, 250 above) witness—the tendency of what Nietzsche called the 'herd' (i.e. the Tory
party and the *élite* of London society) to rise and crush the greater,
unique and original, personality. That was why he tried to avoid
further persecution by a futile defence: 'Who can bear refutation?'
(p. 123). He not only trained and disciplined himself to an almost
excessive humility—we may recall his life-long horror of egotism
(pp. 51, 91)—but also strove to mask his stature by a studied self-
mockery and self-denigration. This Teresa herself saw as, in part, a
technique for disarming malice, though its root cause she read
differently (II; VI, 103–5). Arnold takes the Stranger's advice. For the
rest, all is easy. Valour he does not request, since he already possesses
it. He had been about to kill himself when the Stranger appeared:

You lately saw me
Master of my own life, and quick to quit it;
And he who is so is the master of
Whatever dreads to die.   (I, i.)

An admirable commentary on Byron at Ravenna (pp. 173–5).

The play's continuance, though interesting on other grounds, is
not directly relevant to our present purpose, except to observe that
the Stranger, who is a kind of devil, takes (i) the deformed shape of
Arnold and (ii) the name of Caesar. He henceforth represents the
darker, more Napoleonic, aspect of the Byronic ambition. 'Caesar',
being a name belonging to 'empires' and 'the world's lords', is called
'fittest for the devil in disguise' (i, i). With a more than Mephisto-
phelean cynicism ranging over the horrors of blood and battles, he
functions, like Mephistopheles, as a necessary but distasteful companion, corresponding, we may suggest, to the hideous threat of
blood-action looming on the horizon of Byron's personal destiny.

To return to our opening. From Byron's youth, the choice of
directions, with its various military, civic (or social) and poetic possibilities, had been a problem (Teresa, II; IX, 160); and here we find
Byron-Arnold repudiating various masks, or aspects, of his personality, *including the superman,* his final choice falling on a figure repre-
senting the softer side of his own nature and the spirit of Greece;
though, even so, he realized that the appearance of *too obvious and outstanding a virtue* must be studiously avoided. When Trelawny told
him that his body would be claimed by Westminster Abbey, he
answered: 'No—they don't want me—nor would I have my bones
mingled with that motley throng'; and he named a rocky islet off
Maina where he would like his bones to lie (Trelawny, XVII). He
was beyond such things (Blessington, 280), and alone; as surely born
for desolation as the fire of Manfred's spirit, which, like 'the red-hot
breath of the most lone simoon', was happiest among 'barren sands'
which 'bear no shrubs' for its fierce life to 'blast' (*Manfred,* III, i). So
now, with an image harking back to his youthful lines to Becher
(pp. 234–5),

> The fire that on my bosom preys
> Is lone as some volcanic isle;
> No torch is kindled at its blaze—
> A funeral pile.
>
> (*My Thirty-Sixth Year.*)

Byron tried from youth onwards to master, even to deny, his own
greatness, and his last thoughts were thoughts of simplicity, and of
Greece.

This studied rejection of Demetrius Poliorcetes demands our
closest attention. Byron had *moods* when knowledge of his own

stature possessed him, when, as Stendhal observed, he would 'pretend to everything', only to become soon after 'the sublime poet and the man of sense' (LJ, III, App. VIII, 440); when, in the Countess Albrizzi's words, 'his thoughts and feelings were more stupendous and unmeasured' than Napoleon's (LJ, IV, App. II, 442). At the marriage crisis his wife accused him of 'love of power', 'a boundless and *impious* pride' (italics mine), and a 'glorying' in wickedness (The Marriage Separation, LJ, III, 297, 300, 310). During January 1816, Augusta was sending bulletins to Lady Byron regarding Byron's supposed madness. Here is an extract quoted by Ethel Colburn Mayne in her *Life of Lady Byron:*

'He talked of you quite coolly and of his intention of going into a lodging by himself . . . in short, looked black and gloomy, nobody could tell why or wherefore, the rest of the night. One of the things he said was . . . that he considered himself "the greatest man existing". G. (George Byron) said laughing, "except Bonaparte". The answer was, "God, I don't know that I do except even him!" I was struck previously with a wildness in his eye' (XIV, 207).

This is of central importance. Observe that Byron shows here no self-satisfaction whatsoever, but rather agony of mind in face of an awe-inspiring recognition. Miss Mayne notes acutely that Lady Byron would have known well that her husband was not thinking of the despised poetry, but rather of 'something in his nature' to do with what she saw as an antagonism to Divinity (XV, 226). They realized that Byron's assertion, if formulated, must take the form of a Messianic challenge. In better mood, after commenting on his own and Shelley's rejection, Byron once, if we are to believe Trelawny, remarked: 'Man is the same rancorous beast now that he was from the beginning, and if the Christ they profess to worship reappeared, they would again crucify Him' (Trelawny, VII). What is the meaning of these extraordinary hints?—Or this: 'The secret were too mighty for your souls' (*Marino Faliero*, V, 1)? Such was the appalling problem with which Byron was struggling throughout his life.

And here we may place a very remarkable incident that occurred in Cephalonia. We rely on reports by Trelawny and the Mr. S—— quoted by Charles Mackay (for Charles Mackay, see Nicolson, VI, 126). Trelawny's book is well known; the other, an account of Byron's visit to Ithaca and return to Cephalonia in 1823, is quoted by Edgcumbe (I, V, 48–63). Mr. Harold Nicolson's narrative has already grouped together the passages I am to quote illustrating (i) Byron's arrival at a monastery on the Hill of Samos in Cephalonia on his return from Ithaca, as narrated by Trelawny, and (ii) the narrative by Mr. S—— of Byron's extraordinary behaviour on that occasion.

Trelawny recounts how the Abbot greeted Byron with the words, 'Christ has risen to elevate the cross and trample on the crescent in our beloved Greece'; and proceeded to intone a long eulogium on the English lord, boys swinging censers of incense before him:

'Byron had not spoken a word from the time we entered the monkery; I thought he was resolved to set us an example of proper behaviour. No one was more surprised than I was when suddenly he burst into a paroxysm of rage, and vented his ire in a torrent of Italian execrations on the holy Abbot and all his brotherhood. Then, turning to us with flashing eyes, he vehemently exclaimed:

' "Will no one release me from the presence of these pestilential idiots? They drive me mad!" Seizing a lamp, he left the room.

'The consternation of the monks at this expression of wrath may be imagined . . .' (Trelawny, xix).

Irritation on such an occasion is not surprising; but this was more than irritation. It acted as a knife twisted torturingly into a body, for it had touched Byron's central 'complex', the inmost torment of his existence. He was being greeted as a saviour, and at least closely *associated* with Christ. The result was remarkable. For next we have *the one explicit and detailed account preserved to us of Byron's violent behaviour;* the kind of behaviour that caused his wife first to think him mad and next to insist on a separation; and *it was brought on directly by these monks according him almost divine honours,* such as Athens had accorded Demetrius Poliorcetes. Here is our sequel, from the narrative by Mr. S——:

'Lord Byron retired almost immediately from the *sala*. Shortly afterwards we were astonished and alarmed by the entry of Dr. Bruno, wringing his hands and tearing his hair . . . It appeared that Lord Byron was seized with violent spasms in the stomach and liver, and his brain was excited to dangerous excess, so that he would not tolerate the presence of any person in his room. He refused all medicine, and stamped and tore all his clothes and bedding like a maniac. We could hear him rattling and ejaculating. Poor Dr. Bruno stood lamenting in agony of mind, in anticipation of the most dire results if immediate relief were not obtained by powerful cathartics, but Lord Byron had expelled him from the room by main force. He now implored one or more of the company to go to his lordship and induce him, if possible, to save his life by taking the necessary medicine. Trelawny at once proceeded to the room, but soon returned, saying that it would require ten such as he to hold his lordship for a minute, adding that Lord Byron would not leave an unbroken article in the room. The doctor again essayed an entrance, but without success. The monks were becoming alarmed, and so, in truth, were all present. The doctor asked me to try to bring his lordship to reason. "He will thank you when he is well," he said, "but get him to take this one pill, and he will be safe." It seemed a very easy undertaking, and I went. There being no lock on the door, entry was obtained in spite of a barricade of chairs and a table within. His lordship was half undressed, standing in a far corner like a hunted animal at bay. As I looked determined to advance in spite of his imprecations of "Back! out, out of my sight! fiends, can I have no peace, no relief from this hell! Leave me, I say" —and he lifted the chair nearest to him, and hurled it direct at my head. I escaped as I best could and returned to the *sala*' (Edgcumbe, I, v, 61; Nicolson, IV, 132; texts vary slightly).

Eventually Byron took the medicine, and, on waking in the morning, 'was all dejection and penitence' (Edgcumbe, I, v, 63). Observe how closely Byron's phraseology here ('fiends', 'hell') recalls the conclusion to *Manfred*.

Exactly what the monks had meant by their ceremonious welcome is not very clear; but certainly Byron's advent suggested to others such words as 'Messiah' and 'avatar' (pp. 215–16); it was a 'miniature crusade' (p. 214). Parry tells us that he knew perfectly well that he could at any time assume a far more spectacular leadership than he chose (p. 212). But such thoughts he repudiated and at the limit *feared*. Less than two days after his attack in the monastery, roused from sleep by Trelawny's shouts, he started up in 'terror', 'staring wildly' and muttering: 'I have had such a dream! I am trembling with fear. I am not fit to go to Greece. If you had come to strangle me, I could have done nothing.' Beside his bed were—as always—his pistols and his Bible (Trelawny, XIX). 'I am not fit to go to Greece': we can best understand these incidents by deliberately reading into that phrase a depth beyond Trelawny's intention.

There was, indeed, 'something unearthly' (*Childe Harold*, iv, 137) about him, witnessed by numerous descriptions. Teresa refers to 'that kind of supernatural light which seemed to surround him like a halo' (i; ii, 78). To women he appeared regularly as a creature beyond humanity: we may remember the effect exercised on 'Miss S.' (p. 228). Caroline Lamb in *Glenarvon* has a typical description:

'It seemed as if the soul of passion had been stamped and printed on every feature. The eye beamed into life as it threw up its dark ardent gaze, with a look nearly of inspiration, while the proud curl of the upper lip expressed haughtiness and bitter contempt; yet, even mixed with these fierce characteristic feelings, an air of melancholy and dejection shaded and softened every harsher expression . . . Calantha felt the power, not then alone, but evermore . . . She could have knelt and prayed heaven to realize the dreams, to bless the fallen angel in whose presence she at that moment stood' (quoted Drinkwater, iii, 232).

'Fallen angel' exactly corroborates the statement of *Manfred*, suggesting an identity of excellence and disaster; an excellence which is, on our plane, or at least appears, disastrous, as in Shelley's 'bright blot' (p. 254). A less tragic pen-picture is left us by Miss Jane Porter who was struck by his voice as 'the most melodious' she had ever heard. His face she would 'never forget':

'The features of the finest proportions. The eye deep set, but mildly lustrous; and the complexion what I at the time described to my sister as a sort of moonlight paleness. It was so pale, yet with all so softly brilliant' (LJ, ii, 331–2, Note).

Teresa says that his eyes were in turn blue, grey and violet, varying with his thoughts (i; ii, 76). Moore's first impressions recorded nobleness of bearing, beauty, 'gentleness' of 'voice and manners', and kindness. He observed 'the pure, spiritual paleness of his features, in the expression of which, when he spoke, there was a perpetual play of lively thought, though melancholy was their habitual character when in repose' (Moore, xiii, 145; LJ, ii, 67, note).

The recurring quality may be called 'spiritual'. We have, too, Teresa's remarkable account of Byron's appearance at the news of Allegra's death:

'A mortal paleness spread itself over his face, his strength failed him, and he sunk into a seat. His look was fixed, and the expression such that I began to fear for his reason; he did not shed a tear; and his countenance manifested so hopeless, so profound, so sublime a sorrow, that at the moment he appeared a being of a nature superior to humanity . . .
'. . . I found him on the following morning tranquillized, and with an expression of religious resignation on his features . . . "It is God's will—let us mention it no more"' (LJ, VI, 52, note).

A similar sublimity was felt by Gamba after Byron's death: 'Immediately after his death, his countenance had an air of calmness, mingled with a severity, that seemed gradually to soften; for when I took a last look of him, the expression, at least to my eyes, was truly sublime' (Gamba, VI, 277–8). It was not only to the women that Byron appeared a being of superlative, spiritual, often tragic, beauty. During the outcry in 1816 Coleridge wrote: 'If you had seen Lord Byron, you could scarcely disbelieve him—so beautiful a countenance I scarcely ever saw . . . his eyes the open portals of the sun—things of light for light' (Drinkwater, IV, 259). Scott said that when Byron was gloomy, he would wait until the shadows 'left his countenance like the mist rising from the landscape' (LJ, III, App, IV, 415). To him Byron's beauty was something to make one 'dream'; and Stendhal called its power 'divine' (Teresa, I; II, 76, 78).

As for the darker, more passionate, occasions, both aspects, the beautiful and the tempestuous, are finely rendered for us by the Countess Albrizzi:

'It would be to little purpose to dwell upon the mere beauty of a countenance in which the expression of an extraordinary mind was so conspicuous. What serenity was seated on the forehead, adorned with the finest chestnut hair, light, curling, and disposed with such art, that the art was hidden in the imitation of most pleasing nature! What varied expression in his eyes! They were of the azure colour of the heavens, from which they seemed to derive their origin. His teeth, in form, in colour, in transparency, resembled pearls; but his cheeks were too delicately tinged with the hue of the pale rose. His neck, which he was in the habit of keeping uncovered as much as the usages of society permitted, seemed to have been formed in a mould, and was very white. His hands were as beautiful as if they had been the works of art. His figure left nothing to be desired, particularly by those who found rather a grace than a defect in a certain light and gentle undulation of the person when he entered a room, and of which you hardly felt tempted to enquire the cause. Indeed it was scarcely perceptible—the clothes he wore were so long . . .

'His face appeared tranquil like the ocean on a fine spring morning; but, like it, in an instant became changed into the tempestuous and terrible, if a passion (a passion did I say?), a thought, a word, occurred to disturb his mind. His eyes then lost all their sweetness, and sparkled so that it became difficult to look on them. So rapid a change would not have been thought possible; but it was impossible to avoid acknowledging that the natural state of his mind was the tempestuous' (LJ, IV, App. II, 441–2).

That one state was more 'natural' than the other we need not assert; but we shall not deny that both were there. To Hazlitt, Byron's 'brow' collected 'the scattered gloom' and his eye flashed 'livid fire'. In him we recognize a 'demon'; and that, said Hazlitt, 'is the next thing to being full of the God' (*Lectures on Living Poets*; quoted Lovelace, I, 6).

These strange descriptions suggest a personality not easy to assess in normal categories. Lady Blessington told him that his denunciations resembled rather those of a 'fallen angel' than an ordinary mortal; at which he was amused, saying, with remembrance probably of the London press, that the title was, at least, an improvement on 'demon' (Blessington, 332). In defining poets as resembling 'creatures of another sphere' strangely allied with 'mortals' (Blessington, 71), Byron was certainly thinking of himself. Indeed, he was often seriously *embarrassed* by himself, as his journals witness; and was forced into fiction to attempt definitions which he was reluctant to apply directly. Hence we have in *Manfred* such phrases as 'I am not of thine order', 'This man is of no common order', 'The order which thine own would rise above', 'There is an order of mortals on the earth' (II, i; II, ii; II, iv; III, i). Manfred's passions and 'powers' make him a stranger among men with little in common with 'breathing flesh' (II, ii). In contact with human beings, he says,

> I felt myself degraded back to them
> And was all clay again.
>
> (II, ii.)

Hence, too, the various 'Promethean' poems; and the descriptions, so impregnated with personal significances, of the Apollo (p. 261),

Demetrius Poliorcetes and Achilles (p. 272). Byron's 'eagle spirit' was, in Shelley's phrase, if not blinded, yet seriously troubled, 'by gazing on its own exceeding light' (p. 252). If, as could be argued, he was what might be defined as the next Promethean man in Western history after Christ, he had reason to be embarrassed; and the more so since the culture of his time possessed no thought-structure in which his significance could be placed. Our suggestion may appear bold, but no one else fulfils the conditions. The great men of the Christian tradition cannot be said to *add* anything to the life of Christ; the men of action are not poets, and the poets not— at least in the sense that Byron was—men of action. In Byron you get something new, in which poetry and action, aristocracy and revolution, Christianity and statecraft, each raised to a high autono-mous power, co-exist within one single human, yet magical, person-ality. This is exactly what, in the Renaissance world, should constitute 'the new Prometheus of new men'; for, finally, Byron's greatness is less a greatness, his goodness less a goodness, of selection than of *inclusion;* or, as Teresa aptly puts it, 'an exceptional assembly of rare qualities which met for the first time in one man, and which, shining in the midst of a most corrupt society, constituted almost an anomaly which became a real defect, hurtful however to himself only' (I; I, 52). She spoke probably more wisely than she knew, since the 'rare qualities' involved must certainly include essences that are—or seem—immoral. These we cannot here discuss, though I hope later to show how Byron as man and poet diversely covers without any straining of evidence the whole gamut of Shake-spearian passion and Shakespearian humour; which is, one might suppose, as good a qualification for Promethean stature in our time as one could wish for. There were, naturally, difficulties. He suffered, says Parry (x, 262), from censure by surroundings 'quite unable to appreciate all the nobleness of his character'. But at the supreme occasions of his story these diverse, often lurid, colours were, very clearly, constituent to a single goodness and purity of staggering power: 'His very virtues', says Teresa, 'mystified the world' (I; I, 52).

VI
GOD AND CAESAR

OORE once distinguished Byron's genius as a poet from
what he called his mysterious 'poetry of character', compact of youthful, 'fresh' and 'unworldly' feelings, together with a certain 'ennobling light of imagination'
which, despite all his professed scorn of man, nevertheless 'gave a
lustre' to 'all on which it rested' (XL, 468). As though by some extension of what Teresa called the 'Pythagorean abstinence which he
had laid down as the rule of his life' (I; III, 129), Byron bended his
own tumultuous nature to the service of this delicate excellence.
One of his meditations reads, she says, like 'the confession or soliloquy of some Christian philosopher' (I; X, 452). And he succeeded
where Napoleon failed:

> An empire thou couldst crush, command, rebuild,
> But govern not thy pettiest passion, nor
> However deeply in men's spirits skill'd
> Look through thine own, nor curb the lust of war,
> Nor learn that tempted Fate will leave the loftiest star.
>
> (*Childe Harold*, III, 38.)

Whatever instincts were in him, they were understood and, normally, were controlled; more, given the occasion, they were harmonized; and the harmonization of such diverse and Shakespearian
instincts as Byron's—how diverse and Shakespearian we cannot
here discuss—touched a supreme virtue rich in power and magic,
continuous with his own youthful idealism.

Such virtue, however, exacts its cost. Byron was now more alone
than ever. The compulsion '*aut Caesar aut nihil*' had taken a new
form, but not been dispelled. Indeed, the conquest of one sort of
Caesarism only the more firmly instated him in another. For, however strong his will to humility, he could in practice only meet mankind by stooping.

Moore saw Byron as belonging to a class 'so set apart from the
track of ordinary life' and 'so removed, by their very elevation, out
of the influences of our common atmosphere' (XXIII, 270), that social

intercourse was hard: 'How easily', he wrote, 'his gigantic spirit could be, if not held down, at least entangled, by the small ties of society' (xv, 162). Such a man had, finally, to act and speak from above: contact was only possible in so far as his eminence was recognized, and hence, in part, his liking for association with admitted inferiors. Lady Blessington saw him as a man wrestling with spiritual problems 'too elevated to allow of any reciprocity', there being an 'immeasurable distance between his genius and others' (395); and sometimes his manner made you aware of it (404). But it was not so with those who needed sympathy. His heart was always 'yearning' towards his fellow-men:

'Byron warred only with the vices and follies of his species; and if he had a bitter jest and biting sarcasm for these, he had pity and forbearance for affliction, even though deserved, and forgot the cause in the effect. Misfortune was sacred in his eyes, and seemed to be the last link in the chain that connected him with his fellow-men' (236).

'The last link': Byron was, from first to last, related to man as the helper, the patron, the giver. But his bounty was, and is, not solely material. Lady Blessington remarked that he had no 'small change' for social intercourse, since his 'gold' was in 'ingots' (49). The image appears to be his own from his reported statement later contrasting the 'weighty metal of thought' with the 'small money of conversation', comparing himself to a man in a story who suffered all the miseries of poverty while possessing a huge diamond which from its size could find no purchaser; so excellent a symbol of his troubled life, that he followed it up with a laughing disclaimer—'Bless me, how I have been holding forth . . .' (123).

Let us, in conclusion, glance briefly at one of those 'ingots', something so simple, so small in appearance and yet so large in meaning, that misunderstanding is easy; a sonnet compacting perfectly Byron's own achieved synthesis of power with gentleness to define once and for all that peculiar sweetness, or softness, with which he willed to penetrate the harsh world of government. If Byron had behaved cavalierly to the Regent, he certainly made amends with a poetic tribute than which nothing nobler has ever been offered to an English sovereign. Towards his life's close the puritanical and moralistic Wordsworth penned a sonnet-sequence—strange choice—in support of the death penalty. The direction taken by Byron's warmer, more sexually-impelled, genius was more human, more gentle. Our Sonnet praises the Regent for an act of generosity and mercy and simultaneously defines that peculiar royalty which Byron himself exercised at Missolonghi, whereby he was as interested in the saving of individuals or humanizing the punishment of a single offender as in the victorious campaign. It could, perhaps, only have flowered from an aristocratic tradition; it is innately, superbly, aristocratic, in the full and best meaning of a word which by derivation means the 'power' of the 'best'. But it is also personal and intimate; the very use of the sonnet form marks the will to plant the sweets of personal feeling in the soil of statesmanship. Its valuation of mercy and will to address the Sermon on the Mount not to the lowly but to the seats of power are unmatched outside Portia's speech in *The Merchant of Venice* and certain passages of *Measure for Measure*.[1] These passages Byron knew well. After telling Bowring that no money gathered for the Greeks could be considered as wasted, since, even if failure were to result, there would be the alleviation of distress and the finding of new homes in new countries for the destitute, he added that such actions would 'bless both those who gave and those who took', as 'the bounty both of justice and of mercy' (12 May 1823; VI, 208–9; *The Merchant of Venice*, IV, i). On such acts of mercy his mind was always dwelling. And he had often enough seen, as had Shakespeare in a passage he himself twice quoted (Note to *Childe Harold*, II, i; speech on the Roman Catholic Claims; see p. 132), 'proud' man, 'dress'd in a little brief authority', playing his 'fantastic tricks before high Heaven' (*Measure for Measure*, II, ii); and so have we all, on every level of human organization. Often enough, such 'tricks' pass for justice; but our Sonnet offers something different, of which Byron himself was, in all his doings, an exemplar. It is the supreme expression of patron and protégé; of government become personal; or, we might say, of Gospel replacing Law, not merely in religion, but in statesmanship. It is entitled *Sonnet to George the Fourth on the Repeal of Lord Edward Fitzgerald's Forfeiture*.[2] Framed in its jaunty prose setting (a letter to Murray, 12 August 1819; LJ, IV, 345), it makes a perfect miniature of the complete Byron:

'So the Prince has been repealing Lord Edward Fitzgerald's forfeiture? *Ecco un' Sonetto!*

1. To these we should add the one surviving drama of the Incas, *Apu-Ollantay,* a great work flowering from a culture-soil of Byronic quality.
2. For Lord Edward Fitzgerald see Medwin, 270–3; and Journal, 10 March 1814; LJ, II, 396.

To be the father of the fatherless,
   To stretch the hand from the throne's height, and raise
   His offspring, who expired in other days
To make thy Sire's Sway by a kingdom less—

This is to be a Monarch, and repress
   Envy into unutterable praise.
   Dismiss thy Guard, and trust thee to such traits,
For who would lift a hand, except to bless?

Were it not easy, Sir, and is't not sweet
   To make thyself beloved? and to be
   Omnipotent by Mercy's means? for thus
Thy Sovereignty would grow but more complete:
   A Despot thou, and yet thy people free,
   And by the Heart, not Hand, enslaving us.

'There, you dogs: there's a Sonnet for you: you won't have such as that in a hurry from Mr. Fitzgerald. You may publish it with my name, an' ye wool. He deserves all praise, bad and good; it was a very noble piece of principality.'

On the Sonnet's literary perfection, its exact fitting of thought to form, its unobtrusive ease of natural, yet winnowed, speech, it would indeed be tempting to expand; but the temptation must be resisted. Without claiming, then, to do justice to the nobility and graciousness of its manner, let us turn to its statement.

It is a statement of power; but without power there is no government at all. Parry tells us that Byron reacted less against any *theory* of government than against particular governments in practice (pp. 194, 202); against specific acts of despotism and inhumanity. Byron was no theorist, any more than Christ himself. Our sonnet should be read therefore less as an argument for good dictatorial government than as a plea for a certain *way* of governing by all the numerous dictators, big and little, that go to form *any* government: or, indeed, institution of any kind, political, social, educational, or domestic. Again we are reminded of Pope's:

> For Forms of Government let fools contest;
> Whate'er is best administer'd is best.
>
> (*Essay on Man*, III, 303.)

The great cry of the Renaissance world is for leadership that is not corrupted by power, Byron's 'leader in talent and truth' (p. 237).

The greatest imaginative thinkers—Plato, Dante, Milton, Shaw—
are concerned less to insist on a science of good government than
to lay emphasis on the kind of men needed to govern. Ibsen and
Nietzsche demanded less new politics than new men; both could
regard the 'state' as anathema; and in *Emperor and Galilean* the
attempt to found the great Third Empire pointing Christianity and
paganism beyond themselves failed precisely because Julian lacked
the necessary stature, did not remain uncorrupted by power; sway-
ing, moreover, from tyranny to literary propaganda, thus substituting
for the high synthesis of action and imagination what Byron in his
early satire called 'the mighty instrument of little men'; and so failing
utterly, to adapt a phrase of Nietzsche, to become a 'Roman Caesar
with the soul of Christ'. Until such men, at least in embryo, exist
to lead us, what Tennyson in *Becket* called 'the long-tugg'd, thread-
bare-worn, quarrel of Crown and Church' must persist. Power
there must be. The Byronic virtues themselves, as indeed is always
true of genius, could only mature when he was accorded, within
his context of action, recognition, faith, and therefore power; when
at once he became, in a deeper than the sense intended, a 'mine'
from which all 'could extract gold at their pleasure' (p. 206). So
our Sonnet defines *a power which is not corrupt*. It hints a way to the
'freedom' which Ibsen desired from that unending conflict of liberty
and tyranny which constitutes politics (Brandes, 20 Dec. 1870;
204); it suggests a possibility wherein that particular antimony ceases
to exist; where human government, in Shakespearian phrase, 'shows
likest God's', and service becomes perfect freedom: 'A despot thou
and yet thy people free.' The Sonnet thus points secular ordinance
towards divine excellence. Its statement is accordingly Christian,
and yet in a sense, the sense negatively defined in *Emperor and Galilean,*
transcends Christianity. The New Testament leaves us with God
and Caesar as separated and unrelated; but throughout his life, and
pre-eminently in this Sonnet which, as Teresa observes, so exactly
'reveals the aspirations of his great heart' (Teresa, II; VII, 142–3),
Byron would render unto God the things that are Caesar's, and
demand of Caesar the things that are God's.

INDEX A: LORD BYRON

I. Animals: love of, 3–16, 170, 190, 247; menageries, 4, 10–11; poetry, 11–15, 112; blood-sports, 11–13, 15, 107, 121, 124, 158, 183, 197; compared with people, 6–7, 15–16, 23, 35, 75–7, 79, 106, 115, 158, 169, 184, 188, 190, 210, 225, 241, 251; dogs, 5, 7–10, 216; horses, 5–6, 10, 14, 40, 118; wolf and bear, 4, 7; the elephant, 6–7; the geese, 11.

II. Courage: 27–9, 94, 114, 118, 182, 273–4, and see V; risks duelling, 53, 117–18, 120–2; fights, 114–16, 120; assassination, 27, 115–16, 168–9, 173–5, 274; arrest, 27, 169, 171–5; the elements, 114–15, 118–19, 205–9; as saviour, 68–9, 72, 118–19; with caution, 94; calmness, 63 (note), 94, 116, 170–4, 184, 207–9.

Moral Courage: at Missolonghi, 182, 199–202, 209; during anxiety, 63; refuses blood-sports, 13, 107, 197, 200; attacks the great, 30, 95, 128, 133–4, 138–41, 174, 263; opposes conventions, 31, 105, 140, 251; lack of (to hurt), 58, 65–6, 75, 87.

III. Endurance and Exercise: on travels, 42, 108, 203, 265; fasting, 13, 108, 203, 206, 246, 265, and see IV, 'asceticism'; training, 107–8, 177, 265; as spiritual relief, 106, 108, 265; boxing and fencing, 106, 144; riding, 5, 40, 103, 107, 158, 174; shooting, 12–13, 106–7, 174, 197, 210; the water, 107–14, 158, 174; seamanship, 119, 207; sea-poetry, 109–13, 150–1.

IV. Goodness: 38, 41–2, 44, 51, 92, 94, 122, 228–9 ('kalos').

Benevolences: 286. Assistance to writers, 52–62; financial generosity, 62–6, 85–93 (Venice, Ravenna), and see V, VI; money 'to do good', 92, 186; care and persistence, 58, 86, 92, 98, 171, 180, 186, 188; to those despised, 60–1, 66, 229, 256; irrespective of party, 87, 226; in secret, 87–9, 98–9, 266.

Education, 39, 53–5, 61, 67–73, 77–9, 85–6, 92–3, 132–3, 176, 190, 214, 232, 245, 263, 267; for the workers, 232, 245; protection, 58, 67–9, 72–5, 77–8, 83, 118, 121, 128, 136, 160; saving, 61, 68–9, 72, 77–8, 85, 87, 93, 118–22, 200, 252–3, and see V; consideration for servants, 70, 73–5, 78, 87, 128, 211; courtesy and tact, 29, 61–3, 86, 95, 99 and note, 192, 200, 204–5, 228–9, 256, 266; and see V.

Morality: 44–7. Moved by instances of virtue, 94–7, 235, 269; early idealism, 39; anger at lack of moral charity, 38, 96–7, 270, 286; will to ethic, 44–5; his poetry moral, 39, 95, 267.

Irritability denied, 43; and licentiousness, 42, 43 (note), 265; 'no vices', 41, 265; Venetian dissipation, 41 (note), 255–6, 259; questioned, 108; complexity of love-affairs, 265; will to moral uplift, girls, 98, 228–9; others, 57–8, 59–61, 190, 201, 236, 263, 267. Asceticism, 42, 265, 271, 285, and see III, 'fasting'; self-mastery, 107, 160, 243, 263, 265, 285, and see V, 'self-discipline'; humility, 51–3, 57, 95, 124, 154, 226–7, 232, 237–8, 240, 246, 252, 263–4, 268, 270, 273, and see V; self-accusations, 41–3, 57, 79, 136–7, 270, 273; caused by moral idealism, 45, 63, 136–7, 263–4, and see 51.

General defence, 34–7; asserts goodness, 89–91; 'Judge of me by my actions', 33, 193, and see 44, 51, 77, 89, 164; attainment of highest virtue, 44–5, 99, 240, 247–8, 264–7, 270, 281; beyond good and evil, 33–4, 39, 158, 160, 240, 247–8, 256–7, 269 (note), 281; blamed for his virtues, 28, 65–6, 201, 250, 281.

Magnanimity: 29, 43, 124–5, 207. Repudiates egotism, 51, 53, 91, 122, 273; absence of jealousy, 29, 53–7, 95; of selfishness, 52, 91, 98; pleasure in others' success, 52, 54–6, 94–5; respect for others' interests, 62–4, 122–4, 215; for enemies, 119, 171, 179, 197–200; repudiates early satire, 53, 124, 267; refuses to repeat it, 124, 267; dislikes defences, 91, 116, 123, 266–7; welcomes honest attacks, 122–3; accepts criticisms, 52; admits error, 227; gratitude, 64; forgiveness of wrongs, 37, 80, 97, 249, 253, 260, 264, 266 (John Scott); of tyrants (Nero), 83; makes allowances for cowardice, 172–3, 200; for inefficiency, 172–3, 180–1, 187, 208; for ingratitude, 61, 98, 172, 196.

Openness, 28, 95, 140, 187, 209–10; honour, various, 44, 94, 117, 120–4, 137, 197, 201, 214, 234, 264; as mediator, 120–2, 129, 147, 187, 190, 201, and see V; balances opposites, 44–5, 115, 120–1, 124, 146–7, 151–2, 158, 160, 185, 187, 195, 203, 214, 218, 227, 230, 238, 240, 247, 261, 270, 281, 289; blends pacifism and war, 117, 121, 124, 158, 175, 177, 184, 197, 200, 218; above conflicts, 171, 191, 197, 200; sacrificial purpose, 30, 160, 170–2, 176, 182–3, 215, 236, 261, 270–1.

V. Greek Campaign, The: 80–1, 87, 92–3, 121, 179, 261, 289. The early poetry, 164, 179, 183, 215, 220; offer of service, 184; motives, 179–80, 183; purposes, 122, 180, 185, 188, 190, 198–9.

Qualities: realism, 179–80, 183–4, 191–2, 203, 239; statesmanship, 129, 184, 189–95, 212–13; caution, 181–2, 189, 193–5, 204; question of military ability, 168, 177, 181, 183–4, 195–6, 208; leadership and example, 196, 201, 203–6, 209–13; tact and mediation, 122, 187–90, 192, 201, 209–13; self-discipline, 203–4; expectation of death and courage, 180, 182–3, 207–9, 271, and see II, 'moral courage'; patience, endurance, illness, 196, 201, 203–9; humility, 183–4, 196, 203–4, 208, 212, 270; consideration and humanity, 89, 93, 197–200, 204–5, 207, 211, 287; popularity, 93, 196, 207, 211.

Actions: finances campaign, 87, 92, 119, 184–7, 193, 196, 206; letter to the Greek government, 92, 188; reconciles factions, 179–80, 184–5, 187–93, 212–13; plans constitution, 190–1, 194–5, 221; freedom not enough, 193–4; humanizes war (prisoners, etc.), 77, 185, 192, 198–9, 207–8, 212–13, 287; Hato, 77–8, 199, 207; humane punishment, 200–2, 207; tracts and Testaments, 207.

General: the London Committee, 77, 184, 188–9, 191, 195, 206; the Loan, 186–8, 190, 196–7, 206, 213; Ionian Government, 187, 193–4, 213; Greek governments, Central and Western, 186–90, 192, 212; Lepanto, 190, 196, 204, 210; Salona, 205; Greek fleet, 185–6, 197; Capt. Yorke, 194; papers of the liberation, 185, 193; the English artificers, 116, 200, 204, 207; fractious Suliotes and Europeans, 196, 198, 200–1, 204–6, 209–12; mutinies, spies, treachery, 187, 204–6, 212; week of trials, 205; the elements, 205, 207–9, 261.

Conclusions: Byron's death, 216–18; reactions in England, 213, 216–18; nature of his success, 182, 184, 211–16; its technique, 203, 214; an 'individual', 184, 202–3, 213; Moore's assessment, 182, 213–14, 216; the cause defined, 195, 214; religious associations, 182, 192, 195, 214–18; Makriyiannis' *Apomnimonévmata*, 218–21. See also XII, 'approach personal'.

INDEX

VI. Italian Revolution, The: 23, 121. Unrest, 168; the Neapolitan Constitution, 147, 168; offer of service, 87, 147, 168, 184; the cause meditated, 170–2; financial assistance, 87, 168, 172; consideration for enemies, 119, 171, 179, 197; the shot commandant, 119; as 'chief', 169, 173–4; arms stowed, 172; irresponsibility and lack of unity, 168–9, 171–3, 179; failure of Bologna, 169, 172, of Neapolitans, 172–3; revolution fails, 106, 172; sentences on revolutionaries, 173; Byron's assistance, 173; Byron's risks, 169, 173–5; the forest rides, 27, 115–16, 169, 171, 174–5; the peasant woman, 171–3.

VII. Literature and Life: *The Poetry*, 3, and see XI. Antagonism of friends, works destroyed, etc., 32–3, 123, 250, 255, 259, 267; of enemies, 32, 64, 123, 201, 215, 267. Impulse and composition, 7, 52, 104, 215, 244; scorn of writers, 103–4, 122; of poetry, 103, 106, 125, 183, 240, 260, 275, 289; his own decried, 53–5, 61–2, 95, 104–5, 140–1, 183, 260, 267; fame no pleasure, 104, 140–1; irritation, 105, 168, 173, 183, 237; rejects identification, 91, 105; eminence asserted, 57, 238.

Actuality: realism desired, 23–4, 104, 108, 113 (myths); historical equipment, 16–27; poetry below religion, 125; and goodness, 57, 97, 173; and action, 104–6, 125, 228.

The Fusion: poetry as truth, 176, 183; use of 'philosophy', 'wise', 'thought', 'mind', 125, 157–8, 167, 175–7, 183–4, 188, 225, 237, 244–5, 248, 271; a 'mental being', 265, and see 243; mental fire, 245; related fire-symbolisms, see XIV.

Poetic action: 106, 109, 113–14, 152, 158–60, 167, 169, 172 ('the very poetry of politics'), 175–9, 182–3, 186, 188, 190, 195, 202–3, 214, 260 ('puzzle the philosophers of all ages'), 281; Hellespont, 113–14, 158; Ravenna forest, 175; Byron as poetry incarnate, 3, 27, 31, 45, 48, 78, 152, 159, 183, 197, 203, 218, 226, 230–1, 244–5, 247, 259, 262, 270, 280, 285; and see 233.

Miscellaneous: The Prose, 3; style, 22, 79, 83, 96, 136, 174, 287; its pregnancy, 30, 154, 230–1, 238.

The Memoirs, 32, 46, 63, 124; Journals destroyed (Boyhood, Greece), 32. *The Present State of Greece*, 145; *Remarks on the Romaic*, 72 (note); translation from the Armenian (Pauline Epistles), 26. Literary criticism, 57, 60, 183; the Bowles Controversy, 44, 57, 171–2, 176, 233 (note).

The theatre, 35, 52–3, 59, 65; music, 170.

VIII. Marriage Separation, The: 30, 33–7, 62–3, 80, 117, 123–4, 249, 253, 264, 275.

IX. Napoleon: 17, 24, 97, 220, 246, 263. Byron's admiration, 97, 153–5, 159–60, 225; magic and drama, 16, 154, 157–60, 225–6, 240, 243, 271; as racial symbol, 153, 159, 237–9, 251; positive achievement, 153, 158, 167–8; contrasted with good leaders, 160, 225–6, 242; as tyrant, 133, 155–6, 159–60, 242–3; poetic diagnoses, 154–60, 238–42, 285; disgust at failure and survival, 154–5, 157–60, 236–9, 241–2.

Byron and Napoleon, 159–60, 211, 227, 230, 232, 236–9, 263, 265, 271, 274; his 'Napoleonic' carriage, 229; relationship of lover, 159, 225; difference in technique, 188, 190, 192, 201; 'greater than Napoleon', 160, 226, 246, 275, 285. See also XIV.

X. Nations, foreign: 124, 163–4, 167 ('a citizen of the world'), 176, 191–2, 217. Oppressed nations, 22–3; will to their awakening, 61, 92, 164–6, 188–95, 201, 263; hatred of tyrannies, 153, 155–6, 166–9, 175–8, 236, 257; criticisms of British policy (Castlereagh, etc.), 122, 147, 155–7, 164–8; the Holy Alliance,

INDEX

168. See also XII, and XIV, 'enlightener of nations'. Linguistic attainments, 18, 163–4; *Remarks on the Romaic*, 72, note, and see 55.

Places and Peoples: Albania, 25, 32, 114–15, 219; America, 17, 25, 145–6, 163, 171, 177–8, 195, 213–14, 232, 237; Armenia, 26, 114; Assyria, 25, 150; Austria, 17, 27, 86, 163, 167–73, 193; Carthage, 25, 150; Denmark, 163; France, 17, 18 (*Le Cid*), 146, 163–4, 166–7, 177, 179, 192, 219, 237, 242; Germany, 17, 86, 163, 171, 173, 179, 201, 204–5, 209 (note), 214, 227; Greece, ancient, 16, 17, 22–3, 25, 70, 113, 150–1, 155, 166, 171, 180, 237, 261, 272; modern, 7–8, 12, 22–3, 70–3, 77, 80–1, 92–3, 114, 107–8, 119, 129, 145, 163–4, 166–7, 179–221, 226, 229, 239, 261, 270–2, 275–7, and see V; Holland, 166, 171, 237; Iceland, 163; Incas, 164, 287 (note); India, 17, 18, 25, 163; Ireland, 16, 18, 23, 89, 122, 131–4, 167, 214; Italy, 4, 11, 17, 23–7, 79–80, 87–90, 107–20, 147–51, 158, 163–4, 167–76, 178–9, 192, 214, 226, 251–6, 260, and see VI; Venice, 6, 25–6, 35, 41 (note), 86–90, 107–8, 110–11, 113–14, 147–51, 237, 251–60; see Rome, below; Jews, 23, 180; Levant, the, 163; Moors, 165; Portugal, 17, 114, 145, 153, 167, 177; Rome, ancient, 16, 22, 24, 150–1, 157, 164–6, 172, 178, 237, 260–1; Russia, 17, 166, 168, 179, 204, 214, 219, 220; Spain, 17, 145, 164–8, 171, 177, 186; Switzerland, 17, 118–19, 163, 177; Turkey, 6, 17, 19, 23, 77, 129, 163, 167, 180, 197–9, 214, 219, 227; and see V; Plans for 'the East', 236.

XI. Poetical Works: *Age of Bronze, The*, 26, 155–60, 164–6, 190, 242; *An Ode to the framers of the Frame Bill*, 131; *Bride of Abydos, The*, 54, 109; *Cain*, 13–15, 32, 83–4, 96, 105, 112–13, 123, 201, 247; *Childe Harold's Pilgrimage*, 13, 16, 26, 32, 51–3, 55, 69 (note), 73, 75, 80, 84–5, 104–5, 109, 111–12, 113–14, 124, 136, 150–1, 155–6, 158–9, 164, 175–6, 178–9, 183, 190, 197, 220–1, 236, 239–40, 242–3, 245, 247–50, 253–5, 258–62, 267, 278, 280, 285; notes and preface, 22–3, 55, 72, 164, 167, 176, 180, 191, 197, 220–1, 287; *Childish Recollections*, 68; *Condolatory Address to Sarah, Countess of Jersey*, 139; *Corsair, The*, 8, 14, 56, 66, 81, 104, 109, 139; *Curse of Minerva, The*, 52, 221, 245; *Deformed Transformed, The*, 14, 151, 178, 234, 261, 271–4, 276, 281; *Destruction of Sennacherib, The*, 13; *Don Juan*, 11–14, 32, 57, 67, 78, 80–3, 104, 107, 109, 119, 122, 139, 155–7, 164, 167, 175, 177, 186, 197, 201, 227–8, 238, 245, 262, 264, 267–8; notes, 12, 21, 105, 119; cantos destroyed, 32; Juan and Haidée episode, 67, 82–3; Leila, 78; *Don Leon* poems, The, ix; *English Bards and Scotch Reviewers*, 53, 59, 97, 105, 117, 124, 267; postscript and preface, 117, 121, 267; *Epitaph on a Friend*, 68; *Fare Thee Well*, 35, 266; *Giaour, The*, 14, 55, 237, 243, 248; *Heaven and Earth*, 14, 111–12; *Hebrew Melodies, The*, 26; *Hours of Idleness*, 67, 145; *Inscription on the Monument of a Newfoundland Dog*, 8–9; *Irish Avatar, The*, 139, 158; *Island, The*, 109–10, 155; *Lament of Tasso, The*, 26, 178; *Lara*, 53, 67, 81, 248; *Lines addressed to the Rev. J. T. Becher*, 234–5, 274; *Lines to a Lady Weeping*, 138; *Lines Written After Swimming from Sestos to Abydos*, 107; *Manfred*, 7, 67, 96, 141, 150, 240–1, 243, 247–8, 253, 256–7, 260, 274, 277–8, 280; *Marino Faliero*, 14, 24, 26, 63 (note), 104, 113, 138, 143, 145, 147–50, 169, 178, 183, 227, 246, 260, 265, 275; preface, 21–2; *Mazeppa*, 14; *Monody on the Death of Sheridan*, 26, 38, 248, 260, 273; *Napoleon's Farewell*, 158; *Ode on Venice*, 113, 178, 257, 260; *Ode to Napoleon*, 26, 154–5, 159, 238–9, 241–2; *On This Day I complete my Thirty-Sixth Year*, 93, 216, 231, 270–1, 274; *Parisina*, 62; *Prisoner of Chillon, The*, 14; *Prophecy of Dante, The*, 26, 151, 164, 178, 244, 261; notes, 33 (note). *Prometheus*, 243–4, 247, 257, 261; *Sardanapalus*, 15, 23–4, 26, 81, 85, 120,

Related to gentleness, 243–4; to education, 241, 245–6; to liberty, 178, 242–3; contrasted with Napoleon, 159, 226, 241–4, 246, and see IX, 'difference in technique' and 'greater than Napoleon'. Byron as Prometheus, 141, 159, 178, 226, 241, 243–50, 254, 257–62, 271, 281; 'enlightener of nations', 141, 226, 241, 243–4, and see 126, 176, 220–1, 226, 235–7. See also X, XIX.

Related symbolisms: light, 39, 220–1, 243, 245, 252, 255, 262, 278–9, 281; fire, 234, 241, 245–8, 257, 259, 262, 269, 274; spark, 170, 177, 241, 243–5; lightning, 124, 243, 248–9, 257, 262, 268; electric, 215, 248; flame and Phoenix, 234–5; 'intellectual fire', 245. Sun, 239, 261, 272; star, 229, 239, 285; 'golden ray' or centre, 46; golden star, 160; gold, 227, 286, 289; diamond, 38, 286. See also VII, 'philosophy', etc.

XV. Psychological characteristics: *General:* two main Byrons, 96, 252, 287; inclusiveness, 31, 44–6, 48, 124, 135, 146–7, 151–2, 171, 281, and see IV, 'balances opposites'; Shakespeare's world covered, see XVII; variability, 38, 44, 46. Principles of unity: truth, 45–6, 99, 235, 253, 255, 263; hatred of cant, 38, 263, 269; generosity, 38, 46, 99, 255, 263; tenderness, 97; liberty, 38, 44 (note), 263; religion, 44 and note.

Tender qualities: 38, 83, 94, 98–9, 188, 197, 272; bisexuality, 96; femininity, 67, 81, 94–5; avuncular, 76; maternal, 81–5, 160; nurse-like, 8, 70–1, 74–5, 79, 86; youthful emotions crushed, 38, 66–7, 83, 97–8; boyishness, 48, 72, 78; liking for youth, 29, 57–8, 72, 74, 83, 132; youth key to existence, 67, 70, 268, 285; Harrow, 18, 20, 48, 68, 70, 72, 118, 125, 135, 145–6, 153, 233–4, 241.

Romantic friendships, 67–74; children, 29, 75–8, 80–4; his own, 78–81, 85; love-affairs (normal), 43, 265, 271–2; started by others, 70, 76–7; shyness, 43, 136, 181, 238.

Sweetness of disposition, 85, 260, 270, 285–6; contradicts reputation, 85–6, 209, 228; sympathy with suffering, 10, 14, 89, 94, 99, 100, 119, 127, 175, 197–9, 247, 252–3, 269–70, 286–7; hatred of punishments, 10, 87, 128–31, 200–2; of cruelty, 10, 94, 171, 197–9; of bloodshed, war etc., 15, 72, 77, 121, 124, 128–9, 144, 150, 157–8, 160, 169, 175, 183, 197–9, 242, 264, 274; duels, 120–1, 197, 264; animals, see I; tendency to tears, 10, 81, 95, 199, 272.

Humour, 40, 48, 96, 239, 268–9, 281; erotic challenge, 155–6, 286–7. As universal lover, 67, 97–8, 211, 233, 252–4, 286. See also XII, 'Approach personal'.

Robust qualities: Intuition of energies, 6, 7, 13, 16, 106, 133, 160, 262; vigour and virility, 97, 100, 117. Rejects sentimentality, 43, 79, 81–3, 97, 136; also heroics and romanticism, 43, 94, 97, 116, 144, 179, 183–4, 191–2, 203, 239. Bitterness, 38–9, 249–50, 275; scorn and mockery, 43, 81, 96–8, 128, 131–5, 144, 173, 235, 237, 239, 253, 258, 273, 278, and see XIII; pride, 43, 104, 126–7, 187, 227, 238, 240–1, 251–3, 258, 263–4, 266 (spiritual), 275; ambition, 126, 234–5, 240–1, 265, 271, 274; from maternal impulse, 230; pugnacity, 96, 116–18, 120–1, 174–5; 'lust for duelling', 121; accepts war, 124, 152–3, 157–8, 175, 177, 197. Resentments violent, 37, 97, 144, 249, 260, 266–7, 270; passions, 37, 118, 144, 231, 276–7, 280; madness, 32–3, 62–3, 137, 252–5, 259, 275–7.

Miscellaneous: Reading and scholarship, 16–27; memory, 16–21; conversation, 95, 252, 268–9; uncanny penetration, 191, 268–9; 'a mental being', 265. Self-persecution, see IV, 'self-accusations'; lameness, 234, 247, 271, 274, 279–80. Business instincts, 92, 98, 104, 186, 206, 229.

INDEX

XVI. Religion: Fletcher's account, 74; Teresa's account, 42, 132 (note); Kennedy, 77, 96; general, 44, 72, 88, 125, 132, 215, 243, 275. His reading, etc., 18, 20, 26, 68–9.

'The Deity', 'Providence', etc., 44 (note), 79, 132, 151, 193, 208, 215, 235, 247, 279; horror of atheism, 79; 'eternity' and 'immortality', 48, 111, 147–52, 160, 214–15, 242–4, 261–2; related to freedom, see XII. Affinities with Catholicism, 23, 79, 82–3, 85, 131–3, 151, 178; the Inquisition, 165; Calvinistic up-bringing, 132, 247; Ishmael complex and damnation, 48, 83, 96, 246–7, 267; related to tenderness, 15, 83–4, 243, 247; rejection of Hell, 30, 83–4, 96–7; respect to true Christianity, 29, 96–7, 99, and see 185, 287; Mrs. Sheppard, 96–7; anger at lack of moral charity, see IV (Morality). The Bible, 20, 86; his own, 20, 132, 277; Sermon on the Mount, 117, 218, 287; Jehovah and the Flood, 14–15, 84, 111–12, 247; St. Paul, 176 (note), 180; with 'the Christ', 232.

Speech for Catholic emancipation, 131–4; distribution of Testaments and tracts, 207; the convent at Athens, 71–2; Armenian monastery at Venice, 114; monks at Cephalonia, 275–7. Fears of Messianic status, 275–8.

See also V, 'religious associations'; XII, *Conclusions;* XIX, 'Christ', 'Satanism'; and Index B, Christ, St. Paul.

XVII. Shakespeare, William: His world covered, 44–5, 281, 285; other comparisons, 3, 16, 84, 180, 231; *Measure for Measure,* 202, 287; *The Merchant of Venice,* 287; *The Winter's Tale,* 84. Compared with Cassius, 114, 158; Hamlet, 48, 85, 105–6, 120, 131, 138, 147, 232, 238; Macbeth, 48; Prospero, 30; Puck, 48; Timon, 8, 30, 48, 58, 63, 99, 260.

Byron's references and quotations: 55, 105, 154, 227, 251 (note); handled ironically, 103, 115–17, 128, 136, 144, 155, 230–1. *Hamlet,* 105, 115; *1 Henry IV,* 103, 169–70; *2 Henry IV,* 55–6; *Henry V,* 116; *Henry VIII,* 128, 230; *Julius Caesar,* 153–4, 237; and see 158; *King Lear,* 154; *Macbeth,* 55, 133, 136, 155, 157–8, 171, 185–6, 231, 251; *Measure for Measure,* 132, 287; *The Merchant of Venice,* 113, 133, 287; *Othello,* 106, 113, 128, 176; *Richard III,* 143, 157–8; *Romeo and Juliet,* 105, 113, 116, 144; *The Tempest,* 60; *Timon of Athens* (?), 227; *Twelfth Night,* 117. The tragedies and Napoleon, 157–8.

XVIII. Society: 227–8; descent royal, 230–2, 270; noble, 35, 226–7, 230; crests and trappings, 39, 108, 229–30; Byron's interest, 147, 227, 229–33, 270; symbolic radiations, 226, 228, 230–3; related to 'the Christ', 232; nobility fused with poetry, 233.

His own charm, 95, 226, 228–9, 251–2, 271, 278; the 'dandies', 227–8, 271; the aristocracy criticized, 227–8, 233; and social functions, 227–8, 256; fondness for social inferiors, 67–75, 128, 142, 171–3, 232, 256, 286; social ostracism, 30, 34–7, 46, 249–51, 266–7, and see XII, 'press vituperation' and XIX, 'rouses hostility'.

XIX. Superman: general conception, 159, 237–9, 272; in Nietzsche, 256, 272; maternal impulse, 230.

Byron as life-genius: 30–9, 248–51, 271; as leader, 238–41, and see V, 'leadership' and XII, 'ideal government'; rouses hostility and misrepresentation, 30–3, 37–9, 42, 66, 91, 196, 201, 205–6, 215, 244, 248, 250–1, 273; in Shelley, 255; today, 3–4, 16, 27–9, 33, 41–2, 46–7, 93–7, 132 (note), 181–2, 184, 267. Rejection by London, 30, 34–7, 46, 131; compared with Dante's, 30, 33 (note); and see XII, 'press vituperation', etc.

Byron as superman: 3, 48, 141, 216, 228–9, 238–41, 251–62, 271–81, 285–6; self-embarrassment, 31, 37, 138, 227, 238–41, 249–50, 252, 273, 280–1; repudiation, 263, 272, 274, 276–7. As Messiah, 215, 275, 277; compared with Christ, 31, 46, 182, 192, 216–17, 256, 275–7, 281, 288; St. Paul's 'the Christ', 232; St. Paul, 176 (note), 195; Socrates, 31, 183, 271; Gandhi, 183; Prometheus, see XIV; Nietzsche's Zarathustra, 176 (note), 179 (note), 269; as Titan, 29, 246–7, 259; Satanism, 32, 54, 141, 201, 246–7, 254, 256, 275, 280; Shakespearian drama personified, 44, 281, 285. See also VII, 'Byron as poetry incarnate'; IX, 'greater than Napoleon'; XII, 'thwarted'.

Personal beauty, 228, 261–2 (the Apollo), 272, 278–80; magnetism and power, 95, 163, 192, 200, 211, 215, 226, 233, 252, 255, 260, 271, 289; inspires devotion, 211, 233. Superlative assertion, 249–50, 260 ('the philosophers of all ages'); posthumous power claimed, 249, 259 ('something unearthly'). Thoughts and deeds prophetic, 127–9, 131, 133, 135, 146–7, 152, 156–7, 167–8, 170–1, 177–9, 182, 184, 191–2, 195, 201, 213–15, 217, 233, 236; long-range effects, Italy, Greece, etc., 179, 182, 213–14, 218–20, 226, 259. Westminster Abbey not impressed, 217–18, 233; and see 94, 274.

INDEX B: GENERAL

Where citations are indirect, the original authorities only are given. Correspondents, as such, are not indexed; nor is the bulk of the historical, geographical, and literary material of pp. 16–26.

INDEX

Fox, Henry: 76

Franklin, Benjamin: 25, 237, 242

Galt, John: 4, 13, 20, 31, 42-3, 52, 85-6, 106, 114, 115 (note), 118-19, 137, 139, 181, 183-4, 187, 190, 198, 213, 270

Gamba, Count Pietro: xi, 13, 29, 107, 170, 172, 206, 221; quoted, 5, 10-11, 19, 20, 33, 56, 77, 80, 85-6, 88-9, 93, 106-7, 118-19, 132, 159, 179-80, 183-216, 221, 238, 279

Gandhi, Mahatma: 183

George III: 25, 152

George IV: *see* Index A, Prince Regent

Gifford, William: 52-3, 58, 123

Giraud, Nicolo: 71-2, 77

Glover, Richard: 125

Godwin, William: 62-3

Goethe: 26, 52; *Faust:* 240, 271

Gordon, Charles O.: 68

Gordon, Lord George: 142

Greek Chronicle, The (also *Telegraph): see* Index A, V

Grenville, Lord: 135

Guiccioli, Count: 6, 27, 115-16, 174

Guiccioli, Teresa: x, xi, 23, 37, 93-4, 115-16, 170, 174, 271-2; qualities as a biographer, 40-1, 46-7, 60, 95, 98, 234; *My Recollections of Lord Byron,* x, 40-1; *La Vie de Lord Byron en Italie,* 41; quoted, 9-11, 13, 20, 40-7, 51-2, 55-8, 60-8, 72, 76, 78, 80, 85, 88-9, 97-9, 107-8, 116-18, 132 (note), 173-4, 180, 191, 228-9, 234-5, 250-1, 254-6, 260, 263-6, 268-73, 278, 281, 285, 289

Hall, Capt. Basil: 86

Hampden, John: 64

Hannibal: 24, 157, 184, 225, 242

Hanson, John: 125

Hanson, Newton: 4

Harley, Lady Charlotte ('Ianthe'): 75

Harness, William: 43 (note), 68-70, 73, 92

Hato (or Hatagée): 77-8, 92, 199, 207

Hazlitt, William: 280

Heliogabalus: 141

Henley, John ('Orator'): 142, 225-6

Henry VIII: 141

Henson, Bishop H. H.: 267

Herod: 29

Hobhouse, John Cam (Lord Brough-ton): xi, 32, 64, 75, 94-5, 108, 114, 115 (note), 118, 121, 123, 141-2, 241, 250, 265; quoted, 32, 42, 56, 62, 75, 94-6, 114, 211, 213, 216, 235, 265-6

Hodgson, Francis: 58, 62-3

Holland, Lord: 127, 135, 138-9

Homer: 97, 113, 125, 182, 193

Hoppner, R. B.: 75-6, 87-8, 90, 200; the 'Hoppner scandal', 27-9, 65

Hunt, Henry ('Orator', 'Bristol'): 142, 146, 225-6

Hunt, John: 63-6, 92, 123, 138, 176-7, 214-15

Hunt, Leigh: 16, 22, 33 (note), 61-6, 137-8, 158, 206, 259; quoted, 16, 120

Hussein Bey: 76

Ibsen, Henrik: 31, 289; *Emperor and Galilean,* 247, 262, 289

Iley, —: 98

Irving, Washington: 42

Jackson, John ('Gentleman'): 106

James II of Scotland: 231

Jeaffreson, J. C.: 13, 20, 30

Jeffrey, Francis, Lord: 58, 60, 117

Jesus Christ: *see* Christ

Johnson, Samuel: 17, 140

Joy, Henry: 85

Julian the Apostate: 25, 184

Julius Caesar: *see* Caesar

'Junius': 135

Juvenal, 139

Karaiskaki: 205, 210, 212

Kean, Edmund: 35

Keats, John: 57, 245

Kennedy, Dr. James: 20, 52, 77, 190, 192, 206-7; quoted, 40, 43, 64-5, 72, 78, 80-1, 85-7, 96, 106-7, 119, 147, 180, 188, 191, 196-8; Int., 216

Kennedy, Mrs.: 77

Kinnaird, Douglas: 65-6, 146, 176, 185-6

INDEX

Knight, G. Wilson: Works cited, ix, 3,
15 (note), 24 (note), 30-1, 47, 70
(note), 135 (note), 147, 180 (note),
231 (note)
Knight, H. G.: 52

Lamb, Lady Caroline: 117, 278
Leander: 108, 113
Leigh, Augusta: 5, 20, 63, 77, 80, 136,
253, 275
Leigh, Georgiana: 76
Le Mesurier, Edward: 9
Leonidas: 25, 220, 225
Liberal, The: 63-6
Liverpool, Lord: 6
London Magazine, The: 98
Long, Edward Noel: 70
Loukas: 72-3, 206, 216
Lucretius: 63
Lusieri (the artist): 71
Luther, Martin: 26, 132
Lycurgus: 220
Lyttleton, Lord: 125

MacDermott, Marshall: 114
Mackay, Charles: 275
Makriyiannis, K.: 218-21
Mahmout Pasha: 76-7
Mahomet: 25, 153
Marat: 142
Matthews, C. S.: 4
Maturin, C. R.: 56, 62
Maurois, André: xi, 8, 29, 42, 72, 74,
114, 163, 182
Mavrocordato, Prince: 19, 93, 187, 189,
192, 194, 196, 209-10, 212, 215
Mayne, Ethel Colburn: 98, 275
Medwin, Capt. Thomas: x, 4, 7, 10-11,
28-9, 33 (note), 40, 42, 52, 60, 75,
78, 80, 106-8, 113-14, 116-19, 121,
141, 145-7, 158-9, 166-7, 172,
174-5, 177-8, 180, 197, 243, 246
Melbourne, Lady: 81, 139-40
Mengaldo, Chevalier: 107
Merimée, Prosper: 98
Meyer, Dr. J. J.: 193
Milbanke, Miss Annabella: *see* Lady
Byron

Millingen, Dr. Julius: 20, 77-8, 85, 180,
182, 193, 198, 205, 209, 211, 215-16,
218
Miltiades: 25, 225
Milton, John: 24, 29, 147, 176, 195, 257,
262-3, 289
Mirabeau: 237
Moore, Dr. John: 22
Moore, Thomas: x, xi, 29, 33, 39, 42,
45-6, 53, 58, 64, 95, 103, 105, 117,
123, 141; encouraged by Byron,
53-5, 67, 92; the *Memoirs*, 63;
quoted, 5, 16-18, 28, 31-3, 42-4,
48, 52-3, 56, 61-3, 68, 72-5, 78-81,
83, 85-8, 92-3, 95, 98, 104, 106-8,
114, 118, 132, 135, 138, 147, 153,
168, 182-3, 185, 187, 191-2, 195,
206-8, 210-11, 213-14, 216-17,
226, 230, 238, 255, 264-5, 267-8,
272, 278, 285-6
Morning Chronicle, The: 131
Morning Post, The: 153
Mule, Mrs.: 74
Murray, Joe: 8, 73-4
Murray, John (Byron's publisher): 52-3,
61-2, 64-6, 91-2, 122-3, 186,
267
Murray, John, 'Junior' (1858): 66 (note)
Murray, Sir John (editor of *Lord Byron's
Correspondence*): 27, 69 (note), 203

Napier, Col. Charles: 181, 184, 192,
201, 213
Napoleon: *see* Index A
Nathan, James: 5
Nemesis: 23, 249
Nero: 25, 83, 141
Newstead Abbey: 4, 7, 11, 42, 62, 67,
69, 75, 163
Nicolo: *see* Giraud
Nicolson, Harold: xi, 3, 12-13, 29, 33
(note), 64, 66 (and note), 96-7, 179,
181-2, 184, 187, 192-3, 203, 206,
208, 213, 275-7
Nietzsche, Friedrich: 31, 33, 47, 160,
195, 247, 262, 269, 273; *Thus Spake
Zarathustra*, 176 (note), 179 (note),
256, 269; *The Will to Power*, 289
Noël, Lady: 144

302

INDEX